MCSE Guide to
Microsoft SQL Server 2000 Administration

Mathew F. Raftree

COURSE TECHNOLOGY

THOMSON LEARNING

Australia • Canada • Mexico • Singapore • Spain • United Kingdom • United States

COURSE
TECHNOLOGY
TM
THOMSON LEARNING

MCSE Guide to Microsoft SQL Server 2000 Administration

by Mathew F. Raftree

Contributing Authors:
Robert Brooks
Mark Lepper
Rich Ranna

Managing Editor:
Stephen Solomon

Product Manager:
Laura Hildebrand

Technical Editor:
Atul Mistry

Production Editor:
Debbie Masi

Quality Assurance Manager:
John Bosco

Associate Product Manager:
Elizabeth Wessen

Editorial Assistant:
Janet Aras

Marketing Manager:
Toby Shelton

Text Designer:
GEX Publishing Services

Compositor:
GEX Publishing Services

Cover Design:
Efrat Reis

Disclaimer
Course Technology reserves the right to revise this publication and make changes from time to time in its content without notice.

ISBN 0-619-03553-6

BRIEF

Contents

TABLE OF
Contents

Preface

Welcome to the *MCSE Guide to Microsoft SQL Server 2000 Administration!* This book provides in depth coverage of the knowledge and skills required to pass Microsoft certification exam 70-228: *Installing, Configuring and Administering Microsoft SQL Server 2000 Enterprise Edition.* The course of study prepares database administrators to work with SQL Server 2000 in medium to very large computing environments. Databases play a central role in every organization whether they manage financial, customer or inventory information, and SQL Server 2000 has gained considerable market share over the last few years with its competitive features and relatively inexpensive price tag. As a result, the demand for qualified professionals to manage and develop databases using SQL Server 2000 has increased considerably making the 70-228 certification quite sought after.

The Intended Audience

This book is intended to serve the needs of those individuals interested in learning more about Microsoft SQL 2000 Enterprise Edition, as well as individuals who are interested in obtaining Microsoft certification on this topic. This book provides a thorough introduction to the issues and operations revolving around the implementation and ongoing maintenance of SQL Server 2000 databases.

Chapter 1, "An Introduction to SQL Server 2000" gives a brief overview of the history of SQL Server and the various features offered in the latest 2000 release.

Chapter 2, "Installing and Upgrading SQL Server 2000" covers the installation process in detail. When you have completed the end of chapter materials you will be able to successfully install multiple instances of SQL Server 2000 Enterprise Edition. Additional topics covered include upgrading from versions 7 and 6.5.

In **Chapter 3**, "Administering and Configuring SQL Server 2000" shows you how to configure various options that control how an instance of SQL Server 2000 operates. This chapter also exposes you to the various underlying components that power an installation.

Chapter 4, "SQL Server 2000 Database Architecture" provides you with a thorough understanding of the inner workings of SQL Server 2000. This chapter discusses the physical storage mechanisms used by databases as well as the transaction architecture that provides data consistency in a multi-user environment. This chapter also includes an overview of the common database objects and what they are typically used for.

Chapter 5, "Creating SQL Server 2000 Databases" takes the information in Chapter 4 one step further by providing detailed information on creating and configuring databases on an instance of SQL Server 2000. After a detailed discussion of database objects such as tables and views, hands-on projects at the end of the chapter allow you to apply what you've just read and create these objects.

Chapter 6, "Optimizing and Troubleshooting Databases" outlines various considerations for tuning a database for maximum performance. In addition to hardware considerations like RAID hard drive arrays, the chapter explains the pros and cons of index and table placement and prepares you for troubleshooting transaction related problems.

Chapter 7, "Performing Disaster Recovery Operations" covers the backup and restore process native to SQL Server 2000. Various strategies for disaster recovery planning are discussed as well as the operations and configurations required to implement these strategies. This chapter also covers the database maintenance plan wizard and shows you how to easily create and schedule backups and routine maintenance tasks.

Chapter 8, "Security in SQL Server 2000" provides you with a thorough overview of the security constructs within SQL Server 2000 and will prepare you for managing access to a SQL Server 2000 instance and its associated databases. This chapter also shows you how to use various tools to audit user activity.

Chapter 9 "Extracting and Transforming Data with SQL Server 2000" describes various methods for moving data in and out of databases. The sections on replication provide a good foundation on planning and implementing distributed data delivery and synchronization between databases. The chapter also discusses Microsoft Data Transformation Services in detail, providing you with the skills needed to effectively import and export data from a SQL Server 2000 database. In addition, the chapter outlines new XML features of SQL Server 2000 and how these features are configured.

Chapter 10 "Automating and Monitoring SQL Server 2000" covers the SQL Server Agent service and how it is used to schedule and automate administrative tasks. The Windows 2000 System Monitor is also discussed, to provide you with the skills needed to diagnose hardware and troubleshoot common problems.

Features

To ensure a successful learning experience, this book includes the following pedagogical features:

- **Chapter Objectives:** Each chapter in this book begins with a detailed list of the concepts to be mastered within that chapter. This list provides you with a quick reference to the contents of that chapter, as well as a useful study aid.

- **Illustrations and Tables:** Numerous illustrations of server screens and components aid you in the visualization of common setup steps, theories, and concepts. In addition, many tables provide details and comparisons of both practical and theoretical information and can be used for a quick review of topics.

- **End-of-Chapter Material:** The end of each chapter includes the following features to reinforce the material covered in the chapter:

  - **Summary:** A bulleted list is provided which gives a brief but complete summary of the chapter

  - **Review Questions:** A list of review questions tests your knowledge of the most important concepts covered in the chapter

  - **Key Terms List:** A list of all new terms and their definitions

 Hands-on Projects: Hands-on projects help you to apply the knowledge gained in the chapter

 Case Study Projects: Case study projects take you through real world scenarios

- **On the CD-ROM:** On the CD-ROM you will find **CoursePrep®** exam preparation software, which provides 50 sample MCSE exam questions mirroring the look and feel of the MCSE exams, and **CourseSim®** simulation software, which allows you to perform tasks in a simulated SQL Server 2000 environment.

Text and Graphic Conventions

Wherever appropriate, additional information and exercises have been added to this book to help you better understand what is being discussed in the chapter. Icons throughout the text alert you to additional materials. The icons used in this textbook are as follows:

 Tips are included from the author's experience and provide extra information on installation.

 The Note icon is used to present additional helpful material related to the subject being described.

 Each Hands-on Project in this book is preceded by the Hands-on Project icon and a description of the exercise that follows.

Case Project icons mark the case project. These are more involved, scenario-based assignments. In this extensive case example, you are asked to implement independently what you have learned.

Instructor's Materials

The following supplemental materials are available when this book is used in a classroom setting. All of the supplements available with this book are provided to the instructor on a single CD-ROM.

Electronic Instructor's Manual. The Instructor's Manual that accompanies this textbook includes:

- Additional instructional material to assist in class preparation, including suggestions for classroom activities, discussion topics, and additional projects.
- Solutions to all end-of-chapter materials, including the Review Questions, Hands-on Projects and Case Projects.

ExamView® This textbook is accompanied by ExamView, a powerful testing software package that allows instructors to create and administer printed, computer (LAN-based), and Internet exams. ExamView includes hundreds of questions that correspond to the topics covered in this text, enabling students to generate detailed study guides that include page references for further review. The computer-based and Internet testing components allow students to take exams at their computers, and also save the instructor time by grading each exam automatically.

PowerPoint presentations. This book comes with Microsoft PowerPoint slides for each chapter. These are included as a teaching aid for classroom presentation, to make available to students on the network for chapter review, or to be printed for classroom distribution. Instructors, please feel at liberty to add your own slides for additional topics you introduce to the class.

ACKNOWLEDGMENTS

This book has been a tremendous learning experience for me and I would like to thank all of the people who helped in the process. First, thanks to Stephen Solomon, managing editor, and Laura Hildebrand, product manager, for making this project happen. Also, thanks to Atul Mistry, the technical editor whose keen eye and extensive knowledge are felt in nearly every page of this book. To the reviewers and the quality assurance team, I thank you for your hard work and diligence—this book could not have been published without your significant efforts. And to Debbie Masi, my production editor, who transformed the manuscript into its clean format.

To my contributing authors, Rich Rana, Mark Lepper and Rob Brooks, your help on chapters 9, 5, and 7 respectively was immeasurable. Your efforts took a lot of the pressure off when I most needed it and I thank you all.

Last but certainly not least, I must thank my wife Robin for all of her encouragement throughout the process. Her support has bolstered all of my efforts; without her in my corner I would be lost. Thank you Robin, I couldn't have done it without you.

DEDICATION

The book is dedicated to Gus and Shirley Walter. I love you and miss you both.

Read This Before You Begin

To the User

Whether you are working towards Microsoft certification like MCDBA or MCSE, or are simply looking to increase your knowledge of SQL Server 2000 installation and administration, this book will make it easy to achieve your goals. Ideally you will have access to a classroom lab containing computers configured in the following way:

- **Windows NT Server, Windows 2000 Server, or Windows 2000 Advanced Server.** An Internet connection is helpful and will be required for some of the case projects.

- **Microsoft SQL Server Enterprise Edition** – You can download an evaluation copy from the SQL Server Web site at **www.microsoft.com/sql**

- **Data Disk**. Some of the chapters in this book have additional materials that supplement the end of chapter projects. The CD included with this book contains these supplemental files. They can also be obtained electronically from the Course Technology Web site by connecting to **http://www.course.com**, and then searching for this book title.

Visit Our World Wide Web Site

Additional materials designed especially for you might be available for your course on the World Wide Web. Go to **http://www.course.com**. Search for this book title periodically on the Course Technology Web site for more details.

To the Instructor

When setting up a classroom lab, make sure each workstation has Windows NT or 2000 Server, Internet Explorer 5.5, and Microsoft Outlook 97,98, or 2000. Students will install SQL Server 2000 Enterprise Edition on these computers in the course of working through the book. On top of that, students will need administrative rights on the workstations to perform many of the operations covered in the hands on projects throughout the book.

AN INTRODUCTION TO MICROSOFT SQL SERVER 2000

After reading this chapter and completing the exercises, you will be able to:

♦ Discuss the functionality of relational database management systems

♦ Define SQL

♦ Understand important features of SQL Server 2000

There isn't a business system today that doesn't run some kind of database. With the incredible number of interconnected people (via the Internet) and the sheer volume of data that exists today, where would we be without databases? Databases are responsible for everything from managing our accounts at banks and brokerages to analyzing data for medical research. One could argue that the database is the single most important business application in the world today.

If you have ever searched for airline tickets online or bought a book from a Web site, you have interacted with a database. Databases are the quintessential "Back End" system and the "blood and guts" of e-commerce and management information systems. By storing data in a standardized way and allowing access to this data through several user interfaces, database systems are often the cornerstone of a production-quality business application.

Microsoft's implementation of a relational database management system, SQL Server 2000, is one of the most popular and powerful products in the industry. If you are a database administrator or are planning on working with databases in the future, knowledge about administering the product will be a valuable asset.

WHERE IT ALL BEGAN: A BRIEF HISTORY OF THE STRUCTURED QUERY LANGUAGE

The **SQL** language was originally developed by IBM in a prototype relational database management system, System R, in the mid-1970s. The original SQL language (SEQUEL2) was described in the November 1976 *IBM Journal of R&D*. The premise behind the new language was to provide a way for people to access data through simple English language statements. The language was embraced by the high-tech industry, and over time, it became standardized in the form of the language we know today. The **American National Standards Institute (ANSI)** is the primary group responsible for publishing the SQL standards. Comprised of American industry and business groups, ANSI develops trade and communication standards for the United States. The latest version to be standardized is known as ANSI-92 SQL, because it was finalized in 1992. It is important to realize that the SQL standard does not take into account the complex features required by today's applications. In order for new features to be implemented in database products, vendors oftentimes add extensions to their own SQL language interpreter. In general though, vendors implement the ANSI-92 standard (which defines a core group of language constructs).

The database market has grown considerably over the years, and most vendors in this space offer a product that is SQL-enabled. Companies like Microsoft, IBM, Oracle, Sybase, and Informix all offer high-end database management systems. However, each one implements SQL in a slightly different way. Microsoft SQL Server 2000 is compliant with ANSI-92 SQL, but it offers functionality above and beyond the ANSI-92 standard as well. The unique flavor of SQL used in Microsoft database management systems is known as **Transact-SQL** or **T-SQL** for short. This book will have many examples of T-SQL statements used to perform operations like creating a database, querying a table of records, and checking the disks that a database resides on.

DATABASE ARCHITECTURE

At its simplest, a database is a file used to store information. An Excel spreadsheet with a list of customers could be considered a database. However, the term database usually refers to a software application that consists of two parts:

- Files used to store physical data
- An application for managing and accessing these files

The software that manages the data files is what makes a database a database management system (DBMS).

 There are several relational database management system (RDBMS) software packages available today. The most common of these are Microsoft SQL Server 2000, Oracle, Sybase, and DB2 (IBM).

The application is responsible for handling data requests and committing changes to the data. It is also responsible for enforcing the structure of the database including:

- Ensuring data is stored properly, and that the rules for defining data are not violated

- Providing some level of disaster recovery by which data can be restored to a consistent state

- Maintaining relationships between data entities residing in the database

These requirements are adhered to by several classes of database software (for example: file based, object based, and relational), however the most prolific of these classes is the relational database.

RELATIONAL DATABASE CONCEPTS

The theory underlying all of the relational database systems in use today was developed by a scientist name E. F. Codd in the early 1970s. While working for IBM, Codd came up with his theory based on two types of mathematics known as "set theory" and "predicate logic." His work has been a core element of the database software market for the last 30 years. SQL Server 2000 is itself a relational database management system (RDBMS), and a solid understanding of relational database design concepts is imperative when working with the product.

In abstract terms, a database is a collection of various entities that may or may not be related. An **entity** is defined as some object comprised of various pieces of data.

In a customer management system, the database would contain information about each customer. Consequently, each customer can be thought of as an entity. Each customer is comprised of various pieces of information (data), including name, address, and phone number. These pieces of data are considered **attributes** of the customer. The customer management system also stores customer orders (each customer will have one or more orders associated with it). In this case an order becomes an entity. Some likely pieces of information that define an order are: OrderID, OrderDate, ShipCity, etc.

It is assumed that each customer can have from zero to many orders. This being the case, each order record would have an attribute that denotes which customer is the owner of the order. In this example there is a relationship between the customer entity and the order entity. The relationships between entities are stored in the database and are used when pulling data out of the system through queries.

Within the database system, each entity would be implemented as a table, and each piece of information (attributes) would be implemented as columns in a table. A full collection of all of the attributes makes up a row or a record. Figure 1-1 illustrates the relationship between the Customers and Orders tables.

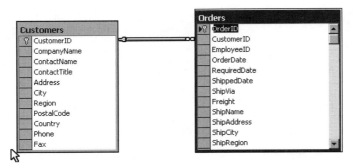

Figure 1-1   Simple table structure from the NorthWind database in SQL Server 2000

Notice how the Orders table has a field called CustomerID. By storing the CustomerID value in the Orders table, the customer can be identified and all of the associated information about that particular customer can be accessed.

The CustomerID field in the Orders table would be populated with a valid CustomerID from the records in the Customers table. Storing data in this format makes it easy to navigate through related entities. With just an OrderID value, an application could access the Orders record and from that record, get the CustomerID and consequently access the appropriate Customer record. Allowing data entities to be defined this way provides a very flexible environment for defining the structure of business information.

INTRODUCING MICROSOFT SQL SERVER 2000

Microsoft SQL Server 2000 has matured considerably over the years and is currently one of the most robust and cost-effective database servers on the market. While earlier versions of the product were based on the Sybase relational engine, SQL Server 7.0 was a complete rewrite of the original codebase from the ground up. The results were greatly improved performance and scalability, as well as an improved administrative and development functionality. SQL Server 7.0 was well received in the marketplace and gained instant credibility as a top-of-the-line database.

 Microsoft purchased the rights to the engine in order to get a foothold in the database market.

SQL Server 2000 builds on SQL Server 7.0 foundation to provide even greater performance and impressive new Internet capabilities. This latest version of the product offers a level of scalability that rivals that of any competitor in the world. SQL Server 2000 is already the most used database on the Web and is making headway into the high-end market with features like improved scalability and failover clustering support.

FEATURES OF SQL SERVER 2000

Microsoft SQL Server 2000 is a robust, feature laden database server that can support even the most demanding applications.

The robust administrative tools and simple installation processes make it one of the easiest database servers to configure and deploy. The following sections will discuss the key features of SQL Server 2000 broken down by Scalability and Availability, Database Features, Administrative Features, Internet Enabled Features, and Data Warehousing Features.

Scalability and Availability

In order to compete with some of the larger players in the database world (like Oracle and IBM), SQL Server 2000 provides even better performance and scalability than previous versions of the product. With the increasing need for 100% "uptime" (**availability**) and the ability to easily expand to handle an increasing user volume over time (**scalability**), SQL Server 2000 is ready to meet the needs of even the most demanding application requirements.

Scalability Features

SQL Server 2000 is built to run on all of the latest Microsoft operating systems, including Windows NT 4.0, Windows 2000, Windows 98, and Windows ME. This being the case, a database application would function the same when installed on any of the operating systems mentioned. A simple deployment of SQL Server 2000 could use the cheaper Windows ME. More costly and robust operating systems can be implemented if the need to support a larger workload increases over time.

 Some features of SQL Server 2000 are not supported on Windows 98 and Windows ME, mostly due to limitations in the operating systems themselves. Performance of SQL Server 2000 will be better on Windows 2000 Server and Windows NT Server, due to the improved I/O operations of those operating systems.

SQL Server 2000 supports **federations** of database servers. A federation is a group of computers that cooperate to process a single workload (see Figure 1-2). Using a federation of servers allows data to be distributed across physical machines, but to be queried as if it were all residing on a single server. For example: XYZ Company has a product catalog that they store in a SQL Server 2000 database. The catalog is comprised of 30 million products. Leveraging SQL Server 2000 federated database features, three separate computers running SQL Server 2000 are set up to share the workload of product queries. Each server will hold 10 million records of the product table in a local table. The collection of local tables (one in each server) is then grouped into a **distributed partition view** that allows SQL queries to treat the group of tables as if it were one table. Federations allow the largest databases (multiple terabytes) to be supported using SQL Server 2000.

Federation of SQL Servers
(Three product tables contain different segments of the overall product information. The three tables appear as a single table to external applications and queries)

Figure 1-2   Federated database servers

SQL Server 2000 Enterprise Edition is now capable of supporting a single database instance on as many as 32 CPUs. Improvements in the way SQL Server 2000 performs parallel operations allow SQL Server 2000 to take advantage of the most advanced multiprocessor computers available today. SQL Server 2000 can break down a single complex operation into multiple parts and run each part on a separate processor, thus improving outright performance considerably.

SQL Server 2000 Enterprise Edition scales up to 64 gigabytes of RAM. Keeping a database in RAM (or as much of it as you can at least) while it is running provides much better performance over constant hard disk I/O.

Availability Features

Today, business systems must be reliable and constantly available. As more and more systems are being built for the Internet, availability has become a key concern alongside scalability. The Web introduces a new environment where anyone with an Internet connection is a potential customer. There is no longer the idea of "business hours," as customers want access to goods and services any time of day or night. System downtime is no longer acceptable in today's business environment. With this in mind, SQL Server 2000 provides the highest levels of reliability through features like online backups, log shipping, and failover clustering.

SQL Server 2000 offers online differential database backup support. Online backups allow users to perform database backups while still connected to the system. This allows the data in the database to be backed up without having to make the system unavailable as the backup operation executes. Differential backups only save the data that has been changed since a previous backup has been performed. By only backing up the bare minimum of data, differential backups take less time to execute and result in backup files that are smaller in size.

Log shipping is a new feature of SQL Server 2000 that allows transaction logs to be backed up and automatically sent and applied to another server. This functionality can be used to set up a "standby" server, or set of servers that are synchronized regularly with the production system. In the event of a system failure, an administrator can activate the standby server quickly to minimize downtime. Log shipping is also helpful in situations where a reporting server is used. The production system would handle all of the normal transaction processing, but the standby server could be used to perform larger queries used by management reports, thereby reducing the load against the production system.

SQL Server 2000 implements failover clustering based on the features of the Microsoft Clustering Service (MSCS) available in Windows NT 4.0 and Windows 2000.

Failover clustering allows multiple computers running SQL Server 2000 to be run concurrently with a shared set of hard disks that house the database. In a clustered environment, when one server fails, the operating systems resources and SQL Server 2000 are transferred to an operational server in the cluster. This ensures that the system will be available even in the event of a hardware failure. The administrative tools offer simplified interfaces for managing failover clusters of SQL Server 2000, making the addition and removal of servers from a cluster a straightforward task.

Database Features

The Microsoft SQL Server 2000 database engine can meet the needs of the largest and most demanding application environments. With a focus on supporting large scale implementations, SQL Server 2000 provides several enterprise database features that optimize performance and ensure the integrity of vital data.

In order to provide absolute data integrity and the highest level of performance when modifications to data are made (especially in concurrent user situations), SQL Server 2000 implements dynamic row-level locking. **Locking** is used to restrict access to a resource in a multiuser environment. SQL Server 2000 locks users out of a specific row, column, or table automatically to prevent concurrent data modification problems.

 Locking doesn't prevent a user from accessing data if the particular data is being affected by another query. If two users both attempt to modify the same row in a table at the same time, then both modifications will be applied. Whichever modification request is received first will be executed while the other request is locked out. When the first modification finishes, the second will be applied automatically. All of this happens transparent to the user.

Depending on the particular query executed, the database engine will dynamically determine the best possible locking scheme to ensure the fastest response and least impact on overall performance. For example, if a query were accessing a few rows in a large table, the database would use row-level locking to ensure that only the rows being used by the query are locked while it executes. If a query is going to modify almost all of the rows in a table, then the database would implement a table lock until the query finishes (a table lock requires much less overhead to create and therefore allows the query to execute faster). Locking architecture will be discussed in greater detail in Chapter 4.

To ensure that data integrity is maintained, every data modification is performed within a transaction. In addition, SQL Server 2000 can take part in **distributed transactions**, where modifications to multiple disparate data sources can be handled as a single transaction. This feature is especially valuable when data in two systems must be synchronized in real time.

Replication allows specified data sets to be mirrored to multiple locations. Implemented as a Publisher/Subscriber metaphor, SQL Server 2000 replication will allow the various data sources to make changes to local datasets and automatically synchronize the changes to other locations. Replication is often used in situations where satellite offices in different geographic locations need to share their data with a central office database.

Administrative Features

One of the best features of SQL Server 7.0 was its ability to dynamically tune itself. In SQL Server 7.0, the database monitors itself and adjusts memory usage, lock resources, and file sizes to ensure that only the resources the database actually needs at any given point in time are consumed. SQL Server 2000 adds to this feature through improved tuning algorithms that interact with various subsystems to determine how to tune the database on the fly.

Another important feature that cannot be overlooked is the best-of-breed GUI administrative tools that are shipped with SQL Server 2000. The most important administrative tools included with SQL Server 2000 are:

- Enterprise Manager: Enterprise Manager is the primary management tool for SQL Server 2000. It allows an administrator to perform the following tasks:
  - Register individual servers in a group
  - Configure all SQL Server 2000 options for each registered server
  - Create and administer all SQL Server 2000 databases, objects, logins, users, and permissions in each registered server
  - Define and execute all SQL Server 2000 administrative tasks on each registered server
- SQL Query Analyzer: SQL Query Analyzer offers a graphical user interface for designing and testing T-SQL statements, batches, and scripts interactively. It provides the following functionality:
  - A Free-form text editor for typing out T-SQL statements, including color-coding of T-SQL syntax to improve the readability of complex statements
  - An object browser and templates to speed up the process of developing T-SQL scripts by exposing the structure of the database and providing T-SQL "shells" for common tasks like creating tables or performing inserts

- A graphical SHOWPLAN diagram that presents the logical steps of an execution plan for a particular T-SQL statement. This is particularly useful when diagnosing poorly performing parts of a query for optimization.

- SQL Profiler: The profiler is a tool that captures events that occur for a particular instance of SQL Server 2000. The trace files it generates are helpful when diagnosing actions that lead to a problem with the database. Trace files can also be used to monitor the performance of SQL Server 2000 and determine where optimizations may be required.

- Import/Export Data (DTS): The Import and Export Data item in the SQL Server 2000 program group activates the Data Transformation Services (DTS) Wizard. This tool allows an administrator to easily create import or export routines for a given SQL Server.

The administrative applications shipped with SQL Server 2000 provide database administrators with unmatched ease of use and access to nearly every administrative function of the database server.

New Security Features

In an Internet environment, security is one of the largest concerns in any system. SQL Server 2000 has many security enhancements that allow a system to operate under the highest level of security commercially available. When installed in a Windows 2000 environment, SQL Server 2000 leverages the integrated security offered by the operating system. SQL Server 2000 also offers the following security enhancements:

- Role-based security for server, database, and application profiles

- Security auditing tools

- Tracking of 18 different security events and additional subevents

- **Secure Sockets Layer (SSL)**: A protocol designed to enable encrypted, authenticated communications across the Internet. SSL provides three important things: privacy, authentication, and message integrity. SSL leverages public key cryptography to provide security through encrypted communication. Within this architecture, one key is used to encrypt (public) and one is used to decrypt (private). The public key is passed out to all people so that they can encrypt data prior to sending it to an application. When a client connects with a server, the public and private keys are used to ensure authentication, and then a more efficient secret key is generated to facilitate ongoing communication between the two computers. This type of security is common on the Internet, where consumers often send credit card information to a site.

 URLs that begin with *HTTPS://* instead of *HTTP://* are using SSL.

■ **Kerberos**: A system developed by MIT that lets two parties on a network communicate securely. Kerberos provides both user authentication and mutual client server authentication. This protocol relies on secret key encryption, and the key is usually generated from the user's password.

All of these features (especially encryption) have helped SQL Server 2000 to achieve the U.S. government C-2 level security certification. This is the highest level of security available in the high-tech industry.

Internet Enabled Features

Extensible Markup Language (XML) is a language for creating documents containing structured information. Basically it is a standardized way to format data so that any application that supports the XML format can handle the data. XML has a similar syntax to HTML in that it is tag based. For example, a simple comma delimited data set may look like this:

```
12,John,Smith,555-4534.
```

In XML, the same data would like this:

```
<Customer ID="12" FirstName="John" LastName="Smith"
Phone="555-4534">.
```

SQL Server 2000 offers native support for XML. With this feature, data is returned from the database in XML format for use with Internet applications and integration services like BizTalk server. In addition, SQL Server 2000 integrates directly with Microsoft Internet Information Service (IIS) to provide HTTP access to data stored in the database. In this way, the database can be queried by specifying a URL in a browser. Through IIS, SQL Server 2000 can be accessed in a number of ways, including the new XPath query syntax. The relational database engine also supports retrieving and writing data through XML based queries.

Data Warehousing Features

Companies gather information through normal business operations. This data can be consolidated and organized into a data warehouse.

Data warehouses are usually built from a variety of data generated by various systems within an organization. These systems could include Online Transaction Processing (OLTP), Accounting, customer relationship management, and spreadsheets.

The data warehouse can be used to analyze large volumes of historical data in complex ways. A data warehouse is used to ask questions that will help drive business decisions. For example, a data warehouse could be queried to determine the best-selling products in a given month for a specific customer segment. The results of the query would then be used to drive a decision to offer a discount on those products in that month to drive sales even higher. Analysis Services in SQL Server 2000 provide full data warehousing and Online Analytical Processing (OLAP) capabilities.

Components of SQL Server 2000

Almost all of the SQL Server 2000 functionality is provided by the four primary components of the product:

- SQL Server database engine (MSSQLServer service)
- SQL Server Agent (SQLServerAgent service)
- Microsoft Distributed Transaction Coordinator (MS DTC service)
- Microsoft Search service

Each of these components is implemented as a Windows **service**. A service is an application that is usually launched when a computer is booted up and continues to run while the computer is on. Services typically do not have a user interface because they perform activities that do not require interaction with a desktop application. A key feature of services is that they can run under the auspices of a particular user account on a computer or network. In this way, the access that services have to network and machine resources can be easily restricted. Windows NT and Windows 2000 allow an administrator to set up user accounts and then associate services with a particular account. In general, any program that must run constantly while the computer is powered on should be implemented as a service. The SQL Server 2000 components each adhere to this definition and are therefore implemented as Windows services.

 In later chapters, managing the services that make up the SQL Server 2000 components will be discussed in detail.

SQL Server Database Engine (MSSQLServer Service)

When SQL Server 2000 is installed on a machine, a service named **SQL Server database engine (MSSQLServer service)** is added to the operating system. This service is responsible for the basic operation of the database itself. The service itself manages all of the files that house data and transaction logs for the database. In addition, the MSSQLServer service handles all T-SQL requests that are sent to the server from client applications (like Enterprise Manager or a COM component used by a Web site). As the backbone of the relational database system, the MSSQLServer service is responsible for allocating system resources to multiple concurrent users and ensuring the integrity of the data by preventing multiple users from updating the same piece of data simultaneously.

Whenever a database is queried, the MSSQLServer service is interpreting the T-SQL and returning data or performing some database related task. Tasks such as database creation, query execution, and data updates are all performed by the MSSQLServer service. The other components that make up SQL Server 2000 extend the database functionality inherent in the MSSQLServer service.

SQL Server Agent Service

One of the biggest challenges when implementing a large scale database system is administration. Certain people within an organization need to be alerted when there is a server failure or other problem that requires human interaction. Also, most systems require certain processes to be executed at regular intervals in time (e.g., backups, index rebuilds) to ensure disaster recovery and optimized performance of the database. The **SQL Server Agent service (SQLServerAgent)** is the component of SQL Server 2000 that handles these types of processes.

SQL Server Agent Service allows administrators to define the following objects:

- Jobs: Jobs consist of one or more steps to be performed and can be scheduled to execute at regular intervals. A typical job would be a backup consisting of several steps that include backing up each database on the server as well as the transaction logs.

- Alerts: A user-defined response to a SQL Server event. The SQL Server Agent service allows an administrator to define actions that are executed when a certain event occurs. Events can be anything from a particular error occurring on the system to a maximum storage threshold that has been reached. Responses can be e-mails, calls to pagers, or execution of defined tasks.

- Operators: Operators are people that can be defined by their e-mail address or pager number in the database. This information is then used to forward alerts to the appropriate administrative person.

In later chapters, the various uses of the SQL Server Agent service will be discussed.

Microsoft Distributed Transaction Coordinator

The **Microsoft Distributed Transaction Coordinator (MS DTC service)** manages transactions across multiple data sources. The MS DTC provides services that applications can use to provide transaction management for particular operations, especially situations where data in multiple systems must be updated at the same time. The MS DTC is responsible for distributed transactions, and it's primary function is either to permanently save a set of database changes if all of the operations complete successfully or to cancel all of the changes if any single operation fails.

Microsoft Search Service

The **MS Search service** provides full text indexing and search engine capabilities. The search service supports indexing of database tables as well as documents on a network. Full text indexes comprised of specific tables and columns in a SQL Server 2000 database are defined and constructed by configuring the Search service. These indexes are used when performing text queries. In addition to creating full text indexes, the Microsoft Search service supports querying of indexes. The Search service determines which entities in the full text indexes meet the search criteria provided by a user or application.

CHAPTER SUMMARY

Structured Query Language (SQL) is a standardized programming language for accessing data. The version of the language implemented by Microsoft SQL Server 2000 is known as T-SQL. T-SQL adheres to the ANSI-92 standard for SQL and offers functional extensions specific to Microsoft SQL Server 2000.

A database is comprised of files that house data and applications that manage and access these files. Relational databases allow data entities to be defined in tables. Each attribute of an entity is defined as a column within a table. A set of all of the attributes for a given entity is defined as a row in a table (a collection of column values). Relational databases perform the following functions:

- Ensuring data is stored properly, and that the rules for defining data are not violated

- Providing some level of disaster recovery by which data can be restored to a consistent state

- Maintaining relationships between data entities residing in the database

SQL Server 2000 is a robust product capable of scaling up to the growing needs of any organization. Most of the core functionality of SQL Server 2000 is provided by the following components:

- SQL Server database engine (MSSQLServer service)

- SQL Server Agent (SQLServerAgent service)

- Microsoft Distributed Transaction Coordinator (MS DTC service)

- Microsoft Search service

SQL Server 2000 supports up to 32 processors and 64 gigabytes of RAM. Through clustering technology and improved backup functionality, SQL Server 2000 is capable of high availability and scalability.

KEY TERMS

American National Standards Institute (ANSI) — An organization of American industry and business groups that develops trade and communication standards for the United States. Through membership in the International Organization for Standardization (ISO) and the International Electrotechnical Commission (IEC), ANSI coordinates American standards with corresponding international standards.

attribute — A piece of information that describes a data entity. For example, for a customer entity, the associated attributes could consist of name, address, and phone number.

availability — The ability of a system to be constantly accessible by it's users. Using redundant technologies like failover clustering increases availability.

distributed partition view — A single queriable entity that is horizontally partitioned and housed on multiple physical computers.

distributed transactions — Transactions that group queries that affect data on multiple servers.

entity — An object comprised of various pieces of data and stored in a database.

Extensible Markup Language (XML) — A language for creating documents containing structured information.

federation — A group of servers that cooperate to process a single workload.

Kerberos — A system developed by MIT that lets two parties on a network communicate securely. Unlike in SSL, which uses two static keys (public key and private key), Kerberos generates a unique key for each communication session.

locking — The process by which access to a resource in a multiuser environment is restricted. SQL Server 2000 locks users out of specific rows, columns, or tables automatically to prevent data modification problems from concurrent activity.

log shipping — Process by which transaction logs of a database are backed up and applied to a secondary database server. The goal of log shipping is typically to have a standby server (relatively in sync with the main server) that can be activated in the event of a primary server failure.

Microsoft Distributed Transaction Coordinator (MS DTC service) — A component of SQL Server 2000 that provides transaction management services that facilitate including several different sources of data in one transaction.

MS Search service — A full text indexing engine that is bundled with SQL Server 2000. It generates and maintains full text indexes as well as handles queries that access them.

replication — A process that copies and distributes data to another and then synchronizes information between databases for consistency.

scalability — The ability to easily grow in size to support a growing user base. For example, XYZ Company sets up a database driven application and wants to have a system that not only works with the initially estimated user population size, but can be easily expanded to support the growing user population in one year, five years, or ten years.

Secure Sockets Layer (SSL) — A protocol that uses public key cryptography to enable encrypted, authenticated communications across the Internet.

service — An application that starts when a computer is booted up and continues to run while the computer is on. Services do not require graphic user interfaces and run invisibly to the user.

SQL Server Agent service (SQLServerAgent service) — The component of SQL Server 2000 that supports features allowing the scheduling of periodic activities (like database backups), or the notification to system administrators of problems that have occurred with the server.

SQL Server database engine (MSSQLServer service) — The SQL Server 2000 service manages all of the files that comprise the databases owned by an instance of SQL Server 2000. It is the component that processes all Transact–SQL statements sent from SQL Server 2000 client applications.

Structured Query Language (SQL) — A language used to insert, retrieve, modify, and delete data in a relational database. SQL also contains statements for defining and administering the objects in a database. SQL is the language supported by most relational databases, and is the subject of standards published by the International Organization for Standardization (ISO) and the American National Standards Institute (ANSI).

Transact–SQL (T-SQL) — The version of the SQL language implemented by Microsoft SQL Server 2000.

REVIEW QUESTIONS

1. Who is the primary group responsible for publishing standards for the Structures Query Language (SQL)?

    a. Microsoft

    b. IBM

    c. World Wide Web Consortium (W3C)

    d. American National Standards Institute (ANSI)

2. Which of the following is not a primary component of SQL Server 2000?

    a. SQL Server database engine (MSSQLServer service)

    b. SQL Server Agent (SQLServerAgent service)

    c. SQL Server 2000 Enterprise Manager

    d. Microsoft Distributed Transaction Coordinator (MS DTC service)

    e. Microsoft Search service

3. What is the mechanism used by SQL Server 2000 to prevent data corruption in the event of concurrent updates to the same piece of data?

    a. locks

    b. distributed transactions

    c. Secure Sockets Layer (SSL)

    d. XPath Queries

4. Which of the following can not be created and managed by SQL Server Agent?

   a. jobs

   b. operators

   c. clusters

   d. alerts

5. SQL Server 2000 is capable of being run on up to how many processors (CPUs)?

   a. 1

   b. 8

   c. 32

   d. 64

6. Which SQL Server component supports the creation of full text indexes?

   a. SQL Server database engine (MSSQLServer service)

   b. SQL Server Agent (SQLServerAgent service)

   c. Microsoft Distributed Transaction Coordinator (MS DTC service)

   d. Microsoft Search service

7. Which of the following is a language for creating documents containing struc-tured information?

   a. SQL

   b. T-SQL

   c. XML

   d. SSL

8. The SQL Query Analyzer tool is used to:

   a. configure SQL Server options

   b. diagnose a problem with the database to identify the actions leading up to a problem

   c. test and debug T-SQL statements

   d. develop export routines for data in a SQL Server 2000 database

9. Which one of the following features of SQL Server 2000 provides scalability?

   a. failover clustering

   b. log shipping

   c. database federations

   d. native XML support

1

10. XYZ Company has a main office in Dallas and two regional offices in New York and Chicago. Each office has its own SQL Server 2000 database and the regional offices need to be able to synchronize their data with the main office at the end of each business day. Which SQL Server feature should be implemented to handle this requirement?

   a. log shipping

   b. replication

   c. Data Transformation Services

   d. XML

11. Which of the following is not a core responsibility of a relational database:

   a. ensuring data is stored properly, and that the rules for defining data are not violated

   b. providing some level of disaster recovery by which data can be restored to a consistent state

   c. integrating directly with the Internet

   d. maintaining relationships between data entities residing in the database

12. Which term applies to minimizing downtime for a SQL Server 2000 deployment?

   a. scalability

   b. availability

13. True or False: The primary components of SQL Server 2000 are implemented as services.

14. Which type of security generates new encryption keys for every communication session?

   a. Secure Sockets Layer (SSL)

   b. Kerberos

   c. both

15. Which component of SQL Server 2000 is responsible for ensuring that changes to data in multiple databases are committed or cancelled as a single operation?

   a. SQL Server database engine (MSSQLServer service)

   b. SQL Server Agent (SQLServerAgent service)

   c. Microsoft Distributed Transaction Coordinator (MS DTC service)

   d. Microsoft Search service

Hands-on Projects

Project 1-1

In this hands-on activity you will familiarize yourself with SQL Server Books Online. You will need access to a computer that has the SQL Server administrative tools installed on it.

To use SQL Server Books Online:

1. Click the **Start** button on the lower-left side of the screen.

2. Highlight **Programs** and then **Microsoft SQL Server**.

3. Notice the various programs that can be run from this application group to administer and configure SQL Server 2000. The primary applications discussed in this book are Books Online, Enterprise Manager, Query Analyzer, Import/Export Data, and Profiler. Each of these will have hands-on labs in later chapters.

4. Click the **Books Online** application item from the Microsoft SQL Server group (see Figure 1-3). It is vitally important that an administrator of SQL Server 2000 is familiar with the documentation for the product.

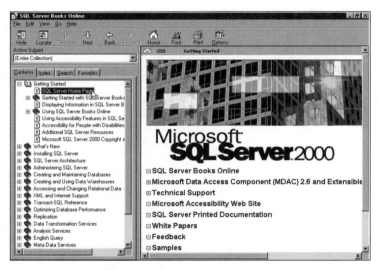

Figure 1-3   Home Page of SQL Server Books Online

5. Click on the **Getting Started with SQL Server Books Online** heading (see Figure 1-4).

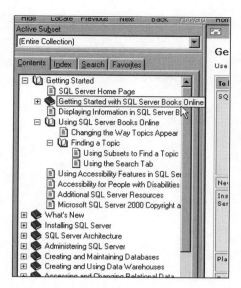

Figure 1-4   Select a topic in SQL Books Online

6. Read through all of the sub listings with regard to using Books Online.

Project 1-2

In this hands-on activity you will use the search feature of SQL Server Books Online to find out which features of SQL Server 2000 are supported by the different editions on the product. You will need access to a computer that has the SQL Server administrative tools installed on it.

To perform a text based search in SQL Server Books Online:

1. Start SQL Server Books Online by pressing the **Start** button and highlighting **Program Files** and then **Microsoft SQL Server**. Highlight and click the **Books Online** item from the group.

2. Click the **Search** tab and enter **Features Supported** in the text box.

3. Click the **List Topics** button to execute the search using the words you just provided. (The search should yield 78 results.)

4. To narrow the search, click the **Search Titles Only** check box in the lower-left side of the Books Online search interface (see Figure 1-5).

5. Reexecute the search by clicking the **List Topics** button beneath the text box where you typed in "Features Supported."

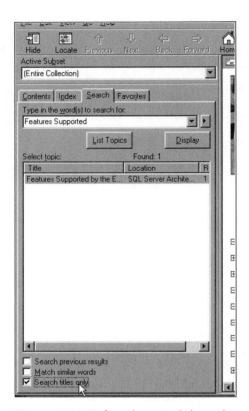

Figure 1-5   Refine the search by only searching the titles of articles

6. There is only one result now, titled "Features Supported by the Editions of SQL Server." Double-click this item to view the information in the right half of the Books Online interface.

Project 1-3

In this hands-on activity you will go on the Web and take advantage of Microsoft's free training seminars on SQL Server 2000. You will need a computer that has access to the Internet and supports Windows Media Player.

To view Microsoft's free training seminars on SQL Server 2000:

1. Make sure your computer is connected to the Internet and then start your browser.

2. Type the following URL in your browser's address text box: *http://msdn.microsoft.com/training/seminars/DataAccess.asp.*

3. View the **Keynote** seminar by clicking either the 56 Kbps or the 110 Kbps link.

> If you are using a modem to access the Internet, then use the 56 Kbps link.
> If you connect to the Internet through a cable modem or LAN, then select the
> 110 Kbps link. The content is the same for each link, but the video and sound
> quality of the 110 Kbps link is better.

4. Watch and read along as Paul Flessner (Vice President, Microsoft SQL Server),
   discusses the role of SQL Server 2000 in the new Microsoft application frame-
   work known as .Net (pronounced "Dot Net").

CASE PROJECT

As a SQL Server 2000 consultant, you have been hired to help a client in choosing a
database vendor. The project will be an Internet-based initiative. Address the following
requirements of the client with the features of SQL Server 2000 that meet each need.

1. The client has a Web consulting company contracted to build an Internet site.
   They plan on building the site using XML to pass data to Web pages for display.

2. The client will require high availability of their vital Web data. They want to
   ensure that their Web site is always available for use, even in the event of a hardware failure.

3. The client expects the user base for their Web application to start out modestly and
   continue to grow over the months and years ahead. They want to make sure they
   choose a database system that can scale with the needs of their growing business.

4. The client is running a customer management system on an existing SQL Server
   in house, and they want to be able to integrate that system with the new Web system. Ideally, data in both systems could be updated at the same time, ensuring that
   the two are always in sync. Identify the features of SQL Server 2000 that will help
   the client achieve this goal.

OPTIONAL CASE PROJECTS FOR TEAMS

Team Case One

You and your team are charged with creating a pricing summary for SQL Server 2000. Using the Internet (*www.microsoft.com/sql*) compile a spreadsheet of the different pricing models for SQL Server 2000 for all of the editions of SQL Server 2000. Also, discuss the differences between the pricing models. Finally, determine which is cheaper for the following scenario:

A company wants to buy SQL Server 2000 to support an application that will have 75 users within the organization. For performance reasons, the computer running SQL Server 2000 will have two processors. Determine if it is cheaper to purchase licenses based on CPUs or client access licenses.

Team Case Two

As a team, generate a list of valuable Web sites that have SQL Server 2000 information. On the list, name the Web site, the URL, and provide a brief summary of the type of information or audience that the site is geared toward.

2

INSTALLING AND UPGRADING SQL SERVER 2000

After reading this chapter and completing the exercises you will be able to:

◆ Understand hardware and software requirements before installing or upgrading SQL Server 2000

◆ Install SQL Server 2000

◆ Upgrade an existing installation of SQL Server 2000

◆ Troubleshoot installations and upgrades

The process of installing SQL Server 2000 can be a very simple one. However, without a thorough understanding of the various installation options available, it is easy to make mistakes that will affect how the database operates. The default installation options will meet the needs of most companies, but every SQL Server 2000 implementation has different goals and requirements.

Before popping the SQL Server 2000 disk into your CD-ROM drive and rushing through an installation, take the time to get acquainted with the various editions of the product. Also, be sure to familiarize yourself with some of the most often overlooked installation options like collations (for internationalization) and multiple instances. In this chapter, upgrading to SQL Server 2000, along with the most important installations considerations, will be discussed and a full installation scenario will be illustrated.

HARDWARE AND SOFTWARE REQUIREMENTS OF SQL SERVER 2000

Like all applications, SQL Server 2000 has minimum hardware and software requirements that must be met prior to beginning a successful installation. Remember that the minimum requirements are just that. Each individual deployment of SQL Server 2000 will have different hardware requirements to meet storage and performance needs.

Table 2-1 lists the minimum hardware requirements for installing SQL Server 2000. In addition to the hard drive space, more hard disk space will be required, depending on the volume of data being stored in user databases.

Table 2-1   Minimum Hardware Requirements

Hardware	Minimum Requirements
Computer	Intel or compatible Pentium 166 MHz or higher
Memory (RAM)	**Enterprise Edition:** 64 MB minimum, 128 MB or more recommended **Standard Edition:** 64 MB minimum **Personal Edition:** 64 MB minimum on Windows 2000, 32 MB minimum on all other operating systems **Developer Edition:** 64 MB minimum **Desktop Engine:** 64 MB minimum on Windows 2000, 32 MB minimum on all other operating systems
Hard disk space	**SQL Server database components:** 95 to 270 MB, 250 MB typical **Analysis services:** 50 MB minimum, 130 MB typical **English Query:** 80 MB **Desktop Engine only:** 44 MB
CD–ROM drive	Required

SQL Server 2000 Windows CE Edition has the following hardware requirements:
- Microsoft Windows CE operating system version 2.11 or later for Handheld PC Pro (H/PC Pro) or Palm-size PC (P/PC) devices
- Windows CE 3.0 or later for Pocket PC devices
- 1–3 MB of available storage space, depending on processor type, operating system version, and components installed

In a typical production environment, a machine with at least two Pentium processors and 256 MB of RAM is a good rule of thumb. Depending on the requirements of a specific deployment, you need to test the performance of any system with simulated workloads to ensure the best results in a production environment.

Table 2-2 shows the various operating systems that the various editions of SQL Server 2000 can run on.

Table 2-2   Operating System Requirements

Operating System	Enterprise Edition	Standard Edition	Developer Edition	Personal Edition/ Desktop Engine	Windows CE Edition
Windows 2000 DataCenter Server	Yes	Yes	Yes	Yes	No
Windows 2000 Advanced Server	Yes	Yes	Yes	Yes	No
Windows 2000 Server	Yes	Yes	Yes	Yes	No
Windows NT Server	Yes	Yes	Yes	Yes	No
Windows 2000 Professional	No	No	No	Yes	No
Windows NT Workstation	No	No	No	Yes	No
Windows 98/ME	No	No	No	Yes	No
Windows CE	No	No	No	No	Yes

Additional Software Requirements

The following are some of the additional software requirements for SQL Server 2000 installations:

- All SQL Server 2000 editions require Internet Explorer 5. Internet Explorer 5 is used by both the graphic administration tools (e.g., Enterprise Manager) and the HTML help files in SQL Server Books Online.

- If SQL Server 2000 is being installed on Windows NT Server, Service Pack 5 or higher must be installed prior to installation.

- If the XML features are going to be used, Internet Information Services must be installed prior to a SQL Server 2000 installation.

INSTALLING SQL SERVER 2000

The following pages walk through a basic installation scenario of SQL Server 2000 Enterprise Edition on a Windows 2000 Advanced Server computer. For this installation, the following assumptions are made:

- The SQL Server will be used by a large-scale Web site for storing catalog information and processing transactions.

- The target computer will be running Windows 2000 Advanced Server and has two processors. (This installation scenario will also work on a computer running Windows 2000 Server with a single processor.)

- The target computer has a single hard drive (designated as C:\).

Each step and any resulting decisions are outlined and explained in detail. However, there are several considerations that you must address before putting in the SQL Server 2000 CD-ROM:

- Be sure that the computer on which SQL Server 2000 will be installed meets the hardware and software requirements outlined in the previous section.

- If you are installing the program on a machine that already has a version of SQL Server installed (especially when upgrading from a previous version), back up the current installation.

- Understand the availability requirements for the installation and plan accordingly. If failover clustering is required, then be sure to read all of the documentation regarding failover clustering installations. Later in this chapter, failover clustering will be discussed in further detail, but it will not be covered by the installation scenario.

- Depending on what languages data will be stored in, choose the appropriate **collation** during the installation process. The physical storage of character data is controlled by collations in SQL Server 2000. A collation specifies the binary patterns that represent each character available and the rules by which characters are sorted and compared.

In addition, make sure the following requirements are met prior to beginning the setup process:

- Log on to the operating system with an account that has local administrator rights on the computer. In the case of the installation scenario described in this chapter, it is assumed that the person performing the installation is logged on to the computer using the local administrator account.

- Be sure to shut down any instances of the operating system Event Viewer and Registry Editors that may be open.

- Be sure to shut down any services on the computer that are dependent on SQL Server. These services include anything that is using Open Database Connectivity (ODBC), including Internet Information Services.

The Internet Information Service can be shut down by going to the Services Manager and clicking Program Files, pointing to Administrative Tools, and clicking Services in Windows 2000. The same Services Manager can be accessed in Windows NT by clicking the Start button, pointing to Settings, clicking Control Panel, and clicking on Services. The name of the service that needs to be stopped is called World Wide Web Publishing Service.

- Create one or more valid domain user accounts that will enable the SQL Server 2000 components to log on and provide network access to the SQL Server 2000 installation. In the case of the installation scenario in this chapter, you will create an account for each of the SQL Server 2000 components that require them. This will be discussed in detail a little later on.

Running the Setup Program

Begin the installation process by simply placing a SQL Server disc in the CD-ROM drive, and the screen shown in Figure 2-1 appears. If the Installation Wizard does not start, navigate to the root of the installation folders (or the root of the CD) and double-click the Autorun.exe program.

Figure 2-1   SQL Server 2000 Enterprise Edition installation screen

Once the Autorun program executes, the installation menu screen offers several options. The SQL Server 2000 Components option opens a screen with various installation options. The SQL Server 2000 Prerequisites option opens a screen where the Common Controls Library Update is located. This option is only necessary if the installation is being done on a Windows 95 computer. Clicking the Browse Setup/Upgrade Help button will bring up SQL Server Books Online with the Installation Help section automatically highlighted. The Read the Release Notes option opens the ReadMe.txt file in the default text file viewer (usually Notepad). The View Our Web Site option simply opens a browser to the SQL Server homepage (*http://www.microsoft.com/sql/*). In order to perform an installation of SQL Server 2000, click the SQL Server 2000 Components menu item from the initial set of options.

Figure 2-2   SQL Server Components installation options

The SQL Server Components screen, shown in Figure 2-2, is the starting point for installing any of the following:

- *Install Database Server*: This option will begin the installation process for the database engine and administrative tools. This is the option that is selected in this installation scenario.

- *Install Analysis Services*: This option will begin the installation process for the data warehousing components of SQL Server 2000.

- *Install English Query*: This option installs a special set of facilities that allows users of SQL Server 2000 to query the database using logical English language statements. More information on English Query Services can be found at SQL Books Online.

Begin the installation process by clicking the Install Database Server option. Then click the Next button on the Welcome screen. The Computer Name screen appears, as shown in Figure 2-3.

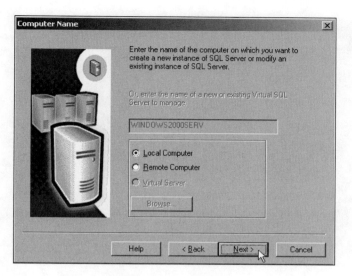

Figure 2-3   Computer Name screen

Installing SQL Server on a Local Computer

In this installation scenario, SQL Server 2000 Enterprise Edition is installed on the local computer (for this example, the local computer is named WINDOWS2000SERV). Select the Local Computer option, which defaults to the name of the computer that the installation program is running on. Notice that the application components can be installed on a remote machine by selecting that option and browsing to another computer on the network. In addition, if clustering services are available, the Virtual Server option can be selected to install an instance of SQL Server 2000 directly into an existing cluster.

The Virtual Server option will be selected by default if the installation program detects that Microsoft Clustering service (MSCS) is running on the computer on which you are performing the installation. The option is unavailable if MSCS is not detected.

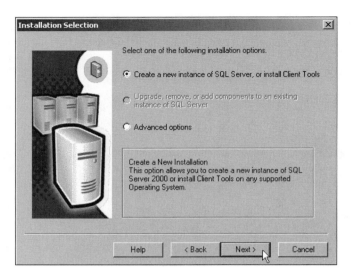

Figure 2-4 Installation Selection screen

Once the local machine is designated as the target for the installation process, click the Next button to display the Installation Selection screen shown in Figure 2–4. Here the administrator is offered a few choices regarding the type of installation he plans to run. The following options are available:

- Create a new instance of SQL Server, or install Client Tools: This is the option used in the example, since an initial installation is being performed.

- Upgrade, remove, or add components to an existing instance: This option is only enabled if an existing instance of SQL Server is detected by the Setup program.

- Advanced options: This option provides access to advanced installation tasks like rebuilding the registry, recording an unattended installation file (with a file extension of .ISS), or maintaining virtual servers for clustering.

Leave "Create a new instance of SQL Server, or install Client Tools" selected and click the Next button. The User Information screen shown in Figure 2-5 prompts for a person's name and company name. Typically the name of the administrator of the SQL Server install will be entered along with the appropriate company name.

Click the Next button to link through two screens. The first is the Software License Agreement page. Read through it and click the Yes button, and the CD-Key screen appears. Enter in a valid 25 digit CD-Key found on the back of the CD case, and click the Next button.

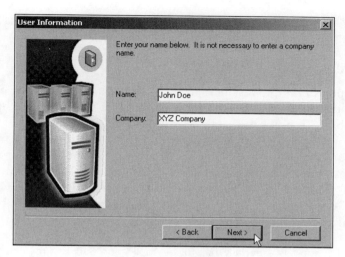

Figure 2-5   User Information screen

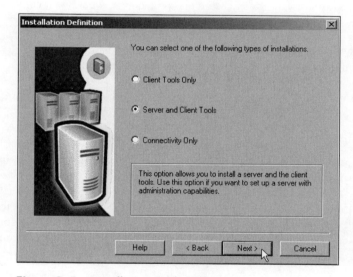

Figure 2-6   Installation Definition screen

The Installation Definition screen, shown in Figure 2-6, provides the following options:

- Client Tools Only: Installs only the client management tools like Enterprise Manager and Query Analyzer, as well as the client connectivity components. This option would be used when an administrator plans to manage SQL Server instances from his workstation on the network.

- Server and Client Tools: This option will install the database components and the client tools. It provides access to a wide array of installation options and is the selection made in this installation scenario.

- Connectivity Only: This option will simply install the Microsoft Data Access Components (MDAC 2.6) and network libraries.

Multiple Instances in SQL Server 2000

SQL Server 2000 supports multiple instances of the database engine running on a single computer. Each individual instance can be accessed as if it were installed on a separate machine. Reliability is improved due to the fact that each instance operates independently. The isolation between instances ensures that only the application using a particular instance is affected in the event of a database problem. Another valuable use of multi-instance support is with application development. A development, quality assurance, and staging environment can all be set up on a single machine, saving time (moving code changes across instances) and money (hardware costs associated with three separate physical environments).

 Multi-instance support is especially helpful in Application Service Provider (ASP) environments. An **Application Service Provider (ASP)** is a company that hosts and supports software for its customers. An example would be a company that has an Internet-enabled customer management system. The company's clients would pay a monthly fee to use the customer management application. With multiple instances, the ASP can leverage hardware by using one machine to support the SQL Server 2000 instances of multiple clients.

When multiple instances of SQL Server 2000 are installed on a single computer, a unique set of the following resources are created for each instance:

- System and user databases
- SQL Server and SQL Server Agent services (When multiple instances are installed, the names of these services includes the instance names. For example, if an instance is named CustomerDatabase, then the MSSQL Server service will be named MSSQL$CustomerDatabase and the SQL Server Agent service will be called SQLAgent$CustomerDatabase.) Since these services are uniquely named, they can be shut down and started independently of other instances.
- Registry keys associated with the MSSQL and SQL Server Agent services
- Network connection addresses used by applications to connect to specific instances of SQL Server 2000

Although multiple instances can operate independently on a single server, there are some components that are shared by multiple instances:

- Only one instance of the Administrative Tools is installed on any single computer. Also, the registry settings for the client applications (Administrative Tools) are not duplicated.
- Only one copy of the MS Search Service is installed on a computer with multiple instances of SQL Server 2000. The single MS Search Service provides

full-text indexing and searching for all of the instances of SQL Server installed on a single computer.

- Only a single copy of English Query and Analysis Services is installed on a machine with multiple instances of SQL Server 2000.

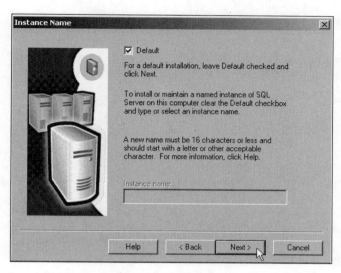

Figure 2-7   Instance Name screen

Notice in Figure 2-7 that the default instance is chosen. This selection is made automatically when a preexisting instance of SQL Server 2000 is not detected on the target machine. Click the Next button to continue on the Setup Type screen.

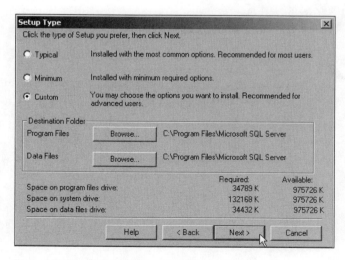

Figure 2-8   Setup Type screen

The Setup Type screen, shown in Figure 2-8, offers three choices for the installation type and provides an interface for specifying file locations for the files that will be used by the instance being installed.

- Typical: This option will install all of the components of SQL Server and assumes the default installation options. This option is sufficient for most installations to a single server.

- Minimum: This option only installs the minimum components required to run SQL Server 2000. It is usually only chosen when hardware limitations (hard drive space) prevent the installation of all of the components.

- Custom: This option allows an administrator to explicitly select components and subcomponents as well as customize the collation settings for an installation.

The file locations are prepopulated with the default file path of C:\Program Files\Microsoft SQL Server\. In this scenario the default file locations are sufficient, but they can be changed based on the hardware configuration of the target machine.

Typically, the program files of SQL Server 2000 are installed on the system hard drive (the drive that contains the \WINNT folder and the data files are stored on a second physical hard drive (D:\ or F:\ usually). Also, it is important to note that there are some issues with installing the program files on a cluster disk. Be sure to read the installation documentation thoroughly prior to installing in a clustered environment.

In this installation scenario, the typical installation will be performed, but the Custom Setup option is selected. The Typical Setup doesn't show all of the options available in an effort to simplify the process. The Custom Setup defaults the input screens with the options of the Typical Setup but shows additional screens not offered by the Typical Setup. Click the Next button to continue to the Select Components screen.

Components of SQL Server 2000

The following section describes all of the components and subcomponents available for an installation of SQL Server 2000, as shown in Figure 2-9.

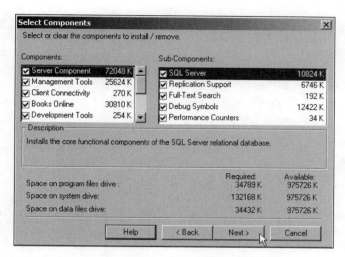

Figure 2-9 Select Components screen

Server Components   The following Server components are included when the option for Server and Client Tools is selected as an initial installation definition.

- SQL Server: Installs the core functional components of SQL Server relational database

- Upgrade Tools: Installs the SQL Server Upgrade Wizard, used to upgrade SQL Server version 6.5 databases to version 2000

- Replication Support: Installs the files required for replication

- Full-Text Search: Installs the Microsoft full-text search engine (Microsoft Search service), which provides improved searching facilities for character data stored in the databases

- Debug Symbols: Installs the debug symbols for installations

- Performance Counters: Installs performance counters for use with SQL Server

Management Tools   The following Management tools are included when the Client Tools option is selected as an initial installation definition.

- Enterprise Manager: The primary management tool for SQL Server 2000

- Profiler: Used to monitor and audit SQL Server 2000 database activity

- Query Analyzer: The standard query tool provided by SQL Server 2000. It is used to execute and test T-SQL statements and queries on a database.

- DTC Client Support: Used to extend database transactions across multiple servers

- Conflict Viewer: Used in replication scenarios to view and change the way synchronization conflicts are resolved

Client Connectivity   The Client Connectivity component is used to facilitate communication between clients and servers. It installs the Microsoft Data Access Components (MDAC) and the DB-Library, OLE DB, and ODBC network libraries.

Books Online   The Books Online component installs both the SQL Server Books Online for SQL Server 2000 and online Windows-style Help. These resources are indispensable when working with SQL Server 2000.

Development Tools   The Development Tools component installs tools that are useful when programming applications for SQL Server 2000. Typically these would only be installed if the SQL Server was going to be used for development.

Code Samples   The Code Samples component installs a set of programming examples that demonstrate common programming tasks associated with developing applications with SQL Server 2000. In this installation, all of the default components are included. Click the Next button to access the Services Accounts screen.

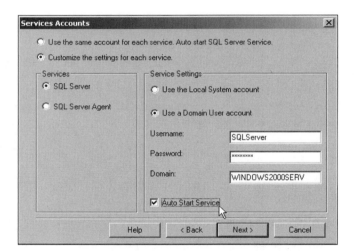

Figure 2-10   Services Accounts screen

The Services Accounts menu allows the configuration of user accounts used by the SQL Server and SQL Server Agent services (see Figure 2-10). The default option is to use a single account for both services.

Creating Windows User Accounts for Use by SQL Server 2000

In this installation scenario, we create two user accounts for use with the SQL Server and SQL Server Agent services. Also, we configure both services to start automatically when the server is started up, by clicking the Auto Start Service check box for each service.

2

The differences between using the local system account and a domain user account can drastically affect how SQL Server 2000 will operate. The local system account does not have network access, since it is only known to the resources on the local machine. A domain user account lets the service log on to the network and access network resources, as well as interact with other SQL Servers. Network access to other computers allows SQL Server 2000 to store and back up data across several machines. It also allows SQL Server 2000 instances to interact directly with other SQL Server 2000 instances on a network, enabling activities like replication and heterogeneous queries. The following powerful features can only be implemented if the services are configured to use a domain user account:

- Replication

- Remote procedure calls

- Backups to network hard drives

- Heterogeneous joins across servers

Before we can configure the SQL Server services to use domain user accounts, we must create the user accounts using the Computer Management application of Windows 2000. This application is accessed by clicking Start, highlighting Programs, highlighting Administrative Tools, and clicking Computer Manager.

We are making local system accounts in this example, but the process is the same for domain user accounts (except the accounts are made on a domain controller).

Using the user management facilities of the Computer Management program (Figure 2-11) in Windows 2000, two users are created: SQLServer and SQLAgent. In this example we set the password never to expire to ensure that the services will always start properly when the SQL Server computer is rebooted.

Each of these user accounts must have the following rights on the computer on which SQL Server 2000 is being installed:

- "Log on as a service" permissions

- Permission to modify the registry keys associated with SQL Server 2000 (Administrative rights on the local machine provides these permissions)

- "Access and Change" permissions on the SQL Server installation folder and the drives and folders on which the database and log files reside.

The rights are all granted if the Windows User Accounts are added to the Local Administrators group.

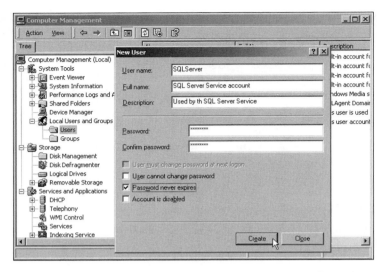

Figure 2-11   Creating domain user accounts in Windows 2000

Associating Windows Logons with SQL Server 2000 Services

Now that we have created the two accounts in Windows 2000, we can associate them with the SQL Server and SQL Server Agent services in the Setup program.

First, select the option labeled "Customize the settings for each service" and then enter the appropriate user name, password, and domain. This SQL Server computer will be used for a production database system, and as such, SQL Server and its associated services should start when the machine boots up. To achieve this, check the Auto Start Service check box.

Once all of the correct user account information is set for the SQL Server service, select the SQL Server Agent service from the left side of the screen and provide the appropriate user account information on the right side. Click the Auto Start Service check box for the SQL Server Agent service.

When the Auto Start Service check box is checked for the SQL Server Agent service, a warning message will appear. It simply states that the SQL Server Agent has a dependency that requires the SQL Server services to be running when the Agent service starts. This situation may cause problems when trying to shut down the SQL Server manually. This usually doesn't affect typical installations and will be fine for this installation scenario, but the dependency can be deactivated after the installation is complete if required.

Click the Next button to proceed to the Authentication Mode screen of the installation program shown in Figure 2-12.

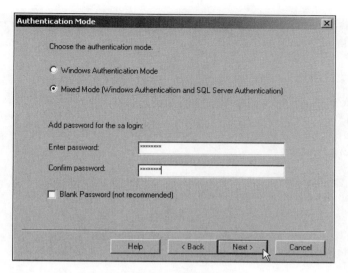

Figure 2-12   Authentication Mode screen

SQL Server 2000 Authentication Modes

SQL Server 2000 authenticates user logons in one of two ways: Windows Authentication Mode or Mixed Mode. Under **Windows Authentication Mode**, a user logs on to the SQL Server using either a Windows NT or Windows 2000 user account. With **Mixed Authentication Mode**, both Windows and SQL Server-based authentication are implemented.

When a user attempts to access a SQL Server instance that implements Windows authentication, SQL Server validates the account through the Windows security mechanism that houses user account information for both individual computers as well as entire Windows domains.

Mixed Authentication Mode supports standard Windows authentication, but it also provides support for SQL Server user accounts. This is provided for backward compatibility with earlier versions of SQL Server. Many applications written for earlier versions of SQL Server (typically versions 6.5 and 7.0) use the user name and password features of SQL Server instead of network user accounts.

Many developers and database administrators prefer to use SQL Server Authentication because of their familiarity with a previous version of SQL Server. Since all access to a database instance is controlled through SQL Server, there is no need to coordinate with network administrators to set up security schemes. However, Windows Authentication Mode is strongly recommended with SQL Server 2000 and provides the following benefits over SQL Server authentication:

- Secure validation and encryption of passwords
- Auditing

- Password expiration and minimum password length
- Account lockout after multiple invalid logon requests

Collation Considerations

As stated earlier, collations control the physical storage of character data in SQL Server 2000. In almost all cases, the default collation chosen by the SQL Server Setup application is acceptable. The default collation is based on the Windows **locale** of the computer on which SQL Server 2000 is being installed.

 The Regional Options item in the Windows Control Panel shows the Windows locale of a computer.

In this installation, the collation options are left unchanged because the default selections are acceptable (Figure 2-13).

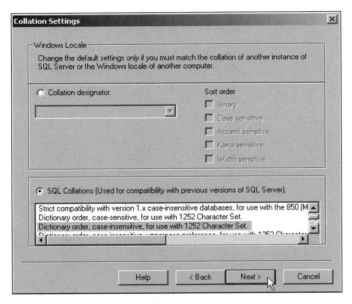

Figure 2-13   Collation Settings screen

Collation Components

There are several aspects of collations that are important to understand before making any choices about the collation option that SQL Server 2000 will use. The first of these is how character data is stored on computer memory. Each character is stored as a sequence of ones and zeros that uniquely identifies it. Each one and zero is called a bit, and 8 bits make up a byte. So in a single-byte character there are 8 ones or zeros that define the character. With single-byte characters (made up of 8 bits each) there are only $256(2^8)$ possible unique combinations. **Code pages** define a set of bit patterns for letters, numbers, and symbols. Each European language, such as German or Spanish, has its own single-byte code page. Different languages have different unique characters. To support this condition, numerous code pages are available to support different languages. Most Western languages have a single-byte code page offering 256 unique characters.

Languages that have more than 256 unique characters (especially Asian languages) have double-byte code pages which support over $65,000(2^{16})$ unique characters.

As the Web becomes the medium of choice for delivering applications, there is an increasing need to store data in multiple languages in a single location. In an effort to address the problems involved with storing multilingual data in one database, a 2 byte character set called **Unicode** has been developed by independent standards organizations. SQL Server 2000 supports Unicode through the use of special character data types that are specified for individual columns in database tables (nchar, nvarchar, and ntext).

 Unicode data types require twice as much physical space as typical datatypes because they implement 2-byte characters. However, the extra space required is a small price to pay when you consider the fact that Unicode eliminates the need to convert characters between code pages.

In addition to code pages, collations also have sort orders. **Sort orders** define the sequence in which characters are sorted and how characters are evaluated in comparison operations. A sort order specifies things like:

- Dictionary order: "a" comes before "b"
- Case sensitivity: "a" does not equal "A"

Collations specify three things:

- Sort order for Unicode data
- Sort order for non-Unicode data
- Code page used for non-Unicode data

Selecting an Appropriate Collation

When determining the appropriate collation to choose when installing SQL Server 2000, the first place to look is to the group of people who will use the system. In general, if all of the users speak the same language, choose the specific collation for that language. For example, if all of the users of a system speak Polish, then choose the Polish collation. If the user group speaks multiple languages, choose the collation that will support all of the languages. For example, most of the western European languages are supported by the Latin1_General collation.

The Custom Setup type must be chosen from the SQL Server 2000 Setup program to modify the default collation settings for an installation. Collations can be changed using the Collation Settings screen of the Setup program. Notice the default collation is Latin1_General (the default for U.S. English) because the Windows locale on the computer is "ENGLISH (United States)." Only change the default collation if it must match the collation settings of another SQL Server instance (required for interactivity like replication between SQL Servers).

An important improvement of SQL Server 2000 over earlier versions, is that collations can be selected for instances, databases, and even individual columns. For each of these, the collation will default to the collation of the previous object. For instance, a column will inherit the collation of the database that houses it, and a new database will default to the collation of the SQL Server instance that owns it. Click the Next button to continue to the Network Libraries screen.

Networking Libraries   The Network Libraries screen shown in Figure 2-14 allows network libraries to be installed for an installation of SQL Server 2000. Network libraries are used to facilitate communication between clients and SQL Servers using various interprocess communication mechanisms (IPC).

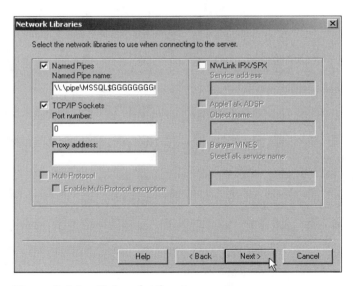

Figure 2-14   Network Libraries screen

The following list outlines the various network libraries available through the SQL Server 2000 Setup program:

- **Named Pipes**: Required when installing SQL Server 2000 in Windows 2000 or Windows NT. Named Pipes permits access to shared network resources.

Named Pipes is not supported in Windows 98.

2

- **TCP/IP Sockets**: Allows communication through standard Windows sockets. The default port for default instances of SQL Server 2000 is 1433. For named instances, a port will be dynamically assigned each time the service starts unless a static port number is assigned. The proxy address allows SQL Server 2000 to listen for requests through a proxy server.

- **Multi-protocol**: A single library that offers support for TCP/IP, Named Pipes, and NWLink IPX/SPX. Multi-protocol is not supported for named instances of SQL Server 2000.

- **NWLink IPX/SPX**: Provides support for Novell NetWare clients connecting to SQL Server 2000

- **AppleTalk ADSP**: Allows clients on an AppleTalk network to communicate with SQL Server 2000. It is not supported with named instances of SQL Server 2000, and it will not be supported in future releases of SQL Server.

- **Banyan VINES**: Supports Banyan Vines clients. It is not supported with named instances of SQL Server 2000, and it will not be supported in future releases of SQL Server.

In this installation scenario, the defaults we select are Named Pipes and TCP/IP. These choices are the most common and provide support for most typical networks. Unless specific support for Netware, AppleTalk, or Banyan Vines clients is required, always use the default settings.

Once the network libraries are selected and the Next button is clicked, a message-only screen announces that the installation program has enough information to install the instance of SQL Server 2000. Before you start copying files onto the target machine, choose a licensing mode.

Licensing Options for SQL Server 2000 SQL Server 2000 has two licensing schemes. One is based on the number of devices connecting to a database instance, and the other is based on the number of processors that the SQL Server computer has (see Figure 2-15).

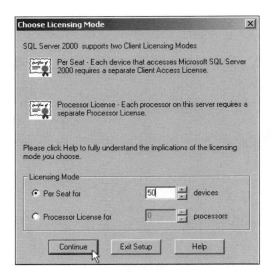

Figure 2-15 Licensing Mode screen

Per Seat licensing is based on the number of devices that will connect to SQL Server 2000. A device could be a desktop workstation, terminal based application, or any other device that uses an application that connects to an instance of SQL Server 2000. Per Seat is usually cheaper in situations where individual clients are connecting to multiple SQL Servers, because a licensing fee is paid per user instead of per SQL Server computer.

With Processor Licensing, fees are paid based on the number of processors (CPUs) that the SQL Server computer has. There is no limit to the number of devices that can connect to SQL Server 2000 under this licensing model. Processor Licensing is often implemented when SQL Server 2000 is used as the back end for a Web site with a large user population.

Licensing Modes of SQL Server 2000

In this installation scenario, SQL Server 2000 is being installed to support a large-scale Web site on a computer with two processors so Processor License is chosen. The appropriate selections are made on the Choose Licensing Mode screen of the installation program and the Continue button is clicked to begin the installation of SQL Server 2000.

 The SQL Server 2000 installation program begins by installing the connectivity components (**Microsoft Data Access Components (MDAC)**). The MDAC setup program automatically detects and identifies any active processes that may be using files needed for installation. It is recommended that these processes be shut down prior to installation, but it is not required. However, if you chose not to shut them down, the computer will have to be rebooted when the SQL Server 2000 installation finishes for changes to take affect.

When the installation program finishes, SQL Server 2000 is installed on the target machine. This includes all of the database engine components as well as the suite of administrative tools. (The tools can be accessed by clicking Start, highlighting Programs, and selecting SQL Server.)

Failover Clustering Considerations

Failover clustering is implemented with SQL Server 2000 when there is a high availability requirement for a deployment. When SQL Server is used as the database back end for large-scale, high-volume systems, failover clustering will help to ensure that users will have access to data even in the event of a hardware or software failure. All of the clustering functionality implemented by SQL Server 2000 is based on the Microsoft Clustering service (MCSC) available in Windows NT 4.0 Server and the Windows 2000 Server family.

In a clustered environment, multiple SQL Server computers share a common set of cluster resources (usually hard drives). Each SQL Server computer in a cluster is called a **node** and shared resources of the cluster are referred to as **cluster groups**. All of the nodes in the cluster communicate with each other by sending small network messages known as **heartbeats**. The heartbeat messages are used by the cluster services to determine which nodes are operational. In the event that a heartbeat is not received from a node, MSCS considers the node as "failed" and transfers the shared resources in the cluster group to another operational node in the cluster. In this way, database processing can continue without the end user noticing.

Advanced Installation Options

When the Advanced options selection on the Installation Selection screen is selected, three choices are offered:

- Record Unattended .ISS file
- Registry Rebuild
- Maintain a virtual server for failover clustering

Unattended Installation

The "Record Unattended .ISS file" option allows an unattended installation file to be created. When this option is chosen, all of the typical prompts for an installation are provided but the selections are used to build an unattended installation file instead of actually installing SQL Server 2000. The file generated has an extension of ".iss" (the default file name is Setup.iss) and is stored in the \WINNT folder of the computer. This file is used by running SQL Server Setup directly from the command prompt. Sample batch files are included on SQL Server 2000 CDs to perform common installations. Table 2-3 lists these sample files.

Table 2-3   Sample Unattended Installation Batch Files on the SQL Server 2000 CD

Type of unattended installation	Batch File Used
Typical installation of SQL Server	Sqlins.bat
Client tool only: Includes management tools, client connectivity, and other tools (no server is included)	Sqlcli.bat
Custom installation of SQL Server: All components included	Sqlcst.bat

These batch files contain a command line call to the SQL Server 2000 Setup program. To execute a .iss file that is recorded manually, you must call the SQL Server Setup program from the command prompt with the proper options. Assume that an unattended installation file has been generated and that the SQL Server 2000 CD is in the CD-ROM drive (Drive letter E:\). The command below runs the SQL Server 2000 Setup with the options specified in the setup.iis file.

```
E:\x86\setup\setupsql.exe −s −f1 "C:\WINNT\setup.iss"
```

The *−s* argument makes setupsql.exe run silently (with no user input required). The *−f1* argument and following file paths specify the unattended installation file to use.

Rebuilding the Registry

The Registry Rebuild option will rebuild the registry entries for a corrupted SQL Server 2000 installation. This option will prompt the user for all of the typical installation options and then repair the registry accordingly. It is important to note that the same choices used to perform the initial installation must be made to restore the registry to a correct state.

 The Registry Rebuild option will not repair any data errors or the master database.

SQL SERVER 2000 UPGRADES

Performing upgrades from previous versions of SQL Server is a very straightforward process. Tools that come with SQL Server 2000 allow easy upgrades from versions 7.0 and 6.5 as well as between editions of SQL Server 2000 (i.e. upgrading Standard Edition to Enterprise Edition). Selecting the "Upgrade, remove, or add components to an existing instance of SQL Server" option triggers SQL Server 2000 Setup to detect which version of the product is currently running on a computer and provide the appropriate options (where existing installations are version 7.0 and 2000). A straightforward process for upgrading version 6.5 databases to version 2000 is also provided. For added stability, the Setup program has built-in recovery processes that resume an upgrade automatically in the event of a failure.

Upgrading from SQL Server 7.0

There are two ways to upgrade databases to SQL Server 2000 from version 7.0. The most obvious is to upgrade all of the underlying components, as well as existing databases, by running a standard upgrade using the SQL Server 2000 Setup program. The second option involves using the Copy Database Wizard to move databases from a version 7.0 installation to an existing version 2000 instance.

Upgrading a SQL Server 7.0 Installation

An installation of SQL Server 7.0 can be fully upgraded or overwritten by SQL Server 2000. The Setup program will detect if SQL Server 7.0 is present and the upgrade option will be available. The steps to perform the upgrade are almost identical to a typical installation like the scenario covered in this chapter.

The result of the upgrade is that all of the program files from SQL Server 7.0 are upgraded and all the existing databases are preserved. In effect, the SQL Server 7.0 instance is replaced with a SQL Server 2000 instance. After the upgrade is complete, the full-text catalogs used need to be repopulated (if they were used in SQL Server 7.0), and the statistics of the database need to be updated. These tasks are not completed automatically by the upgrade because they can be time-consuming; but not executing them manually can result in poor performance from a newly upgraded SQL Server 2000 instance.

 The only way to get back to the original SQL Server 7.0 installation is to uninstall SQL Server 2000, reinstall SQL Server 7.0, and then manually restore the databases that were backed up prior to upgrading in the first place.

Copy Database Wizard

The Copy Database Wizard is used to copy or move databases between multiple instances of SQL Server 2000 and to upgrade databases from SQL Server version 7.0 to SQL Server 2000. You can access the Wizard through Enterprise Manager by right-clicking on a registered SQL Server, selecting All Tasks, and then clicking the Copy Database Wizard option. As with an installation upgrade, the statistics of a database copied to an instance of SQL Server 2000 must be updated to ensure optimal performance.

 Only user databases can be moved from version 7.0 to version 2000 using the Copy Database Wizard. The system databases (master, model, and msdb) cannot be moved or copied with the Wizard.

Upgrading from SQL Server 6.5

Upgrading to SQL Server 2000 from version 6.5 is quite different from the process of upgrading from version 7.0. The architectural differences between versions 6.5 and 7.0 are so great that a straight upgrade cannot be performed from version 6.5 to SQL Server 2000.

In this type of upgrade, the SQL Server 2000 components are installed without affecting the existing version 6.5 installation. In fact, the databases and some SQL Server settings are actually *copied* to the 2000 version installation. To perform this type of upgrade, you must first install SQL Server 2000 on the same machine as the version 6.5 installation, and then you must execute a series of steps to migrate both the database structure and raw data.

Once you have installed an instance of SQL Server 2000 on the SQL Server 6.5 computer, you can use the SQL Server Upgrade Wizard to upgrade the version 6.5 databases (click Start, highlight Programs, and select Microsft SQL Server – Switch). The Wizard upgrades any or all user databases housed in a version 6.5 installation, transferring all the objects and user data. It will also maintain replication settings, SQL Server Agent settings, and any SQL Server 6.5 configuration options that are still applicable in SQL Server 2000.

When you have successfully completed the upgrade using the Upgrade Wizard, the computer will have both a SQL Server 2000 instance and the preexisting SQL Server 6.5 installation. Both will be fully operational and can be managed from unique sets of the graphical administrative tools.

Upgrading Editions of SQL Server 2000

When working solely with SQL Server 2000, you can easily accomplish upgrades in functionality and upgrades to other versions. You can add components that are not installed to an existing installation by running the Setup program and selecting the "Upgrade, remove, or add components to an existing instance of SQL Server" option. The screens that follow prompt you to either upgrade the current edition or to add components that are not already installed. Table 2-4 lists the edition to edition upgrades supported.

Table 2-4 Edition Upgrade Chart

Installed Version	Can Upgrade To
SQL Server 7.0 Desktop Edition	SQL Server 2000 Personal Edition
	SQL Server 2000 Standard Edition
SQL Server 7.0 Standard Edition	SQL Server 2000 Standard Edition
	SQL Server 2000 Enterprise Edition
SQL Server 7.0 Enterprise Edition	SQL Server 2000 Enterprise Edition
SQL Server 2000 Developer Edition	SQL Server 2000 Enterprise Edition
SQL Server 2000 Standard Edition	SQL Server 2000 Enterprise Edition
SQL Server 2000 Personal Edition	SQL Server 2000 Standard Edition

TROUBLESHOOTING INSTALLATIONS AND UPGRADES

Even with all of the automation and detection facilities of the Setup program, things can still go wrong during an installation or upgrade. This section identifies where to find answers if problems occur during execution of the Setup program or while upgrading databases.

In addition to the useful troubleshooting information in SQL Server Books Online, Microsoft has a special TroubleShooters Web site that offers the latest information. If a problem occurs that is not documented in the Books Online, access the TroubleShooters Web site at *http://support.microsoft.com/support/tshoot/*.

Most problems are caused by too little disk space, conflicts with other running applications, or shared files that are locked. These types of things can usually be avoided if all pre-installation requirements are met. These include hardware and software requirements of SQL Server 2000 (discussed earlier) and programs known to cause conflicts when SQL Server 2000 Setup is run.

Useful Files for Diagnosing Problems

SQL Server Setup will create three files that can provide information about problems that occur during an installation or upgrade:

- Sqlstp.log: This file is located in the \WINNT folder on the system drive of the target machine. It records any errors that occur during the configuration portion of Setup.

- Setup.log: This file is located in the \WINNT folder on the system drive of the target machine.

- Errorlog: The most recent error log for SQL Server 2000. It can be found in the \Log folder off of the installation directory (Default is C:\Program Files\Microsoft SQL Server\Mssql\Log\Errorlog).

A special log file is generated for upgrades from version 6.5 to 2000 using the SQL Server Upgrade Wizard. During the SQL Server Upgrade process, all custom stored procedures, logons, users, and permissions are validated. If any problems are detected, a dialog box appears alerting the user that a problem has occurred. When errors or warnings occur, error logs (with a .err file extension) can be found in the following location: C:\Program Files\Microsoft SQL Server\Mssql\Upgrade\<servername>_<date>_<time>

An additional date/time specific directory is generated every time the Upgrade Wizard is run.

CHAPTER SUMMARY

❏ Installing and upgrading SQL Server 2000 is a straightforward process based mostly on an intuitive Setup program that comes with every edition of SQL Server 2000. The various editions provide a wide array of functionality designed to suit the needs of any sized company. Every Microsoft operating system (including Windows CE) has an edition of SQL Server 2000 suited to it. Proper analysis of business and technical requirements aids in selecting an edition of SQL Server 2000 that will work best for a given situation.

❏ Enterprise Edition offers the most functionality and supports the most hardware of any edition of the product. The Developer Edition allows programmers to design and test applications that leverage all of the functionality of the Enterprise Edition but only pay for a reasonably priced developers license. Standard Edition offers everything but the scalability and availability features of the Enterprise Edition. The Personal and Desktop Engine editions are deployed on workstation computers that are running applications that required local database storage.

❏ The SQL Server Setup program is a very stable application that performs several different types of installations and upgrades for SQL Server 2000. It prompts a user with several screens for pertinent information (most of which is defaulted based on thorough detection mechanisms). Some of the options available include specific components to install, authentication modes, network libraries, and user accounts used by the SQL Server 2000 components.

❏ Unattended installations allow a file containing specific setup options to be used by the Setup program in lieu of user input. Selecting the Advanced Options selection in the Setup program generates an unattended installation file. The file that is generated is named setup.iss.

❏ In order to easily resolve problems encountered during an installation or upgrade, several log files are generated by the Setup program to provide detailed information of what occurred during a process.

KEY TERMS

AppleTalk ADSP — Library allowing clients on an AppleTalk network to communicate with SQL Server. It is not supported with named instances of SQL Server 2000 and it will not be supported in future releases of SQL Server.

Application Service Provider (ASP) — A company that hosts and supports software for its customers or provides an application that can be "leased" by its customers.

Banyan VINES — This library supports Banyan Vines clients. It is not supported with named instances of SQL Server 2000 and it will not be supported in future releases of SQL Server.

cluster group — Term used to refer to shared sets of resources (usually hard drives) used by a SQL Server failover cluster.

2

code page — Defines the bit patterns that represent specific letters, numbers, and symbols. Some are single byte, consisting of 256 unique values. Others are double byte and offer over 65,000 unique values.

collation — Specifies the binary patterns that represent each character available and the rules by which characters are sorted and compared.

heartbeat — Simple network messages passed between nodes on failover clusters that are used to determine which nodes are operational.

locale — The Windows operating system attribute that defines certain behaviors related to language. The locale defines the code page, used to store and sort character data, as well as language-specific items such as the format used for dates and time and the character used to separate decimals in numbers.

Microsoft Data Access Components (MDAC) — The key technologies for enabling data access across a network. MDAC is installed as a suite of connectivity tools for accessing data in a variety of formats.

Mixed Authentication Mode — One of two mechanisms used to validate user connections to SQL Server instances. Users are identified by their Windows domain logon or SQL Server logon information.

Multi-Protocol — A single network library that offers support for TCP/IP, Named Pipes, and NWLink IPX/SPX. Multi-Protocol is not supported for named instances of SQL Server 2000.

Named Pipes — A network library that is required when installing SQL Server in Windows 2000 or Windows NT. Named Pipes permits access to shared network resources.

node — Term used to refer to a single SQL Server computer within a failover cluster

NWLink IPX/SPX — The NWLink network library provides support for Novell NetWare clients connecting to SQL Server.

sort order — The set of rules used by a collation to define how characters are sorted and evaluated by comparison operations.

TCP/IP Sockets — The TCP\IP network library allows communication through standard Windows sockets. The default port for default instances of SQL Server 2000 is 1433. For named instances, a port will be dynamically assigned each time the service starts, unless a static port number is assigned. The proxy address allows SQL Server to listen for requests through a proxy server.

Unicode — Unicode defines a set of letters, numbers, and symbols by using two bytes per character. Two-byte characters allow Unicode to offer more that 65,000 possible values compared to single-byte character sets, which only allow 256. Unicode includes characters for most modern languages.

Windows Authentication Mode — One of two mechanisms used to validate user connections to SQL Server instances. Users are identified by their Windows user or group when they connect.

REVIEW QUESTIONS

1. What is the recommended amount of RAM for SQL Server 2000 Enterprise Edition?

   a. 32 MB

   b. 64 MB

   c. 128 MB

   d. 256 MB

2. What defines the set of rules for how characters are sorted and evaluated by comparison operations?

   a. sort order

   b. code page

   c. Unicode

3. Single-byte code pages support how many unique characters?

   a. 256

   b. 1024

   c. 32768

   d. over 65,000

4. What is used to upgrade a version 7.0 installation to a version 2000 installation?

   a. Copy Database Wizard

   b. DTS

   c. SQL Server 7.0 Setup program

   d. SQL Server 2000 Setup program

5. In a high-volume Web site scenario, which licensing option is typically chosen?

   a. Processor Licensing

   b. Per Seat Licensing

6. What is the default installation folder for SQL Server 2000?

   a. C:\Program Files\SQL2000\

   b. C:\Program Files\Microsoft SQL Server\

   c. C:\WINNT\Microsoft SQL Server\

   d. C:\MSSQL\

7. When multiple instances of SQL Server 2000 are installed on a single computer, which of the following is one of the resources that is shared across instances?

   a. SQL Server service

   b. SQL Server Agent service

2

c. MS Search service

d. transaction logs

8. Which of the following features is not affected by setting up the SQL Server service to log on using the local system account?

a. replication

b. backups to network hard drives

c. exporting data using Data Transformation Services (DTS)

d. heterogeneous joins across servers

9. What software do the graphic administration tools and SQL Server Books Online require?

a. Notepad

b. Windows NT Service Pack 5

c. Internet Explorer 5

d. Netscape Navigator

10. Which of the following cannot be accomplished with the SQL Server 2000 Setup program?

a. install a new instance of SQL Server 2000

b. upgrade a version 7.0 installation to version 2000

c. upgrade a version 6.5 installation to version 2000

d. install OLAP Services

11. What is the name of the log file containing errors that occurred during the Setup program?

a. Setup.log

b. ErrorLog.txt

c. Sqlstp.log

d. Setup.iss

12. The default collation for a new installation of SQL Server 2000 is based on?

a. the edition of SQL Server 2000 being installed

b. the Windows locale of the local machine

c. nothing, the default is always U.S. English

d. whether English Query Services are being installed or not

13. What application must be installed on a computer prior to installing SQL Server 2000 if the XML features are going to be used?

a. Internet Information Server 5 (IIS 5.0)

b. Microsoft Data Access Components (MDAC)

    c. Event Viewer

    d. SQL Server 2000 Enterprise Manager

14. Which of the following is not an option on the Installation Definition screen of the Setup program?

    a. Client Tools Only

    b. Server and Client Tools

    c. OLAP Tools

    d. Connectivity Only

15. What is the file extension for an unattended installation file?

    a. .exe

    b. .mdf

    c. .iss

    d. .log

16. Which feature of SQL Server 2000 is especially important to Application Service Provider (ASP) companies?

    a. log shipping

    b. multiple instances

    c. OLAP services

    d. Full-text searching

17. A company uses SQL Server 7.0 to manage research information. Each of the users has access to SQL Server through a logon and password that are managed by SQL Server. The IT department wants to upgrade to SQL Server 2000 and it wants to continue to use the logons provided by the previous SQL Server 7.0 installation. Which authentication mode should you choose when upgrading their version 7.0 installation?

    a. Mixed Mode

    b. Windows Authentication Mode

18. A company wants to install SQL Server 2000 Standard Edition on three separate computers in three different countries. The three installations will not interact with each other, and each one will have users that speak a different language (requiring a different collation). However, all three of the computers will reside in a single hosted facility and have the same Windows locale. Which installation strategy should be used in this situation?

    a. perform a typical installation on each computer

    b. perform a minimum installation on each computer

    c. perform a custom installation on each computer

HANDS-ON PROJECTS

All of the following hands-on projects can be performed using a single Windows 2000 Advanced Server computer.

2

Project 2-1

To determine if a computer meets the minimum hardware requirements for an installation of SQL Server 2000:

1. Click **Start**, highlight **Programs**, highlight **Administrative Tools**, and select **Computer Management**.

2. Expand the System Information item by clicking the **+** icon next to it.

3. Click the **System Summary** item below System Information. Notice how the system information is displayed on the right side of the screen in Figure 2-16.

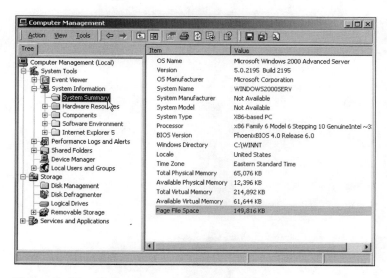

Figure 2-16   System summary information

4. Check the OS Name, Processor, and Total Physical Memory items to ensure that they meet the minimum hardware requirements for an installation.

This screen will also show the Windows locale used to determine the default collation when SQL Server 2000 is installed.

Project 2-2

To verify that the services (SQL Server and SQL Server Agent) have been set up properly, using the installation scenario from this chapter:

1. Click **Start**, highlight **Programs**, highlight **Administrative Tools**, and select **Computer Management**.

2. Expand the **Services and Applications** item.

3. Click the **Services** item. (The list of services is easier to read if you click the **View** button at the top of the window and then click on the word **Detail**).

4. Scroll down to the **MSSQLSERVER** service and double-click it to bring up the service properties screen shown in Figure 2-17. Verify that the service status is Started.

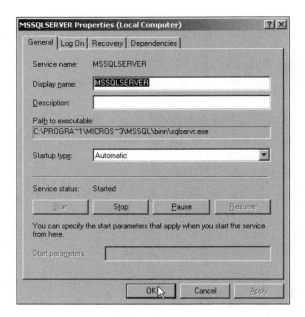

Figure 2-17   MSSQLServer service properties

5. Repeat the above steps for the SQLSERVERAGENT service.

Project 2-3

To review the directories created by the installation scenario in this chapter:

1. Start Windows Explorer (click the **Start** button, highlight **Programs**, highlight **Accessories**, and click **Windows Explorer**).

2. Navigate to C:\Program Files\Microsoft SQL Server\MSSQL and familiarize yourself with the folders and their contents.

3. Read the item entitled "Locating Directories and Files" in SQL Server Books Online to learn more about each folder.

2

Project 2-4

To inspect the registry entries created by the installation scenario in this chapter:

1. To start the Registry Editor **Open** text box first click the **Start** button and then click the **Run** button.

2. Enter **regedt32** in the **Open** text box and click the **OK** button. (The Registry Editor will open.)

3. Select the **HKEY_LOCAL_MACHINE** window from the windows that are open in the Registry Editor.

4. Navigate down to folders by following these steps: Click **HKEP_LOCAL_MACHINE**, select **SOFTWARE**, select **Microsoft**, and then select **MSSQLServer**.

5. Navigate around the various folders and key values to familiarize yourself with the registry changes made when SQL Server 2000 is installed.

Project 2-5

To verify an installation by connecting to SQL Server 2000 with the Query Analyzer Tool and executing a query:

1. Start the Query Analyzer by clicking the **Start** button, highlighting **Programs**, highlighting **Microsoft SQL Server**, and clicking **Query Analyzer**.

2. In the logon dialog, enter the correct server name (WINDOWS2000SERV in the installation scenario), select **Windows authentication**, and click the **OK** button.

3. When the Query Analyzer appears, type the following command in the query window:

   "SELECT @@SERVERNAME"

4. Execute the query by clicking the green triangle button on the top toolbar. (This executes queries.)

5. The results appear in the bottom half of the query window. The server name (WINDOWS2000SERV in the case of the installation scenario) should be the only thing returned by the query.

6. Verify that the following query also returns information about the version of SQL Server that is installed:

   "SELECT @@VERSION"

Project 2-6

To use the SQL Server Licensing tool to change the licensing information for an installed instance of SQL Server 2000:

1. Click the **Start** button, highlight **Settings**, and click **Control Panel**.

2. From the Control Panel, double-click the **SQL Server 2000 Licensing Setup** item.

3. The Choose Licensing Mode screen from the Setup program appears allowing licensing information to be specified. The current licensing information is populated in the screen.

4. Change the number of processors to "**4**" and click the **Continue** button. That's it! The licensing information has been changed.

CASE PROJECTS

Case One

XYZ Company has hired you to assess their requirements and come up with a detailed plan for installing SQL Server 2000. They needed a database engine that offers top-notch processing speed and data storage facilities to be used with a Human Resources application that is being developed by programmers in-house. The HR application will be available on the company intranet and have over 1000 users. XYZ has purchased two separate computers on which to install SQL Server 2000: one for the live application, and another for development and testing (used by the internal programmers). Since it is being used over the company intranet, every user who accesses the application will be supplying a Windows-based user name and password. Currently the budget will not cover a clustered failover installation, and the development team plans to perform backups often to ensure data will not be lost. Based on these requirements, what types of installations should be done on each of the computers? Which licensing model makes the most sense for each SQL Server being installed?

Case Two

You are part of a team of SQL Server consultants that is meeting a potential client. The client needs to select a database system to support a growing Web site and has some concerns that you will address in your meeting. First of all, in an effort to penetrate other global markets, they want to support multiple languages for their Web site, but they are worried about the costs associated with such an initiative (the possibility of additional hardware to support languages other than English). Also, with the incredible growth in user activity the company has seen over the last few months, they want to implement a database that can offer scalability (their concerns focus on both hardware and database size limitations). Finally, since they host a commercial-grade Web site, they want to ensure that the system is always up and running, even if a hardware error occurs. Your job is to come up with a proposal discussing the features of SQL Server 2000 that will help the client achieve their goals. In addition to the information provided in this chapter, read case studies and testimonials on the SQL Server home page (*www.microsoft.com/sql*) to provide real-world examples of how SQL Server 2000 is being used by other companies to solve similar problems.

Case Three

You are the managing database administrator for a company that is rolling out SQL Server 2000 to multiple offices. There are 10 offices including the headquarters where you work. The other offices only have one or two IT staff and they are not very knowledgeable about SQL Server 2000. SQL Server 2000 will be installed on identical hardware with the same options at each satellite office. What are your options for ensuring that all of the installations are performed correctly? What are the pros and cons of each option?

2

3

ADMINISTERING AND CONFIGURING SQL SERVER 2000

After reading this chapter and completing the exercises you will be able to:

♦ Identify the applications installed with SQL Server 2000

♦ Configure SQL Server 2000 with the Enterprise Manager and SQL Query Analyzer

♦ Configure SQLMail and SQLAgentMail

♦ Create a linked server

Configuring and Managing SQL Server 2000 can be a very complex endeavor, but the Administrative Tools and documentation installed with SQL Server 2000 are designed to simplify things. Getting familiar with these tools is the first step toward becoming an effective, certified SQL Server 2000 professional. When working with SQL Server 2000, tools like Enterprise Manager and Query Analyzer are used extensively to perform such tasks as configuring SQL Server, creating and altering databases, and managing security information.

In this chapter, the various applications found in the SQL Server program group (installed when SQL Server 2000 is installed) are identified. Some of the more important administrative features will also be covered to provide a basis of understanding for using the client tools to administer various instances of SQL Server 2000.

CLIENT APPLICATIONS INSTALLED WITH SQL SERVER 2000

Once SQL Server 2000 is installed on a computer, a SQL Server program group is created to organize all of the client applications associated with SQL Server 2000 (see Figure 3-1). Each of these programs is accessible through the start menu by clicking the Start button, highlighting Programs, and then highlighting Microsoft SQL Server.

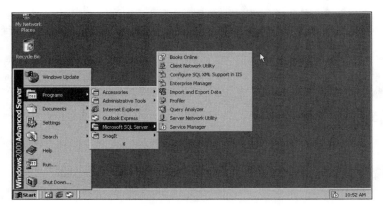

Figure 3-1   The SQL Server 2000 program group

Books Online

Books Online contains the documentation and help files associated with SQL Server 2000 and its various functions. All of the information contained in Books Online is accessed through an HTML interface similar to Windows Explorer. Locating information in the documentation is facilitated through a hierarchical menu (similar to folders on a computer file system) and through full-text searching.

Client Network Utility

The Client Network Utility is used to determine the versions of various network libraries installed on a computer and to set up server aliases, as well as some more advanced configurations. Network libraries are used by a client application to connect to SQL Server 2000. Client applications include all of the Administrative Tools, as well as any custom programs that connect to a SQL Server 2000 instance.

Configure SQL XML Support in IIS

This allows SQL Server 2000 to be configured to accept requests directly over the Internet. It opens a program called "IIS Virtual Directory Management for SQL Server," which allows SQL Server 2000 to be configured to listen for requests over the **Hypertext Transfer Protocol (HTTP)**. This functionality will be discussed in detail in later chapters.

Enterprise Manager

Enterprise Manager is a robust management tool for administering and configuring SQL Server 2000 instances. It functions as a "command center" when working with SQL Server 2000 and is a starting point for just about any task a database administrator may be charged with. The most important feature of Enterprise Manager is that it allows multiple local and remote SQL Server 2000 instances to be managed from a single computer. In addition, Enterprise Manager provides an interface for creating and configuring databases, managing permissions on database objects, setting SQL Server 2000 configuration parameters, and much more. Throughout this book, various important features of Enterprise Manager will be discussed in detail.

Import and Export Data

The Import and Export Data item in the SQL Server 2000 program group invokes the Data Transformation Services (DTS) Import/Export Wizard. The wizard simplifies the process of importing, exporting, and transforming data and database objects between disparate sources (like two different SQL Servers or a SQL Server database and an Oracle database). DTS and the Import/Export Wizard will be discussed in Chapter 8.

Profiler

The Profiler program is used to capture events that occur on an instance of SQL Server 2000. It can be set up to generate a trace file that records a list of all the actions performed against an instance. You can then analyze trace files to determine problems or even "replay" them as a series of steps leading up to a specific event. The tool is typically used to perform the following types of actions:

- Diagnosing queries that are not running at acceptable speeds
- Recording a set of actions that lead to a problem and then replaying the steps to replicate the problem. (This is useful when determining the cause of problems with a SQL Server 2000 application.)
- Monitoring how queries perform under specific workloads
- Security auditing of actions that are occurring on a SQL Server 2000 instance for later review

Profiler will be discussed in detail in later chapters in the context of troubleshooting and optimization.

Query Analyzer

The Query Analyzer is the standard SQL query tool for use with SQL Server 2000. It is used to design and test T-SQL statements that are run against an instance of SQL Server 2000. The tool itself is optimized for working with SQL statements and has several features that automate the process and save time. There are also features to aid in the optimization of statements being written, including a graphical query plan generator and index tuning wizard. Throughout this book, the Query Analyzer will be used to execute T-SQL statements that perform different operations.

Server Network Utility

The Server Network Utility is used to change the network libraries for an installed instance of SQL Server 2000. It allows an administrator to activate, deactivate, and reconfigure server network libraries used to listen for clients accessing the database over various network protocols. It offers similar functionality to the SQL Server Setup program and includes support for changing the protocols used by specific instances of SQL Server 2000.

Services Manager

The Services Manager tool allows the various services associated with SQL Server 2000 to be stopped, started, and paused. The services supported by the Services Manager are used with the various SQL Server components installed with a particular instance. Depending on the various components that were installed during setup, the Service Manager has access to the following services:

- SQL Server service

- SQL Server Agent service

- Microsoft Search service (Windows NT and Windows 2000 only)

- MS DTC service (Windows NT and Windows 2000 only)

- MSSQLServerOLAPService service (Windows NT and Windows 2000 only)

 MSSQLServer LapService and Search Service are only available if installed.

EXPLORING ENTERPRISE MANAGER

The Enterprise Manager application is used to perform virtually all of the administrative tasks that are required of a SQL Server 2000 instance. This section provides a basic introduction to navigating around Enterprise Manager and configuring instance-level options. Figure 3-2 shows the default view when the Enterprise Manager application is started.

Server Groups

Different instances are assigned to server groups to aid in organization. Groups can organize related servers in the same way that folders on a file system help organize files. Commands can then be executed against groups instead of single instances to save time on common administrative tasks. The default group created when Enterprise Manager is installed is called SQL Server Group. You can add additional or custom groups easily by right-clicking on Microsoft SQL Servers and then clicking New SQL Servers Group in the Enterprise Manager, as shown in Figure 3-3.

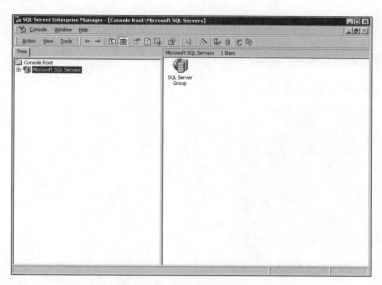

Figure 3-2   SQL Server Enterprise Manager

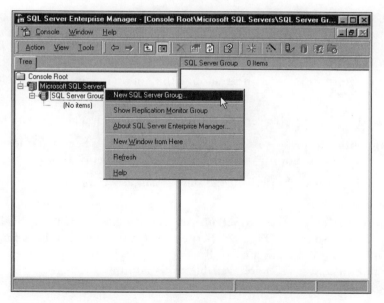

Figure 3-3   Creating Server Groups in Enterprise Manager

A group does not have many properties, since it is only used to organize SQL Server 2000 instances; therefore, the Server Groups window for creating new groups is very simple. The only information it requires is a group name and, optionally, whether the new group is a top-level group or if it exists as a sub-group beneath another group in the hierarchy (identical to subfolders on the file system). The Server Groups window is shown in Figure 3-4.

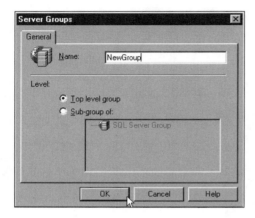

Figure 3-4   Server Groups screen

Registering Servers

Enterprise Manager allows multiple SQL Server instances to be registered and made available for administration from a single interface. Before you can manage an instance, you must register it with Enterprise Manager. This is a simple process that can be performed either through a wizard interface or a simple data entry screen. In order to complete a successful registration, you must supply the following information about an instance:

- The name of the SQL Server 2000 instance (must be available on the network)
- The authentication mode used to connect to the SQL Server (either Windows Authentication Mode or SQL Server Authentication)
- The server group within which the new instance will reside in Enterprise Manager

Once an administrator enters the proper information in the Registered SQL Server Properties dialog box, as shown in Figure 3-5, the server is registered and residing within the server group specified. At this point all of the configuration properties, database properties, and administrative tasks are available to an administrator.

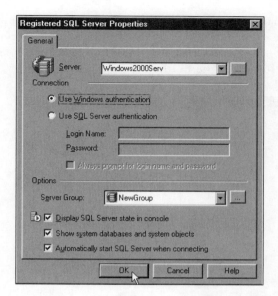

Figure 3-5 Registered SQL Server Properties screen

QUERY ANALYZER

The SQL Server Query Analyzer tool is used for developing and executing T-SQL statements. The text editor interface uses color codes based on T-SQL syntax to improve the readability of statements being developed. In addition, there is a simple object browser that allows a SQL programmer to easily view the name and structure of any object in a database from the query tool itself, thus reducing development time. Query Analyzer is often used side-by-side with Enterprise Manager to configure and maintain SQL Server 2000 instances and databases.

The Query Analyzer tool can be started in the following ways:

- By entering the command isqlw in a command prompt window or from the Run prompt, accessed by clicking the Start button

- By clicking Start and navigating to Programs, highlighting Microsoft SQL Server, and then clicking on Query Analyzer

- By clicking the Tools menu in Enterprise Manager and then clicking on SQL Query Analyzer

Unless the Query Analyzer is started from Enterprise Manager (from the tools menu), login information must be specified. The login screen requires the name of the SQL Server that the connection is being established as well as login credentials.

The query view of the Query Analyzer tool shown in Figure 3-6, is the default when the application starts. Queries are typed into the large text box and are executed by clicking the Execute Query button (green triangle) or pressing the F5 key. The results of queries are returned in tabular format at the bottom of the screen.

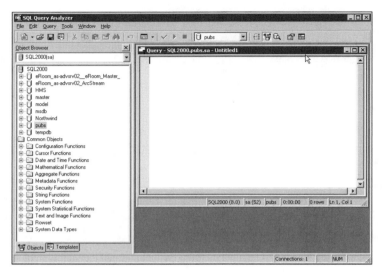

Figure 3-6   SQL Query Analyzer

The Query Analyzer includes several time-saving features like templates and automatic object-based scripts. Templates provide skeleton statements for creating objects in a database, as well as performing management functions, such as adding a linked server. An object-based script is used to generate the syntax for performing inserts, updates, and deletes on particular tables in a database.

Configuring a Registered SQL Server

Once a SQL Server is registered, the wide array of configuration options can be accessed easily by right-clicking on the server node in Enterprise Manager and selecting the Properties option as shown in Figure 3-7.

The SQL Server Properties (Configure) window provides access to several server-wide configuration options. Figure 3-8 shows how the various types of configurations are segmented by different tabs on the screen (Memory, Server Settings, Connections, etc.).

General Tab

The General tab shown in Figure 3-8 displays the various software and hardware properties of the computer on which SQL Server 2000 is installed.

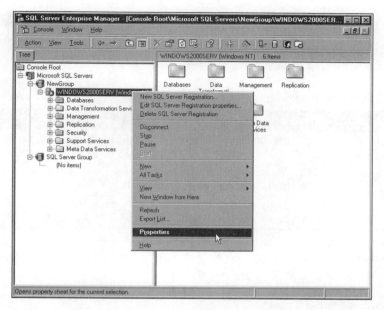

Figure 3-7   Accessing the Properties of a registered instance of SQL Server 2000

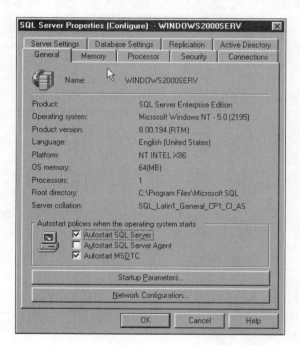

Figure 3-8   General tab of the SQL Server Properties screen

The startup parameters for the SQL Server are accessible from this tab as well. Startup parameters are used to determine file locations and certain behaviors of SQL Server 2000 instances when they are started. When SQL Server 2000 is first installed, three default startup parameters are set, as listed in Table 3-1.

Table 3-1   Default Startup Parameters

Default Startup Options	Description
-d*master_file_ path*	The fully qualified path for the master database file (typically, C:\Program Files\Microsoft SQL Server\MSSQL\Data\Master.mdf)
-e*error_log_ path*	The fully qualified path for the error log file (typically, C:\Program Files\Microsoft SQL Server\MSSQL\Log\Errorlog)
-l*master_log_path*	The fully qualified path for the master database log file (typically C:\Program Files\Microsoft SQL Server\MSSQL\Data\Mastlog.ldf)

There is also a set of additional startup parameters that are available for various purposes. The most common of these are listed in Table 3-2.

Table 3-2   Additional Startup Options

Other Startup Options	Description
-c	Reduces startup time by starting an instance of SQL Server 2000 independently of the Service Control Manager (SQL Server does not run as a service if this option is specified)
-f	Starts an instance of SQL Server 2000 with a minimized set of configurations. This option is useful if an incorrect configuration has been made and it is preventing SQL Server 2000 from starting.
-m	Starts an instance of SQL Server 2000 in single-user mode. This option is helpful if there are problems with system databases that should be repaired.
-s*instancename*	Allows a named instance of SQL Server 2000 to start. If the -s parameter is not set, only the default instance will try to start.
-x	Disables CPU time and the recording of cache-hit ratio statistics. This allows SQL Server 2000 instances to operate with maximum performance.

Server Setting Tab

The Server Settings tab shown in Figure 3-9 allows several instance wide options to be viewed or modified. It is the place where the default language for SQL Server messages is specified. This tab is also where a **query governor threshold** is set. The query governor is a component of SQL Server 2000 that enforces time-based restrictions on query execution. The "cost" value specified in the query governor represents the maximum number of seconds that a single query is permitted to run. SQL Server 2000 estimates the cost of a query prior to execution so that long-running queries can be canceled before they start. This helps to prevent poorly designed or resource-intensive queries from degrading the overall performance of a server.

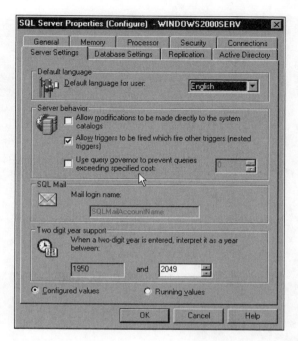

Figure 3-9 Server Settings tab of the SQL Server Properties screen

The way in which SQL Server 2000 handles two-digit years is set from the Server Settings tab. Two-digit years are handled in the following way:

- Two-digit years that are less than or equal to the last two digits of the cutoff year are in the same century as that of the cutoff year.

- Years greater than the last two digits of the cutoff year are in the century previous to that of the cutoff year.

- The rules are not applied for explicit four-digit years.

For example, if the two-digit year support range is between 1950 and 2049 (default value), then a date sent to SQL Server 2000 as "01/01/75" would be translated to "01/01/1975". Similarly, a date sent to SQL Server as "01/01/34" would be translated to "01/01/2034".

 Several of the tabs in the SQL Server Properties windows have the dual radio buttons at the bottom ("Configured values" and "Running values") displayed in Figure 3-10. When you select the "Configured values" option, the various options on the tab are enabled, and modifications are allowed. If you change any values on a tab, clicking the "Running values" option shows whether the changes have taken effect. If they have not, then you must stop and start the instance to ensure that any configurations are committed.

Figure 3-10   Configured values and Running values

Memory Tab

SQL Server 2000 can dynamically allocate memory as required for operations. The Memory tab, seen in Figure 3-11, allows a minimum and maximum size parameter for the amount of memory that SQL Server 2000 will use. By default, SQL Server 2000 instances are configured to use as much memory as the system allows. For machines that are dedicated to SQL Server 2000, the minimum amount should be set to zero. If the computer housing SQL Server is also used for additional services (e.g., network printing) the minimum amount of memory should be set above zero to ensure that response times from SQL Server 2000 won't degrade to unacceptable levels when the load on the computer from other services is too great. The "Minimum query memory" setting specifies the minimum amount of memory that a query will get for execution. The default value setting of 1024 KB is an acceptable value for most cases, but should be adjusted to meet application and user needs.

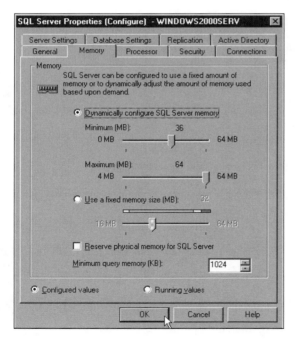

Figure 3-11   Memory tab of the SQL Server Properties screen

Database Settings Tab

The Database Settings tab seen in Figure 3-12 allows several global properties for databases across an instance. The bulk of the options have to do with index creation and tape backup, which will be discussed in detail in later chapters. The Recovery Interval option is used to determine how many minutes per database are permitted when SQL Server 2000 performs recovery.

Each time an instance of SQL Server 2000 is started, each database on that instance is "recovered." The process consists of committing or rolling back transactions that have not been written to disk when the instance stopped. The recovery interval is used when an instance is running to force transactions in memory to be committed to disk. When transactions are committed to disk it is known as a checkpoint in SQL Server 2000. Checkpoints occur when the volume of transactions not committed to disk has reached a certain threshold. For example, a reporting system (where modifications are not often made) would have very few checkpoints, but an instance of SQL Server 2000 used to support a transactional system where data is constantly being modified, checkpoints would occur frequently. It is recommended that the recovery interval setting be left at zero, which allows SQL Server 2000 to automatically determine when checkpoints are executed. The only reason to change it is if checkpoints are occurring too frequently and are impairing system performance. In this case, increase the recovery interval amount incrementally until an acceptable level of overall performance is reached.

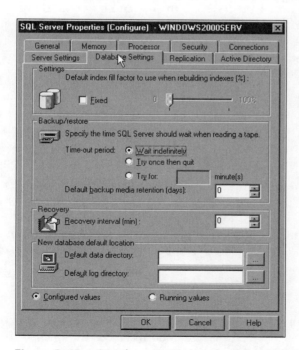

Figure 3-12   Database Settings tab of the SQL Server Properties screen

This Database Settings tab also allows default directories to be specified for new databases to store their log and data files.

Processor Tab

This tab, shown in Figure 3-13, shows all of the processors available for use by a SQL Server 2000 instance, as well as a set of configuration options for optimizing performance. The maximum worker threads option allows a specific number of operating system **threads** to be used by a SQL Server 2000 instance. SQL Server 2000 will use several threads for intrinsic operations like handling requests from multiple networks, performing checkpoints, and handling multiple concurrent users. SQL Server 2000 also takes advantage of the thread pooling facilities of Windows NT or Windows 2000. Thread pooling provides optimized performance when a high volume of users are connected simultaneously to a SQL Server 2000 instance.

 Typically, each client connecting to a SQL Server 2000 instance is provided a thread. In situations where there are hundreds or even thousands of concurrent users, threads are placed in a pool, doled out to handle client requests, and returned to the pool when the requests have completed. This provides much better performance in high-volume systems.

The "Boost SQL Server priority on Windows" option allows a SQL Server 2000 instance to run at a higher priority than other processes on the operating system. By default, SQL Server 2000 will run at a priority of 7, but when the checkbox is checked, it will run at a priority of 13 (which gives it precedence over other running applications on a server). It is recommended that this option only be checked if the computer is dedicated to SQL Server 2000 and SQL Server 2000 will be using multiple processors.

This tab allows SQL Server 2000 to be configured for parallelism (using multiple processors for executing queries). Parallel query support allows SQL Server 2000 to execute a single query using multiple threads on more than one processor (CPU). This feature increases the performance of complex queries handling large amounts of data. By default, SQL Server 2000 instances will use all available processors on a computer.

The "Minimum query plan threshold" option allows a specific query cost value to determine whether a parallel query plan is generated for a query. Before a query is executed, SQL Server estimates its "cost of execution." This initial "cost" value is based on using only a single thread to perform the operation. If the cost is higher than the minimum query plan threshold, a parallel query plan is generated to take advantage of multiple operating system threads and computer processors.

Security Tab

The Security tab seen in Figure 3-14 provides an interface to alter the authentication type and security auditing level of a SQL Server 2000 instance.

3

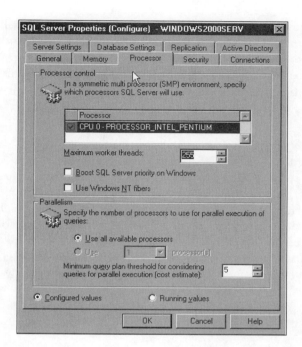

Figure 3-13   Processor tab of the SQL Server Properties screen

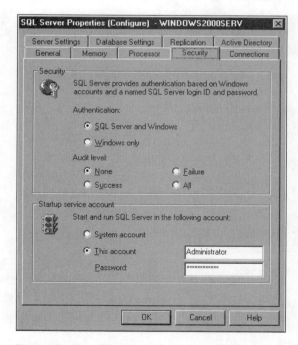

Figure 3-14   Security tab of the SQL Server Properties screen

Security auditing writes the results of login attempts to log files. "Success" will log all successful attempts to log in to a SQL Server 2000 instance (both Windows and SQL Server authentication). "Failure" will log only failed login attempts (bad user name or password). The "All" option logs every login attempt. The default value for this option is "None," no security auditing is performed. From this tab, the login account used by the SQL Server 2000 service can be modified as well.

Connections Tab

The Connections tab displayed in Figure 3-15 allows a maximum number of simultaneous user connections to be specified. By default this value is set to zero, which makes SQL Server 2000 dynamically create connections as needed up to a maximum amount of 32,767. The default setting is recommended in most cases and should not be changed. However, in situations where the number of concurrent users is hindering performance of a SQL Server 2000 instance, the user connection limit can be set. Take note that if a maximum amount is specified, users over that number will receive an error message from SQL Server 2000 until an available connection can be assigned to them.

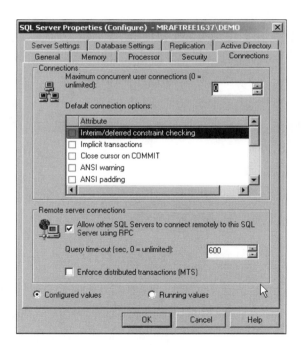

Figure 3-15   Connections tab of the SQL Server Properties screen

Configuring Server Options with Sp_configure

Most of the configuration options modified in the SQL Server properties screen are available through a system-stored procedure called sp_configure. This procedure can be called from the Query Analyzer application to make changes to the settings of SQL Server 2000. The procedure takes two parameters:

- @configname: The name of the configuration setting to change

- @configvalue: The new value to assign to the specified configuration setting

Table 3-3 describes common configurations and value ranges for use with the sp_configure systems stored procedure. To set the "recovery interval" configuration using sp_configure, use the following T-SQL syntax:

```
sp_configure 'recovery interval', '5'
GO
RECONFIGURE
```

The RECONFIGURE statement causes the new setting to take effect on the running server (unless the setting requires that the instance be started and stopped).

Table 3-3 Configuration Names for Use with Sp_configure

Configuration Option	Minimum	Maximum	Default
affinity mask	0	2147483647	0
allow updates	0	1	0
awe enabled	0	1	0
c2 audit mode	0	1	0
cost threshold for parallelism	0	32767	5
cursor threshold	-1	2147483647	-1
default full-text language	0	2147483647	1033
default language	0	9999	0
fill factor	0	100	0
index create memory	704	2147483647	0
lightweight pooling	0	1	0
locks	5000	2147483647	0
max degree of parallelism	0	32	0
max server memory	4	2147483647	2147483647
max text repl size	0	2147483647	65536
max worker threads	32	32767	255
media retention	0	365	0
min memory per query	512	2147483647	1024
min server memory	0	2147483647	0
using nested triggers	0	1	1
network packet size	512	65536	4096
open objects	0	2147483647	0
priority boost	0	1	0

Table 3-3   Configuration Names for Use with Sp_configure (continued)

Configuration Option	Minimum	Maximum	Default
query governor cost limit	0	2147483647	0
query wait	-1	2147483647	-1
recovery interval	0	32767	0
remote access	0	1	1
remote login timeout	0	2147483647	20
remote proc trans	0	1	0
remote query timeout	0	2147483647	600
scan for startup procs	0	1	0
set working set size	0	1	0
show advanced options	0	1	0
two-digit year cutoff	1753	9999	2049
user connections	0	32767	0
user options	0	32767	0

CONFIGURING E-MAIL FOR SQL SERVER 2000

SQL Server 2000 has facilities to generate and send e-mail messages, as well as the ability to receive and process e-mails. There are two services of SQL Server 2000 that provide mail functionality: SQLMail and SQLAgentMail. SQLMail is used by the SQL Server service to send and receive e-mails. SQLMail can be used to send e-mail with T-SQL statements. It can also be used to receive e-mails containing queries and send a response e-mail containing the results of the query. SQLAgentMail is used by SQLServerAgent to send e-mails when certain events occur on a SQL Server instance. It is typically set up for such tasks as sending an informational e-mail to an administrator when a certain alert condition is raised (configuring SQL Server 2000 alerts is discussed in Chapter 10).

Both SQLMail and SQLAgentMail function by connecting as a client to an e-mail server. Each service operates independently and is therefore configured separately. Both can connect to any of the following e-mail server types:

- Microsoft Exchange Server
- Microsoft Windows NT Mail
- Post Office Protocol 3 (POP3)

The first step to configuring e-mail services for SQL Server is setting up a mail profile in either Windows NT or Windows 2000. This is done by clicking Mail on the Control Panel.

The Mail option in Control Panel is only available if Microsoft Outlook is installed.

3

Hands-on Project 3-3, at the end of this chapter, will cover the exact process for setting up a mail profile. A single profile can be set up for use by both SQLMail and SQLAgentMail, or two separate profiles can be configured. Once a mail profile is set up properly, the two mail services are configured easily by selecting a profile name for each to use.

SQLMail is configured from Enterprise Manager by opening the Support Services folder and right-clicking on the SQLMail option. From this screen, displayed in Figure 3-16, the proper profile is specified and a test can be performed to ensure that the service is operational. When a test is executed, an e-mail is sent to the profile's e-mail box confirming that a mail session has been started and stopped successfully with the profile.

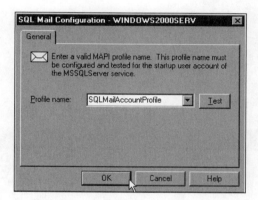

Figure 3-16   SQL Mail Configuration screen

You can configure SQLAgentMail from the SQL Server Agent Properties window seen in Figure 3-17. To access this window, expand the Management folder in Enterprise Manager, right-click on SQLServerAgent, and then select Properties.

Sending Mail With SQLMail

Once SQLMail is set up and functioning properly, you can call **extended stored procedures** from stored procedures, triggers, or simple T-SQL batches. This will automatically build and send an e-mail, as well as process mail that has been sent to the SQLMail account. The various extended stored procedures used to handle mail services are outlined in Table 3-4.

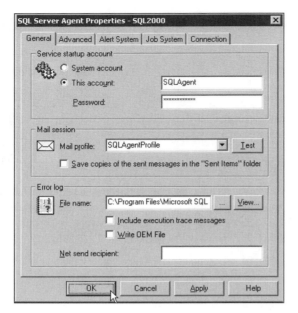

Figure 3-17   SQL Server Agent Properties screen

Table 3-4   SQL Server 2000 Extended Stored Procedure for E-mail

Procedure Name	Function
xp_startmail	Starts a SQLMail session. **Note:** This procedure is not usually needed because SQLMail is usually already running.
xp_stopmail	Stops a SQLMail session..
xp_sendmail	Used to send e-mails including query results and files as attachments
sp_processmail	This procedure is called to handle any incoming e-mail. E-mails sent to SQL Server 2000 are expected to have a valid SQL Server T-SQL query in the message body. This procedure can be scheduled to run at certain times or regular intervals to process any e-mail sent to SQL Server. **Note:** Sp_processmail calls the extended stored procedures xp_findnextmsg, xp_readmail, and xp_deletemail to iterate through the messages in an inbox. It also calls xp_sendmail to send reply e-mails with query results.

Xp_sendmail Examples   Xp_sendmail takes several parameters to allow access to most of the features of any e-mail client, like Microsoft Outlook or Netscape Mail. Xp_sendmail takes the following parameters:

- @recipients: The e-mail addresses (separated by semicolons) that the e-mail is sent to

- @message: The body of the e-mail message to be sent

- @query: A valid T-SQL query. The results of the query are returned in the e-mail (optional)

- @attachments: A semicolon-delimited list of the paths for files that will be added to the e-mail message as attachments (optional)

- @copy_recipients: A semicolon-delimited list of e-mail addresses to which the message will be copied (CC'd) (optional)

- @blind_copy_recipients: A semicolon-delimited list of e-mail addresses to which the message will be blind copied (BCC'd) (optional)

- @subject: The subject of the e-mail message to be sent (optional)

- @type: The e-mail message type (optional)

- @attach_results: Specifies whether the query results are returned in the body of the e-mail or as an attached file. A value of "true" causes the query results to be added to the e-mail as a text file attachment. A value of "false" causes the query results to be appended to the message body (optional)

- @no_header: Specifies whether the column headings are returned with the query in the e-mail body. The default value is "false," which makes SQL Server 2000 include the column headings with the query results. If the parameter is set to "true," then only the results of the query are returned without the column headings (optional)

- @width: Specifies the line width of the output of a query to prevent line breaks from being inserted into query output (optional)

- @seperator: The text column separator used to format the results. A comma could be specified to force the results of a query to be returned in comma-delimited format (optional)

- @echo_error: Appends any error messages encountered from the execution of the query to the body of the e-mail message

The following examples illustrate the basic T-SQL syntax for call xp_sendmail. This code can be executed by opening the Query Analyzer application and typing it into a query window.

- Sending a basic text e-mail

```
EXEC xp_sendmail @recipients = 'jsmith@XYZ.com',
                 @copy_recipients = 'ljames@XYZ.com',
                 @message = 'SQL Mail is properly
                 configured',
                 @subject = 'SQL Mail Configured!!'
```

This code will send an e-mail with the subject and message above to *jsmith@XYZ.com* and copy *ljames@xyz.com* on the message. Obviously, all of the parameters can be modified to send e-mail to any valid e-mail address with customized subjects and message bodies.

- Sending query results in an e-mail

```
EXEC xp_sendmail @recipients = 'jsmith@XYZ.com',
                 @subject = 'Contents of the Customer
                 Table',
                 @query = 'SELECT * FROM Customer'
```

This code will send an e-mail to *jsmith@XYZ.com* with the output of the SELECT statement in the body of the message.

- Sending query results as an attachment to an e-mail

```
EXEC xp_sendmail @recipients = 'jsmith@XYZ.com',
                 @subject = 'Contents of the Customer
                 Table',
                 @query = 'SELECT * FROM Customer'
                 @attach_results = 'TRUE',
                 @separator = ','
```

This code will send an e-mail to *jsmith@XYZ.com* with the output of the SELECT statement as an attached file. The @separator parameter specifies the field separator in the generated text file (in this case it is a comma, so the resulting file would be a comma-delimited text file containing all of the data from the Customer table).

LINKED SERVERS

One of the most powerful features of SQL Server 2000 is the ability to perform distributed queries. Distributed Queries access data from multiple heterogeneous data sources across the local machine and remote machines on the network. **OLE DB** (pronounced "Oh Lay Dee Bee"), the Microsoft specification for an application programming interface (API) for universal data access, supports the processing of distributed queries. OLE DB is used to access data in relational databases, spreadsheets, mail stores, or any data repository that has an OLE DB Provider. **OLE DB Providers** are software components that provide access to various data source types. For example, there are OLE DB providers for SQL Server 2000, Oracle, Excel spreadsheets, and Exchange Server (e-mail).

OLE DB support in SQL Server 2000 allows queries executed in SQL Server 2000 to access data housed in remote or foreign data sources. For example, a table in an Oracle database could be queried from SQL Server 2000, and the results could be returned with additional data from the SQL Server itself. The integration possibilities are endless and fairly easy to design due to the standards-based approach of OLE DB. Remote data sources are configured in SQL Server 2000 as objects called "linked servers."

A linked server allows SQL Server 2000 to execute commands against any data source accessible through OLE DB. This functionality allows a single distributed query executed from a SQL Server 2000 instance to update multiple, disparate data sources. It is also the foundation for distributed partition views (database objects used to increase performance of queries against large tables by segmenting the data across multiple SQL Servers to leverage additional hardware resources). This section will cover the process of setting up linked servers with SQL Server 2000 and accessing remote data through T-SQL statements.

Figure 3-18 illustrates how SQL Server 2000 and OLE DB work together to gain access to remote data stores for distributed queries. SQL Server 2000 uses OLE DB and, based on the types of remote data stores, the appropriate OLE DB providers.

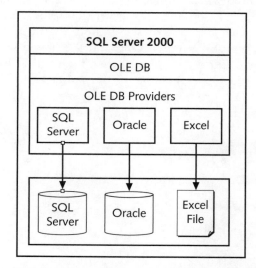

Figure 3-18   SQL Server linked server architecture

Setting Up a Linked Server

Linked servers are set up through either a graphic interface in Enterprise Manager or by executing system-stored procedures with proper parameter values. New linked servers are configured from the Linked Servers item under the security folder in Enterprise Manager displayed in Figure 3-19.

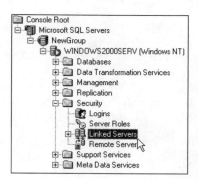

Figure 3-19   Linked Servers in Enterprise Manager

Right-clicking on Linked Servers and selecting the New Linked Server option activates the screen for setting up new linked servers shown in Figure 3-20. This screen consists of three tabs for inputting general data source information, security information (used by the local SQL Server 2000 instance to log on to the linked server), and configuring server settings.

The General tab provides an interface for selecting an OLE DB provider and then providing the associated information required when connecting to an OLE DB datasource. It also has the option of directly linking to other SQL Server 2000 instances. When adding another SQL Server 2000 instance as a remote server, only the instance name needs to be supplied and the SQL Server server type selected. If the linked server is a different type of data source (i.e., Oracle, Excel, Access, etc.) then the OLE DB properties must be supplied. Each of these is specific to the type of data source being added as a linked server. Based on the OLE DB provider selected, the various fields have provider-specific help information displayed in the bottom gray box.

Figure 3-20   General tab of the New Linked Server screen in Enterprise Manager

A linked server can also be created through the use of a system-stored procedure called sp_addlinkedserver. This procedure takes the following arguments (the equivalent of the text boxes provided by the General tab of the New Linked Server screen):

- @server: The system name of the server being added as a linked server. (If there is more than one instance of SQL Server 2000 on the machine, use the convention "servername\instancename.")

3

- @srvproduct: The product name of the OLE DB provider (e.g., Oracle). NOTE: This parameter is not required when linking to other SQL Server 2000 instances.

- @provider: The programmatic identifier for the OLE DB provider specified by @srvproduct. The set of provider identifiers is found in SQL Server Books Online. NOTE: This parameter is not required when linking to other SQL Server 2000 instances.

- @datasrc: The data source name as interpreted by the OLE DB provider. When linking to SQL Server 2000 instances, the value should be the network name of the computer housing SQL Server 2000 (default instance) or the servername\instancename syntax for named instances. This value depends on the type of provider, so check Books Online when working with data sources other than SQL Server 2000.

- @location: The location of the data source as interpreted by the OLE DB provider. NOTE: This parameter is not required when linking to other SQL Server 2000 instances.

- @provstr: The provider-specific OLE DB connection string that identifies a data source. NOTE: This parameter is not required when linking to other SQL Server 2000 instances.

- @catalog: The name of the database that resides on the linked server. This option only effects the SQL Server 2000 and DB2 OLE DB providers, but is not required when linking SQL Server 2000 instances to other SQL Server 2000 instances.

When the following procedure is called from a Query Analyzer window with the following syntax, the instance called NewInstance on the SQL Server Windows2000SERV is linked to the current SQL Server.

```
sp_addlinkedserver 'Windows2000SERV\NewInstance'
```

In a distributed query, the local SQL Server connects to the link server by providing a login and password that is valid for the linked server. By default, calling sp_addlinkedserver will set up the local server to connect to a linked server by emulating the current user login. When the local SQL Server and the linked server do not share login information (like Windows logins and passwords on a network), explicit login mappings must be set up to ensure that queries requested from the local server can authenticate with the linked server. The Security tab of the Linked Server Properties screen (displayed in Figure 3-21) allows logins of the host server to be mapped to logins on the remote linked server. When the local server attempts to connect to the linked server to execute a query, it will send the mapped login information to authenticate. For example, in Figure 3-19, the local login "sa" is mapped to a remote user name ("admin") and password. When a user that is logged in to the local server with the "sa" login executes a query against the linked server, the local SQL Server will send the mapped remote user name and password when it connects to the linked server to process the query.

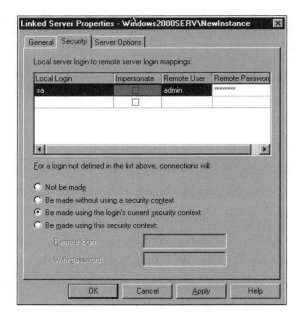

Figure 3-21   Security tab of the New Linked Server screen in Enterprise Manager

Once security configurations have been made, clicking the Tables item beneath the linked server in Enterprise Manager can test the linked server setup. If a list of tables appears in the right pane of Enterprise Manager, then the linked server can be accessed from the local server; otherwise an error message appears.

All of the security information can also be set up using a system stored procedure called sp_addlinkedsrvlogin. This procedure takes the following arguments:

- @rmtsrvname: The name of the linked server that login applies to

- @useself: Specifies the name of the login used to connect to the linked server. If this parameter is set to TRUE, then the remote login and password values (@rmtuser and @rmtpassword parameters) are ignored. If it is set to FALSE, then the remote user credentials will be used when authenticating with the remote server.

- @locallogin: The login on the local server. A value of NULL supplied for this parameter will map all local logins to the remote credential supplied in the @rmtuser and @rmtpassword parameters. If not NULL, this parameter should have a valid SQL Server or Windows login provided as its value.

- @rmtuser: The user name used to connect to the linked server if the @useself parameter is set to "false"

- @rmtpassword: The password associated with the login supplied for the @rmtuser parameter

The following code example will create a linked server to the NewInstance named instance of SQL Server 2000 on the server named Windows2000SERV. It then creates a login mapping that specifies that the local "sa" login emulate the user name "admin" when connecting to the linked server.

```
sp_addlinkedserver 'Windows2000SERV\NewInstance'
sp_addlinkedserverlogin 'Windows2000SERV\NewInstance',
'false', 'sa','admin', 'mypassword'
```

COMMAND LINE UTILITIES

Several command line utilities are installed with SQL Server 2000. Most of these utilities are used to perform administrative tasks and test installed instances.

Osql Utility

The osql utility allows T-SQL statements to be run from the command line as shown in Figure 3-22. While the Query Analyzer tool is better for designing and testing T-SQL queries, the osql utility is often used to access the database through batch files on the operating system. The program is accessed by typing "osql" into a command prompt window.

Figure 3-22   Osql Command Line utility

You can easily access a command line window in Windows-based operating systems by clicking Start and then clicking the Run option. Typing cmd in the Open field and pressing OK opens a command line window.

Various options are available to specify connection information and control the behavior of the program.

The following is a list of the most commonly used options (options are case sensitive):

- –L: Lists the locally configured servers and the names of the servers broadcasting on the network

- –U: The login name used to connect to SQL Server 2000

- –P: The password for the login (osql will prompt the user for a password if this option is not specified)

- –E: Causes osql to connect to SQL Server 2000 using a trusted connection (Windows authentication) instead of requesting a password

- –S *server_name*[*instance_name*]: The name of the instance of SQL Server 2000 osql will connect to. Only *server_name* is required to connect to the default instance. But *server_name\instance_name* must be specified to connect to a named instance of SQL Server 2000. If no value is specified for this option, osql connects to the default instance of SQL Server 2000 on the local computer. If a remote SQL Server is being connected to from osql this option must be specified.

- –d *database_name*: The name of the database that the query will execute against

- –l *time_out*: The login timeout (in seconds) for osql. The default timeout value is eight seconds.

- –t *time_out*: The query time (in seconds) used by osql. If a value is not specified, commands do not time out.

- –s *col_separator*: Specifies the character used as a column separator (a blank space by default). For example, to produce comma-separated output from a query run in osql, use the –s option with a comma (,).

- –w *column_width*: The screen width for output from queries. The default is 80 characters. When an output line exceeds this value, it is broken up into multiple lines.

- –q "*query*": Executes the query specified when osql starts, but does not exit osql when the query completes

- –Q "*query*": Executes the query specified when osql starts, and causes osql to exit when the query completes

- –i *input_file*: The full path of a file that contains SQL statements or stored procedures

The less than (**<**) comparison operator can be used in place of –i.

- –o *output_file*: Identifies the file that receives output from osql

The greater than (>) comparison operator can be used in place of -o.

- -p: Includes performance statistics when queries are run

OSQL Examples

This section contains examples of using osql from the command line.

Example 1

```
OSQL -E -dPubs
```

This line will start osql in interactive mode. It uses the –E option and therefore uses a trusted connection to authenticate with SQL Server 2000. It will connect to the local default instance of SQL Server 2000 because the –S option is not specified. The –d option is used to connect to the Pubs database.

Example 2

```
osql -dnorthwind -Swindows2000serv -E -Q"select
employeeid, lastname, firstname, title from employees"
-oc:\testsql.txt
```

Example 2 will connect to the Northwind database on the default instance of SQL Server 2000 on the computer named "Windows2000Serv" on the network. The –Q option specifies a query to run and that osql will exit when the query is finished. The results of the query are written to the text file Testsql.txt on the C drive of the local computer.

SQLDIAG Utility

The SQLDIAG utility generates an informational file consisting of diagnostic information and query trace information (if a query is running). The purpose of the utility is to generate information that Microsoft Product Support will use to help diagnose problems with a SQL Server 2000 implementation. The default file created by SQLDIAG is C:\Program Files\Microsoft SQL Server\MSSQL\log\SQLdiag.txt.

 SQLDIAG can only be run on the local server. It can access individual instances but they must reside on the local machine.

The file generated by SQLDIAG contains the following pieces of information:

- Text of all error logs
- Registry information

- DLL version information
- Output from:
  - sp_configure
  - sp_who
  - sp_lock
  - sp_helpdb
  - xp_msver
  - sp_helpextendedproc
  - sysprocesses
- Input buffer SPIDs/deadlock information
- Microsoft Diagnostics Report for the server, including:
  - Contents of <servername>.txt file
  - Operating System Version Report
  - System Report
  - Processor List
  - Video Display Report
  - Hard Drive Report
  - Memory Report
  - Services Report
  - Drivers Report
  - IRQ and Port Report
  - DMA and Memory Report
  - Environment Report
  - Network Report
- The last 100 queries and exceptions

CHAPTER SUMMARY

- SQL Server 2000 is supported by several graphical and command prompt-based applications. The most important of these is Enterprise Manager. Enterprise Manager is the primary tool for configuring SQL Server 2000 instances and managing databases. Query Analyzer is used to develop, test, and run T-SQL scripts. Together these tools allow just about every task associated with instance management to be performed.

3

❏ Microsoft SQL Server 2000 is a database management system and as such offers a multitude of configuration settings to control its behavior. Improvements to the underlying architecture of the product allow most of the configurations to be dynamic (self configuring), but there are many cases where explicit configuration settings are made through Enterprise Manager or by calling various system stored procedures like sp_configure and sp_addlinkedserver.

❏ SQL Server 2000 has the ability to send and receive e-mail on its own. Through the use of an e-mail profile set up in Windows, SQL Server 2000 connects to a valid mail server and has access to an inbox as well as outbound message delivery. The two components of SQL Server that have e-mail capabilities are SQLMail and SQLAgent Mail. SQLMail can process incoming e-mail and reply to messages containing queries with the results. SQLMail is also used to provide programmatic access to e-mail through T-SQL (extended stored procedures like xp_sendmail). When SQLAgentMail is configured, events on the server can trigger automatic e-mails to be sent to various administrators, alerting them of the problem.

❏ Linked servers allow multiple disparate data sources to be managed or accessed through SQL Server. By using **OLE DB**, the Microsoft programmatic standard for data access, linked servers can be accessed from a local server through the use of T-SQL commands. Linked servers are useful for integrating multiple data sources (e.g., performing updates in multiple places when data is changed in a single SQL Server 2000 instance).

KEY TERMS

checkpoint — An event that causes data modifications stored in the transaction log to be committed to disk. When a checkpoint occurs, all changes to data that have occurred since last checkpoint (and have not yet been committed to disk) are written to disk. Checkpoints can be triggered automatically by SQL Server 2000 if the instance is configured for this (recovery internal set to zero). They can also be triggered by an explicit recovery interval (specified by an administrator), or when requested by a user or a system shutdown.

extended stored procedure — A function that is part of an external software object (DLL), which is coded using the SQL Server 2000 Extended Stored Procedure API. The function can then be called using Transact-SQL from SQL Server 2000, using similar statements to those used to execute Transact-SQL stored procedures. Extended stored procedures are often developed to provide functionality that is not supported by T-SQL.

Hypertext Transfer Protocol (HTTP) — The most common protocol used to transfer information from Web servers to Web browsers. Because of this protocol, most URLs begin with HTTP://.

OLE DB — The application programming interface (API) for accessing data stored in any format (databases, spreadsheets, text files, e-mail stores).

OLE DB Provider — A software component that provides access to data from a particular type of data source through the standard OLE DB API (e.g., SQL Server databases, Access databases, or Excel spreadsheets).

query governor threshold — Signifies the maximum query cost a query can have while still being able to run. Query cost refers to the estimated time (in seconds) required for a query to be executed based on the hardware configuration of the computer.

thread — An operating system component that allows multiple simultaneous requests to a multiuser application to execute as separate tasks. The SQL Server 2000 relational database engine leverages multiple threads to make use of multiple processors and optimize performance when multiple, concurrent user connections are performing operations. Threads ensure that some user connection is executing even when other connections are blocked (e.g., when waiting for disk reads and writes to complete).

REVIEW QUESTIONS

1. Which startup option will make SQL Server 2000 start in single-user mode?

   a. –m

   b. –l

   c. –e

   d. –d

2. What is associated with SQLMail and SQLAgentMail to configure them to send and receive e-mail?

   a. a Windows login account

   b. the SQL Server service

   c. a Windows mail profile

   d. a network library

3. SQL Server 2000 instances registered in Enterprise Manager can be organized with SQL Server _____.

   a. folders

   b. groups

   c. icons

   d. Network Utility

4. What is it called when all transactions are written from memory to disk?

   a. database backup

   b. checkpoint

   c. log shipping

   d. thread

3

5. What is the maximum amount of concurrent user connections that SQL Server 2000 can support?

    a. 1024

    b. 2048

    c. 32,767

    d. 131,072

6. Which system-stored procedure is used to set up a login mapping for a linked server?

    a. sp_configure

    b. sp_addlinkedserver

    c. sp_addlinkedsrvlogin

    d. sp_addalias

7. Which e-mail server type is supported by SQLMail or SQLAgentMail?

    a. Microsoft Exchange Server

    b. Microsoft Windows NT Mail

    c. Post Office Protocol 3 (POP3)

    d. all of the above

8. What piece of information is not required to register a SQL Server 2000 instance in Enterprise Manager?

    a. the name of the SQL Server 2000 instance

    b. authentication information (user name and password or Windows login)

    c. the network protocol to connect the instance with

    d. the SQL Server Group in which registered instance will reside

9. What does the query governor threshold help to prevent?

    a. illegal access to a SQL Server 2000 instance

    b. poor performance due to poorly performing queries

    c. conflicts that arise from concurrent user activity

    d. query plans that don't take advantage of multiple processors

10. What is the Microsoft specification for an application programming interface (API) for universal data access?

    a. Active Data Objects (ADO)

    b. SQL Distributed Management Objects (SQL-DMO)

    c. OLE DB

    d. named pipes

11. Which stored procedure is used to set the configuration properties of a SQL Server 2000 instance?

    a. sp_statistics

    b. sp_serveroption

    c. sp_configure

    d. sp_dboption

12. What will the following code do?

```
EXEC xp_sendmail @recipients = 'john@xyz.com',
                 @query = 'SELECT * FROM NewSales',
                 @subject = 'Sales Report',
                 @message = 'The contents of
                 INFORMATION_SCHEMA.TABLES:',
                 @attach_results = 'TRUE',
                 @separator = ','
```

    a. send an e-mail with the results of the query in the message body

    b. send an e-mail signifying that the specified query has been run

    c. produce an error in SQL Server 2000

    d. send an e-mail with the query results as a comma-delimited file attachment

13. A company wants to keep a log of all attempts to log in to an instance of SQL Server 2000, regardless of the result of the login attempt (success or failure). What has to be done to achieve this?

    a. Nothing, SQL Server 2000 does this by default.

    b. Select "All" from the Security tab (Audit Level section) of the SQL Server Properties screen.

    c. Start SQL Server 2000 using the -e startup parameter.

    d. Use sp_configure to configure the Login Auditing option.

14. An instance of SQL Server 2000 needs to be accessed remotely from a local SQL Server. Both servers use the SQL Server Windows account to login. What must be done to ensure that a connection between the two servers can be established?

    a. nothing, since the two computers reside on the same network

    b. The remote server must be added as a linked server on the local server.

    c. The remote server must be added as a linked server on the local server. The local server must be configured to impersonate the "sa" account on the linked server.

    d. The remote server must be added as a linked server on the local server, and the local server must be added as a linked server on the remote server.

3

15. Which statement sets the minimum amount of memory allotted to execute a query to 2048 kb?

   a. `sp_addlinkedserver 'Windows2000Serv'`

   b. `sp_configure 'min memory per query', '2048'`

   c. `sp_configure 'querymemory', '2048'`

   d. `sp_addlinkedsrvrlogin 'false', 'sa', 'sa', 'password'`

16. Which system–stored procedure is used by SQL Server 2000 to handle incoming e-mail messages containing queries?

   a. sp_configure

   b. xp_sendmail

   c. xp_processmail

   d. xp_readmail

17. Which option in osql specifies that a trusted connection be used?

   a. –e

   b. –E

   c. –q

   d. –U

18. Which of the following commands will generate a text file with the contents of the employee table?

   a. `osql -dnorthwind -Swindows2000serv -E -Q"select from employees" -oc:\testsql.txt`

   b. `osql -dnorthwind -Swindows2000serv -E -Q"select from employees"`

   c. `osql -dnorthwind -Swindows2000serv -E -Q"select from employees" -Fc:\testsql.txt`

   d. `osql -dnorthwind -Swindows2000serv -e -Q"select from employees" -Oc:\testsql.txt`

19. Which program is used to produce information that is used by Microsoft Product Support to help diagnose problems with an instance of SQL Server 2000?

   a. mssql.exe

   b. isqlw.exe

   c. bcp.exe

   d. sqldiag.exe

20. What is the default priority of SQL Server 2000 operations in Windows?

   a. 1

   b. 7

   c. 13

   d. 25

HANDS-ON PROJECTS

Project 3-1

To create a SQL Group and then register a SQL Server 2000 instance in SQL Server Enterprise Manager:

1. Start Enterprise Manager by clicking **Start**, highlighting **Programs**, highlighting **Microsoft SQL Server**, and then clicking on **Enterprise Manager**.

2. Click the **Action** menu, and then click the **New SQL Server Group** option shown in Figure 3-23.

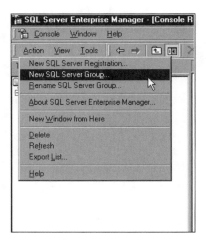

Figure 3-23   Create a new SQL Server group

3. Name the group by typing **Local Servers** in the Name text box of the Server Groups window shown in Figure 3-24.

4. Make the new group a sub-group of SQL Server Group by clicking the **Sub-group of** radio button and clicking on **SQL Server Group**. Click **OK** to save the new group.

5. Click the **Action** menu and then click the **New SQL Server Registration** option.

If the Register SQL Server Wizard appears, click the check box saying you don't want to use it and click the Next button. This will activate the Registered SQL Server Properties window, shown in Figure 3-25.

6. In the Registered SQL Server Properties window shown in Figure 3-25, fill in the name of the local SQL Server 2000 default instance. (In this example it is **Windows2000Serv**. The name of the local server should be entered here.) Click on **Use Windows authentication** and click **OK**.

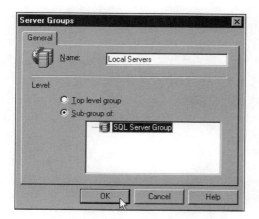

Figure 3-24 Server Groups screen

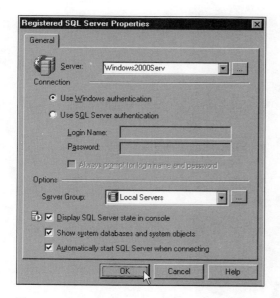

Figure 3-25 Registered SQL Server Properties

7. Register the named instance of SQL Server 2000 that was installed in the previous chapter. The steps are the same as Steps 1–6 above, except that the server name is **Windows2000Serv\NewInstance**.

Project 3-2

To configure the registered SQL Server from the previous exercise for optimum performance:

1. Right-click on the registered SQL Server node in the tree on the left side of the screen and left-click the **Properties** option.

2. Click on the **General** tab of the SQL Server Properties (Configure) screen, and click the **Startup Parameters** button.

3. In the Startup Parameters screen displayed in Figure 3-26, type **-x** in the Parameter text box and click **Add**.

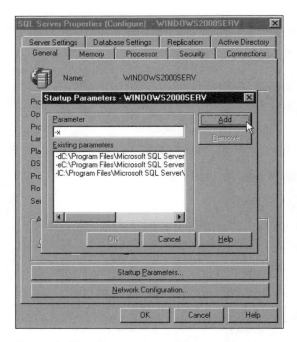

Figure 3-26 Startup Parameters screen

The -x parameter disables CPU time and the recording of cache-hit ratio statistics to allow a SQL Server 2000 instance to operate with maximum performance.

4. Click **OK** to close the Startup Parameters screen.

5. Click the **Processor** tab.

6. Check the **Boost SQL Server priority on Windows** check box and click **OK**, as shown in Figure 3-27.

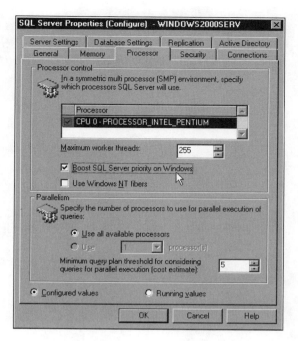

Figure 3-27   Processor tab

At this point, Microsoft SQL Server might alert you that the instance must be stopped and started for the settings to take effect. Click Yes to restart the instance and Yes when asked if dependent services should be stopped and started. If these screens don't appear, follow Steps 7–9 to manually restart the instance.

7. For the settings to take effect, the instance must be stopped and started. Right-click on the **SQL Server instance** node on the left side of Enterprise Manager, and left-click **Stop**.

8. A dialog box appears asking if you are sure you want to stop the instance. Click **Yes**.

When an instance is stopped, the red square appears in the icon as shown in Figure 3-28.

Figure 3-28   Stopped SQL Server instance

9. Right-click on the **instance** node again and left-click **Start**.

Project 3-3

To set up a mail profile in Windows and configure SQLMail to use that profile to send and receive e-mail:

Microsoft Outlook must be installed to complete this exercise.

1. Click **Start**, click on **Settings**, and then select **Control Panel**.
2. In the Control Panel, double-click the item called **Mail**.
3. Click **Add** to start the Microsoft Outlook Setup Wizard.
4. Click the **manually configure information services** radio button as shown in Figure 3-29, and click **Next**.

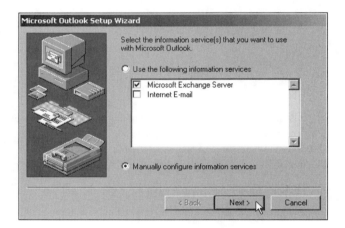

Figure 3-29   Configure e-mail profiles screen

5. Enter the name of SQLMail for the profile that is being created. Click **Next**, and the Profile Properties Window appears.
6. Click **Add**, select **Microsoft Exchange Server**, and click **OK**. This will bring up the Microsoft Exchange Server screen shown in Figure 3-30.

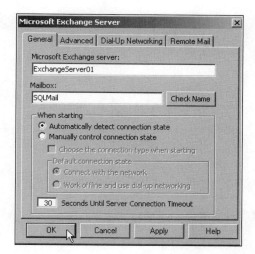

Figure 3-30 Exchange Server Properties

In nine out of 10 cases the mail server used with SQL Server is Microsoft Exchange Server.

Add the name of the Microsoft Exchange e-mail server and the name of the mailbox being used by SQL Server 2000, and click **OK**.

In this example the Exchange Server is named ExchangeServer01 and a mailbox has been created on that server called SQLMail. Typically, a SQL Server administrator would work with the IT department to get a mail account set up for use by SQL Server 2000. The mailbox should be set up to use the same Windows account that the SQL Server and SQL Server Agent services use at startup. Exchange Server profiles can't be created unless a connection to a valid Microsoft Exchange Server can be established.

7. Click **OK** again in the Properties dialog box.
8. Click **Finish** in the Wizard.
9. Click **Close** in the Mail dialog box.
10. Go back to Enterprise Manager, expand the **Support Services** node in the tree.
11. Right-click on the **SQLMail** option and select the **Properties** option to access the SQLMail Configuration screen displayed in Figure 3-31.
12. Enter **SQLMail** as the Profile name for use by the SQLMail service, and click **OK**.

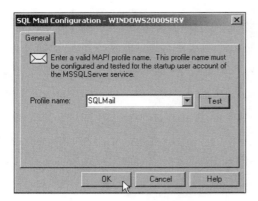

Figure 3-31   General tab of SQL Mail Configuration screen

Project 3-4

To add a named instance of SQL Server as a linked server to the default SQL Server instance:

1. Start Enterprise Manager by clicking **Start**, clicking **Programs**, clicking **Microsoft SQL Server**, and then clicking **Enterprise Manager**.

2. Expand the **Windows2000Serv** node in the tree on the left and then expand the Security folder.

3. Right-click on **Linked Servers** and left-click **New Linked Server**, as shown in Figure 3-32.

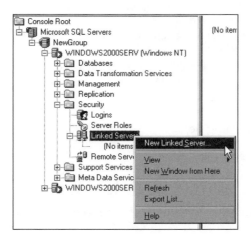

Figure 3-32   Adding a new linked server

4. Click the **General** tab of the Linked Server Properties screen displayed in Figure 3-33. Enter the name of the SQL Server instance (in this case **WINDOWS2000SERV\NEWINSTANCE**, but any valid *SERVERNAME\INSTANCENAME* value will work). Also click the **SQL Server** server type button.

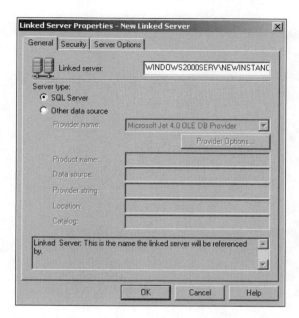

Figure 3-33   General tab of Linked Server Properties screen

5. Click the **Security** tab.

6. Click the **Be made using the login's current security context** button as shown in Figure 3-34.

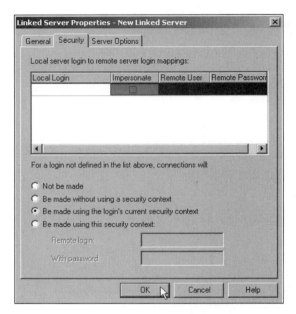

Figure 3-34 Security tab of Linked Server Properties screen

 It is assumed that both instances were set up for Windows Authentication and that they were both installed under the same login: "Administrator on the local machine" in this case.

7. Click **OK** to add the new linked server.

8. Expand the node for the new item under **Linked Servers** in the tree window (left side of Enterprise Manager).

9. Click **Tables** to test the connectivity between the linked servers.

10. If a list of tables appears on the right side of Enterprise Manager, then the linkage is set up properly between the servers.

Project 3-5

To use Query analyzer to change some configuration settings for an instance of SQL Server 2000:

1. Start Enterprise Manager by clicking **Start**, clicking **Programs**, clicking **Microsoft SQL Server**, and then clicking **Enterprise Manager**.

2. Click on a registered instance of SQL Server 2000.

3. Click on the **Tools** menu, and choose **SQL Query Analyzer**.

4. Once in Query Analyzer, type **sp_configure** in the query window and click **Execute Query**, as shown in Figure 3-35.

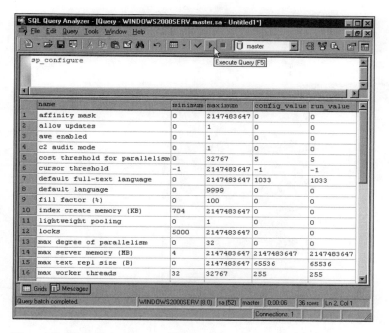

Figure 3-35 Using sp_configure from Query Analyzer

5. Now type **sp_configure 'max worker threads', '500'** and click **Execute**. This will change the number of available worker threads to 500.

6. Read the output message. At this point, for the setting to take effect, the statement **RECONFIGURE** must be executed. Type **RECONFIGURE** in the query window and click **Execute**.

7. To check that the value has changed and is committed, run the **sp_configure** stored procedure again with no parameters. Notice in the results that **run_value** has not changed (it is still 255 and not 500).

8. To commit the change on the instance of SQL Server 2000, the SQL Server must be stopped and started. Go back to Enterprise Manager.

9. Right-click on the default instance (in this case **WINDOWS2000SERV**) and click on **Stop**, as displayed in Figure 3-36. Wait a moment for the shutdown to complete.

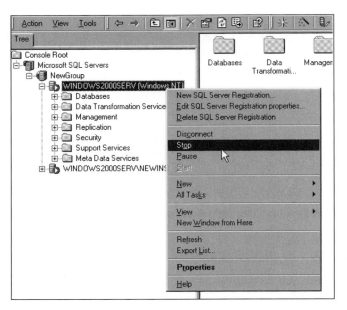

Figure 3-36   Stopping SQL Server 2000

Click Yes to confirm the stopping of the service. Also click Yes to stop the dependent services.

10. Right-click on the default instance (in this case **WINDOWS2000SERV**) and click on **Start**.

11. Go back to Query Analyzer again and run the **sp_configure** stored procedure again. Notice that the **run_value** for the **max worker threads** option has changed to 500.

CASE PROJECTS

Case One

You have been hired as a SQL Server consultant by XYZ company to help them deploy SQL Server 2000 to support a variety of applications. The ability to send e-mails from the database directly is very important to XYZ company. Write up a fact sheet on the e-mail capabilities of SQL Server 2000, the mechanisms for sending e-mail directly from SQL Server 2000, the types of software (i.e., Mail client and Mail servers) that are required to configure SQL Server 2000 for e-mail.

Case Two

XYZ Company has three SQL Servers on separate computers throughout its network. One SQL Server supports the inventory control database, another supports the order management system, and a third is used to support a catalog for an e-commerce Web site. XYZ wants to be able to update both the order management database and the inventory database directly from catalog (Web) database. Develop a proposal for the use of linked servers to support this requirement. Discuss what linked servers are, how they are configured, and any considerations that must be made before successful deployment. Use SQL Books Online to find more detailed information than this chapter provides.

Case Three

ABC Company has two SQL Server 2000 computers that are used in different ways. Both were installed with the default configurations of the SQL Server Setup program. One computer is used exclusively by SQL Server 2000 and should be tuned to provide the highest level of performance possible. The other SQL Server is on the computer that is the file server for the network users. This SQL Server must be configured properly so that the performance of the file server access is not compromised. Generate a set of recommendations for each server, with supporting information from SQL Server Books Online or Web resources.

4

SQL SERVER 2000 DATABASE ARCHITECTURE

After reading this chapter and completing the exercises you will be able to:

♦ Identify how information is physically stored by SQL Server 2000

♦ Discuss the underlying application architecture of the SQL Server 2000 relational database engine

♦ Identify how information is physically stored by SQL Server 2000

♦ Understand the most common database objects and their purposes

♦ Understand transactions and locking

SQL Server 2000 automatically allocates physical storage blocks to house data. There are several types of database objects that are available when defining databases. These objects are used to define the structure of individual data entities, the types of data they contain, relationships between data entities, and to enforce custom business rules on data. In addition to providing a flexible infrastructure for defining databases, SQL Server 2000 offers robust functionality for handling the simultaneous, multiuser activity common to enterprise-level systems. To ensure the integrity of data in a concurrent environment, SQL Server 2000 manages user operations in transactions.

Before forging ahead to create and manage databases, it is important to take a step back to gain an understanding of the application architecture of SQL Server 2000. This chapter discusses high-level architectural concepts that greatly affect the way that SQL Server 2000 operates. A solid understanding of these concepts is crucial when implementing and deploying mission critical databases.

STORING DATA

The primary job of a database system is to store information. It can be any type of information, from financial statistics to retail inventory data. Information is stored physically (as 1s and 0s) in files that are used by SQL Server 2000 databases. Data is not the only thing that makes up a relational database. There are several types of objects that are available in SQL Server 2000 to define the structure and rules for storing data. There are also objects that control how data is manipulated and retrieved through T-SQL queries.

Physical Data Storage

The basic unit of physical storage in SQL Server 2000 is a **page**. The size of each page is 8 KB. Each page contains a 96-byte header that stores information like the amount of free space available, a reference to a database object that owns the data stored within the page, and whether the page is used for data or indexes. A page also has a footer that consists of a set of entries called row offsets. Offsets contain information about where the data rows stored on the page start (the number of bytes from the beginning of the page). The rest of the space in a page is available to store data. When a row is inserted into a table, the individual pieces of data (column data) are written to a page that is owned by the table.

 All data for a row is captured on a single page except for any text, ntext, and image data. These large binary datatypes can exceed the size of a single page and are therefore stored on separate pages.

SQL Server 2000 writes rows sequentially in a page until the page is full (see Figure 4-1). Depending on the size of each row, a single page may store multiple rows of data. In SQL Server 2000, a single row cannot span multiple pages. For this reason, a limit of 8060 bytes per row is applied to database tables so that a single row of data can be written to a single page.

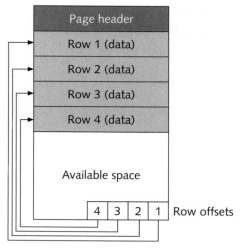

Figure 4-1   SQL Server 2000 data page

Notice how the single page contains multiple data rows and that each data row has a row offset entry at the end of the page that is used to find the starting byte for each row. While the page is the smallest unit of storage in SQL Server 2000, space to store table or index data is allocated in larger blocks called **extents**. An extent consists of eight contiguous pages so each extent is 64 kilobytes in size (8 KB per page × 8 pages per extent = 64 KB per extent). A **uniform extent** is dedicated to a single object. In a uniform extent, all eight pages are used to store data from the same table or index. **Mixed extents** share the pages amongst multiple database objects. Usually when a table is first created it uses pages from a mixed extent. Once the table has enough data to require additional extents for storage, uniform extents are employed.

 The data contained in pages and organized in extents is stored in files that are used by SQL Server 2000 databases. Each database is created with at least two physical files. One of the files is used to store data and database information, and the other is used as a transaction log (transaction logs will be discussed in more detail later). Figure 4-2 shows the relationship of the storage objects in SQL Server 2000.

 While additional data files can be created and associated with a database, only one is needed when a database is first created.

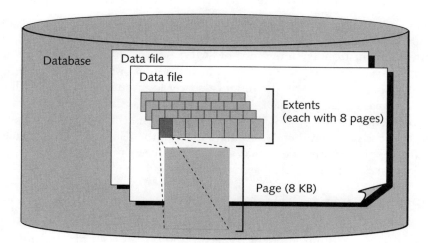

Figure 4-2   SQL Server physical data storage

DATABASE OBJECTS

There are several types of objects that can be implemented in a SQL Server 2000 database, each with its own intended uses and capabilities. These objects are the basic building blocks of databases and perform such functions as storing data, ensuring data integrity, and accessing and modifying data. Objects, like tables and indexes, are used to store and catalog raw data. Constraints, defaults, and data types are database objects that control the relationships between tables and the data values stored in particular columns in a table. Stored procedures, triggers, and user-defined functions allow custom T-SQL logic to be developed to enforce business rules within a database. Views are custom queries (SELECT statements) that are stored in the database and are available for data access as if they were tables.

Tables

Tables are the most common database object and are used to store all raw data. Tables are structured in a very similar fashion to spreadsheets, in that data is organized into a two-dimensional format (columns and rows). As discussed in Chapter 1, a row represents a logical record of data (for example, a customer record). Rows contain one or more discreet pieces of information in columns. For example, a customer table could have columns that store name, address, and phone data. When taken as a group, the information stored in a single row (consisting of the various column data) makes up a record.

System tables are special tables used by SQL Server 2000 to store information about the structure of other tables and objects, security and login information, and various configuration information. Each instance of SQL Server 2000 has a set of system tables (prefixed with "sys") that are used to store information about the configuration of the instance, the databases defined on the instance, server login information, etc. All of these tables exist in a master database that is installed with each instance of SQL Server 2000. Each user-defined database in a SQL Server 2000 instance has its own set of system tables that store the data defining the configuration of the database and all its tables and objects. It is strongly recommended that you do not access these tables directly, as they store vital information that the database engine uses.

Data Types

The columns of each table are defined with a name and data type. The data type specifies what type of data the column stores. SQL Server 2000 offers a set of standard data types for storing different types of data. Data types restrict the type of data that a column can store. For example, a column that is set up to store integers will not store character information. Data types ensure that columns only allow a specific set of data, known as a domain. A **domain** is the valid range of values that a column can store. For example, when creating a column to store birthdays, you would want to make sure that users can only save valid dates.

 Data types are not the only thing that can enforce a specific domain of data values for a column. Constraints (discussed later in this chapter) offer further data integrity by establishing rules for acceptable values in a particular table column.

Table 4-1 outlines the various column data types supported by SQL Server 2000.

Table 4-1   Column Data Types

Type	Domain
Bigint	Whole numbers from −9,223,372,036,854,775,808 to 9,223,372,036,854,775,807
Int	Whole numbers from −2,147,483,648 to 2,147,483,647
Smallint	Whole numbers from −32,768 to 32,767
Tinyint	Whole numbers from 0 to 255
Bit	0 or 1
Decimal	Whole or fractional numbers from -10E38 to 10E38
Float	Approximation from −1.79E308 to 1.79E308
Real	Approximation from −3.40E38 to 3.40E38
Money	Currency from −922,337,203,685,477.5808 to +922,337,203,685,477.5807
Smallmoney	Currency from −214,748.3648 to +214,748.3647
Datetime	Dates from Jan 1, 1753 to Dec 31, 9999
Smalldatetime	Dates from Jan 1, 1900 to June 6, 2079
Char	Fixed-length character, non-Unicode string; max of 8000 characters
Varchar	Variable-length, non-Unicode string; max of 8000 characters
Text	Variable-length, non-Unicode string; max of 2,147,483,647 characters
Nchar	Fixed-length character, Unicode string; max of 4000 characters
Nvarchar	Variable-length, Unicode string; max of 4000 characters
Ntext	Variable-length, Unicode string; max of 1,073,741,823 characters
Binary	Fixed-length binary data; max of 8000 bytes
Varbinary	Variable-length binary data; max of 8000 bytes
Image	Fixed-length binary data; max of 2,147,483,647 bytes
Sql_variant	Can store any SQL data type except text, ntext, timestamp and sql_variant.
Timestamp	Database-wide unique number; updated on every row update
Uniqueidentifer	Globally unique identifier (GUID)

4

In general, text, ntext, and image columns are used to store large blocks of information, like digital images or large files (e.g., documents). To optimize performance, these types of data are stored on separate physical disk space (pages) than the rest of the data that comprises a row. To force these column types to be stored in the same physical space as the rest of the row data, use the "text in row" option of the sp_tableoption system-stored procedure. This can provide performance enhancements by ensuring that the relational engine does not need to go to various physical locations on a hard drive to retrieve the data.

SQL Server 2000 also allows **user-defined data types** to be created. A user-defined data type is a custom data type that is based on the standard SQL Server 2000 data types. User-defined data types are handy when you want to ensure that several columns have the exact same type, size, nullability, default, and rule. You can define the data type once and then use it as if it were one of the standard data types.

Defaults

Defaults are used to provide a value for a column when one is not supplied. For example, a default could be defined for an "insert date" column in a table that contains order information. The default could specify that the current date is inserted into the column if a specific date value is not supplied in an insert statement.

Defaults are often used to prevent NULL values from being saved in the database. NULL values require additional processing overhead when performing actions like comparisons; therefore, whenever possible, it is a good idea to define column defaults instead of allowing NULL values.

Constraints

Constraints are user-defined rules that help enforce the integrity of column data. They are primarily used to restrict the data that is saved in a particular column. There are several types of constraints supported by SQL Server 2000:

- *Check constraint*: Check constraints allow you to restrict column data by evaluating a supplied value prior to saving data in the database. A check constraint could be set up on a "date shipped" column in a table containing order information, to ensure that the value supplied for the "date shipped" is later than the "order date." Check constraints can also be used to specify a range of values that are acceptable in a particular column. For example, a check constraint that ensures that only a value of "male" or "female" is allowed could be set up on the gender column in a table containing employee information. A **rule** is a database object that is very similar to a CHECK constraint. Rules are supported in SQL Server 2000 to provide backward compatibility with older versions of SQL Server. Rules have basically been replaced by CHECK constraints in SQL Server 2000 and are generally not used.

- *NOT NULL constraint:* A NOT NULL constraint is used to prevent null values from being stored in a column or columns of a table.

- *Primary key constraints:* A **primary key constraint** is a column or combination of columns in a table that uniquely identify a data row. Only one primary key constraint can be defined for a table and the column(s) defined in the primary key cannot contain NULL values.

- *Unique constraints:* A unique constraint forces a column or set of columns to be unique. Unique constraints are effective when a primary key already exists on a table, but other columns in the table must be unique. Unlike primary keys, unique constraints allow NULL values to be entered. In a unique constraint, NULL values are simply ignored when validating for uniqueness.

- *Foreign key constraints:* A **foreign key** is used to define relationships between tables in a database. A foreign key references a column in another table and ensures that values provided for a foreign key column exist in the column of another table.

To better understand the relationship established between tables through the use of foreign keys, see Figure 4-3.

Primary key column

Customer table

CustomerID	Name	Zip Code
1	John Smith	02109
2	Bud Green	04563
3	Judy Crane	05673
4	Matthew Rizzo	03452
5	Jennifer White	07512
6	Charles Douglas	04356

Foriegn key column

Orders table

OrderID	CustomerID	Total
10001	2	$10.00
10002	4	$30.00
10003	1	$22.00
10004	1	$38.00
10005	3	$59.00
10006	5	$14.00

Figure 4-3   Table relationships with foriegn keys

In an orders database, you may store information about customers in a Customer table and information about orders in an Orders table. The Customer table implements a primary key on the CustomerID column to ensure the uniqueness of rows. The requirement of the database is that each customer can have zero, one, or more orders associated with him or her. Notice that the Orders table contains a field called CustomerID, which establishes this relationship in the database. This field in the Orders table must contain a valid CustomerID value. To ensure this data and relationship integrity, a foreign key constraint is created on the CustomerID field of the orders table. With a foreign key in place, the CustomerID value supplied when adding rows to the Orders table will be checked against the set of CustomerID values (primary key) in the Customer table. If the CustomerID value supplied for the orders table does not already exist in the Customer table, then an error will occur and data will not be saved in the orders table.

 The requirement for foreign keys is that they reference a unique column in a table. Consequently, foreign key constraints can reference both primary key columns and columns that have a unique constraint defined for them.

Foreign key constraints support **cascading updates** and **cascading deletes** within a SQL Server 2000 database. In a cascading update or delete, changes to a key field are automatically propagated to referencing tables by the database engine. For example, if a CustomerID in the Customer table were changed from a value of 1 to 10001, a cascading update would update the orders table so that every row that has a CustomerID of 1 is updated to have a CustomerID of 10001. If you were to delete a record from the Customer table that had related rows in the Order table, all rows in the order table for that particular customer would be deleted automatically.

Indexes

It is common for a database to store millions of rows of data. In order to provide optimized performance when searching for specific rows of data in tables and views, SQL Server 2000 uses structures called indexes. An **index** in SQL Server 2000 is similar to a book index, in that it allows faster discovery of information. If you want to find a topic in a book index, you navigate to the appropriate letter (book indexes are usually alphabetical) and then find the appropriate topic. By using the index instead of flipping through the entire book, you can avoid a high percentage of extraneous data and execute your search more efficiently. The goal of an index is to improve the searching process by requiring fewer lookups to locate specific information.

Database indexes are physically stored in a B-tree structure. This structure is comprised of multiple (up to millions) database pages that store **index rows**. Index rows are similar to the data rows discussed earlier, except that they contain a key value and a memory pointer to other pages used by the index. Figure 4-4 illustrates the B-tree structure of an index.

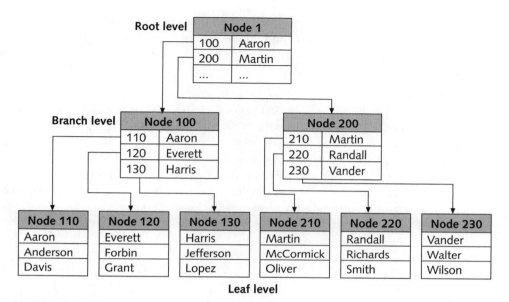

Figure 4-4 The B-tree structure of a database index

The index in Figure 4-4 is defined on the last name started in an imaginary Employee table. To explain how the database engine uses the index, assume that a database user has requested information for an employee whose last name is Richards. When the Employee table is searched with a last name value, SQL Server 2000 first goes to the root level of the index. Notice that at the root level, there is only one index node, known as the **root node**. The supplied value of "Richards" is compared to the values in the root node. Since "Richards" is alphabetically greater than both "Aaron" and "Martin," the "Martin" entry is selected and the database engine traverses down the B-tree to the applicable **branch node** (in this case Node 200). A branch node is similar to a root node and used in much the same way. The lowest level node in an index is known as a **leaf node**. Leaf nodes contain actual data in the case of the clustered index, and pointers to data pages in the case of a nonclustered index. However, while there is only one root node, there can be any number of branch nodes existing on any number of hierarchical levels. In this example there is only one branch level, but in databases with high volumes of data, there are usually several.

The value of "Richards" is again compared with the index rows in Node 200. Since it is greater than both "Martin" and "Randall" and less than "Vander," the "Randall" row is selected and the database engine jumps to Node 220. At this point, the leaf level is reached and the index search is completed. The use of this index by the database engine to execute the query significantly reduces the amount of operations required to locate the "Richards" row in the Employee table. Only three lookups had to be performed (one for each node leading to the leaf level node containing "Richards"). If the index was not defined on the last name column of the table, the database engine would have performed a **table scan**. In a table scan, every row of the table is queried and a comparison is made on each row until a match is found. So by using the index, the number of operations required to locate the record is reduced to three, from possibly millions (if a table scan is used).

The leaf level of an index will store different information depending on the type of index created. There are two general types of indexes: **clustered** and **nonclustered**. Clustered indexes physically store rows from a table in the index leaf nodes. By this design, when a clustered index is defined on a column (or multiple columns), the data on the table is physically stored in order. For this reason, only one clustered index can be defined per table. In a nonclustered index, the leaf level nodes contain pointers to the actual data row instead of the data itself. Since the data is not physically stored in the leaf nodes of a nonclustered index, many nonclustered indexes can be defined per table (up to 249). Nonclustered indexes allow a table to be searched efficiently on columns that are not sorted when persisted to disk.

Views

Views provide a method for abstracting the representation of the tables in a database. A view is implemented as a stored query in the database. The stored query consists of a SQL SELECT statement that retrieves information from one or more tables. When accessed by database users, a view acts just like a table in that it can be queried for specific rows and columns; and it can even be used to insert or delete data from the underlying tables queried by the view.

Views are used to present data to users in different ways from the base table structure. They can be used to restrict the rows or columns that a database user can access. For example, a view could be defined that includes only a subset of customer information like name, address, and phone, while not exposing sensitive information like credit rating. Views can also be secured so that only certain authorized users may access them. There are several reasons that a view would be implemented in a database:

- To restrict the rows in a table that a user is able to access. This type of view is considered **horizontally partitioned** because it provides a subset of table rows. For example, a Customer view could be set up to only return the customers that are assigned to a specific sales person.

- To restrict a user to specific columns. This type of view is considered **vertically partitioned** because it only provides a subset of the columns in a table or set of tables. For example, allow all company employees to see the name, office, work phone, and department columns in an Employee table, but do not expose any columns with salary information.

- To join columns from multiple tables so that they look like a single table. For example, a single view could be set up based on a Customer table and a Salesperson table. The view could contain the name of the customer and the name of the salesperson assigned to the customer.

In Figure 4-5, a view has been developed that returns all customer information except for the credit limit, which may be confidential to most users of the database.

ID	First Name	Last Name	State	Phone	Credit Limit
1	John	Masey	AL	xxx-xxx-xxxx	$10,000
2	Jane	Monroe	AL	xxx-xxx-xxxx	$12,000
3	Jill	Adams	AZ	xxx-xxx-xxxx	$25,000
4	Jack	Scott	CA	xxx-xxx-xxxx	$50,000
5	Kevin	Holmes	CA	xxx-xxx-xxxx	$35,000
6	Hillary	Reed	CA	xxx-xxx-xxxx	$15,000
7	George	Karl	CA	xxx-xxx-xxxx	$10,000
8	Bill	Patterson	CA	xxx-xxx-xxxx	$25,000
9	Chris	Rizzo	NH	xxx-xxx-xxxx	$85,000
10	Lisa	Jones	NH	xxx-xxx-xxxx	$10,000
11	Megan	Smith	NH	xxx-xxx-xxxx	$15,000
12	Scott	Davis	NH	xxx-xxx-xxxx	$20,000

Figure 4-5 Vertically partitioned view

In Figure 4-6, a view has been developed that returns just the customer records from California. Though views appear like standard tables, they are actually generated on the fly, when a user or application requests information.

ID	First Name	Last Name	State	Phone	Credit Limit
1	John	Masey	AL	xxx-xxx-xxxx	$10,000
2	Jane	Monroe	AL	xxx-xxx-xxxx	$12,000
3	Jill	Adams	AZ	xxx-xxx-xxxx	$25,000
4	Jack	Scott	CA	xxx-xxx-xxxx	$50,000
5	Kevin	Holmes	CA	xxx-xxx-xxxx	$35,000
6	Hillary	Reed	CA	xxx-xxx-xxxx	$15,000
7	George	Karl	CA	xxx-xxx-xxxx	$10,000
8	Bill	Patterson	CA	xxx-xxx-xxxx	$25,000
9	Chris	Rizzo	NH	xxx-xxx-xxxx	$85,000
10	Lisa	Jones	NH	xxx-xxx-xxxx	$10,000
11	Megan	Smith	NH	xxx-xxx-xxxx	$15,000
12	Scott	Davis	NH	xxx-xxx-xxxx	$20,000

Figure 4-6 Horizontally partitioned view

Stored Procedures

A **stored procedure** is a group of T-SQL statements that is compiled with a single execution plan. Stored procedures are saved in the database and can be called both from T-SQL queries and from client applications. Since stored procedures can manipulate and maintain table data, they are often used to support business logic associated with data in the database. For example, a stored procedure may be developed to insert order information. Since order information may reside in multiple tables (and even mulitple databases), a stored procedure would help to encapsulate any logic required for maintaining data.

The database engine generates query plans when a stored procedure is compiled. All of the actions contained within the T-SQL statements of a stored procedure are checked by the database engine to determine the fastest way for the code to execute (which indexes to use, least cost in terms of I/O, etc.). Once this plan is determined it is stored for easy reuse whenever the stored procedure is called.

Each instance of SQL Server 2000 contains a group of administrative stored procedures prefixed by sp_. These are called system stored procedures and are provided as a core piece of SQL Server 2000. These stored procedures are used to perform common administrative and monitoring activities, and you can run them from any database.

An **extended stored procedure** is utilized in Transact SQL the same way as a standard stored procedure, but their functionality is implemented in a dynamic-link library (DLL), written in a language like Visual Basic or C++ (rather than Transact-SQL). The xp_sendmail stored procedure discussed in the previous chapter is an example of an extended stored procedure.

Triggers

Triggers are special stored procedures that run when data is modified (inserted, updated, deleted) in a table. Since they run when data is changed, triggers are often used to maintain data integrity and enforce business logic. For example, an insert trigger could be set up on a customer table so that when a new customer record is added, an appropriate sales person (based on location or some other relevant factor) could be associated with the customer.

Triggers are fired automatically when a certain data modification is performed, so there is no need to call them explicitly. Simply performing an insert, update, or delete statement will cause a related trigger to execute.

User-Defined Functions

A **user-defined function** is a set of T-SQL statements that can be reused in other T-SQL scripts. They are very useful for encapsulating commonly performed operations (e.g., data validation). Functions are very powerful in that they can be referenced as if they are a single value, like a date, or as if they were an entire table containing rows and columns. For example, a scalar function that returns an integer could be used in check constraints or as a data type of a table column just as if it were an integer. A function that returns a table can be used in a select statement as part of a view.

TRANSACTION ARCHITECTURE

SQL Server 2000 is responsible for maintaining the consistency of the data it stores. To ensure the highest level of integrity and consistency within a database, transactions are used when statements are processed. A transaction consists of a single or multiple statements that are taken as a single unit of work. For example, observe the following group of statements:

1. Insert an order record in the orders table

2. Update an accounting table with the total for the order

3. Update the inventory database to reflect the purchases included in the order

It is of the utmost importance that all of these operations are performed successfully. If even one of them fails, the consistency of the database is compromised. By setting up these three statements within a transaction, SQL Server 2000 will ensure that all of the operations are committed as a single successful operation, or all of the operations will be rolled back in the event of a single or multiple point failure.

There are four requirements that must be adhered to for a transaction to be valid. These four requirements are referred to as the ACID properties. ACID is an acronym for "Atomicity," "Consistency," "Isolation," and "Durability." These properties are enforced by SQL Server 2000 to ensure the consistency of data and to handle multiuser concurrency issues.

- *Atomicity*: Transactions are handled as the smallest unit of work in SQL Server 2000. All of the individual operations within a transaction must be successful or none of them can be completed.

- *Consistency*: The operations of a transaction must leave data in a consistent state. This means that all data integrity must be upheld and internal objects like indexes must be updated to reflect data changes. If a transaction succeeds, it leaves the database in a new consistent state. If it fails, then the database is returned to the state it was in prior to the transaction executing.

- *Isolation*: In a concurrent environment, transactions must be isolated from one another. Situations can arise where two users are attempting to alter the same pieces of data. SQL Server 2000 ensures isolation by preventing users from accessing data in an inconsistent state. If two transactions that modify the same data execute simultaneously, one of them is forced to wait so that modifications are not made to data that is in the middle of an existing transaction (inconsistent state).

- *Durability*: This property ensures that once a transaction is complete it will be persisted even in the event of a system failure.

SQL Server 2000 ensures the ACID properties are enforced through the transaction management facilities of the database engine, locking mechanisms for handling concurrency issues, and transaction logs.

Transaction Management

SQL Server 2000 performs every operation in a transaction. A single insert statement is treated the same as a more complex set of T-SQL statements grouped in an explicit transaction. The default behavior of the database engine is to operate in autocommit mode, meaning that each statement is either committed as it executes successfully or rolled back if an error occurs. However, programmers can form explicit transactions using standard statements offered by T-SQL.

The BEGIN TRANSACTION statement specifies that a transaction is starting. Various T-SQL statements are then executed within the transaction. If no errors are encountered, then the COMMIT TRANSACTION statement is called to save all of the changes performed by the operations within the transaction. If an error occurs, the ROLLBACK TRANSACTION statement is used to undo any modifications to data caused by the transaction.

Transaction Logs

Transaction logs are used to meet the "Durability" requirement of transactions. All modifications made to data in a database are recorded in the transaction log prior to being written to the database. This is called a **write-ahead transaction log**. The transaction log helps SQL Server 2000 guarantee that all committed transactions are applied and all uncommitted transactions are rolled back in the event of system failure or an application request of a rollback.

Transaction logs for each database are stored in different files than the data, and are not managed with pages and extents like data files. Instead, they store log records that record an action that was performed on the database. These log records are stored serially so they represent the actual chain of events that occurs on a particular database. The log captures all data changes, the end points of all transactions, extent allocation and disallocation, and table/index creation and deletion.

When a transaction begins, a log row is written to the transaction log. None of the modifications executed within the transaction will be written to the database itself until a transaction commit is received in the log. This prevents data corruption, which could be caused if a system failure occurred in the middle of an executing transaction.

Consider the situation where a person is transferring $500 from a savings account to a checking account. Logically, this action requires two operations: one to deduct $500 from the savings account and one to add $500 to the checking account. Both operations must execute successfully to ensure that information is not lost. The use of transactions and the transaction log ensure that the operation is carried out completely or not at all. When the transaction begins, a record is written to the transaction log, and a transaction log record is written for the deduction to the savings account. Then, the credit to the checking account is recorded. Finally, a COMMIT TRANSACTION record is written to the log, and the changes are committed to the database. If the server failed in the middle of the transaction (e.g., after the deduction from savings, but before the credit to checking), then the transaction log will not receive a COMMIT TRANSACTION log row.

Restarting SQL Server 2000 (either by restarting the services or rebooting the computer) will trigger the automatic recovery process. This process checks the transaction log and commits any completed transaction to the database. All transactions that have been rolled back explicitly or do not have a COMMIT TRANSACTION log row (as in the example above) will be rolled back automatically (removed from the transaction log without being committed to the database).

Transactions and the transaction log in SQL Server 2000 help to ensure the Atomicity, Consistency, and Durability of ACID, but they do not address the idea of Isolation. Handling concurrent activity on a database and ensuring isolation are facilitated by database **locking**. Locking is the process by which SQL Server 2000 ensures transactional integrity and database consistency by preventing users from accessing data being changed by other users, and preventing multiple database users from modifying the same piece of data at the same time.

Transactional Locking

Consider a situation where several sales employees in a company are updating an inventory system as they take orders for books from customers. The inventory system tracks the available quantities of certain books, and orders should not be accepted for items that are out of stock. A problem could arise if there is only one copy of a book in inventory but two salespeople take an order for the same book at the same time. Both salespeople could check the inventory system to determine if the book is in stock, and both would see that there is one copy left. However, two orders could not be made since there is only one copy of the book. This type of situation arises often in high-volume transaction processing systems and must be dealt with to ensure data integrity.

SQL Server 2000 uses an object called a lock to manage simultaneous activity on a database. Locks are automatically issued and managed by the Lock Manager process in SQL Server 2000. Locks are granted on a per-user-connection basis, and as such, individual users can acquire locks on certain pieces of data to prevent other users from performing modifications while the lock is held. The lock manager makes sure that users cannot acquire locks that are in direct conflict with a lock held by another user. This means that two users will not be able to hold locks that allow a certain row to be updated at the same time.

There are several levels of granularity that locks can act on. Table 4-2 lists the various levels of locking.

Table 4-2 Locking Levels

Level	Description
Row	The most granular lock. Locks an individual row in a table or index.
Page	Locks a single 8 KB page owned by a table or index
Extent	Locks an extent (8 contiguous data or index pages)
Table	Locks an entire table
Database	Locks an entire database

When high-level locks are used (like table and database locks), concurrent performance decreases because an entire table or database could be locked and therefore inaccessible to other users. When lower level locks are used (page level and row level), concurrency improves because more data is available to other users. Row-level locking is the finest in granularity and provides the best performance when high volumes of concurrent users are accessing a database. It is especially useful for row inserts, updates, and deletes because only the specific rows affected by an operation are locked. SQL Server 2000 will automatically determine what size locks will be allocated as well as the mode of the lock. Lock modes control how a resource can be accessed concurrently. Table 4-3 outlines the various lock modes implemented by SQL Server 2000.

Table 4-3 Lock Modes

Lock Mode	Description
Shared (S)	Used for read-only operations such as a SELECT statement. No other operations are permitted to update the data while the shared lock is held. Once the read operation is complete, the lock is released.
Update (U)	Used when a resource is being updated. Only one update lock can be held at a time for a particular resource. If an update will be performed, then the Update lock is converted to an exclusive lock, otherwise it is converted to a shared lock.
Exclusive (X)	Used for operations such as INSERT, UPDATE, or DELETE. Exclusive locks ensure that concurrent modification cannot be made to the same resource. No other transaction can read or modify data that is locked with an exclusive lock.
Intent	Used to establish a locking hierarchy between concurrent users. Users acquire intent locks for resources, and these locks are evaluated when an operation is requesting a lock on particular resources. If no intent locks exist, then the operation can acquire an exclusive lock and perform modifications. If there are intent locks already held for the table (transactions are waiting for resources to become available), then the operation must wait.
Schema	Used when an operation dependent on the definition of a table is executing. These types of locks are acquired when a column definition for a table is being altered or a stored procedure that accesses tables is being compiled.
Bulk update (BU)	Used when bulk-copying data into a table

Blocks and Deadlocks

Even with the advanced locking capabilities of SQL Server 2000, situations will still arise when concurrent transactions attempt to modify the same resources. One of the most common problems is known as blocking. Blocking occurs when one transaction is holding a lock on a particular resource and a second transaction needs a conflicting type of lock. In this situation, the second transaction will have to wait until the first transaction releases its lock before completing any operations. If a transaction holds a lock for a long period of time, then it is more likely that a blocking situation will occur. When transactions hold locks for a longer duration, several transactions can become blocked, and oftentimes more resources are affected, causing serious decreases in performance. Figure 4-7 illustrates blocking.

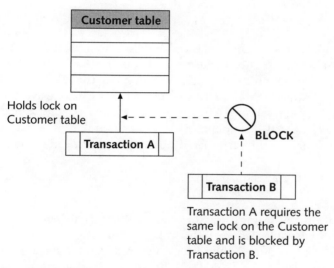

Figure 4-7 Blocking

A **deadlock** occurs when two transactions are blocking each other. Consider the example in Figure 4-8.

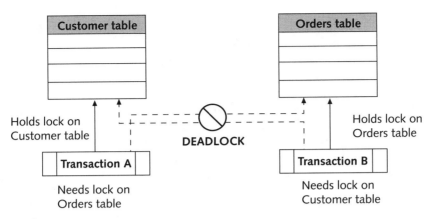

Figure 4-8   Deadlocks

Transaction A already holds an exclusive lock on the Customer table, and it requires a lock on the Orders table before the exclusive lock on the Customer table can be released. Transaction B already holds an exclusive lock on the Orders table, and it requires a lock on the Customer table before it will release its exclusive lock on the Orders table. Since neither transaction will release its lock, a deadlock occurs. SQL Server 2000 automatically detects deadlocks and will terminate a transaction if a deadlock is detected. In this situation the terminated transaction will need to be run again.

CHAPTER SUMMARY

- ❏ The smallest physical unit of storage for SQL Server 2000 databases is the 8 KB page. Pages contain either table data or index information. Pages are organized into groups of eight to form an extent. When data is entered into a table and more space is required for the data to be saved, SQL Server 2000 allocates an extent to the table and the data is written to a page on the extent.

- ❏ SQL Server 2000 databases can contain a wide array of objects. The most common of these is the table. All of the actual data in a database is stored in tables. Stored procedures, triggers, and constraints are objects that ensure business logic is performed and data integrity is enforced when data is modified. Views allow custom presentations of data to be developed. A view can contain a subset of rows or columns from one or more tables and is often implemented to alter the way in which data is presented to database users. Database indexes increase performance of queries by minimizing the amount of I/O operations that must be performed to locate one or more rows of data.

- ❏ SQL Server 2000 offers full transaction management capabilities to ensure data integrity in the event of a server failure. The transaction architecture of SQL Server 2000 also facilitates concurrent database activity by employing locks on resources.

KEY TERMS

branch node — A mid-level node in an index. Branch nodes are traversed to quickly locate specific rows of data.

cascading delete — Records in a foreign key table are automatically deleted when the primary key rows are removed.

cascading update — Changes to a primary key field are automatically made to related foreign key fields.

clustered index — An index that physically sorts and stores the rows in a table. The leaf nodes of a clustered index store actual data rows.

constraints — User-defined rules that help enforce the integrity of column data.

deadlock — A situation arising when two users, each having a lock on one piece of data, attempt to acquire a lock on the other's piece. This circumstance causes the users to block each other indefinitely. To resolve this condition, SQL Server 2000 detects deadlocks and terminates one user's process.

default — A type of constraint that defines a default value for a column in a table.

domain — The valid range of values for a set of data.

extended stored procedure — A special type of stored procedure that is implemented in a dynamic-link library (DLL) and usually written in a language like Visual Basic or C++.

extent — Eight contiguous pages (64 KB). All physical space allocated to tables is done using extents.

foreign key — A column or set of columns that refer to another table for a valid set of values. Foreign keys are a way of enforcing a relationship between tables.

horizontally partitioned — A restriction of rows from a result set.

index — A structure that increases the data retrieval performance of SQL Server 2000 by reducing the amount of I/O operations required to locate specific rows.

index row — Individual entries of an index that are stored in a page and contain a key value and a memory pointer to other pages used by the index.

leaf node — The lowest level nodes in an index. Depending on the type of index (clustered or nonclustered), a leaf node will contain actual data rows or memory pointers to data rows.

locking — Process by which SQL Server 2000 ensures transactional integrity and database consistency by preventing users from accessing data being changed by other users, and by preventing multiple database users from modifying the same piece of data at the same time.

mixed extent — An extent that houses information from multiple tables or indexes on its pages.

nonclustered index — An index that does not physically order the data in a table. Instead of data rows, pointers to data rows are stored in the leaf nodes of the index.

page — The smallest unit of storage employed by SQL Server 2000, measuring only 8 KB.

primary key constraint — A type of constraint applied to a column or set of columns in a table to ensure that each row is unique. No two rows in a table can have the same values in the primary key column or set of columns.

root node — The top-level node of an index. This is the first node that is accessed when an index is being used to locate data.

rules — User-defined rules to enforce data integrity. Rules are provided for backward compatibility.

stored procedures — A group of T-SQL statements that is compiled with a single execution plan.

table — A structure that stores information in a row and column format. A table is the most common database object and is used to store all data in a database.

table scan — A data retrieval operation requiring the database engine to read all of the pages in a table to find the rows that qualify for a query. The database engine performs table scans when a suitable index is not defined.

transaction log — A file that records all changes to a database before they are written to the database itself. Transaction logs allow for internal consistency and recoverability.

trigger — A special type of stored procedure that automatically runs when data is inserted, updated, or deleted from a table. Triggers can be configured to run after data is modified or instead of the data modification statement.

uniform extent — An extent that stores information from only one object.

user-defined data types — A custom data type, based on a standard SQL Server 2000 data type, that can have rules and defaults embedded within it to enforce data validation logic.

user-defined functions — A set of T-SQL statements that can be reused in other T-SQL scripts. User-defined functions can return a single value or a table structure.

vertically partitioned — Restriction of columns from a result set.

views — Logical tables that are based on Transact-SQL statements.

write-ahead transaction log — A log where data modifications are written prior to being committed to the database. When a transaction has been committed in the transaction log, then the data is persisted to the database.

REVIEW QUESTIONS

1. What is the smallest unit of storage that SQL Server 2000 can utilize?

   a. page

   b. extent

   c. unit

   d. kilobyte

2. True or False: Data types can be used to specify that a column accepts integer data only.

3. Which object does SQL Server 2000 use to improve the performance of queries by limiting the amount of I/O operations required to find specific pieces of data?

   a. table

   b. index

   c. default

   d. stored procedure

4. Which type of index physically sorts the table it is defined on and stores the data rows of the table in its leaf nodes?

   a. clustered index

   b. nonclustered index

5. True or False: System-stored procedures are special database objects that are used by the database engine to control transactions.

6. True or False: When two users, each having a lock on one piece of data, attempt to acquire a lock on the other's piece of data, a deadlock occurs.

7. A view that restricts which rows are returned to the user executing a query is considered to be:

   a. vertically partitioned

   b. horizontally partitioned

8. Which two types of constraints ensure that each row in a table is unique? (Select two)

   a. foreign key

   b. primary key

   c. unique constraint

   d. check constraint

9. True or False: A single row in a table can be stored across multiple pages.

10. Which of the ACID properties of transactions requires that all of the individual operations within a transaction must be successful or none of them can?

    a. atomicity

    b. consistency

    c. isolation

    d. durability

11. True or False: Modifications to data are first committed to disk and then written to the transaction log.

12. Which is the most granular locking level offered by SQL Server 2000?

    a. extent

    b. page

    c. row

    d. table

13. Which lock mode is used when a row is being deleted from a table?

    a. shared lock

    b. exclusive lock

    c. delete lock

    d. schema lock

14. Which lock mode is used when the structure of a table is being modified?

    a. shared lock

    b. exclusive lock

    c. delete lock

    d. schema lock

15. Which node of an index does the database engine access first when using the index to locate data?

    a. root node

    b. branch node

    c. leaf node

16. True or False: Deadlocks must be resolved manually by a database administrator.

17. Which of the following requirements could not be satisfied by a view?

    a. returning a subset of rows from a table

    b. preventing users from viewing certain columns in a table

    c. providing cascading delete capabilities

    d. presenting the results of a T-SQL join statement in the same form as a table

18. Which of the four ACID properties of transactions is facilitated through locking in SQL Server 2000?

    a. atomicity

    b. consistency

    c. isolation

    d. durability

19. True or False: The default behavior of SQL Server 2000 is to automatically commit or roll back operations as they complete.

20. Consider a scenario where there is an Employees table with a primary key of EmployeeID. There is also a table called Employees_PhoneNumbers that stores multiple phone numbers for each employee record (Office Phone, Cell Phone, and Home Phone). This table has a foreign key that references the EmployeeID column in the Employees table. If the relationship is configured to perform cascading deletes, what happens when a user tries to delete a "Cell Phone" record from the Employees_PhoneNumbers table?

   a. All of the phone numbers for the Employee record are deleted from the Employees_PhoneNumbers table.

   b. The employee record in the Employees table that the phone number relates to is deleted.

   c. Just the employee phone number is deleted from the Employees_PhoneNumbers table.

   d. An error occurs.

HANDS-ON PROJECTS

Project 4-1

To display the isolating properties of transactions by using Query Analyzer to perform T-SQL statement updates to a database table:

1. Start Query Analyzer by clicking **Start**, highlighting **Programs**, highlighting **Microsoft SQL Server**, and clicking the **Query Analyzer** item.

 Log in to your local instance of SQL Server 2000 through the Log in dialog box.

2. Select the **Northwind** database from the database menu at the top of the screen.

3. Type the following query into the query window and execute it by clicking **Execute Query** on the toolbar, as shown in Figure 4-9:

```
BEGIN TRANSACTION
UPDATE Employees
SET Title = 'Regional Sales Manager'
WHERE EmployeeID = 4
```

This query will start a transaction and then update the title column of the record in the Employees table with an EmployeeID of 4.

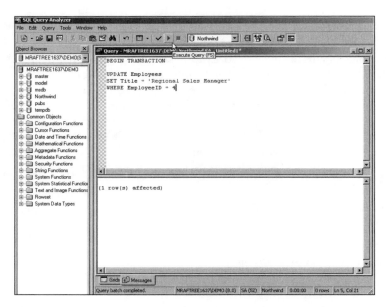

Figure 4-9   Executing an update query in Query Analyzer

4. Open a new query window in Query Analyzer by clicking **New Query** on the toolbar or using **Control-N**.

5. In this new query window type the following query and click **Execute Query** on the toolbar.

```
UPDATE Employees
SET HomePhone = '(206) 555-9482'
WHERE EmployeeID = 4
```

This query will attempt to update the same Employees table record as the previous query (EmployeeID = 4). Figure 4-10 shows that the new query is not permitted to finish executing because the first query is still in the middle of a transaction. Notice how the Cancel Query Execution toolbar button remains available because the query cannot complete executing until the first query finishes its transaction.

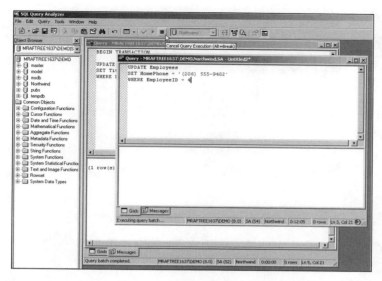

Figure 4-10 A query can't complete its execution because it is blocked by another query accessing the same data in the middle of a transaction.

6. Return to the original query window in Query Analyzer by using the Window menu or typing **Control-Tab**.

7. Erase the original query from the query window and type the following:

    COMMIT TRANSACTION

8. Execute the query by clicking **Execute Query** on the toolbar. Notice that the other window has now completed its query, as evidenced by the "(1 row(s) affected)" message in the query window (see Figure 4-11).

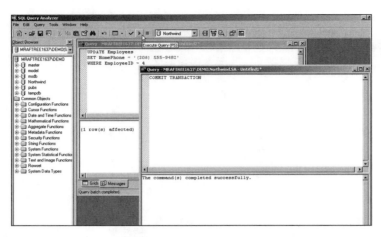

Figure 4-11 Once the transaction is committed, the second query can finish executing its update operation because the locks held by the transaction are released.

Project 4-2

In this project, we inspect views and the underlying tables that they access in Enterprise Manager. The exercise will enable you to easily identify how a particular view differs from a table it is based on structurally. The T-SQL SELECT query that the view is based on will also be inspected.

1. Start Enterprise Manager by clicking **Start**, highlighting **Programs**, **Microsoft SQL Server**, and then clicking the **Enterprise Manager** item.

2. Navigate to the Northwind database by expanding the Databases folder of a registered SQL Server 2000 instance and clicking the **Northwind** database item as shown in Figure 4-12.

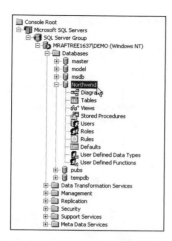

Figure 4-12   Accessing the Northwind database in Enterprise Manager

3. Click the **Tables** item in the tree pane on the left side of the Enterprise Manager window to access a list of available tables to the right.

4. Right-click on the **Products** table and click the **Design Table** option from the context-sensitive menu that appears. The Design Table window appears as shown in Figure 4–13.

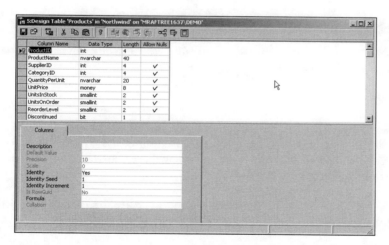

Figure 4-13   Design Table window in Enterprise Manager showing information about the Products table

5. Close the **Design View** window.

The Products table has many columns containing information about a single product.

6. Next, you will inspect a view that is based on this table. Click the **Views** item under the Northwind database in the tree pane of Enterprise Manager.

7. From the list of views on the right side of the window, right-click on the view named **Current Product List**, and click the **Design View** item from the context-sensitive menu. The Design View window appears (as shown in Figure 4-14).

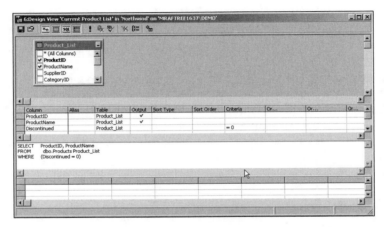

Figure 4-14   Design View window in Enterprise Manager showing information about the Current Product List view

8. Close the **Design View** window.

 The view is based solely on the Products table, but it is both horizontally and vertically partitioned. The only columns it returns are ProductID and ProductName. It limits the rows returned to only those with a value of "0" in the Discontinued column.

9. Start Query Analyzer by clicking **Start**, highlighting **Programs**, highlighting **Microsoft SQL Server**, and clicking the **Query Analyzer** item.

 Log in to your local instance of SQL Server 2000 through the Log in dialog box.

10. Select the **Northwind** database from the database menu in the toolbar.

11. Type the following query in the query window and execute it:

```
SELECT *
FROM Products
```

 All of the columns are included in the results. Also note that 77 rows are returned.

12. Open a new query window in Query Analyzer by clicking **New Query** on the toolbar or using **Control-N**.

13. In this new query window, type the following query and execute it:

```
SELECT *
FROM [Current Product List]
```

 The square brackets [] are required when accessing an object with spaces in its name. This query only returns two columns, ProductID and ProductName, and only returns 69 rows.

Project 4-3

In this project, cascading deletes are configured for a table, and the functionality is tested by deleting a row in a parent table and verifying that the associated rows have been deleted from the child table. In this scenario, the Northwind database is used and the Orders table is the parent table, while the Order Details table is the child.

To configure cascading deletes for a table:

1. Start Enterprise Manager as done in Step 1 of Hands-on Project 4-2.

2. Navigate to the Northwind database by expanding the Databases folder of a registered SQL Server 2000 instance and clicking the **Northwind** database item.

3. Click the **Tables** item in the tree pane on the left side of the Enterprise Manager window to access a list of available tables to the right.

4. Right-click on the **Orders Table** and click the **Design Table** option from the context-sensitive menu that appears.

5. Click **Manage Relationships** on the toolbar as shown in Figure 4-15.

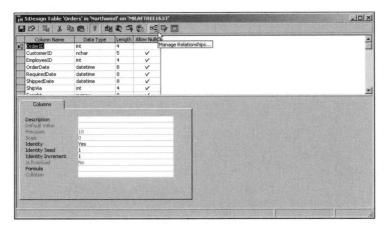

Figure 4-15   The Manage Relationships toolbar button of the Table Design window

6. Click the **Relationships** tab of the Properties window and select the **FK_Order_Details_Orders** relationship in the **Select relationship** menu. Click the **Cascade Delete Related Records** check box as shown in Figure 4-16.

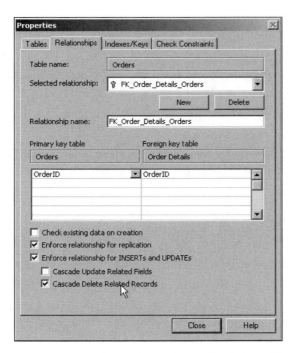

Figure 4-16   The Relationships tab of the table Properties window

7. Click **Close** on the Properties window.

8. Close the **Design Table** window for the Orders table.

9. Click **Yes** to save the changes you made to the table.

10. Click **Yes** again when the Save confirmation window appears (shown in Figure 4-17).

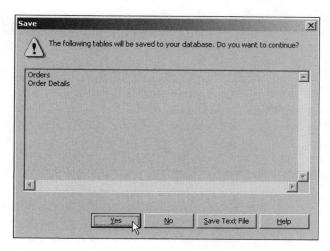

Figure 4-17   The Save confirmation window

11. Open Query Analyzer by clicking the **Tools** menu in Enterprise Manager and then clicking the **SQL Query Analyzer** item. (Make sure the **Northwind** database is selected from the Database menu in the toolbar of Query Analyzer.)

12. Type the following query into the query window and click **Execute** on the toolbar:

```
SELECT *
FROM Orders
WHERE OrderID = 10250
```

There is a single order in the Orders table with an OrderID of 10250.

13. Delete the previous query from the query window, type the following query, and click **Execute** on the toolbar:

```
SELECT *
FROM [Order Details]
WHERE OrderID = 10250
```

There are three rows in the Order Details table relating to the record in the Orders table (they all share the same OrderID of 10250).

14. Delete the previous query from the query window, type the following query, and click **Execute** on the toolbar:

```
DELETE
FROM Orders
WHERE OrderID = 10250
```

Since the cascade delete functionality was activated earlier on the relationship between the Orders and Order Details tables, the three rows in the Order Details table with an OrderID of 10250 should have been deleted automatically when the row in the Orders table was deleted.

15. To verify that the Order Details rows have been deleted, rerun the following query:

```
SELECT *
FROM [Order Details]
WHERE OrderID = 10250
```

There are no rows returned by this query. The rows from the Order Details table were deleted automatically through the cascade delete functionality of SQL Server 2000.

CASE PROJECTS

Case One

Using the content from this chapter and further information in SQL Server Books Online, describe what happens to User A in the following scenario:

Database User A needs to update a row in the Customer table. Database User B is already holding an exclusive table lock on the Customer table when User A initiates its update operation. Assume that User B will finish its operation in two seconds.

What happens when User A first attempts to execute his query?

What happens when User B finishes her operation?

Case Two

Using the content from this chapter and further information in SQL Server Books Online, research design considerations for building databases/tables. Write a document summarizing your findings. Be sure to discuss normalization and the four types of data integrity (including the database objects that help implement them).

Case Three

Figure 4-18 shows the column names of three tables. Using the information from the data types table in Table 4-1 and the information in this chapter and SQL Server Books Online regarding primary and foreign keys, add more detail to the diagram in Figure 4-18. Discuss which data type would best match the columns. Note that the character-based columns of the tables must support international characters (Unicode double-byte characters). Identify which fields should be primary keys, and draw lines between the tables to show the relationships between the primary and foreign keys.

4

Customers*
CustomerID
CompanyName
ContactName
ContactTitle
Address
City
Region
PostalCode
Country
Phone
Fax

Orders*
OrderID
CustomerID
EmployeeID
OrderDate
RequiredDate
ShippedDate
ShipVia
Freight
ShipName
ShipAddress
ShipCity
ShipRegion
ShipPostalCode
ShipCountry

Shippers*
ShipperID
CompanyName
Phone

Case Four

Using the information in this chapter, and through additional reading in SQL Server Books Online, create a document that outlines index architecture in SQL Server 2000 and makes recommendations about where to use each type of index. Begin by identifying the difference between clustered and nonclustered indexes. Go on to list the scenarios where clustered and nonclustered indexes will provide the most benefits.

5

CREATING SQL SERVER 2000 DATABASES

After reading this chapter and completing the exercises you will be able to:

♦ Define the different types of databases SQL Server 2000 supports

♦ Create and manage a SQL Server 2000 database

♦ Create and manage database objects

The primary responsibility of SQL Server 2000 is to provide a robust software infrastructure for creating databases and maintaining data. A single instance of SQL Server 2000 supports multiple databases defined by users. In addition to these user-defined databases, a number of system databases are automatically created when an instance is installed. The database engine uses these system databases to perform instance-wide operations like maintaining database definitions and supporting monitoring processes like alerts. **Databases** are created through the graphical user interface of Enterprise Manager or through the use of T-SQL statements like CREATE DATABASE. Like SQL Server 2000 instances, each database has it own set of configuration options to control how it operates. These options can be set when the database is created and modified at any time through the use of Enterprise Manager or system-stored procedures. Each database is initially created by appointing or creating specific files to store data and transaction log information. Database objects like tables and constraints are added to logically organize data and enforce relationships and business rules. This chapter illustrates the methods for creating and modifying databases in an instance of SQL Server 2000.

TYPES OF DATABASES

There are two general types of databases: **user-defined databases** and **system databases**. A user-defined database is a database created to store application-specific data. User-defined databases can be logically related or separate. For example, you could create a customer database that just stored customer information and an orders database that just held orders. You could also create a single database that stored both customer information and orders.

Every SQL Server 2000 instance has four system databases, necessary for SQL Server to operate. The four system databases are:

- Master
- Tempdb
- Model
- Msdb

The **master database** stores all of the system-level information for a SQL Server 2000 installation. It stores login accounts, configuration settings, and the names and locations of all user-defined databases for the installation. The master database also stores all system-stored procedures and information about extended stored procedures. We will discuss system and extended stored procedures later.

The **tempdb database** is used as a temporary processing location. Tempdb is used to store temporary data (data that does not need to be persisted), temporary code, and as workspace for some querying operations.

The **model database** is used as a template for new database creation. All databases that are created in SQL Server 2000 are based off of model. Unless overridden at the time of creation, a new database will copy the model database's size and options. Also, user-defined objects in model are copied to the new database.

The **msdb database** is used by the SQL Server Agent to store scheduled alerts and jobs information.

In addition to the system databases, the **pubs** and **Northwind** sample databases are created for every SQL Server 2000 installation. These are referenced extensively in SQL Server Books Online, so it is a good idea to get to know them.

You can review information about the databases for a given SQL Server 2000 installation by running the sp_helpdb system-stored procedure in SQL Query Analyzer. When run without any parameters, this procedure returns sizing and ownership information for all the databases on the server. When run with a database name as an input parameter, the procedure returns sizing and physical file information for the specified database.

FILES AND FILEGROUPS

As discussed in Chapter 4, SQL Server 2000 databases use files to physically store data and log information. These files are grouped into filegroups to help organize and consolidate the information they manage.

Files

SQL Server 2000 databases are mapped to two or more operating system files, which are referred to as **files**. SQL Server 2000 supports three file types:

- Primary data files
- Secondary data files
- Log files

All databases are created on a single primary data file. The **primary file** holds the data and system tables for the database. Primary files are usually files with an .mdf extension. You may choose to use secondary data files for a database as well. **Secondary files** (.ndf) allow databases to be expanded onto more than one file. This feature offers added flexibility by allowing tables and indexes to be placed in specific files. This could be beneficial in scenarios where you have multiple physical disks. You could choose to put some high transaction tables on their own disk to reduce contention.

 Files and filegroups cannot be shared across multiple databases.

The transaction log for the database is stored on one or more log files (having .ldf file extensions). Transaction log information and data cannot be stored on the same file so, each database must have at least one log file. Transaction log files cannot be associated with filegroups either.

When creating files, a size parameter is specified that defines how large the initial file will be. Files can be expanded manually or configured to grow automatically. Automatic expansion allows you to configure a file to grow by fixed amounts or by a percentage of its size. The growth of a file may be capped at a defined size, or it may be unlimited.

The location of files associated with a database is maintained in the master database, as well as on the primary file for the database. In most cases, the file information located in the master database is used, except in scenarios where the information is not available or accurate. Information from the primary file of the database would be used in the following scenarios:

- When attaching to an existing database (described later in this chapter)
- When restoring the master database
- When upgrading from SQL Server 7.0

SQL Server 2000 files have a logical and a physical name associated with them. The logical name is used when referring to the file in T-SQL statements. The name must follow the rules for **regular identifiers**; that is to say that the name must be unique and less than 128 characters in length. Though it must start with either a letter, underscore, "at" sign (@), or number sign (#), subsequent characters can include numbers. Spaces are not allowed. Names that don't meet the above restrictions must be delimited with double quotes or brackets. These are called **delimited identifiers**. The physical name is the filename; it must conform to the operating system file-naming rules.

Filegroups

Filegroups are designed to help administer data files. Filegroups allow data files to be grouped together and referenced as a single entity. A file may be a member of only one filegroup. Once a filegroup is defined, you may place tables, indexes, text, and image data on that filegroup. Note that transaction logs are never associated with filegroups. Transaction logs are managed as individual files. There are two types of filegroups: primary and user-defined. A **primary filegroup** contains the primary file and any other files not associated with another filegroup. A **user-defined filegroup** contains any additional files as specified during database creation or later alteration. There is always one **default filegroup**. Pages allocated for new table and index space come from the default filegroup when no filegroup is specified for the table or index.

User-defined filegroups may be marked as read-only. This can be useful in scenarios where data exists that shouldn't be modified. For example, historical data may be stored on a read-only filegroup to avoid accidental modification.

 The primary filegroup cannot be marked read-only since it contains the database system tables.

CREATING A DATABASE

SQL Server 2000 databases are created by using Enterprise Manager or T-SQL statements. Most tasks can be accomplished within the intuitive GUI of SQL Enterprise Manager. There, however, are some tasks that can only be accomplished with code, so it is a good idea to be familiar with the T-SQL commands used when creating and modifying databases. This chapter will illustrate how to perform tasks with SQL Enterprise Manager as well as T-SQL code.

To see a list of the databases on your server, expand the SQL Server Group node in SQL Enterprise Manager until you find the name of your server. Expand the databases node by left-clicking on the plus sign next to Databases. The tree should expand, revealing the existing databases, as shown in Figure 5-1.

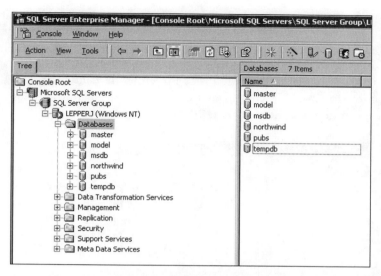

Figure 5-1   Viewing database information with SQL Enterprise Manager

The same information is available through the sp_helpdb system-stored procedure in SQL Query Analyzer, as shown in Figure 5-2.

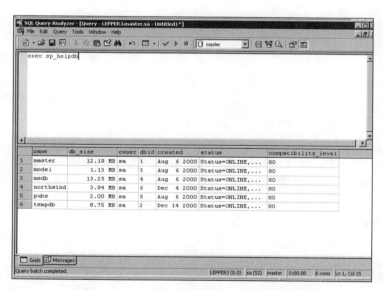

Figure 5-2   Viewing database information with SQL Query Analyzer

To create a new database in Enterprise Manager, right-click on Databases and select New Database from the context-sensitive menu. This displays the Database Properties dialog box, shown in Figure 5-3.

In the General tab, type the name for the database. The information in the Database and Backup sections of the General tab will be empty until you save the database. In the Maintenance section, you should choose a default collation for the database. The collation for a database is the default collation that will be used for character data that is used in the database. Collations define the sort order for Unicode data as well as the code pages and sort orders for non-Unicode data. Since there is a default collation defined for the server, you can generally leave this as "(Server default)".

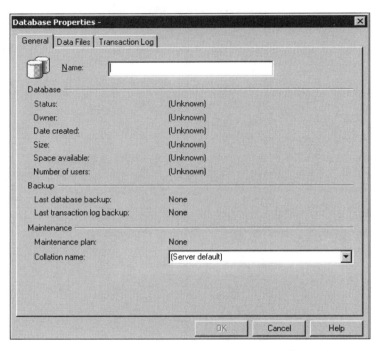

Figure 5-3   General tab of Database Properties dialog box

Managing Files and Filegroups

The Data Files tab shown in Figure 5-4 is used to create the primary and secondary files that are used to store the database on a hard drive or set of hard drives.

Each row in the Database Files grid represents a separate physical file for the database. The first row of the grid must contain information for the primary database file. The File Name column stores the logical filename for the data file. The Location column is the full path and filename for the file. The Initial size (MB) column is the starting size for the file. The default value for the size is taken from the model database. The size parameter is measured in megabytes and must be a whole value. The Filegroup column stores the name of the filegroup of which the file will be a part. For the first file, the value must be primary. If you plan to use more than one file for the database, you need to add a row to the Database Files grid for each file.

You can choose to store these extra files on the primary filegroup or on a new filegroup. To create a new filegroup, change the name of the Filegroup column.

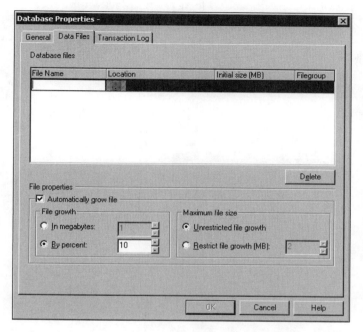

Figure 5-4 Data Files tab of Database Properties dialog box

 Though SQL Server 2000 gives you the flexibility to have multiple files spread over disks, most databases will operate sufficiently with one data file and one transaction log file. Filegroups are often used in scenarios where performance must be optimized. Filegroups (and therefore database objects) can be placed on separate physical drives to leverage the I/O capabilities of multiple hard drives. This topic will be discussed in greater detail in Chapter 6.

SQL Server 2000 data files can be configured with a static size or with a directive to automatically grow to accommodate more data as required. To configure how files grow, select a file in the Database Files grid. The "File properties" controls on the bottom of the screen allow the file to be configured for automatic file growth. When a data file is configured this way, SQL Server 2000 will automatically increase the size of the file when it fills (either by a percentage of current size or fixed size in megabytes). To configure data files to remain fixed in size, the "Automatically grow file" check box should be unchecked. The size of the file can be altered manually later if more space is required.

If data files are configured to grow automatically, it is a good idea to set a maximum file size. Otherwise, it is possible that the file could grow until it filled the hard drive.

SQL Server 2000 returns an error when an insert operation is performed against a database that does not have any available space.

Each database has at least one data file and at least one transaction log file. To configure a transaction log file for a database, select the Transaction Log tab as shown in Figure 5-5. Transaction log files are defined in much the same way as data files except that they don't belong to filegroups.

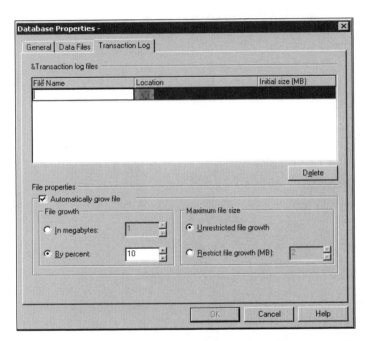

Figure 5-5   Transaction Log tab of Database Properties dialog box

Since all data modifications are written to the log, the transaction log tends to fill up. You can truncate the log to remove the committed portion of the log. SQL Server 2000 can then reclaim the truncated space.

Clicking OK initializes the database. Initialization includes overwriting any previous data on the disk space occupied by the data and transaction files to zeros.

Creating Databases with T-SQL Statements

You may also create a database by using the CREATE DATABASE T-SQL command. To use this command, open a query window with SQL Query Analyzer. The following Transact-SQL statement creates a database called Orders with one data file of 100 MB and one log file of 200 MB.

```
USE master
GO
```

```
CREATE DATABASE orders
ON PRIMARY
( NAME = orders_data,
    FILENAME = 'c:\program files\microsoft sql
server\mssql\data\orders_data.mdf',
   SIZE = 100,
   MAXSIZE = 200,
   FILEGROWTH = 25 )
LOG ON
( NAME = orders_log,

    FILENAME = 'c:\program files\microsoft sql
server\mssql\data\orders_log.ldf',
  SIZE = 200,
  MAXSIZE = 500,
  FILEGROWTH = 50 )
GO
```

If the database does not show up under Databases in SQL Enterprise Manager, right-click on Databases and choose Refresh from the context-sensitive menu. This will refresh the screen and the database should show up.

The following code uses the CREATE DATABASE T-SQL command to create the same Orders database, but with multiple data files spread across several disks.

```
USE master
GO
CREATE DATABASE orders
ON PRIMARY
( NAME = orders_prim,
    FILENAME = 'c:\program files\microsoft sql
server\mssql\data\orders_prim.mdf',
   SIZE = 100,
   MAXSIZE = 200,
   FILEGROWTH = 25 ),
FILEGROUP order_history
( NAME = order_hist1,
    FILENAME = 'd:\program files\microsoft sql
server\mssql\data\order_hist1.ndf',
   SIZE = 50,
   MAXSIZE = 100,
   FILEGROWTH = 25 ),
( NAME = order_hist2,
    FILENAME = 'd:\program files\microsoft sql
server\mssql\data\order_hist2.ndf',
   SIZE = 50,
   MAXSIZE = 100,
   FILEGROWTH = 25 )
```

5

```
LOG ON
( NAME = orders_log,
    FILENAME = 'c:\program files\microsoft sql
server\mssql\data\orders_log.ldf',
  SIZE = 200,
  MAXSIZE = 500,
  FILEGROWTH = 50 )
GO
```

This creates an orders database with two filegroups. The primary filegroup contains one 100 MB data file on the server's C: drive. It is configured to a maximum size of 200 MB and will automatically grow in 25 MB increments. The second filegroup, named order_history, contains two 50 MB files on the server's D: drive. They are each configured for a maximum size of 100 MB and can grown in increments of 25 MB. In this configuration, you could choose to put the order history details table on the order_history filegroup to help boost performance for order history inquiries.

MODIFYING DATABASES

To provide flexibility, SQL Server 2000 databases are easily modified after their creation. The physical size of a database may be changed to meet the needs of a particular installation. Database options may need to be altered to control how a particular database operates. You may need to move databases from one instance of SQL Server 2000 to another. Enterprise Manager and T-SQL statements are used to easily handle these conditions.

Expanding Databases

Databases can be configured for automatic file expansion by using the growth parameters for the database. While this simplifies database maintenance, it may not always be desirable, especially when disk space is at a premium. Fortunately, data and log files can be manually expanded at any time.

There are several options for database expansion. One option is to physically enlarge the files used by the database. Alternatively, new files or filegroups can be added to the database definition to increase the available data space.

To increase the file sizes for the database using SQL Enterprise Manager, right-click on the database and choose Properties from the context-sensitive menu. This loads the Orders Properties dialog box, shown in Figure 5-6.

Both the data or log portions of a database can be expanded from this interface. If you wish to expand the data portion of the database, select the Data Files tab. If you wish to expand the log portion of the database, select the Transaction Log tab. Both of the screens display a grid that lists all of the physical files that make up the database. You may modify the Space allocated (MB) column to make any file larger. Note that you cannot decrease the file size from this interface.

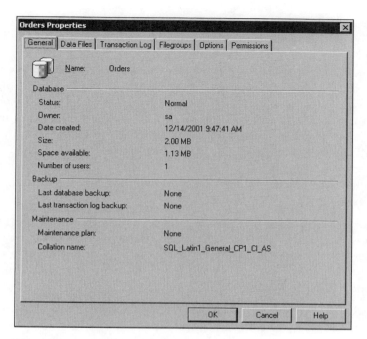

Figure 5-6   Orders Properties

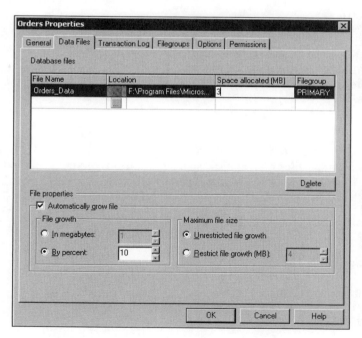

Figure 5-7   Expanding database file size

To add new files to the data portion of the database, select the Data Files tab, as shown in Figure 5-7. The Database Files grid will display all the current files in use by your database. To add a new file, simply add a new row to the grid. Note that by convention, secondary files use an .ndf extension. The Space allocated (MB) column is the starting size for the file. The size parameter is measured in megabytes and must be a whole number. The Filegroup column stores the name of the filegroup of which the file will be a part. You can choose to store the extra file on the primary filegroup or on a new filegroup. To create a new filegroup, change the name in the Filegroup column. If you would like automatic file growth, check the **Automatically grow file** check box in the File properties section and specify the various properties associated with automatic file growth. If you prefer to handle file sizes on your own, uncheck the "Automatically grow file" check box.

To add an additional transaction log file, choose the Transaction Log tab of the Database Properties dialog box. Add a new row to the Transaction Log files grid. You may choose to have the log automatically grow as needed by selecting the "Automatically grow file" check box. As with data files, you can specify the file to grow unrestricted (Unrestricted file growth) or capped (Restrict file growth (MB)).

The T-SQL ALTER DATABASE command is used to expand a database. ALTER DATABASE provides the ability to add, delete, and modify the basic structure of a database (including files and filegroups). For example, the following code would change the size of a data file named orders_data to 200 MB and the transaction log named orders_log to 300 MB:

```
USE master
GO
ALTER DATABASE orders MODIFY FILE
  (NAME=orders_data, SIZE=200MB)
ALTER DATABASE orders MODIFY FILE
(NAME=orders_log, SIZE=300MB)
GO
```

The following example adds a new filegroup called NewFileGroup. The filegroup will add two fixed-sized database files of 100 MB each. In addition, the code will add a new log file of 100 MB configured to grow automatically by 10% until it caps out at 200 MB.

```
USE master
GO
ALTER DATABASE orders ADD FILEGROUP NewFileGroup
GO
ALTER DATABASE orders
ADD FILE
  ( NAME = new_data1,
    FILENAME='d:\data\new_data1.ndf',
    SIZE=100MB,
    FILEGROWTH=0),
  ( NAME = new_data2,
```

```
   FILENAME='d:\data\new_data2.ndf',
   SIZE=100MB,
   FILEGROWTH=0)
 TO FILEGROUP NewFileGroup


ALTER DATABASE orders
ADD LOG FILE
( NAME = new_log1,
   FILENAME='d:\data\new_log1.ldf',
   SIZE=100MB,
 MAXSIZE=200MB,
   FILEGROWTH=10%)
GO
```

Shrinking a Database

There are times when it is necessary to shrink a database because disk space is limited and unused disk space within a database is needed for other purposes. Removing unused space from a database will also optimize backup operation by limiting the size of the files that are backed up. Fortunately, both the data and log portions of a database can be shrunk. This can be done manually, or it can be configured to occur automatically.

The simplest way to shrink a database is to have it done automatically. Automatic database shrinking occurs as a background process and should not affect normal usage. To set a database to automatically shrink with SQL Enterprise Manager, right-click on the database and choose Properties from the context-sensitive menu. Select the Options tab and check the Auto shrink check box.

 Since a database set to automatically shrink cannot shrink below its initial size, make sure your initial database size makes sense. For example, in a development environment, you probably would want to keep the database file small for quicker backup and recovery. You can always expand the database later.

Alternatively, the ALTER DATABASE command with the SET option can be used to set the database to shrink automatically. For example,

```
USE master
GO
ALTER DATABASE orders SET AUTO_SHRINK ON
GO
```

For better results and more flexibility, it is generally better to shrink the database manually. Manual shrinking allows you to specify how much space you would like to free. It also gives you the ability to shrink individual files in a database.

To shrink a database manually, right-click on a database in SQL Enterprise Manager and choose All Tasks and Shrink Database from the context-sensitive menu. This opens the Shrink Database dialog box shown in Figure 5-8.

Figure 5-8   Shrink Database dialog box

The "Maximum free space in files after shrinking" box is the desired percentage of free space that you would like in the database. Clicking OK at this stage will cause the database to release any unused space to the operating system, but it will only shrink up to the last allocated extent in the database. You may also choose to schedule the shrink for off hours by selecting the "Shrink the database based on this schedule" check box.

The individual files in the database can be shrunk by clicking Files. This opens the Shrink File dialog box shown in Figure 5-9.

Manual shrinking of databases can also be accomplished with the T-SQL command DBCC SHRINKDATABASE and DBCC SHRINKFILE. For example, to shrink a database by 25% with page reallocation, you would use:

```
DBCC SHRINKDATABASE('orders', 25)
```

To shrink a transaction log file down to 100 MB, you would use:

```
USE ORDERS
GO
DBCC SHRINKFILE('orders_log', 100)
```

When shrinking multiple file databases, you can decide to remove files to reduce size. If this is the strategy, make sure to use DBCC SHRINKFILE with the EMPTYFILE option. This will move all data in the file to another file. You can then run ALTER DATABASE to remove the empty file.

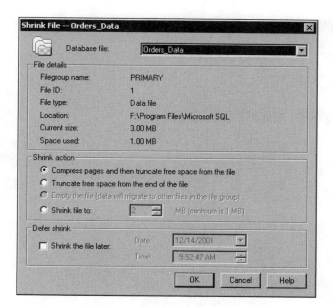

Figure 5-9   Shrink Files dialog box

Changing the Default Filegroup

The default filegroup is where new pages are allocated when a table or index does not explicitly define a filegroup. To change the default filegroup, right-click on your database in SQL Enterprise Manager and choose Properties from the context-sensitive menu. This loads the Properties dialog box shown in Figure 5-10. The Filegroup tab displays a list of all filegroups in the database. The Default check box is available to change the default filegroup for the database.

In the example below, the ALTER DATABASE command is used to modify the default filegroup.

```
USE master
GO
ALTER DATABASE orders MODIFY FILEGROUP
[NewFileGroup] DEFAULT
```

Configuration Settings

Each database has a set of options that govern its behavior. You can modify many database options by using the Database Properties box in SQL Enterprise Manager. There are subsets of options not available through SQL Enterprise Manager; these can be changed using ALTER DATABASE.

To modify options using SQL Enterprise Manager, right-click a database and select Properties from the context-sensitive menu. This loads the Orders Properties dialog box. Select the Options tab shown in Figure 5-11.

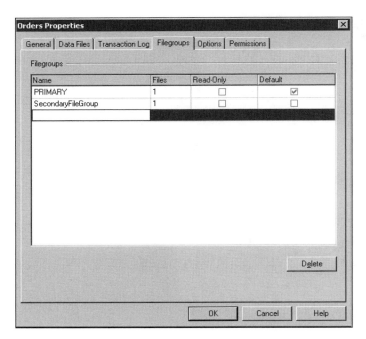

Figure 5-10   Database filegroups

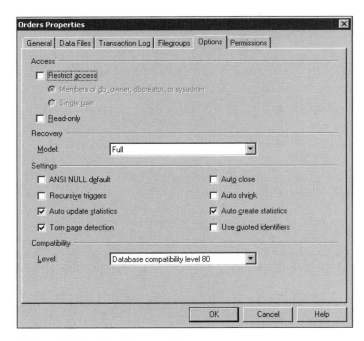

Figure 5-11   Database options

Table 5-1 describes the various options available in this screen and what they control.

Table 5-1   Database Options

Option	Description
Restrict access	Allow either members of the db_owner, dbcreator, or sysadmin or allow a single user to access the database.
Read-only	Data cannot be modified.
Recovery Model	Full: All operations, including bulk operations such as SELECT INTO, are fully logged. This provides for full recoverability with appropriate data and transaction log backups. Bulk-Logged: Reduced logging of bulk operations like SELECT INTO. This results in better database performance and smaller log files, but sacrifices full recoverability. Simple: The database can be recovered only to the last full database backup or last differential backup.
ANSI NULL default	Checking this box causes all new database columns to allow null values by default
Recursive triggers	Checking this box allows triggers to fire recursively.
Auto update statistics	Checking this box causes query optimization statistics to be updated automatically when they are out of date.
Torn page detection	Checking this box allows SQL Server 2000 to find incomplete pages that may have been due to power failures and outages.
Auto close	Checking this box automatically shuts down the database when the last user leaves.
Auto shrink	Checking this box causes SQL Server 2000 to periodically attempt to shrink the database.
Auto create statistics	Checking this box allows missing query optimization statistics to be built automatically.
Use quoted identifiers	Checking this box specifies that identifiers (e.g., column names) can be delimited by double quotes and character strings must be enclosed in single quotes.
Compatibility	Determines the compatibility level of the database with previous versions of SQL Server.

5

To set database options through code, you can use ALTER DATABASE. For example, to put a database in single-user mode, you would use:

```
USE master
GO
ALTER DATABASE orders SET SINGLE_USER
```

To change the recovery model being used,

```
USE master
GO
ALTER DATABASE orders SET RECOVERY BULK_LOGGED
GO
```

A full list of the options available through the SET statement can be easily found in SQL Server Books Online by searching with the following phrase: "Setting Database Options".

 You may set database options with the sp_dboption system-stored procedure. This is provided for backward compatibility reasons. The recommended method to change database options in T-SQL is ALTER DATABASE.

Attaching and Detaching Databases

You may move databases from server to server by attaching and detaching. When a database is detached, it become inaccessible. All references to the database are removed from the system tables on that server. Once detached, the physical database files may be moved to another server where they can be attached for use with that server.

 Detaching a database is not the same as taking a database offline. An offline database, whether taken offline manually or through the sp_certify_removable system-stored procedure, is still a part of a SQL Server 2000 instance. Once a database is detached, SQL Server 2000 no longer knows anything about it.

When attaching a database, all information about the file composition is obtained from the database file containing the primary filegroup. When attaching, you must tell SQL Server 2000 which database file has the primary filegroup information.

To detach a database, right-click on the database in SQL Enterprise Manager and choose Detach Database from the All Tasks option in the context-sensitive menu. This opens the Detach Database dialog box shown in Figure 5-12.

The Detach Database dialog box is rather simple. If there are users connected to the database, you can remove them by clicking Clear. The statistics used by the database engine to optimize queries can be updated before detaching the database by checking the "Update statistics prior to detach" check box. When ready, click OK, and the database will be detached. Note that it is removed from the database list in Enterprise Manager.

To attach to a database file, right-click on the Databases node in SQL Enterprise Manager and choose Attach Database from the All Tasks option in the context-sensitive menu. This loads the Attach Database dialog box shown in Figure 5-13.

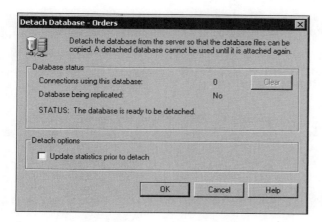

Figure 5-12   Detach Database dialog box

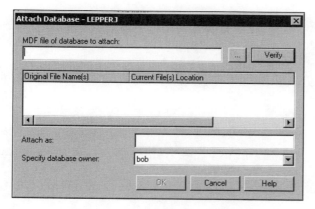

Figure 5-13   Attach Database dialog box

To attach to a database, you need to know the .mdf file that contains the primary file-group. You can use the Ellipses button to navigate to the file. If you choose the correct file, the grid should load with all the files that make up the database. The Verify button refreshes the grid. You can name the database using the "Attach as" text box and set the owner with the "Specify database owner" list arrow. Clicking OK will install the database. You should see the database name show up under the Databases node in Enterprise Manager.

To move removable databases, use the sp_certify_removable stored procedure to certify that the database is configured appropriately and to mark the
database as offline. Once offline, you can copy the database files to another
server. You can then attach the database to the new server. The file containing the system tables stores information concerning the file composition of
the database.

Databases can also be detached and attached using the sp_detach_db and sp_attach_db
system-stored procedures. For example,

```
USE master
/* Detach the database */
EXEC sp_detach_db 'orders'
GO
```

To attach a database, you will need to specify all the physical files that make up the database. For example,

```
USE master
EXEC sp_attach_db 'orders',
'c:\programfiles\microsoftsqlserver\mssql\data\orders_data.mdf',
'c:\programfiles\microsoftsqlserver\mssql\data\orders_log.ldf'
GO
```

Renaming Databases

Databases can be renamed using the sp_renamedb system-stored procedure. The following example renames the Orders database to Oldorders.

```
USE master
EXEC sp_renamedb 'orders','oldorders'
GO
```

Deleting Databases

There may be times when a database is no longer needed. To remove a database, right-
click on the database in SQL Enterprise Manager and choose Delete from the context-
sensitive menu. This loads the Delete Database dialog box shown in Figure 5-14.

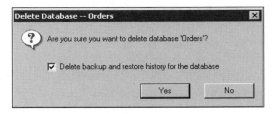

Figure 5-14   Delete Database dialog box

You may choose to remove all backup and restore history for the database by checking the "Delete backup and restore history for the database" check box. Click OK to delete the database.

You may also delete a database with the DROP DATABASE Transact-SQL command:

```
USE master
GO
DROP DATABASE orders
GO
```

 You cannot delete a database while users have connections. Make sure to close all connections to the database before trying to delete it.

DATABASE OBJECTS

Now that you have created a database, it is time to look at what a database contains. As previously mentioned, a database is a collection of data and objects that help to maintain and manipulate that data. To view the objects that a database supports, select the database in SQL Enterprise Manager and click on the plus sign to expand it, as shown in Figure 5-15.

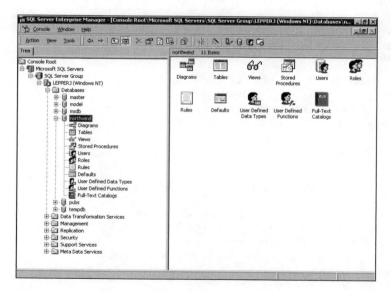

Figure 5-15   Database objects

The only required objects for a database are tables to hold data and users to access the data. All other objects are used to support the data.

General Considerations

The following sections provide some general guidelines when considering database objects. To summarize, they are:

- Ownership
- Object naming
- Permissions
- Viewing object information
- Deleting objects
- Renaming objects

Ownership

In general, the user name of the user who creates an object is the object's owner. The full name of the object is the object name prefaced by the owner name. For example, if a user named Bailey creates a table named Orders, then the full table name is Bailey.Orders. Another user named Madeline could create an Orders table as well; that table's name would be Madeline.Orders. A third Orders table created by the **database owner** would be named dbo.Orders. All references to the object need to specify the owner information. The exception to that rule is if the user name you are logged in with owns the object; in that case you can neglect the ownership information and just reference the object by its name. This holds true for all objects in a SQL Server 2000 database.

As an example, if a user named Bailey creates a table called Orders, queries by Bailey to retrieve the data can use either of the following statements and receive results:

```
/* User Bailey wants to review orders */
/* Access data by full name */
SELECT * FROM bailey.orders
/* Access data by object name. This works because Bailey
owns the table */
SELECT * FROM orders
GO
```

For Madeline to access Bailey's table, the full table name must be used.

```
/* User Madeline wants to review orders */
/* Access data by full name — this works */
SELECT * FROM bailey.orders
/* Try to access data by object name only.
***This fails*** */
SELECT * FROM orders
GO
```

To see an object's owner in SQL Enterprise Manager, left-click on the node you are interested in. This will load the right-hand pane with a list of the objects. The Owner column lists the user name of the owner.

Object Naming

All database objects created by a user need to follow the rules for identifiers. That means the following:

- The first letter of the name must be a letter, underscore, at sign (@), or pound sign (#).
- The rest of name must follow first letter rules, but may also include numbers.
- No spaces are allowed.
- The name cannot be a Transact-SQL reserved word.
- The names must be less than 128 characters.

Names that follow these rules are called regular identifiers. Names that do not follow these rules must be enclosed by double quotes or square brackets. These are called delimited identifiers.

Permissions

In addition to needing access to a database, a user needs explicit permission to create objects in a database. By default, permission to create an object is granted to members of the db_owner and db_ddladmin fixed database roles. In most cases, members of the sysadmin fixed server role can give users explicit permissions to create objects.

To grant users explicit permissions to create objects in a database, open SQL Enterprise Manager and navigate to your database. Right-click on the database and choose Properties from the context-sensitive menu. Then select the Permissions tab shown in Figure 5-16.

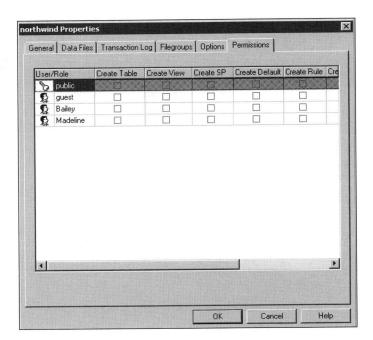

Figure 5-16   Database permissions

The Permissions tab allows you to grant create rights to users in the database. For example, to allow users to create a table, click the Create Table check box next to the user's name. To allow stored procedure creation, use the Create SP column. Click OK to grant the permissions.

Viewing Object Information

To view information about an object in the database with SQL Enterprise Manager, expand your database by left-clicking on the plus sign next to the database name. Left-click on the object of interest. For example, if you want to see all tables in the database, click on the Tables node. The right-hand panel of SQL Enterprise Manager will display a list of all objects of that type along with other object-specific information. You can refresh the information in the panel by right-clicking on the object and choosing Refresh from the context-sensitive menu.

You can also use the sp_help system-stored procedure in SQL Query Analyzer to gain information about database objects. If you run it by itself, you will get a list of all the objects and their owners in the database. If you run the procedure with the name of an object, you will receive more detailed information about the object itself.

Deleting Objects

To remove an object from the system with SQL Enterprise Manager, expand your database by left-clicking on the plus sign next to the database name. Left-click on the object of interest. For example, if you want to delete a stored procedure, click on the Stored Procedures node. The right-hand panel of SQL Enterprise Manager will display a list of all objects of that type. Left-click on the object you want to delete. You may choose several items to drop at once by holding down the control key as you left-click on the objects to drop. When you have selected the objects to delete, right-click to choose Delete from the context-sensitive menu. This will open the Drop Objects dialog box shown in Figure 5-17.

The Drop Objects dialog box displays a list of all the objects that you have selected. If you want to review the dependencies between the selected objects and other objects in the database, click Show Dependencies. To delete the selected objects, click Drop All.

To drop objects with Transact-SQL, you generally run a DROP statement tailored to the specific object you are trying to drop. For example, to drop a table you would use:

```
DROP TABLE orders
GO
```

To drop a store procedure named pr_MySproc you would use:

```
DROP PROCEDURE pr_MySproc
GO
```

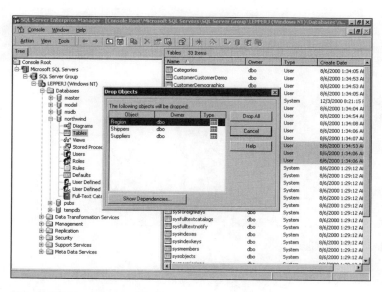

Figure 5-17   Drop objects

Renaming Objects

To rename an object with SQL Enterprise Manager, expand your database by left-clicking on the plus sign next to the database name. Left-click on the object that contains the item that needs to be renamed. For example, if you wanted to rename a view, click on the Views node. This will load the right-hand panel with a list of all the objects of that type. Right-click on the object you want to rename in the right-hand panel and choose Rename from the context-sensitive menu. The name will be editable.

You can also rename an object by using the sp_rename system-stored procedure. The following example renames a view named "vw_AllOrders" to "vw_AllOrders2000."

```
EXEC sp_rename 'vw_AllOrders','vw_AllOrders2000'
```

Creating Tables

To create a table, expand a database node in SQL Enterprise Manager by clicking on the plus sign next to your database. Left-click on the Tables node; this will display all the tables in the database in the right-hand panel. Right-click on the Tables node and choose New Table from the context-sensitive menu. This loads the New Table screen, as shown in Figure 5-18.

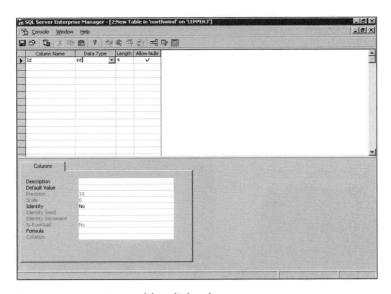

Figure 5-18   New tables dialog box

Adding Columns to Database Tables

Each row in the grid represents a column in the table. The Column Name column stores the name for the field. The Data Type column displays a list of the available data types for the column. The Length column is the width of the field (this is only editable for columns with data types like varchar and char that can be configured with a maximum size). The Allow Nulls check box determines if the column will permit null values.

Each field has additional properties that can be set in the Columns tab. The Description row is a text description of the field, which is stored as an extended property. An **extended property** is a user-defined value that can be attached to almost any object. You can store any number of properties and values with objects in the database. Extended properties are added to the system using the sp_addextendedproperty system-stored procedure.

The Default Value row is the default value for the column when data for the column is not specified on an insert. The list arrow will display any defaults defined globally. The Precision and Scale rows are used for decimal and numeric columns. **Precision** determines the total number of decimal digits that can be stored (both to the left and right of the decimal point). **Scale** determines the maximum number for decimal digits to the right of the decimal point. The Identity, Identity Seed, and Identity Increment rows are used if the column will be used as an auto-generated unique identifier. Identity columns are filled automatically by the database engine with sequential, unique numeric values. You can define one identity column per table based on decimal, int, numeric, smallint, bigint, or tinyint data types. The Identity Seed value is the initial starting point for the column. The Identity Increment is the value of the increment.

The Is RowGuid row is used when you want to generate a value that is guaranteed to be unique not only across the database, but also across all databases in the world. This value is called a Globally Unique Identifier, or **GUID**. This property is used in conjunction with the unique identifier data type. You may define one GUID column per table. To generate GUIDS, you must use the built-in function NEWID as the default for the column. The Formula row is used when you want to define a computed column. It can be an expression, a reference to table columns, or a built-in function. The Collation row specifies a collation that is used for a character data column.

You may choose to set a column as the primary key by selecting the rows that will be part of the key and by clicking on the Set primary key button 🔑 on the toolbar. You may select multiple columns by holding down the Control key while you click on rows. This will place a key icon next to the columns in the key, as shown in Figure 5-19.

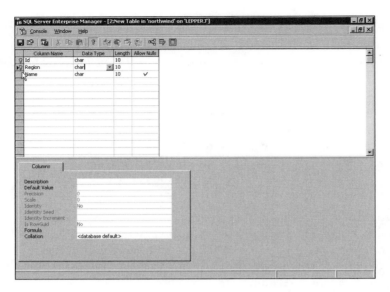

Figure 5-19   Table with multiple-column primary key

Managing Table Properties

The Table and Index Properties button [image] on the toolbar provides access to most other items you will need to manage on your table. The Tables tab (shown in Figure 5-20) lets you manage high-level items on your table.

The "Selected table" list box displays the table you are managing. The Owner list box shows the owner of the table. This list box shows all users in the database as well as all database roles. A new owner is assigned by selecting a user from the list. The "Table name" text box allows you to modify the table name. The Table Identity Column and Table ROWGUID Column list boxes display a list of all columns in the table that could be used as identity and RowGuid columns. You can choose to change the columns used or select the blank option to not use an identity or RowGuid. The Table Filegroup and Text Filegroup list boxes display a list of available filegroups for the database. You can choose to place the table or text data types on any available filegroup. The Description text box is stored as an extended property. It represents a description of the table.

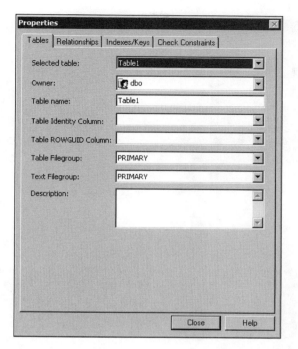

Figure 5-20   Tables tab of Table and Index Properties dialog box

Defining Table Relationships

The Relationships tab shown in Figure 5-21 is used to define primary and foreign keys. To create a new relationship, click New. SQL Enterprise Manager will create a new relationship name in the "Relationship name" text box. The name may be modified, but it must be unique. To define a relationship, choose fields from the two tables you are relating. Select a table in the "Primary key table" list box. In the grid column below, choose each of the fields that make up the relationship. In the Foreign key table list box, choose the related table and the fields that make up the relationship. The "Check existing data on creation" check box validates any existing data in the foreign key table on the relationship fields. The "Enforce relationship for replication" check box assures that the foreign key is enforced when data from the table is copied in a replication scheme. The "Enforce relationships for INSERTS and UPDATES" check box applies the relationship to all data that is inserted, updated, or deleted in the foreign key table. It also assures that data from the primary key table cannot be deleted if rows in the foreign key table refer to it. Updates to primary key values can be automatically propagated to the associated foreign key columns by checking the Cascade Update Related Fields check box. Foreign key rows can be automatically removed if their corresponding primary key rows are deleted by enabling the Cascade Delete Related Records option. Relationships are deleted by selecting the relationship and hitting the delete button.

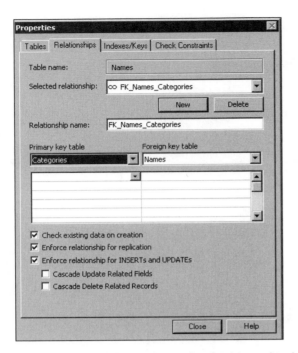

Figure 5-21   Relationships tab of Table and Index Properties dialog box

Managing Table Indexes

The Indexes/Keys tab shown in Figure 5-22 allows you to manage indexes on the columns in the table.

If you created a primary key on the table, there will already be an index created. By default, the primary key will have a clustered index, but this is not a requirement. To create a new index, click New. SQL Enterprise Manager will create a new index name in the Index name field. You may modify this as long as the name is unique. In the grid, select the column(s) that will make up the index. You can choose to order the index data in ascending or descending order. You can also choose which filegroup to store the index on by using the Index Filegroup list box. If you wish to make the index unique, click on the Create UNIQUE check box. If you want to enforce uniqueness via a constraint, use the Constraint option. You may also choose to enforce uniqueness in an index by using the Index option. The **Fill factor** text box determines how full the index pages will be. A value of zero tells the database engine to use the default server setting. The Pad Index check box is available if you are creating a unique index and you have set the fill factor to something other than zero. Pad Index leaves the same percentage of space as the fill factor at other levels of the index. To create a clustered index, use the Create as CLUSTERED check box. Since this physically reorders the table by the index, you can have only one per table.

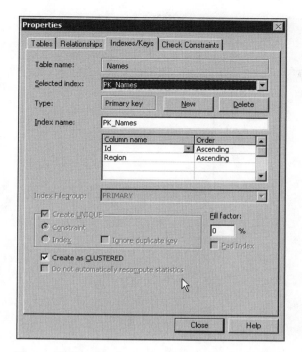

Figure 5-22   Indexes/Keys tab of Table and Index Properties dialog box

Managing Check Constraints

Check Constraints are maintained on the Check Constraints tab shown in Figure 5-23. To add a new constraint, click the New button and type an expression in the "Constraint expression" text box. The expression must evaluate to TRUE or FALSE. You may reference built-in functions as well as other columns in the expression. The "Check existing data on creation" check box will force the database engine to check that existing data satisfies the constraint. "Enforce constraint for INSERTs and UPDATEs" enforces the constraint when data is inserted and updated.

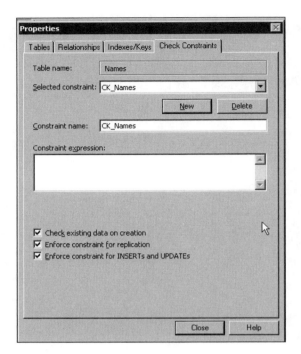

Figure 5-23   Check Constraints tab of Table and Index Properites dialog box

Creating and Modifying Database Objects with T-SQL

Tables can also be added using the CREATE TABLE Transact-SQL command.

The following creates two tables on the primary filegroup. The Customers table has a primary key on an auto-generated ID field. The Orders table stores the customer's unique ID in a foreign key field.

```
CREATE TABLE dbo.Customers
  ( id int NOT NULL IDENTITY (1, 1)
      CONSTRAINT PK_id PRIMARY KEY NONCLUSTERED,
  FirstName varchar(50) NULL,
  LastName varchar(50) NULL,
  Phone varchar(10) NULL
  ) ON [PRIMARY]
```

```
CREATE TABLE dbo.Orders
   (OrderId int NOT NULL IDENTITY (1, 1),
 CustomerId int NULL
       CONSTRAINT FK_CustomerId REFERENCES
dbo.Customers(id),
 OrderDate datetime NULL,
 ProductId char(10) NULL
 ) ON [PRIMARY]
GO
```

Once a table is created, the ALTER TABLE statement can be used to modify it. The following adds a default value of the current system date to the order table OrderDate field.

```
ALTER TABLE dbo.Orders ADD CONSTRAINT
 DF_Orders_OrderDate DEFAULT GetDate() FOR OrderDate
```

Indexes are created using the **CREATE INDEX** statement. The following creates a clustered index on the Last Name field of the Customers table.

```
CREATE CLUSTERED INDEX IX_Customers_LastName ON
dbo.Customers
 (LastName) ON [PRIMARY]
```

The following creates a multi-field nonclustered index on the Orders table with a fill factor of 80%.

```
CREATE NONCLUSTERED INDEX IX_Orders_Date_Product ON
dbo.Orders
 (OrderDate, ProductId) WITH FILLFACTOR = 80 ON [PRIMARY]
```

Views

As discussed in Chapter 4, SQL Server 2000 views are logical tables that are constructed from SQL statements. Though a view acts like a standard table (it has named columns, rows, and it is referenced in Transact-SQL like a standard table), it is actually dynamically generated from standard base tables.

Quite often, views are created to hide the underlying table structure; the view provides a custom view of the data. You could define a view that only shows certain rows of a table. This is often referred to as horizontal partitioning. Similarly, you could vertically partition data by defining a view that displays only select columns from a table. Views can be defined that combine data from many tables and even tables on different servers.

Creating Views in Enterprise Manager

To create a view, expand your database in SQL Enterprise Manager and click on the Views node. This will display all views in the database in the right-hand panel. Right-click on Views and choose New view from the context-sensitive menu.

Views can be based on tables, other views, or user-defined functions. For simplicity, the following discussion will just refer to tables.

The New View screen, shown in Figure 5-24, provides several options to make creating views simpler. The screen is divided into four horizontal panes. The top pane is called the Diagram Pane. The Diagram Pane provides a graphical way to add columns to the view and displays a graphical representation of the tables in the view. It also allows you to define joins between the tables in the view. You can toggle the Diagram Pane on and off by using the Show/Hide Diagram button on the toolbar. The second pane, called the Grid Pane, allows you to determine sort orders, column aliases, and criteria for the view. This is toggled using the Show/Hide Grid Pane button on the toolbar. The SQL Pane is displayed under the Grid Pane. It displays the SQL statement defined by the Diagram and Grid panes. It can be toggled using the Show/Hide SQL Pane button on the toolbar. The last pane displays the results of the SQL statement. The Results Pane can be toggled using the Show/Hide Results Pane button on the toolbar. You test the results of the view by clicking Run on the toolbar.

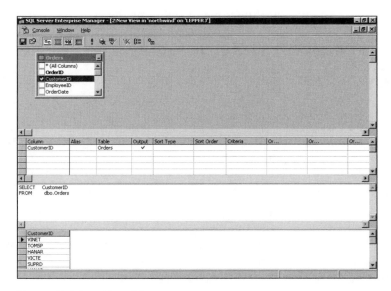

Figure 5-24   New View screen

To add tables to the Diagram Pane, use the Add Table button on the toolbar. This opens the Add Table dialog box shown in Figure 5-25.

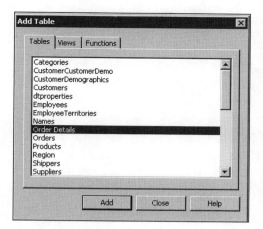

Figure 5-25   Add Table dialog box

If you add tables to the view that have primary and foreign key relationships defined, those relationships will be displayed automatically as shown in the diagram in Figure 5-26.

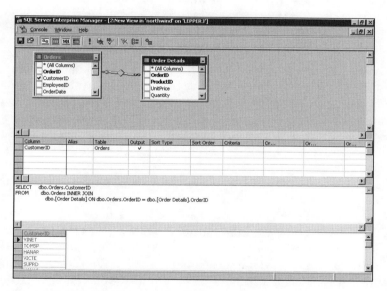

Figure 5-26   One to many join

You can review the join properties by clicking on the join line and then clicking the Properties button ⬚.

The Properties dialog box shown in Figure 5-27 allows you to modify the join properties by changing the join criteria or making outer joins. You can change a join from searching for equivalent values to any comparison operator with the list arrow. You can also create an outer join by checking one of the All rows check boxes. When you are finished with the join, click Close.

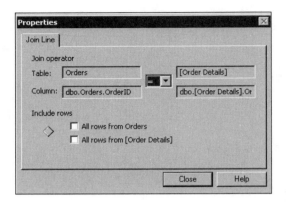

Figure 5-27 Join properties

You can remove a join by right-clicking on the join line and choosing Remove from the context-sensitive menu. You can create new joins by left-clicking and dragging a field in one table to a field in another table. This will generate a join for only the view. It will not change the underlying table relationships.

After tables are added, you can add columns to the result by checking the boxes next to the fields in the tables or by left-clicking and dragging the fields to the Grid pane in the Diagram Pane. The Grid pane represents all the columns that will be part of the view. The Alias column is an alias for the field in the view. In general, this is left blank unless a computed column exists or if you include fields from different tables with the same name in the results. In those cases, you will need to create a unique alias name. The Table column is the name of the table from which the field comes. Check the Output column if you would like to include the column in the results of the view. You may choose to include a column strictly for criteria; in that case, you may not want to show the results in the output. The Sort Type column allows you to sort the view results in ascending or descending order by the field. The Sort Order column displays the order in which the results will be sorted by the columns that have been designated as sorted. The Criteria column holds a search criteria for the column. This can hold an operator like an equals sign, the like operator, etc. For example, to find all last names that start with L, you could enter "like L%". The Or columns are additional search criteria on the column.

You may choose to group by columns by using the Use Group By button ![button] on the toolbar. Grouping allows you to aggregate columns in the result set.

To access the view properties, click on a row on the Grid pane and then click the Properties button 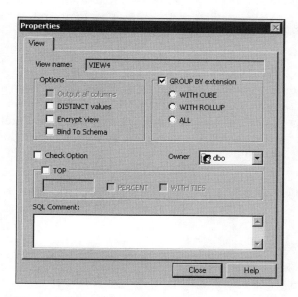 on the toolbar. This loads the Properties dialog box shown in Figure 5-28.

Figure 5-28   View properties

The "Output all columns" check box will add all columns from all tables to the results. This is the same as including the asterisk from all tables. The "DISTINCT values" check box adds the Transact-SQL keyword Distinct. This will remove any duplicate rows from the results. The "Encrypt view" check box allows you to encrypt the view in the database. You can not modify a view definition once it is encrypted.

As you build your view, the SQL pane will update with the equivalent Transact-SQL. When you save the query with the Save button 🖫 on the toolbar, the Transact-SQL is saved to the database.

Creating Views with T-SQL Statements

You can create a view with the CREATE VIEW T-SQL statement. The following example creates a view called vw_USCustomers that displays only US customers.

```
CREATE VIEW dbo.vw_USCustomers AS
SELECT      dbo.Customers.*
FROM        dbo.Customers
WHERE       (Country = 'USA')
GO
```

Stored Procedures

Stored procedures are compiled groups of T-SQL statements that are processed as a single unit of operation. They are typically used to perform business logic and to maintain data in tables. Stored procedures are analogous to functions in other standard programming languages like Visual Basic or C++. Like routines in other languages, stored procedures support input and output parameters as well as return values.

To add a standard stored procedure, expand a database in SQL Enterprise Manager and left-click on the Stored Procedures node. This will display a list of all the stored procedures in the database in the right-hand pane. Right-click on the Stored Procedure node and choose New Stored Procedure from the context-sensitive menu. This loads the Stored Procedure Properties window shown in Figure 5-29.

Figure 5-29   New Stored Procedure window

The Stored Procedure Properties window allows you to type the Transact-SQL code for the stored procedure. The Permissions button allows you to grant permissions to the stored procedure. This is only available after you have saved a stored procedure to the database by clicking OK.

The CREATE PROCEDURE statement in the Stored Procedure Properties window could just as easily be run from a SQL Query Analyzer window, resulting in the creation of the stored procedure.

Triggers

Triggers are a special type of stored procedure that is called when data modifications occur on a table or view. Triggers provide a method of enforcing business rules. Triggers are written in Transact-SQL and can be configured to run when data is inserted, updated, or deleted on a table. Since they are written in Transact-SQL, triggers can enforce more complex business rules than constraints.

There are two type of triggers: **after** and **instead of**. An after trigger fires after an insertion, update, or deletion of data occurs on a table. There can be many after triggers for insert, update, and delete attached to a table. An instead of trigger fires in place of the triggering action and before constraints are enforced. For example, an instead of insert trigger would fire in place of the insertion of data on the table. The trigger could process the data and decide which data should be inserted. Instead of triggers can be defined on tables and views. There can be only one instead of trigger for inserts, updates, and deletes on a table.

To create a trigger, expand the database and left-click on the Tables node. This will display a list of all tables in the database in the right-hand panel. Right-click on the table that will use the trigger and select Design Table from the context-sensitive menu. This loads the Design Table screen. Triggers can be managed by clicking the Triggers button 🔲 on the toolbar. This loads the Trigger Properties dialog box as shown in Figure 5-30.

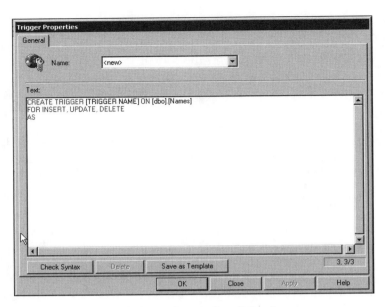

Figure 5-30   New Trigger Properties dialog box

The Name list arrow displays a list of all triggers defined on the table. To create a new trigger, select "<new>". The code for the trigger is typed into the Text text box. The Transact-SQL syntax can be validated by clicking Check Syntax. You may also choose to save the code in the Text window as template for future triggers by clicking Save as Template. When you have finished, click OK.

CHAPTER SUMMARY

- A database is a collection of logically related data and objects that help support and maintain that data. Vital system information is stored in special system databases. The master, model, tempdb, and msdb are examples of system databases. User-defined databases maintain user-specific data.

- Databases are comprised of one or many files that store data and one or many files that hold the transaction log. The transaction log records all modifications to the database to assure recoverability and data consistency. Data files may be organized into a filegroup, which is a named collection of physical operating system files.

- Databases can be configured to automatically grow and shrink in size. This simplifies maintenance. They can also be created to run on removable media like CD-ROMs.

- Databases can contain several types of objects, including tables, views, stored procedures, triggers, indexes, and constraints. These objects are used to store, retrieve, and modify data and to maintain data integrity. These objects can be managed graphically using SQL Enterprise Manager or through T-SQL in SQL Query Analyzer.

KEY TERMS

after trigger — A trigger configured to fire after data modification statements are run.

database — A logical collection of data and objects that are used to support maintenance and use of that data.

default filegroup — The filegroup where space is allocated when a table or index does not explicitly define a filegroup.

delimited identifiers — Names that do not follow the rules for regular identifiers must be delimited with double quotes or square brackets.

extended property — User-defined named value associated with an object in the database.

file — A physical operating system file that stores a database or transaction log.

filegroups — A named grouping of one or more physical data files.

fill factor — The amount of space left in an index page to account for future growth.

GUID — A globally unique identifier.

instead of trigger — A trigger that runs in place of the data modifications that caused it to fire.

master database — A system database that stores login, configuration, and installed database information. The master database stores all system-stored procedures and information about extended stored procedures.

model database — A system database that is used as a template for all user-defined databases.

msdb database — A system database that stores scheduling and alert information.

northwind database — A sample user-defined database installed with SQL Server 2000.

precision — The total number of decimal digits that can be stored in a numeric field in a table (both to the left and right of the decimal point).

primary file — Database file that holds the system tables and data.

primary filegroup — A filegroup that holds the primary data file and any other files not in an explicit filegroup.

pubs database — A sample user-defined database installed with SQL Server 2000.

regular identifiers — A set of naming rules for objects.

scale — The maximum number for decimal digits stored to the right of the decimal point (applies to a numeric field in a table).

secondary files — Additional data files for a database.

system databases — A special collection of databases that store vital system information. The database engine uses system databases to operate.

tempdb database — A system database that is used by the database engine for temporary processing and objects.

user-defined database — *See* database.

user-defined filegroup — A named grouping of files other than the primary filegroup.

REVIEW QUESTIONS

1. The _____ database stores configuration, login, and information about all the databases on SQL Server 2000.

2. True or False: The data and transaction log can be placed on the same file.

3. The system tables for a database are stored on which file?

   a. secondary data file

   b. log file

   c. primary data file

   d. none of these

4. The _____ system-stored procedure provides information about databases and their file sizes.

5. True of False: After creating a database, all users registered with SQL Server may use it.

6. A user named Meredith creates a stored procedure named pr_GetAllTerritories. How would a user named Bailey refer to the procedure?

7. Which of the following is a not a valid table name?

   a. tblOrder

   b. [Order]

   c. #Order

   d. 2000Orders

8. What operation can be used to increase the size of an existing database?

   a. sp_expandDB system-stored procedure

   b. CREATE DATABASE T-SQL statement

   c. ALTER DATABASE T-SQL statement

   d. DBCC GROWDB T-SQL statement

9. Which of the following Transact-SQL commands would be used to configure database options like Read-only and Recovery Model?

   a. sp_configure

   b. sp_changedboptions

   c. ALTER DATABASE

   d. none of these

10. Which T-SQL statement detaches the Customer database?

    a. ALTER DATABASE 'Customer' SET DETACH = TRUE

    b. DROP DATABASE 'Customer'

    c. sp_detach_db 'Customer'

    d. sp_detach 'Customer'

11. Which value specifies the number of digits to allow to the right of the decimal point?

    a. scale

    b. precision

12. When attaching a database, information concerning the database file structure is stored in _____.

13. What type of table column is used to automatically generate sequential numeric row IDs?

    a. Primary Key column

    b. Identity column

    c. Foreign Key column

    d. GUID column

14. True or False: Databases in SQL Server 2000 can be set to grow to a maximum size as data is added to them.

15. True or False: The expression defined for a check constraint must return a value of True or False.

16. Which type of index physically sorts a table by the indexed columns?

    a. clustered index

    b. unique index

    c. nonclustered index

    d. factored index

17. The two sample databases that ship with SQL Server 2000 are called _____ and _____.

18. True or False: You can place a table on a separate hard disk from an index on that table.

19. Which system database is used as a template when new user-defined databases are created in SQL Server 2000?

    a. master

    b. msdb

    c. tempDB

    d. model

20. True or False: Once a database is created, the filegroups that the data files are associated with cannot be changed.

21. Which system-stored procedure returns information about individual database objects?

    a. sp_ObjectInfo

    b. sp_help

    c. sp_who

    d. sp_sysobjects

22. True or False: A single database can only have one log file.

23. Which T-SQL statement would change the name of the CustInfo database to Customers (assume the command is executed from the Master database)?

    a. DBCC DBNAME 'CustInfo', 'Customers'

    b. ALTER DATABASE 'CustInfo' SET DB_NAME = 'Customers'

    c. sp_rename 'CustInfo', 'Customers'

    d. sp_renamedb 'CustInfo', 'Customers'

24. Which T-SQL statement would change the name of the Phone table in the Customer database to Customer_Phone (assume the command is executed from the Customer database)?

    a. sp_renamedb 'Phone', 'Customer_Phone'

    b. sp_rename 'Phone', 'Customer_Phone'

    c. sp_rename 'Customer_Phone', 'Phone'

    d. ALTER TABLE 'Phone' SET NAME='Customer_Phone'

25. Which system database stores information that is used by the SQLAgent service?

    a. master

    b. msdb

    c. model

    d. tempDB

HANDS-ON PROJECTS

Project 5-1

In this project you will create a customer database used to store information about customers and their addresses. The database will have two filegroups, a primary with one file and a secondary with two files. It will also have two transaction logs.

To create a customer database:

1. Start SQL Enterprise Manager. Navigate the tree until you reach the Databases node. Right-click on **Databases** and choose **New Database** on the context-sensitive menu.

2. On the General tab, name the database **Customer**.

3. Select the Data Files tab. In the grid, modify the first row to contain the following data (if necessary):

   File Name: **Customer_Data**

   Location: `C:\Program Files\ Microsoft SQLServer\MSSQL\data\Customer_Data.MDF`

   Initial size (MB): **1 MB**

   Filegroup: **PRIMARY**

4. Click on the first row in the grid to highlight it. In the File properties section, check the **Automatically grow file** check box if necessary, and set the **In megabytes** option to 2 MB. Choose to **Restrict file growth (MB)** to 10 MB.

5. Add a new row with the following data:

   File Name: **Customer_Data_Ext**

   Location: `C:\Program Files\ Microsoft SQLServer\MSSQL\data\Customer_Data_Ext.NDF`

   Initial size (MB): **2 MB**

   Filegroup: **SecondaryFileGroup**

6. Click on the row you just added to highlight it. In the File properties section, check the **Automatically grow file** check box if necessary, and set the **In megabytes** option to 2 MB. Choose to **Restrict file growth (MB)** to 10 MB.

7. Add a second file to the **SecondaryFileGroup**. Configure it to have an initial size of 3 MB. Set it up to automatically grow by 1 MB until it reaches 10 MB.

8. Select the **Transaction Log** tab. In the grid, modify the first row to contain the following data:

   File Name: **Customer_Log**

   Location: `C:\Program Files\ Microsoft SQLServer\MSSQL\data\Customer_Log.LDF`

   Initial Size (MB): **3 MB**

9. Click on the first row in the grid to highlight it. In the File properties section, check the **Automatically grow file** check box if necessary, and set the **In megabytes** option to 2 MB. Choose to **Restrict file growth (MB)** to 15 MB.

10. Add a second transaction log. Configure it to have an initial size of 3 MB. Set it up to automatically grow by 2 MB until it reaches 15 MB.

11. Click **OK** when finished.

Project 5-2

In this project you will add some tables to the Customer database you built in Project 5-1. You will create a customer table and a related address table, in which a customer can have many addresses. The two tables will be related with a primary/foreign key relationship.

To add tables to the customer database:

1. Expand the Customer database by clicking on the plus sign (+). Right-click on **Tables** and choose **New Table** from the context-sensitive menu.

2. In the first row of the **New Table screen**, add a unique ID column by entering the following information:

   Column Name: **CustomerID**

   Data Type: **Int**

   Allow Nulls: **Uncheck**

   Description: **Unique ID for Customers**

   Identity: **Yes**

   Identity Seed: **1**

   Identity Increment: **1**

3. In the second row of the New Table screen, add a **Customer Name** field by entering the following information:

   Column Name: **Name**

   Data Type: **nvarchar**

   Length: **100**

   Allow Nulls: **Uncheck**

   Description: **Customer Name**

4. In the third row of the New Table screen, add an **E-mail address** field by entering the following information:

   Column Name: **E-mail**

   Data Type: **nvarchar**

   Length: **255**

   Allow Nulls: **Check**

   Description: **E-mail Address**

5. Make the CustomerID field the primary key by selecting the row and clicking the **Set primary key** button 🔑 on the toolbar. A key should appear in the selector next to the CustomerID field.

5

6. Save the table by clicking **Save** 🖫 on the toolbar.

7. Enter **Customer** for the table name, click **OK**. Close the Customer Table window.

8. To create the address table, right-click on **Tables** and choose **New Table** from the context-sensitive menu.

9. In the first row of the New Table screen, add a unique ID column by entering the following information:

Column Name: **AddressID**

Data Type: **Int**

Allow Nulls: **Uncheck**

Description: **Unique ID for Addresses**

Identity: **Yes**

Identity Seed: **1**

Identity Increment: **1**

10. In the second row of the New Table screen, add an **Address1** field by entering the following information:

Column Name: **Address1**

Data Type: **nvarchar**

Length: **255**

Allow Nulls: **Uncheck**

Description: **Address1**

11. Add **Address2** and **Address3** fields. These should store up to 255 characters of Unicode data and they should allow nulls.

12. Add a **City** field. The city should hold up to 50 Unicode characters and should allow nulls.

13. Add a **State Code** field. The state code field should only allow a two-letter Unicode state code. It should not allow nulls.

14. Add a **Zip Code** field. It should allow up to 9 Unicode characters and should allow nulls.

15. Add a CustomerID field to relate to a customer.

Column Name: **CustomerID**

Data Type: **Int**

Allow Nulls: **Uncheck**

Description: **Relates to Customer.CustomerID**

16. Make the AddressID field the primary key.

17. Put the address table on the secondary filegroup. Click the **Table and Index Properties** button on the toolbar. On the **Tables** tab, change the **Table Filegroup** list box to **SecondaryFileGroup** and click **Close**.

18. Save the table by clicking the **Save** button on the toolbar.

19. Enter **Address** for the table name, and click **OK**.

20. Add a foreign key constraint that relates the Address Customer ID to the Customer ID. Click the **Table and Index Propertie**s button on the toolbar. Select the **Relationship** tab. Click **New**. In the **Primary key table** list box, choose **Customer**. In the first column in the grid, choose **CustomerID** from the list box. The **Foreign key table** list box should read **Address**. In the second grid column, choose **CustomerID**. Check the **Cascade Update Related Fields** and **Cascade Delete Related Records** check boxes. Click **Close**.

21. Save the table by clicking **Save** on the toolbar. The Save dialog box appears. Click **Yes**.

22. Close the Address Table window.

Project 5-3

In this project you will add some data to the tables to the Customer database. You will also add some check constraints to the Address table to further refine data integrity.

To add data to the tables:

1. To add data to the tables, you must first add some customer records. You cannot add address data first because there is a foreign key that requires an existing customer to be attached to address records. To add data to the Customer table, left-click on the **Tables** node under the Customer database in SQL Enterprise Manager. A list of all the tables in the database should appear in the right-hand pane. If the Customer table is not in the list, right-click on **Tables** and choose **Refresh** from the context-sensitive menu. Right-click on the **Customer table**, choose **Open Table**, and then choose **Return all rows**.

2. Since CustomerID is an identity field, you don't need to add data to the field. Click in the **Name** column and add a name. Then add an e-mail address and add a few rows to the table. Note that the CustomerID field will fill with a sequential integer value as you add each new row.

3. Add some address rows to the Address table. Add two separate addresses for each customer you created. You relate an address to a customer by filling in the customer's CustomerID in the Address table's CustomerID field. If you leave this field blank, or if you type in a value that is not in the Customer table, you will receive an error.

4. Notice that while you can only type in a maximum of two characters in the Address state field, you could still enter a single character. This would be an invalid state code.

To create a check constraint to force the state column to accept only two characters:

1. Close the **Address table**. Right-click on the **Address table** in SQL Enterprise Manager and choose **Design Table** from the context-sensitive menu. This opens the Design Table screen.

2. Click the **Table and Index Properties** button 📨 on the toolbar. Select the **Check Constraints** tab. Click **New**. In the **Constraint expression** text box, type the following constraint:

   state like '[A-Z][A-Z]'

   This constraint only allows two characters to be entered for the state field. Each character must be a letter from A to Z. Change the **Constraint name** to **CK_Address_StateCode**. Since you probably have test data in the table, uncheck the **Check existing data on creation** check box, or you will get an error when the constraint is applied. Click **Close**. Save the table by clicking **Save** 💾 on the toolbar.

3. Test the address table to be sure that you can only enter two-letter characters in the state column.

4. Add a constraint to the zip field on the address table that only allows nine numeric characters to be entered.

Project 5-4

In this project you will create a custom view that displays customer names and their addresses. This allows users to see name and address information without having to look at two tables.

To create a custom view displaying customer names:

1. Expand your database by clicking the plus sign (+). Left-click on the **Views** node to see all views in the database in the right-hand pane. Right-click on **Views** and choose **New View** from the context-sensitive menu. This opens the **New View** screen.

2. Add the Customer and Address table to the view by clicking on the **Add table** button 🔲 on the toolbar.

3. Since a formal relationship has been defined, a one to many join should appear between the two tables in the Diagram Pane. The join should have a key icon attached to the Customer.CustomerID field and an infinity sign attached to the Address.CustomerID field.

4. In the Customer table, check the box next to the **Name** and **E-mail** fields. Both fields should appear in the Grid Pane.

5. Add the following fields to the Grid Pane from the Address table:

   Address1

   Address2

   Address3

   City

   State

   Zip

6. To sort by the **Name** field, choose **ascending** in the Sort Type column for the Name in the Grid Pane.

7. Test your view by clicking **Run** ![run icon] on the toolbar. The Result pane should show a list of names and addresses.

8. Save the view by clicking **Save** ![save icon] on the toolbar.

9. Name the view **vw_NamesAndAddresses**.

10. Close the **New View** screen.

11. To test the view, right-click on the view in the right-hand pane of SQL Enterprise Manager and choose **Open view** and **Return all rows** from the context-sensitive menu.

12. Close the View window when done.

Project 5-5

To detach the Customer database and then reattach it:

1. Right-click on the **Customer database** in SQL Enterprise Manager and choose **All Tasks** and then **Detach Database** from the context-sensitive menu.

2. If there are any open connections to the database, click **Clear**. You will get a dialog box asking if you are sure you want to end all current transactions. Click **OK**. You will then be asked if you want to notify connected users that you are cutting them off. Click **No**.

3. Click **OK** to detach the database. Click **OK** when the confirmation message box appears. Notice that the database is removed from SQL Enterprise Manager.

4. At this point, you could backup the physical .mdf, .ndf, and .ldf files. You don't need to do that for this project.

5. To attach the customer database, right-click on the **Databases** node in SQL Enterprise Manager and choose **All Tasks** and then **Attach Database** from the context-sensitive menu.

6. In the Attach Database dialog, use the **ellipsis** button [...] and navigate to the directory that contains the .mdf, .ndf, and .ldf files.

7. Remember that you need to choose the file that has the primary filegroup on it. Try selecting the **Customer_Data_Ext_Data.NDF** file. You should get an error. You need to select the **Customer_Data.MDF** file.

8. When you select the .MDF file, the grid on the Attach Database dialog box should fill with all the files that make up the database.

9. In the **Attach as** text box, leave the name of the database **Customer**.

10. In the **Specify database owner** list, choose **sa**. This will make the system administrator the dbo.

11. Click **OK**, and then click **OK** again in the confirmation message box. Verify that the database still contains the Customer and Address table. Make sure the customer view **vw_ NamesAndAddresses** still works appropriately.

CASE PROJECTS

Case One

You are sleeping soundly one night when you are awakened by the buzzing of your pager. Unfortunately, you are going to need to take a look at your database server. You review the Windows Event log and notice that it is full of the following errors:

```
Error: 1105, Severity: 17, State: 2
Could not allocate space for object 'OrderDetails' in
database 'Orders' because the 'PRIMARY' filegroup is full.
```

What are your options for fixing the problem? Can you fix the problem remotely? How can you avoid this problem in the future?

Case Two

Read the sections of SQL Server Books Online dealing with estimating database size. The documentation provides detailed formulas for determining the physical space required to store the data in the tables of the database. Based on the table structure shown in Figure 5-31, use the methods for estimation defined in SQL Server Books Online to determine the estimated size of the database.

Assume that the Customer table has 500,000 rows, the Orders table has 2,000,000 rows, and the Order Details table has 5,000,000 rows. For simplicity assume that no indexes exist on these tables.

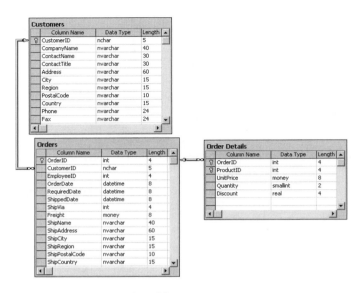

Figure 5-31   Example table structure

Case Three

You are the dba for a project that is developing an application for a client. You are developing the application off-site, but you can connect to the client's network via FTP. The development effort is completed and now the database must be moved to the server in the client's environment. As part of the project, you have been importing data into the new database. You noticed that prior to your import, the database was 100 MB. After the import, the database ballooned to 2 GB, with 1.5 GB in the transaction log alone. You know that moving a 2 GB database over FTP will take an inordinate amount of time. How would you get a copy of the database to your client? What steps would you take to optimize transmission time? How would you load the database onto the client's server?

Case Four

Before addressing the situation defined below, read the sections of SQL Server Books Online that deal with removal databases.

You have created a removable database that stores sales figures. You want to put a copy of the database on a CD-ROM and run it off your laptop. Your laptop is running Windows 2000 Professional. Describe the steps necessary to get a copy of the database onto your laptop. After you create an instance of the database on your laptop, how do you let users back into the database? How will this process affect users using the database? What precautions should you take?

5

6

OPTIMIZING AND TROUBLESHOOTING DATABASES

After reading this chapter and completing the exercises you will be able to:

♦ Use files and filegroups to optimize performance

♦ Discuss common RAID levels

♦ Design optimized indexes

♦ Manage database fragmentation

♦ Understand how SQL Server 2000 uses statistics and execution plans

♦ Troubleshoot transactions and locking

One of the primary responsibilities of a database administrator is to optimize the performance of databases. There are several ways to identify performance problems in SQL Server 2000 databases and various options for resolving them. One of the most common ways to optimize performance is to use hardware effectively. SQL Server 2000 tables and indexes can be placed on different hard drives (through the use of filegroups) to leverage the processing power of more than one disk. Multiple hard drives can be grouped together in redundant arrays to provide performance gains as well as fault tolerance.

Optimization through hardware does have its limits. A poorly designed and maintained database will always have problems in large multiuser environments. Databases that have a high volume of data modifications can become fragmented. Fragmentation results when a single data page fills up and is split into two pages, with each having unused storage space. Regular maintenance of tables and indexes can help to ensure that fragmentation is kept to a minimum.

The SQL Server 2000 database engine has a component known as the **query optimizer**, which analyzes queries prior to executing them in order to determine the most efficient method of execution. The result of this analysis is called an **execution plan**. These plans provide detailed instructions about which indexes to use and which join processes to utilize when a query executes. To create an execution plan, the query optimizer makes decisions based on data distribution statistics and the various indexes defined on the tables in the query. Designing and implementing effective indexes is a complex endeavor, but it can significantly improve the performance of some queries. Knowing the situations that would benefit from indexes, as well as those that would actually suffer from them, is critical to index design.

In addition to various optimization strategies, this chapter discusses troubleshooting tactics that are used with SQL Server 2000. Various hands-on techniques for identifying performance problems and implementing solutions with T-SQL, Enterprise Manager, and SQL Server Profiler are discussed in detail.

OPTIMIZING DATABASES

The design of a database can have serious implications on performance. A sound database schema and properly indexed tables will usually result in optimized performance. Proper placement of tables indexed across multiple physical hard drives will also reduce execution times for queries.

Placing Indexes and Tables

Each database in SQL Server 2000 can store data on multiple data files. Several data files can be grouped logically into a filegroup. The database engine allows objects like tables and indexes to be explicitly placed on filegroups. This is important because it allows hard drives to be leveraged when a query accesses the objects stored across multiple filegroups.

Consider a database that resides on one physical data file, which is stored on the C: drive on a computer. Figure 6-1 illustrates this configuration.

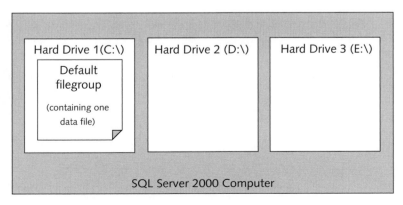

Figure 6-1 Database with one file on one filegroup

In this scenario, a query that searches for and returns a specific set of rows from a table residing on the default filegroup is limited to using only the resources of a single hard drive. However, placing indexes and tables on multiple hard drives (using filegroups and various hardware configurations) will improve performance and is recommended when the hardware is available. The flexible architecture of SQL Server 2000 allows databases to be designed in such a way as to take advantage of all of the hard drives on a computer.

Filegroups and Tables

When a table is created in a database, it is assigned to a particular filegroup. If the filegroup has multiple data files, each residing on multiple hard drives, the table data will be spread across the files. Each of the hard drives can use its own disk controller to scan for data on the hard drive. In the situation illustrated in Figure 6-2, queries will experience increased performance due to the increased capacity offered by multiple hard drives.

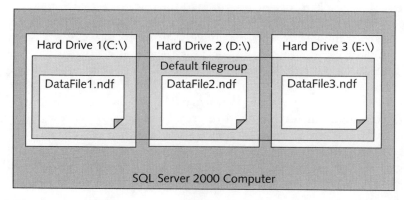

Figure 6-2   Database with multiple data files residing on multiple, separate hard drives

A computer with multiple processors can experience performance gains if tables and filegroups are used intelligently. If a table resides on a filegroup that contains multiple files, and the computer has multiple processors, **parallel scans** of data can be performed. Each processor can start an independent operation on a different data file (located on a different hard drive), thus improving data access performance.

When a query accesses two related tables (through a SQL join operation), performance is better if the tables reside in separate filegroups. Each table can be scanned simultaneously, resulting in better response times. This type of optimization is common when a slow-running query cannot be optimized with better T-SQL code.

Optimization through Index Placement

By default, indexes are stored on the same filegroup as the table on which they are defined, but SQL Server 2000 allows nonclustered indexes to reside in different filegroups from their related table.

A clustered index is stored in the actual data pages of a table and must reside on the same filegroup as the table on which it is defined.

When the database engine uses an index to assist in executing a query, performance gains can be achieved by having the index and table reside on separate filegroups (consisting of data files on separate physical hard drives). Data and index information can be accessed at the same time because the resources of multiple hard drives are available for use.

PERFORMANCE ENHANCEMENTS THROUGH RAID

Redundant array of independent disks (RAID) configurations offer the same type of performance advantage as multiple filegroups across separate physical hard drives. In a RAID system, multiple hard drives are grouped together to provide increased performance and hardware redundancy. RAID is defined as any situation where multiple physical hard drives are combined to create a single logical disk drive. With Windows NT and Windows 2000, the resulting logical drive is treated as a normal hard drive even though, at the hardware level, there are multiple hard drives. Data automatically spreads across the physical hard drives, and when data is retrieved, all of the disks are used to locate data, which results in improved performance. In addition to improved performance, RAID configurations can be used to create a larger logical disk. Using RAID, three 10 GB hard drives can be combined into a single 30 GB drive. RAID devices can be configured in a number of ways, each with its own benefits and limitations. There are several common RAID categories that are classified with a level number (e.g., RAID 0, RAID 1, RAID 2, RAID 3, etc.). The most common of these are described in more detail in the following sections.

RAID 0

RAID 0 is the simplest RAID level. It provides improved performance by using **disk striping** to efficiently distribute and manage the location of data across several hard drives. Disk striping is the process by which data is broken up and stored across grouped hard drives. Data is written to each hard drive in the group in blocks called **stripes**. Each stripe is placed on a separate hard drive as needed in a round-robin fashion. Figure 6-3 illustrates RAID level 0.

RAID 0, while providing increased performance, does not implement disk redundancy. If a single hard drive fails in a RAID 0 configuration, then the entire logical drive will become inaccessible. The sensitivity of critical data in SQL Server 2000 databases typically requires some level of disk redundancy to prevent corruption or data loss. For this reason, RAID 0 is not recommended for use with mission critical databases.

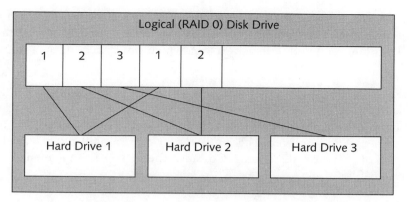

Figure 6-3 RAID 0

RAID 1

RAID 1 provides basic hardware fault tolerance. To accomplish this, two hard drives are used to store separate identical copies of a single set of data. RAID 1 is also referred to as "mirroring" for that reason. Notice in Figure 6-4 that all of the data from a single logical drive is duplicated across two physical hard drives.

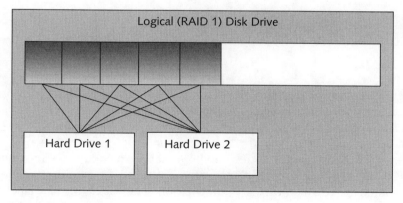

Figure 6-4 RAID 1

Since two sets of data are maintained at all times, the size of the logical drive created from two physical drives is equal to the size of a single physical drive. For example, when two 10 GB hard drives are set up in a RAID 1 configuration, the resulting logical drive would only be 10 GB in size. So for the price of two hard drives, only the storage capacity of a single drive can be utilized. Mirroring can also cause performance degradation because every write operation to a mirrored disk must be performed twice to record the change to both underlying physical drives. Read operations are only performed against a single drive, and both physical drives can be used simultaneously to seek.

RAID 1 is a good solution when one hard drive can hold all of the data. If this is the case, then only two hard drives must be purchased to provide a sound, fault-tolerant solution. RAID 1 is often used with transaction logs, which can usually fit on a single drive.

RAID 5

RAID 5 provides good read performance and fault tolerance. In a RAID 5 disk configuration, **parity** information is stored to recreate lost data. Parity information indicates whether a number is odd or even. This information can be used to recreate lost data through the use of complex algorithms. Consider the RAID 5 implementation illustrated in Figure 6-5.

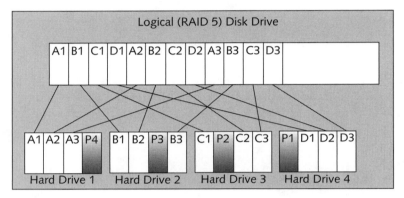

Figure 6-5   RAID 5

In this configuration four hard drives are configured in a RAID 5 disk array. Notice how chunks of data are written out sequentially to the various disks (much in the same way as RAID 0). Each time a block of data is written, the parity information is also written to one of the drives. In Figure 6-5, the first block of parity information (P1) is stored on Hard Drive 4. This parity information can be used to recreate the data for one of the hard drives if it fails. For example, if Hard Drive 2 were to fail, the data residing on it can be regenerated based on the parity information. The block of data labeled B1 is regenerated in its entirety by using the parity information and data blocks A1 and C1. The algorithm used to recreate the lost data compares bit-level data on the remaining data blocks and parity block.

Parity at Work

Consider the RAID 5 configuration in Figure 6-5. Three of the hard drives store data blocks, and one equally sized block on the fourth hard drive is used to store parity information. To simplify things, assume that each block is actually a single bit that can have a value of 1 or 0. Block A1 contains a 1, block B2 contains a 0, and block C1 contains a 0. Parity can be either even or odd. Assuming an odd parity, all of the bits in the various data blocks and the parity block must add up to an odd number. Figure 6-6 illustrates the concept of parity.

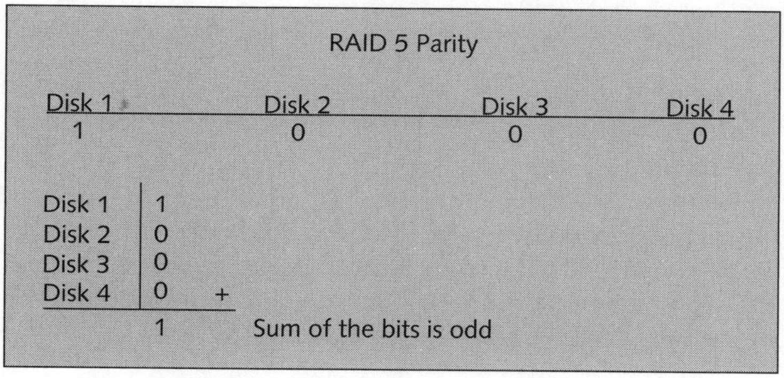

RAID 5 Parity

Disk 1	Disk 2	Disk 3	Disk 4
1	0	0	0

Disk 1	1	
Disk 2	0	
Disk 3	0	
Disk 4	0	+
	1	Sum of the bits is odd

Figure 6-6   Parity in RAID 5

Knowing that an odd sum must be obtained when all of the bits are added up, any bit on the first three disks could be lost and still regenerated correctly by a simple mathematical comparison. For example, if the 0 value on disk 3 is lost, the data values in the remaining drives and the parity information (1,0,0) add up to 1. Since an odd parity is assumed, the data that is lost is easily determined to be a 0 because a 1 would result in an even sum.

RAID 5 is an efficient setup because only the size of one drive in the set is used to provide fault tolerance. In a RAID 5 array with five 10 GB hard drives, a 40 GB logical drive could be created (with 10 GB for parity information). RAID 5 suffers some performance loss on write operations, due to the need to compute parity values and write both the data and parity information. However, the performance of read operations is considerably better than with RAID 1 because multiple hard drives can be used to access data simultaneously. RAID 5 is a good candidate for read-only databases because of the improved read performance and weaker write performance.

RAID 10

RAID 10 combines mirroring from RAID 1 with striping from RAID 0. In a RAID 10 configuration, a striped set of disks is mirrored to another striped set of disks. Basically, each stripe member drive is mirrored for fault tolerance. Figure 6-7 illustrates this concept.

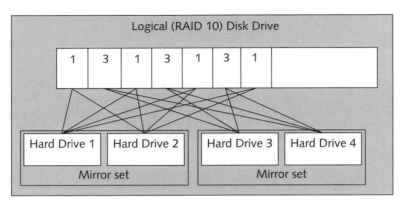

Figure 6-7   RAID 10

RAID 10 offers fault tolerance and good performance. Although there is overhead associated with writing data twice (one for the live drive and one for the mirror), RAID 10 is faster at performing read operations than RAID 5. The only drawback is the additional hardware costs required. RAID 10 requires twice as many drives as a RAID 0 configuration. RAID 10 is recommended for systems where more than 10% of the operations are writes. If the system is mainly used for reading data, then RAID 5 is the preferred option.

Using RAID Arrays and Clustering

We have talked about the redundancy of hard drive resources using RAID disk arrays, but that does not account for situations where servers fail. Failover clustering allows SQL Server 2000 to switch the processing for an instance from a failed computer to a fully operational one. SQL Server 2000 can take advantage of the Microsoft Clustering service (MSCS) available in Windows 2000 and NT.

With MSCS, clustering allows multiple computers to use a shared set of resources like a hard drive. Typically two computers are used, but up to four separate computers can be set up in a cluster (using Windows 2000 Data Center Server). Clustering also supports up to 16 instances of SQL Server 2000 in a single clustered system. Each computer in the cluster is called a **node**, and shared resources (like hard drives) are called **cluster groups**. Each node in the cluster has SQL Server 2000 installed on it, but the data files used by database instances all reside on the shared hard drive. When a node fails, SQL Server 2000 transfers ownership of the cluster group containing the data files to another node.

When SQL Server 2000 is configured for failover clustering, all of the nodes in the cluster can be accessed through the same network identifier (either a computer name or IP address). This allows users to continue their activities without ever knowing that a server has failed. When the cluster group used by the nodes in a clustered configuration consists of a RAID array, SQL Server 2000 has fault tolerance at both the storage and processing level.

INDEXING RECOMMENDATIONS

When properly defined, indexes provide optimized performance in SQL Server 2000. When an index is not used to locate data, the database engine executes a **table scan**. In a table scan, the rows in the table are traversed sequentially until the appropriate row or set of rows is found. An index uses a hierarchical navigation tree to locate data with a minimal number of I/O operations. Consider a table with 100,000 rows of data. In order to find a single row with a particular key value using a table scan operation, up to 100,000 read operations must execute. If an index is used, the maximum amount of read operations would drop by up to 90%.

Understanding when Indexes Are Recommended

Determining the best indexes to create on a table is a very complex process and requires a lot of trial and error testing. In general, queries that return a small set of data will benefit from properly designed indexes. When deciding how to go about creating the indexes that provide optimum performance, consider the types of queries that are likely to be performed. The following types of queries will benefit from indexes:

- Queries that perform an "exact match" search on some key value in a table column and return a small number of records. For example, a query that retrieves a customer record from the Customer table by looking for a specific CustomerID value:

```
SELECT *
FROM dbo.Customer
WHERE CustomerID = 12345
```

- Queries that use a range of values to return rows. For example: a query that searches in the Orders table for order records that have a CreateDate value between October 1, 2001 and November 15, 2001.

```
SELECT *
FROM dbo.Orders
WHERE CreateDate BETWEEN '10/1/2001' AND '11/15/2001'
```

- Queries that use a join operation to retrieve related information in more than one table. For example, a query that generates a data set containing order-specific information from the Orders table and employee-specific data from the Employees table:

```
Select Orders.OrderID, Orders.OrderDate,
Employees.FirstName, Employees.LastName
FROM Orders
INNER JOIN Employees ON
Orders.EmployeeID = Employees.EmployeeID
```

- Queries that return rows in a particular sort order. Remember that a clustered index will physically sort the rows in the table based on the index key values. Consequently, a costly sort operation can be avoided because data is returned in the requested order. For example, a query that returns rows from the Employees table sorted by last name would benefit from a clustered index on the LastName field of the table.

Recommendations for Designing Indexes

One of the most common misconceptions with indexes is that "more is better." However, each index must be maintained whenever there is an insert, update, or delete operation performed on the data in the table. Having too many indexes on a single table can seriously degrade the performance of write operations to the table. For this reason, indexes should be created with caution to ensure that the performance increases achieved through them are not outweighed by the decreased performance of write operations incurred by maintaining them.

Sometimes even one index can be too many. On tables with a few hundred rows or less, using an index to locate data can take longer than performing a table scan (depending on how many levels the index has). Take into account the additional overhead of maintaining the index, and you will find that the index is actually degrading the performance of every operation on the table.

Covering Indexes

When an index includes all of the columns that a query is requesting, the query is considered a **covered query**. Consider a situation where a query only requests the FirstName and LastName columns of a table. A single composite index could contain the data from both columns in its leaf nodes. When the query executes, it does not have to go to the table to retrieve data because all of the values of the columns it needs (as defined in the SELECT clause of the T-SQL statement) are actually stored in the index itself. In this situation, the data is read directly from the index pages and the table is bypassed.

Narrow vs. Wide Indexes

Indexes that key off of very few table columns are called **narrow indexes**. Narrow indexes have the advantage of requiring less overhead for their maintainance (when data is modified in the underlying table) and requiring less disk space for storage. **Wide indexes** are indexes that contain many columns from a table. They offer the advantage of covering more columns and therefore "covering" more queries, but they require more overhead to maintain them.

PAGE SPLITS AND FRAGMENTATION

Indexes are stored as balanced tree structures organized by the key values on which they are based. The leaf nodes of an index store pointers to data rows (in nonclustered indexes) or actual data rows (in clustered indexes). An individual index page can only contain 8 K of information and, as rows are added to an underlying table, leaf nodes in an index begin to fill up. When a page is full and a new row is inserted, SQL Server 2000 makes room for the new row by creating a new page and moving half of the data from the original page to the new page. This operation is referred to as a **page split**. Page splitting hinders performance because of the overhead required to reorganize the full pages. The inefficient use of physical storage that results from page splitting is known as **fragmentation**.

6

Avoiding Fragmentation

As data is inserted, updated, and deleted in various tables (and consequently indexes), the physical location of data becomes spread out on a hard drive due to page splits. Accessing a table that is fragmented provides less than optimal performance because the data itself is not physically stored in the most efficient way. The easiest way to resolve a table fragmentation problem is to rebuild the clustered index on the table (if one exists). Since a clustered index stores the sorted data pages of the table in its leaf nodes, recreating one will result in all of the data in a table being rearranged on the hard drive in an optimal fashion.

 The nonclustered indexes on a table are rebuilt automatically if the clustered index is rebuilt.

There are several ways to rebuild indexes in SQL Server 2000.

- *Use T-SQL DROP and CREATE commands:* The code below drops an index called CompanyName and then creates it again.

```
DROP INDEX [dbo].[Customers].[CompanyName]
GO
CREATE INDEX [CompanyName] ON [dbo].[Customers]
([CompanyName]) ON [PRIMARY]
```

- *Use the DROP_EXISTING option with a CREATE statement:* The DROP_EXISTING option reorganizes the existing index pages. This type of operation eliminates the overhead of deleting an index and then recreating it.

```
CREATE INDEX [CompanyName] ON [dbo].[Customers]
([CompanyName]) WITH DROP_EXISTING ON [PRIMARY]
```

- *Use the DBCC DBREINDEX statement:* This statement rebuilds all of the indexes in a table or a single index in a table. It performs all of the individual recreate operations in a single statement. The statement below rebuilds all of the indexes on the Customers table.

```
DBCC DBREINDEX ('dbo.Customers')
```

Fill Factors with Indexes

The **fill factor** of an index is used to determine how much free space to include on each page of an index. When an index is created or rebuilt, a fill factor specifies the percentage of free space that each leaf node will initially contain (to accommodate new entries without requiring a page split). When specifying a value for the fill factor of an index, 100 means that no free space will be reserved to stored additional rows to the table. A fill factor of 100 is only recommended for read-only tables where no additional rows will be added. A low fill factor (value of 10–20) should only be used when a table has a small portion of the rows that it will eventually have. In this case, index pages with a lot of free space are created. Consequently, page splits can be avoided by having a large amount of available space within the existing pages.

Fill factor is only implemented when an index is created or rebuilt. It is not maintained once the index is rebuilt. When a fill factor of 20 is used to create a new index, the pages of the index will have a lot of free space (80%). However, as rows are added to the underlying table, the index pages will start to fill up and eventually split. The only way to reset the fill factor is to rebuild the index.

Determining an appropriate fill factor can be very complex, as a result, using the default fill factor is highly recommended.

EXECUTION PLANS AND STATISTICS

The SQL Server 2000 **query optimizer** determines the most efficient way to execute a database query. It analyzes database information to find the least expensive way to return the data requested by a query. The optimizer generates **execution plans** for queries that provide instructions for executing a query in the most efficient way.

There are numerous ways to execute a particular query. Consider a table with multiple indexes. Some indexes could help to speed up a particular search operation, while others may not be effective at all. A query is first broken up into smaller logical operations that are simpler to work with. The query optimizer then determines the various steps required to execute a query and the best order in which to perform them.

Statistics

SQL Server 2000 allows the storage of statistical information about the distribution of values in a column. When indexes are created, this information is captured and then used by the query optimizer to determine the cost of using a particular index to perform an operation. The optimizer takes a "least cost" approach when choosing an index and selects the index that statistics indicate to be the most helpful.

Statistics are created when an index is in a certain state (similar to the way fill factor works). Consequently, as data is modified, statistics can become out-of-date and even wrong. This can cause the optimizer to choose an index that may not be the most efficient. To handle this problem, SQL Server 2000 automatically updates statistics by default. The statistical updates are performed regularly to account for data modification on particular columns in a table. Statistics can also be manually updated using the UPDATE STATISTICS T-SQL statement. Executing this statement may be desirable if a table has just been modified in a significant way, for example, if 5000 rows of data were imported in a bulk operation. UPDATE STATISTICS can be used to update the statistics for all of the indexes defined on a table, or for each index individually. The T-SQL code below updates the statistics for the all of the indexes in the Orders table:

```
UPDATE STATISTICS Orders
```

Keeping distribution statistics current will allow the query optimizer to make valid decisions when building an execution plan.

Viewing Execution Plans

There are two ways to view the execution plan for a particular query. The Query Analyzer tool provides an intuitive GUI interface for viewing and analyzing execution plans. Alternatively, the SET SHOWPLAN_ALL T-SQL statement can be used to display a text-based representation of the execution plan of a query.

Consider the following query:

```
Select Orders.OrderID, Employees.FirstName,
Employees.LastName
FROM Orders
INNER JOIN Employees ON
Orders.EmployeeID = Employees.EmployeeID
```

This query performs a simple inner join to return information from two tables in a single request. In this case, the Orders and Employees tables are joined to return the first and last name of employees with the OrderID from the Orders table.

Analyzing Execution Plans with Query Analyzer

To show the query plan for this T-SQL statement in Query Analyzer, simply click the Display Estimated Execution Plan button or use the Control-L shortcut key. Figure 6-8 shows this button on the Query Analyzer toolbar.

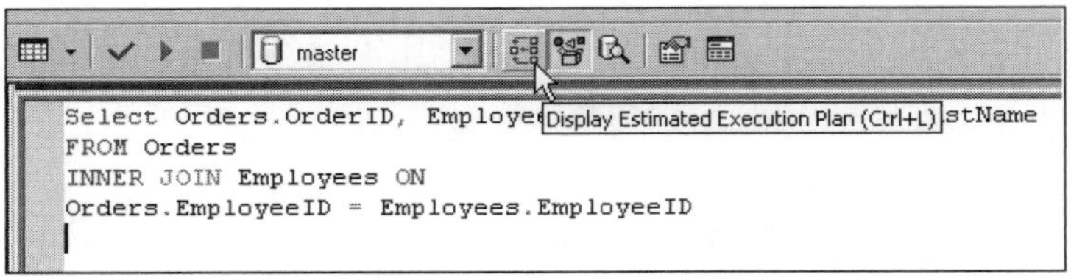

```
Select Orders.OrderID, Employe[Display Estimated Execution Plan (Ctrl+L)]stName
FROM Orders
INNER JOIN Employees ON
Orders.EmployeeID = Employees.EmployeeID
```

Figure 6-8   Display Estimated Execution Plan button

When this button is clicked, the results window of Query Analyzer is filled with a graphical representation of the execution plan for the query. In the case of the query above, the execution plan would look like Figure 6-9.

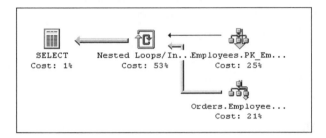

Figure 6-9   GUI display of an execution plan in Query Analyzer

Graphical query plans are read from the upper-right corner to the leftmost icon. In the case of Figure 6-9, two index scans are used to speed up the operation. The first is a full clustered index scan on the Employees table. This operation feeds rows into the Nested Loop operation one at a time. The Nested Loop operation takes the provided EmployeeID value from the clustered index and locates the associated rows in the Orders table. Below the nested loop, notice that a nonclustered index seek operation on EmployeeID in the Orders table is used to quickly locate the orders with a particular EmployeeID value. This process continues until all of the correct rows are returned.

Each operation in the plan is annotated with a cost value specifying how much of the total processing time for the query was needed by a particular operation. Additional information is available about each individual piece of the query by simply rolling the mouse over one of the icons in the execution plan. Figure 6-10 shows the additional information pertaining to each part of the query.

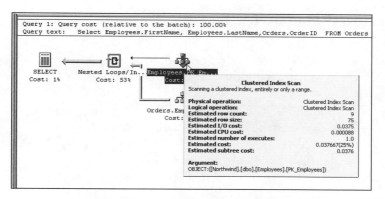

Figure 6-10   Additional information about an individual operation in an execution plan

The additional information shown on this window consists of the following:

- *Physical and Logical operation:* The individual operations that are used to process an operation. Common operations include table joins, index scans, sorts, etc.

 If the physical operation value is shown in red, it means that an error was detected by the query optimizer and the T-SQL should be corrected.

- *Estimated row count:* The estimated number of rows returned by an operation

- *Estimated row size:* The estimated size of the results in bytes

- *Estimated I/O cost:* The estimated I/O resources required to complete the operation

- *Estimated CPU cost:* The estimated CPU resources required to complete the operation

- *Estimated number of executes:* The estimated number of the times that the operation will have to be executed to process the operation

- *Estimated cost:* The estimated cost of the operation given as a percentage of the total estimated cost of executing the query. This value allows individual operations to be quickly identified as bottlenecks.

- *Estimated subtree cost:* The estimated cost of executing the current operation and any other preceding operation(s)

- *Argument:* Any parameters that were supplied with the original T-SQL query

Viewing Execution Plans with T-SQL

The SET SHOWPLAN_ALL ON T-SQL statement outputs similar information, but in a text format. Figure 6-11 shows the T-SQL code required to use SET SHOW-PLAN_ALL ON as well as the execution plan output by the call.

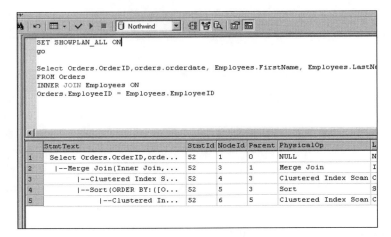

Figure 6-11   Viewing an execution plan with the SET SHOWPLAN_ALL ON statement

Technically, all of the information from the SET SHOWPLAN_ALL ON output is used to generate the graphical execution plan of a query, but it can be difficult to read. The graphical representation offered by the Query Analyzer is a lot easier to work with when diagnosing poorly performing queries.

Viewing execution plans can be very helpful when determining which operation is taking the bulk of the processing time for a query. Execution plans are also helpful for verifying that the most appropriate indexes are being used to perform a particular set of operations. The output shows which indexes are used (or not used) by the query, making it easy to figure out if the optimizer is making the correct choices. For example, an index may not be used by the query because its statistics are not updated to reflect its current state. In the case where a large percentage of values have changed in a table and statistics have not been updated, the query optimizer may not select the index even though it could considerably improve the performance of the query in question.

Using Index Hints to Control Query Plan Creation

The query optimizer will perform calculations to predict the fastest way to execute a query, but the execution plan it generates may not always be the best possibility. SQL Server 2000 lets users optimize queries by using **hints**. Hints allow query writers to control the individual parts of an execution plan. In T-SQL statements, hints can force the execution plan to use certain indexes or join operations.

There are three common types of hints:

- *Join hints:* Specify a type of join operation to be used by the query optimizer

- *Query hints:* Specify a type of query operation to be used by the query optimizer. These hints are used to control operations like sorts and GROUP BY rollup operations.

- *Table hints:* Specify the way in which tables are accessed. A table hint is used to force a particular index to be used by the query optimizer.

Using hints is not an exact science, and second guessing the query optimizer in general is not a good idea. However, when problem queries arise, embedding hints into a T-SQL statement can result in optimized performance. For example, it could be determined that a particular query is not using an index that you suspect will provide the best execution efficiency. The following query uses a table hint to force the SupplierID index to be used to execute the query.

```
SELECT OrderID, SupplierID, OrderDate
FROM Orders WITH (INDEX(SupplierID))
WHERE SupplierID = 12
```

In this query, the WITH option is used to specify a table hint in the FROM clause of the T-SQL statement. The hint specifies which index is to be used by the query optimizer when an execution plan is generated.

Execution Plan Caching

SQL Server 2000 allocates memory to store execution plans for quick access. The pool of memory used to store execution plans is known as the **procedure cache**. The database engine will check the cache every time a query is sent to determine if an execution plan already exists for the query. SQL Server 2000 uses an efficient algorithm to locate existing execution plans quickly. If a plan is found in the cache, then it is used, eliminating the additional overhead of creating an execution plan. The performance offered by using cached execution plans outweighs the extra effort required to locate a cached plan, resulting in an overall improvement in query processing speed.

When certain types of changes are made to a database, execution plans can become inefficient. SQL Server 2000 detects this condition automatically, and cached execution plans are marked as invalid. A cached plan marked as invalid is recompiled and cached the next time it is requested. The following common actions can cause an execution plan to be recompiled:

- Changing the structure of a table or view. For example, when new columns are added to a table.

- Regenerating statistics, either automatically or through a call to the UPDATE STATISTICS T-SQL statement

- Dropping an index used by an execution from the database

- Changing a significant amount of data in a table

When a new index that may improve the performance of stored procedures or triggers is added to a table, SQL Server 2000 does not automatically detect this and recompile the stored procedures or triggers accordingly. In this situation, the objects may benefit from being manually recompiled. The system-stored procedure **sp_recompile** provides this functionality. This procedure can be called to recompile individual stored procedures and triggers, as well as to recompile all of the stored procedures and triggers for a given table. The following T-SQL statement recompiles all of the triggers and stored procedures defined for the Customers table:

```
EXEC sp_recompile dbo.Customers
```

DIAGNOSING DATABASE PROBLEMS

In every system that requires concurrent access to a single data source, there are issues of contention between user requests. As discussed in Chapter 4, SQL Server 2000 uses locks to ensure that concurrent access to data does not result in corruption. One of the most common problems in a multiuser environment like SQL Server 2000 is blocking. Blocking occurs when multiple users require access to the same pieces of information at the same time. If a single user needs exclusive access to a specific set of columns and rows (for example, to perform an update operation), any other users who need access to the same data will be blocked until the original operation has completed. In cases where several users have the same data access requirements, a queue is formed while the blocking operation executes. As locks are freed up by a completed query, the next request is processed, but the queue of waiting requests can grow quite large, resulting in long wait times for users of the system.

To minimize the effects of blocking, queries against the database should execute as quickly as possible. A long-running, commonly used query will almost always cause a blocking issue. Transactions should be managed carefully and designed to execute as a single statement, not relying on user input once a transaction has begun. Leaving a transaction open will always lock resources. Locking problems can be avoided by well-designed databases and efficient T-SQL statements, but in every large-scale system, concurrency issues will arise. There are several options for identifying blocking situations and the queries causing them.

SQL Profiler

SQL Profiler is a powerful monitoring tool that records the operations that occur in an instance of SQL Server 2000. Every action that is performed against a database (including executed queries, stored procedures, etc.) is captured and available in a readable format to determine where problems may exist. This tool allows databases to be easily monitored to determine which requests are hindering performance. The sequence of events against a SQL Server 2000 instance can be captured and then replayed to recreate a particular condition.

SQL Profiler is helpful for performing the following tasks:

- Identifying poorly performing queries
- Monitoring stored procedure activity
- Monitoring locks and determining what is causing a deadlock
- Monitor individual user activity

A specific session of monitoring performed with SQL Profiler is known as a **trace**. Each trace can be configured to capture different types of events and capture the events in a database table or trace file (file extension .trc).

To open SQL Profiler, click Start, highlight Programs, highlight Microsoft SQL Server, and then click on Profiler. It can also be activated from the Tools menu in Enterprise Manager.

Once SQL Profiler is open and connected to an instance of SQL Server 2000, a **trace template** must be defined or selected. A trace template consists of the configurations for a specific trace operation, including which types of activities to record and where to output the captured queries (to a table or to a file).

 SQL Profiler comes with several helpful, predefined trace templates that are useful for performing different types of monitoring. For more information refer to SQL Server Books Online.

Whenever a new monitoring session begins with SQL Profiler, a trace template must be chosen or created. Event classes are chosen to specify which types of SQL Server 2000 events the trace will capture. Figure 6-12 shows the Events tab of the Trace Template Properties dialog box.

An event is any action that occurs in SQL Server 2000. Things like user connections and T–SQL statements are considered events. An event class is a specific piece of event information, like the beginning of a transaction, or the completion of a T–SQL statement. This very granular access to defining what a trace will capture makes SQL Profiler a powerful tool for monitoring SQL Server 2000 databases.

Once you have selected the desired types of events, you should choose the specific pieces of information that a trace will capture. This information can include things like the name of the database an operation was performed against and the user name of the person submitting the request. Figure 6-13 shows the Data Columns tab of the Trace Template Properties dialog.

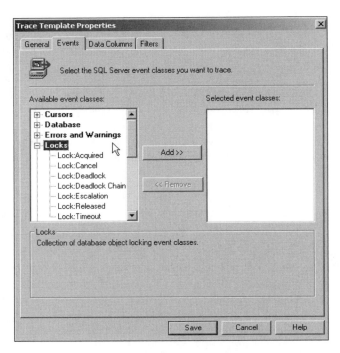

Figure 6-12   Selecting event classes for a trace in SQL Server Profiler

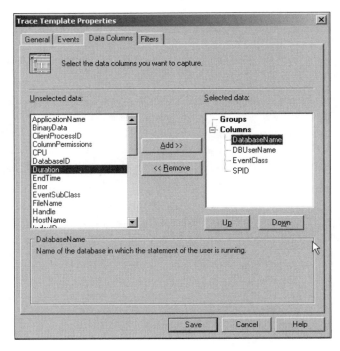

Figure 6-13   Specifying data columns for a trace in SQL Profiler

You can further restrict the events captured by a trace through the use of filters. A filter allows threshold criteria to be specified for a particular event class. The data captured by a trace can become large and unwieldy. A filter helps to further limit the volume of data collected by a trace. You might use a filter to limit recording to only the actions of particular users or groups of users or only long-running queries.

Monitoring Process Activity with Enterprise Manager

SQL Server Enterprise Manager provides a robust management facility for monitoring database activity. By using Enterprise Manager, you can effectively monitor the following types of activity:

- The current users connected to a SQL Server 2000 instance
- The process number and commands that users are running against a database. This includes the status of queries as well as the locks they hold.
- Various objects that are locked and the types of locks held against them

Current activity information is accessed in Enterprise Manager by navigating to the Management folder for a particular instance and expanding the Current Activity item in the tree as shown in Figure 6-14.

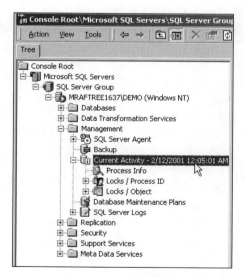

Figure 6-14 Accessing the monitoring capability of SQL Enterprise Manager

The Process Info item shows the current user connections and activity. Each user has a unique number associated with each connection it has to a database. This number is known as a **System Process Identification Number (spid)**. The current state of processes can be viewed (including the database that each process is acting on) from the

Process Info screen. This view of activity also shows if a process is blocked and which other process is blocking it. Locks can also be viewed at the individual process level (per spid) or at the object level by using the Locks / Process ID and the Locks / Object items. Figure 6-15 shows the Process Info information in Enterprise Manager.

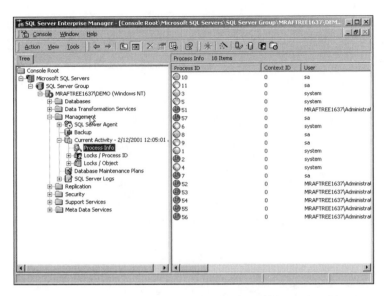

Figure 6-15   Viewing current activity from Enterprise Manager

 SQL Server 2000 manages each connection to a database as a separate process. A single user can hold multiple connections to a database and can therefore own several processes (uniquely defined by a spid) simultaneously. Notice that there are several processes owned by the system administrator user ("sa").

Monitoring Process Activity with System-Stored Procedures

SQL Server 2000 has two system-stored procedures that are helpful in monitoring process activity: **sp_who** and **sp_lock**. The sp_who system-stored procedure returns a snapshot of current user and process activity. It is very similar to the Process Info view in Enterprise Manager, but it returns the information in text format. Figure 6-16 illustrates the results of calling the sp_who system-stored procedure in Query Analyzer.

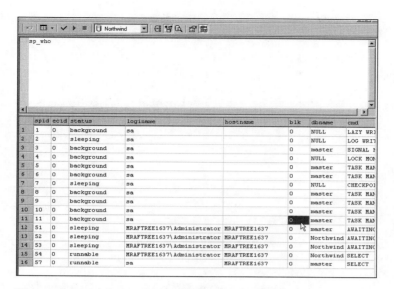

Figure 6-16   Viewing current activity from Query Analyzer

The sp_lock system-stored procedure shows current lock information much in the same way as Enterprise Manager.

Terminating Blocking Processes

When a process blocks other processes, the offending (blocking) process may need to be manually terminated to allow the blocked processes to continue executing. Typically, this situation can happen if a transaction is not committed or if a query is poorly written and goes into an infinite loop. Blocking processes can be terminated from both Enterprise Manager and through T-SQL statements in Query Analyzer. The KILL T-SQL statement is used to terminate a process. It is called with the spid number of a particular process that needs to be manually terminated. For example:

```
KILL 52
```

This statement will actually terminate the process for spid 52. The user connection is dropped, and any query that is running within the process is stopped and rolled back. Killing processes is usually a quick and dirty solution to a larger problem. When blocking situations are encountered frequently, it is usually the result of a poorly designed application.

Chapter Summary

❑ SQL Server 2000 provides various methods for optimizing and troubleshooting database activity. Multiple hard drives can be leveraged to improve performance through proper placement of tables and indexes in filegroups. Alternatively, RAID disk solutions provide optimized hard drive performance for computers running SQL Server 2000. As data is added to tables and indexes, the physical space used to house the information can become fragmented. This can degrade performance because data is stored in the most efficient way on the hard drives.

❑ Understanding execution plans and how the database engine creates them is important when troubleshooting poorly performing queries. The query optimizer chooses the most efficient indexes and the fastest join processes based on the indexes available and the distribution statistics of the data within the indexes.

❑ Poorly performing queries should be identified and optimized to prevent bottlenecks, like blocking in a concurrent environment. SQL Query Analyzer provides a graphical display of query execution plans to easily diagnose problems in slow queries. SQL Profiler, Enterprise Manager, and T-SQL statements provide robust monitoring capabilities to help identify which users or commands are causing overall database performance to degrade.

Key Terms

cluster group — A shared resource in a system configured for failover clustering. Typically a cluster group contains hard drives that are used by the cluster for storage.

covered query — A query whose requested table columns (in its SELECT list) are all stored in a single index. Covered queries can bypass reading data from tables because all of the information it needs resides in the leaf nodes of an index.

disk striping — Also referred to as RAID 0, disk striping involves combining two or more hard drives into a single logical drive and writing chunks of data (stripes) across all of the disks in a round-robin fashion.

execution plan — The step-by-step instructions for executing a query in the most efficient way. Execution plans are generated by the query optimizer.

fill factor — An attribute of an index that defines the amount of free space left on each page of the index when it is created or rebuilt.

fragmentation — The inefficient use of physical storage that results from page splitting.

hints — T-SQL directives used to manually control how an execution plan is generated by the query optimizer.

narrow index — An index that has very few (but at least one) key columns.

node — A single computer running in a cluster configuration.

page split — The process of handling a new insertion to a full index or data page. SQL Server 2000 creates a new page and then moves half of the data from the original page to the newly created one.

parallel scans — The process by which multiple CPUs are used to read data residing in multiple filegroups simultaneously.

parity — An integer's property of being odd or even. Parity checking is used to detect errors in binary-coded data. Parity information is used to rebuild lost data in a RAID 5 configuration.

procedure cache — The pool of memory allocated by SQL Server 2000 to store and reuse compiled execution plans.

query optimizer — The database engine component that generates efficient execution plans for SQL statements.

Redundant Array of Independent Disks (RAID) — A hard drive configuration where multiple physical disk drives are grouped to create a single logical drive. RAID allows for improved performance and fault tolerance through techniques like striping and mirroring.

sp_lock — The system-stored procedure that displays current lock information, including which users hold locks and on which database objects the locks are held.

sp_recompile — The system-stored procedure that is used to force stored procedures and triggers to regenerate a more current execution plan.

sp_who — The system-stored procedure that returns information about current user and process activity.

stripe — An individual block of data used with disk striping.

System Process Identification Number (spid) — A unique number that is used to identify individual processes connected to SQL Server 2000.

table scan — An operation that searches for data in a table by starting with the first row and accessing each row after that until the data is found.

trace — A specific session of monitoring performed with SQL Profiler.

trace template — A set of configurations for a trace. A trace template specifies which types of events to monitor as well as what information is captured with the events.

wide index — An index that has many key columns. For example, a large composite index that is based on seven columns in the table.

6

REVIEW QUESTIONS

1. What data retrieval operation can be avoided through the use of an index?

   a. parallel scan

   b. covered query

   c. table scan

   d. SELECT statement

2. When a covering index is used by a query, what condition results in improved performance?

   a. Data is physically stored in sorted order by the index.

   b. All of the data in the SELECT list is available in the leaf nodes of the index.

   c. The resources of multiple hard drives are leveraged.

   d. Database fragmentation is avoided through the use of the index.

3. Which RAID level is known as *disk striping with parity*?

   a. RAID 0

   b. RAID 1

   c. RAID 5

   d. RAID 10

4. If six 10 GB hard drives are configured in a RAID 5 disk array, how large is the resulting logical drive?

   a. 10 GB

   b. 30 GB

   c. 50 GB

   d. 60 GB

5. Which RAID configuration is recommended for databases that are used primarily for reading data (as opposed to writing data)?

   a. RAID 0

   b. RAID 1

   c. RAID 5

   d. RAID 10

6. True or False: Queries against a table with fewer than 100 rows will benefit from an index.

7. Creating an index with a fill factor of 10 will result in how much space (percentage) being left available on index pages?

   a. 0%

   b. 10%

   c. 50%

   d. 90%

8. Which T-SQL statement will rebuild the indexes defined for a table called Orders?

   a. sp_reindex 'dbo.Orders'

   b. DBCC CHECKTABLE 'dbo.Orders'

c. RECREATE INDEXES ON 'dbo.Orders'

d. DBCC DBREINDEX ('dbo.Orders')

9. Which system-stored procedure shows the current user and process activity for a given instance of SQL Server 2000?

a. sp_lock

b. sp_who

c. sp_recompile

d. sp_help

10. Which of the following tasks is SQL Profiler used for?

a. modifying the database schema

b. adding data to a database

c. monitoring database activity

d. viewing execution plans and optimizing T-SQL queries

11. Which of the following statements best describes distribution statistics in SQL Server 2000?

a. They prevent data from being spread across multiple hard drives.

b. They are used by the query optimizer to choose the indexes that will result in the fastest response time for a query.

c. They store information about the various users connected to different databases on an instance of SQL Server 2000.

d. They are used to sort data in a database table.

12. What does SQL Profiler use to specify which types of events to monitor and what data to capture pertaining to those events?

a. stored procedures

b. trace template

c. execution plan

d. procedure cache

13. Which piece of information from an item in an execution plan identifies the percentage of total processing time that the item uses?

a. estimated cost

b. estimated row count

c. estimated CPU cost

d. estimated I/O cost

14. Which RAID level is best suited for housing transaction logs?

    a. RAID 0

    b. RAID 1

    c. RAID 5

    d. RAID 10

15. Which of the following situations would not cause the execution plan of a query to be recompiled?

    a. A new column is added to a table accessed by a query.

    b. An Index used by a query has been dropped from the database.

    c. A query performs a join operation to return data from multiple tables.

    d. A significant amount of data in a table has been modified.

16. Which of the following tools is not used to monitor the current user and process activity of a SQL Server 2000 instance?

    a. SQL Profiler

    b. Enterprise Manager

    c. Service Manager

    d. Query Analyzer

17. Which of the items below is used to force the query optimizer to use certain operations in an execution plan?

    a. locks

    b. hints

    c. distribution statistics

    d. stored procedures

18. True or False: A user process that is blocking other users can be terminated using the KILL T-SQL statement.

19. You analyze an execution plan and realize that an index is not being used. The index chosen by the query optimizer is newer than the one you would like it to use. What might be the cause of this problem?

    a. The query optimizer is configured to use only clustered indexes.

    b. The distribution statistics on the older index are not up-to-date.

    c. The older index is on an identity column in the table.

    d. A trigger on the underlying table indicates that the older index is not efficient.

20. True or False: SQL Server 2000 can be configured in a clustered configuration with up to 16 nodes.

21. What is the best way to alleviate fragmentation?

    a. using the sp_recompile system-stored procedure

    b. rebuilding a nonclustered index

    c. rebuilding a clustered index

    d. dropping and recreating a table

22. Which statement best describes narrow and wide indexes?

    a. A wide index is used to return more columns from a table, while a narrow index is used to return fewer columns.

    b. A wide index is used to return more rows, while a narrow index is used to return a small set of rows.

    c. A wide index is based on many columns in a table, while a narrow index is based on very few columns in the underlying table.

    d. Wide indexes are clustered and narrow indexes are nonclustered.

23. Which T-SQL query forces the query optimizer to use an index called CustomerID?

    a. `SELECT CustomerID, CustomerName`
       `FROM Orders WITH (INDEX(CustomerID))`
       `WHERE CustomerID = 12`

    b. `SELECT CustomerID, CustomerName`
       `FROM Orders USE (INDEX(CustomerID))`
       `WHERE CustomerID = 12`

    c. `SELECT CustomerID, CustomerName`
       `FROM Orders WITH (CustomerID)`
       `WHERE CustomerID = 12`

    d. `SELECT CustomerID, CustomerName`
       `FROM Orders (USE INDEX(CustomerID))`
       `WHERE CustomerID = 12`

24. What could cause a page split to happen?

    a. using a join operation in a query

    b. using a nonclustered index in a query

    c. rebuilding a clustered index

    d. adding a row to a table

25. What is the pool of memory used by SQL Server 2000 to store compiled execution plans known as?

    a. execution plan cache

    b. tempdb

    c. procedure cache

    d. resource pool

HANDS-ON PROJECTS

Project 6-1

To analyze a simple query with SQL Query Analyzer and add indexes to improve performance:

1. Start Query Analyzer by clicking **Start**, highlighting **Programs**, highlighting **Microsoft SQL Server**, and clicking the **Query Analyzer** item.

2. Log in with a valid administrator account.

3. When Query Analyzer begins, select the **Northwind** database by clicking the database list arrow, as shown in Figure 6-17.

Figure 6-17   Selecting the Northwind database in Query Analyzer

4. Type the following query into the query window of Query Analyzer:

```
SELECT OrderID, CustomerID, OrderDate, ShippedDate
FROM Orders
WHERE ShippedDate > '1998-04-10 00:00:00.000'
```

5. View the execution plan of the query in Query Analyzer by pressing **Control-L** or by clicking the **Display Estimated Execution Plan** toolbar button.

6. Observe that the execution plan indicates that the clustered index on the primary key of the table (OrderID) is being used to perform the query. Roll the mouse over the clustered index scan operation to access specific information about the operation, as shown in Figure 6-18.

7. Since the WHERE clause of the T-SQL statement is restricting rows based on the values in the ShippedDate column of the Orders table, this query may benefit from using an index on ShippedDate instead of the clustered primary key index chosen by the Query Optimizer. Using the Object Browser window of the Query Analyzer, navigate to the indexes folder of the **Orders** table in the **Northwind** database, as shown in Figure 6-19.

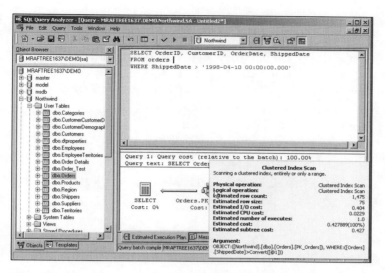

Figure 6-18   The query optimizer chooses the PK_Orders index as shown in the execution plan

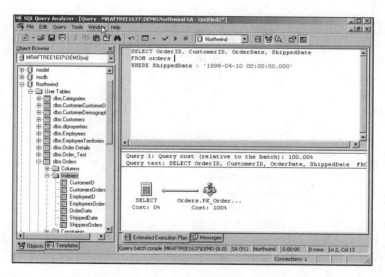

Figure 6-19   Identifying the indexes on the orders table through the object browser pane of Query Analyzer

8. Since there is an index on the ShippedDate column of the table, a query hint can be used to force the query optimizer to use it when executing the query. Alter the T-SQL query in the query window to match the following code:

```
SELECT OrderID, CustomerID, OrderDate, ShippedDate
FROM Orders WITH (INDEX(ShippedDate))
WHERE ShippedDate > '1998-04-10 00:00:00.000'
```

9. Execute the query again by pressing **F5** or by clicking the **Execute** toolbar button.

10. View the execution plan for this modified version of the same query by pressing **Control-L** or by clicking the **Display Estimated Execution Plan** toolbar button. Notice that the execution plan has changed. By specifying the table hint (INDEX(ShippedDate)), the execution is forced to use the ShippedDate index.

11. Roll the mouse over the Orders.ShippedDate operation in the execution plan to view detailed information, as shown in Figure 6-20.

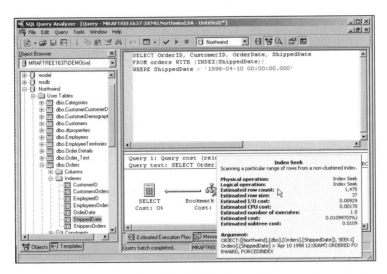

Figure 6-20   Using the table hint to force the execution plan to use the ShippedDate index to process the query

 The query optimizer is a very powerful component of SQL Server 2000 that will usually choose the best possible execution plan for a given query. But the database administrators and programmers are the only people who truly know the table structure and associated data. This knowledge can be used to tailor high-performance execution plans for queries through the use of hints.

12. Close **Query Analyzer** and do not save the queries.

Project 6-2

To use SQL Profiler to monitor the duration of queries running against a database:

1. Start SQL Profiler by clicking **Start**, highlighting **Programs**, highlighting **Microsoft SQL Server**, and then clicking the **Profiler** item.

2. Create a new trace by clicking on the **File** menu, selecting **New**, and then selecting **Trace**.

3. Log in to the local SQL Server 2000 instance.

4. In the **Trace Properties** dialog box shown in Figure 6-21, type a name for the trace and select the **SQLProfilerTSQL_Duration** trace template from the list box.

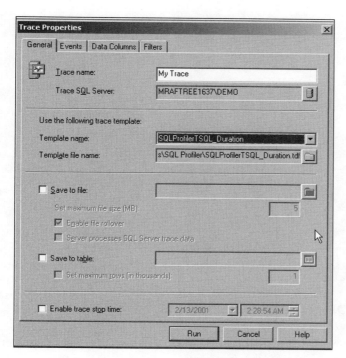

Figure 6-21   Trace Properties Dialog in SQL Profiler

The SQLProfilerTSQL_Duration trace template lists the T-SQL statements that have been executed against a database and the time (in milliseconds) required for those statements to execute.

5. Click **Run** to start the trace. The trace window opens, as shown in Figure 6-22, and the trace awaits requests from database users.

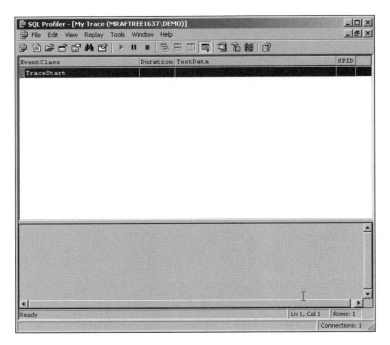

Figure 6-22   Running trace awaiting requests to capture and display information

6. Open SQL Query Analyzer by clicking **Start**, highlighting **Programs**, highlighting **Microsoft SQL Server** and clicking the **Query Analyzer** item. Log in to
   the local instance of SQL Server 2000.

7. Select the **Northwind** database and execute the following query by pressing **F5**
   or by clicking the **Execute** toolbar button:

   ```
   SELECT OrderID, CustomerID, OrderDate, ShippedDate
   FROM Orders
   WHERE ShippedDate > '1998-04-10 00:00:00.000'
   ```

8. Return to SQL Profiler and notice that the trace has captured information about
   the query that was run, as shown in Figure 6-23. (The additional statements captured are issued by opening a new query window in Query Analyzer.) Because of
   the trace template chosen at the beginning of this trace, the information captured
   is limited to the duration of the query, the T-SQL statement itself, and the spid of
   the individual user process that executed the query.

9. Go back to SQL Query Analyzer while still leaving the trace running.

10. Open a new query window by clicking the **New Query** toolbar button or by
    typing **Control-N**. A blank query window should appear.

11. Type the following T-SQL query into the new window and execute it by pressing
    F5 or by clicking the **Execute** toolbar button:

    ```
    SELECT *
    FROM Orders
    ```

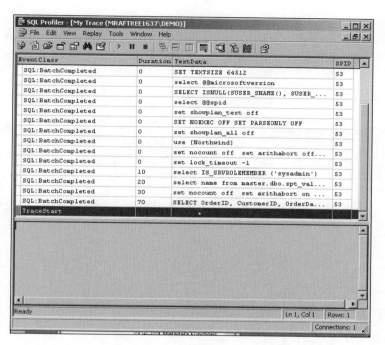

Figure 6-23   The trace captures and displays information about the query that was just executed from Query Analyzer

Figure 6-24 shows two query windows used by Query Analyzer.

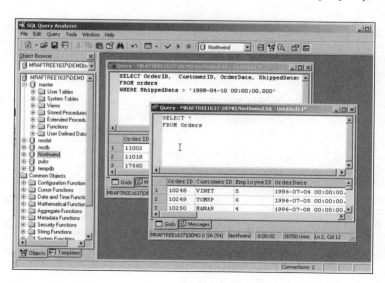

Figure 6-24   Executing a new query from a different query window in Query Analyzer

12. Return to SQL Profiler and observe the numerous entries in the trace that have been added, as seen in Figure 6-25. Notice that there are now queries from two distinct spids being captured. This is the result of having two query windows open in Query Analyzer (each window is handled as a separate user process). Notice that the two longest-running queries (the two used in this exercise) are automatically returned at the bottom of the trace, making it easy to identify long-running queries.

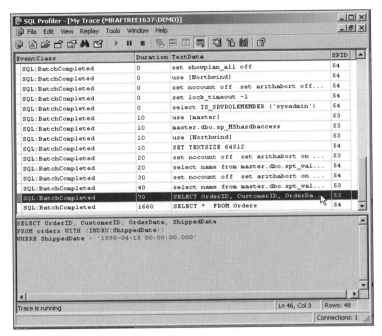

Figure 6-25   The trace has captured information from both open query windows in Query Analyzer

13. Click on the trace entry with **SELECT OrderID, CustomerID, OrderDa...** in the TextData column. Notice that the full query is displayed for convenience in the bottom window of SQL Profiler, as shown in Figure 6-25.

14. Stop the trace and close SQL Profiler without saving.

15. Close **Query Analyzer** without saving the queries.

Project 6-3

To use SQL Enterprise Manager to troubleshoot transactions and locking:

1. In Enterprise Manager, open the **Management folder**, open the **Current Activity** item and then click the **Process Info** item. Notice that there are several current processes, as shown in Figure 6-26.

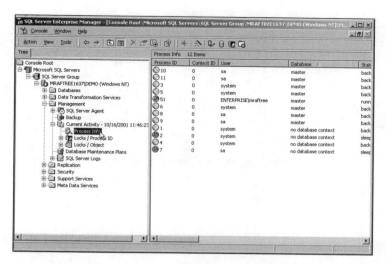

Figure 6-26   The Process Info window in Enterprise Manager shows the current processes connected to SQL Server 2000

2. Open Query Analyzer by clicking the **Tools** menu in Enterprise Manager and highlighting **SQL Query Analyzer**.

3. Click the **Northwind** database from the database list menu in the toolbar of Query Analyzer.

4. Return to Enterprise Manager and refresh the current process information by right-clicking the **Current Activity** item and clicking the **Refresh** option, as shown in Figure 6-27.

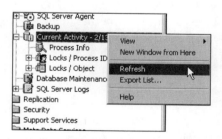

Figure 6-27   Refreshing the current activity information in SQL Server 2000

5. Once the information is refreshed, click the **Process Info** item again to display the current user processes connected to SQL Server. Notice that there is a new process (#52) connected to the Northwind database that represents the open query window in Query Analyzer. See Figure 6-28.

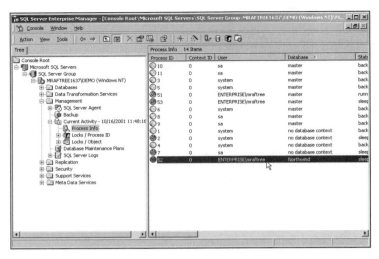

Figure 6-28   Process Info showing a connection to the Northwind database as a result of Query Analyzer

6. Return to Query Analyzer, type the following T-SQL statement, and execute it by pressing **F5** or by clicking the **Execute** toolbar button:

```
BEGIN TRAN
    UPDATE Employees
    SET FirstName = 'George'
    WHERE EmployeeID = 1
```

This code is used to demonstrate the troubleshooting of locking and transactions. A statement should always have a BEGIN TRAN and corresponding COMMIT TRAN or ROLLBACK TRAN statement to ensure that transactions are not left open, holding locks on resources in a database. This statement will actually continue to hold locks on the Employees table even after the update has completed.

7. Return to Enterprise Manager again.

8. Right-click the **Current Activity** item and click **Refresh** as in Step 4.

9. Expand the **Locks / Process ID** item of the **Current Activity** group and then click the **spid 52** item. Notice that the process is holding locks on the Employees table in the Northwind database, as shown in Figure 6-29.

The spid numbers in this example may be different from those on your machine. Be sure to use the proper spid for your system when performing this process.

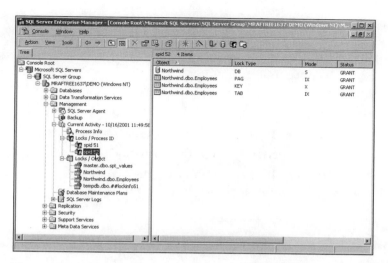

Figure 6-29   Observing locks by process ID with Enterprise Manager

10. Expand the **Locks / Object** item of the Current Activity group and then click the **Northwind.dbo.Employees** item. Notice that process 52 is still holding locks on the Employees table, as shown in Figure 6–30.

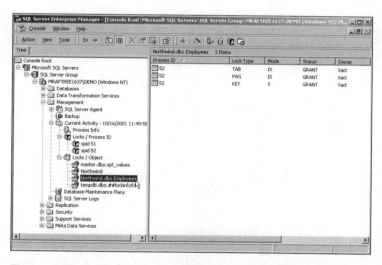

Figure 6-30   Observing locks by database object with Enterprise Manager

The process is still holding locks because the query was executed within a transaction that was not committed or rolled back.

11. Return to Query Analyzer and open a new query window by clicking the **New Query** toolbar button or typing **Control-N**.

12. Type the following query in the new query window and execute it by pressing **F5** or by clicking the **Execute** toolbar button:

```
SELECT *
FROM Employees
```

Notice that this query continues to run and does not return a result set.

13. Return to Enterprise Manager and refresh the current activity as in Step 4.

14. Click the **Locks / Process ID** item in the Current Activity group, and notice that there is a blocking situation, as shown in Figure 6-31.

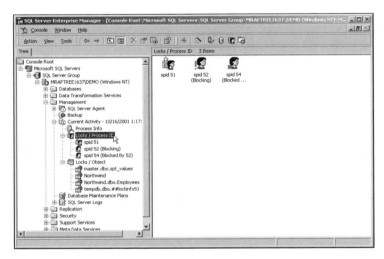

Figure 6-31   Identifying blocking situations with Enterprise Manager

Notice how process 52 (the UPDATE statement) is blocking process 54 (the SELECT statement) because the locks used for the update operation were not released (due to the uncommitted transaction).

15. To resolve the problem, spid 52 must be terminated or *killed*. To kill the process, click the **Process Info** item in the Current Activity group. Right-click on the **process 52** row in the right-hand side of the screen, as shown in Figure 6-32.

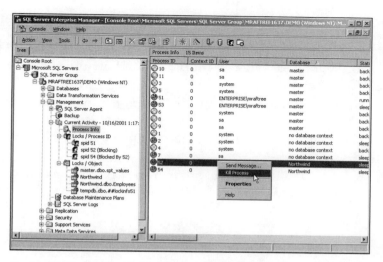

Figure 6-32   Killing a blocking process from Enterprise Manager

16. Click the **Kill Process** item in the set of options and confirm the operation by clicking **Yes** when the confirmation window appears.

17. Right-click on the **Current Activity** item and click **Refresh** as in Step 4. Then click the **Process Info** item again. Notice that process 52 (the one causing the block) does not exist anymore.

18. Return to Query Analyzer and notice that the SELECT query on the Employees table has finished and returned a result set containing all of the information from the table. See Figure 6-33.

19. Close **Query Analyzer** without saving your queries.

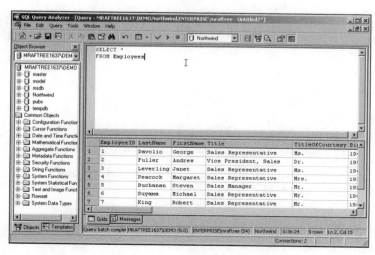

Figure 6-33   The blocked query is allowed to execute because the blocking process was killed

Project 6-4

To use system-stored procedures to troubleshoot transactions and locking:

1. Open Query Analyzer by clicking the **Tools** menu in Enterprise Manager and clicking **SQL Query Analyzer**.

2. Click **Northwind** database in the database list box in the toolbar of Query Analyzer.

3. Open a new query window by clicking the **New Query** toolbar button or typing **Control-N**.

4. Execute the **sp_who** system-stored procedure to view current processes and activity on the instance of SQL Server 2000, as shown in Figure 6-34.

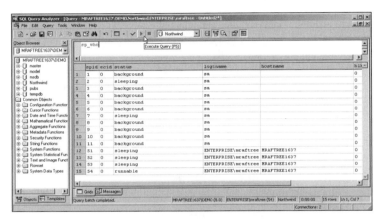

Figure 6-34   Viewing current activity using the sp_who system-stored procedure

5. Return to the first query window that was opened in Query Analyzer, type the following T-SQL statement, and execute it by pressing **F5** or by clicking the **Execute** toolbar button:

```
BEGIN TRAN
     UPDATE Employees
     SET FirstName= 'George'
     WHERE EmployeeID = 1
```

6. Open a new query window by clicking the **New Query** toolbar button or typing **Control-N**. (At this point there are three query windows open.)

7. Type the following query in the new query window and execute it by pressing **F5** or by clicking the **Execute** toolbar button:

```
SELECT *
FROM Employees
```

Notice that this query continues to run and does not return a result set.

8. Return to the query window from which the sp_who system-stored procedure was executed, and execute it again by pressing **F5** or by clicking the **Execute** toolbar button.

9. Notice that the sp_who procedure call shows that a blocking situation has arisen. The blk column of the output shows the spid number of the process that is blocking a current process. Observe that the UPDATE statement process (#52) is blocking the SELECT statement (#55), as shown in Figure 6-35.

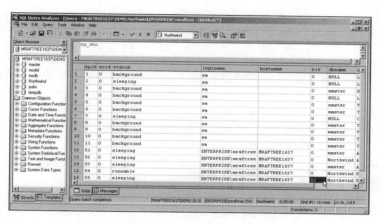

6

Figure 6-35   Identifying blocking situations with the sp_who system-stored procedure

> **Note**
>
> To resolve the problem, spid 52 must be killed. To kill the process, use the KILL T-SQL command with the appropriate spid number. In this case the statement would be **KILL 52**.

10. Open a new query window by clicking the **New Query** toolbar button or typing Control-N. (At this point there are four query windows open.)

11. Type the following query into the window and execute it by pressing **F5** or by clicking the **Execute** toolbar button:

```
KILL 52
```

> **Note**
>
> This will kill the blocking process and allow the blocked process to finish executing. In this case the select statement will now return a result set in Query Analyzer.

12. Return to the query window that was executing the SELECT statement and notice that it has completed processing the query.

13. Return to the query window that was used to execute the sp_who system-stored procedure and reexecute the procedure. Notice that process 52 no longer exists and that process 54 is no longer blocked, as shown in Figure 6-36.

14. Close **Query Analyzer** and Enterprise Manager.

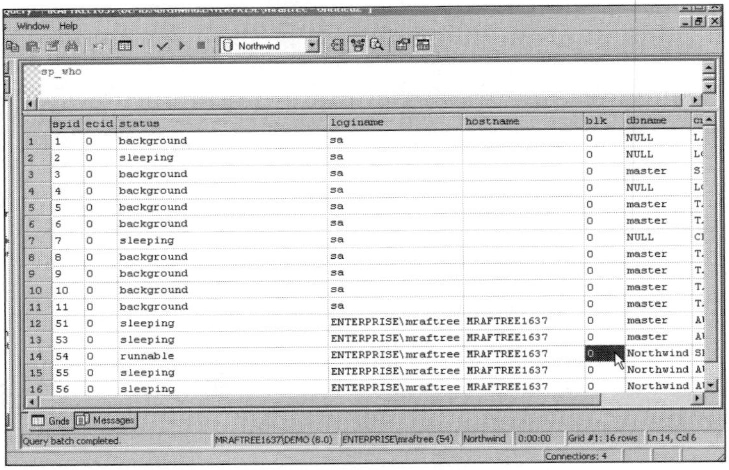

Figure 6-36   The sp_who system-stored procedure shows that the blocking issues have been resolved

CASE PROJECTS

Case One

Consider a situation where SQL Server 2000 will be installed on a server with six 3 GB hard drives available for data storage. A single database will be used for generating reports and will therefore need to be optimized for read operations. Based on the information contained in this chapter and in SQL Server Books Online, research and develop the best strategy using RAID-based hard drive configurations. Keep in mind that different RAID configurations can be used for data and transaction logs.

Case Two

A company has just deployed SQL Server 2000 to house data for its financial systems. As more people within the organization use the system, the response time for operations degrades and users begin to complain that the performance is unacceptable. Assuming that the hard drive configuration and the placement of indexes and tables across filegroups is optimized, poorly performing queries must be the culprit. Based on the information in this chapter and the documentation contained in SQL Server Books Online, define a SQL Profiler trace that will help to identify poorly performing queries. Discuss how to limit the amount of data captured through filters as well.

PERFORMING DISASTER RECOVERY OPERATIONS

After reading this chapter and completing the exercises you will be able to:

♦ Understand backup operations and recovery models

♦ Create database devices

♦ Create full database, differential database, and transaction log backups

♦ Use backups to restore a database

♦ Configure log shipping

♦ Use the Database Maintenance Plan Wizard to create a disaster recovery plan

♦ Ensure the consitency of databases using DBCC T-SQL statements

Database backups are essential to all production-level database environments. Data storage disks can become corrupt or damaged, or just fail. Human errors resulting in data corruption or data deletion are another potential source of problems. Natural disasters are valid concerns, as well. All of these factors lead to the need to return a database environment back to its last consistent state prior to such an event. Minimizing the effects of a database failure is one of the primary responsibilities of a database administrator.

There are several methods of backing up databases in SQL Server 2000, including full backups, transaction log backups, differential backups, and a file or filegroup restore. A full database backup creates a full copy of the database. A transaction log backup only copies the contents of the transaction log. A differential database backup copies the database pages modified after the point in time of the last full backup. A file or filegroup restore has the ability to recover only a portion of the database. These backup operations can be used in conjunction with one another to meet even the most rigorous database availability requirements.

Backing up databases is only half the battle when attempting to maintain a high level of data consistency and database availability. In Chapter 6, we discussed RAID and clustering technologies and how they help to keep SQL Server 2000 instances running in the event of server or hard drive failure, but they are not foolproof. For example, if two hard drives in a RAID array fail, the databases residing on the array become unavailable. In this situation, the hard drives must be replaced and the databases must be restored from backups before users can access them again. Similarly, data corruption can occur within a database, causing it to malfunction. SQL Server 2000 provides a set of T-SQL statements that validate and repair the integrity of databases to prevent unnecessary failure should corruption issues arise. This chapter addresses the issues regarding database backup strategies, backing up and restoring databases, and regularly maintaining databases to ensure they are in a consistent state.

PLANNING FOR DISASTER

Nobody likes to think about system meltdowns (especially database administrators). Fortunately, with improvements in the reliability of both hardware and software, they have become less frequent. However, hardware will fail, and users will make mistakes like deleting important information by accident. The only recourse we have is to plan for such events and minimize their effects on an organization using SQL Server 2000. Backup requirements will differ, depending on the requirements of the organization. For example, a database used to support a reporting system may only be updated weekly, so backing up the entire database every weekend may be sufficient. In the event of a failure, the full backup can be restored in a single operation, bringing the database back to the state it was in when the backup operation was performed. For large mission-critical databases, with data modification occurring constantly during the week, a weekly backup is not sufficient. In this case you would probably back up the transaction log periodically throughout each weekday and perform a full database backup over the weekend. In the event of a failure, the most recent full database backup would be restored first, and then the various transaction log backups are restored in chronological order. This brings the database back to the state it was in after the most recent transaction log backup.

SQL Server 2000 offers a flexible backup architecture that allows database administrators to execute backup operations that meet the data availability requirements of any database.

BACKUP OPERATIONS

SQL Server 2000 provides four different types of backup operations for implementing a suitable backup scheme. The simplest of these is the full database backup operation. This operation creates a backup file containing all of the data in the database at the time when the operation was performed. A differential database backup operation creates a file containing only the data that has changed in the database since the last full backup operation. A transaction log backup stores a recoverable copy of the data changes recorded in the transaction log. The file backup operation allows specific data files within a database to be backed up. This allows individual files to be restored instead of the entire database.

Each of these operations has its own merits and shortcomings. When deciding how to use them, you must consider the following:

- The time it takes to perform the operation (especially when the operation is executed while users are accessing the database)

- The amount of data loss that is acceptable within the system

- The time it would take to restore the database to an operational status in the event of a failure

Full Database Backup Operation

The **full database backup** operation creates an exact copy of all of the data in a database. The entire database can be recreated from the full database backup in the event of a system failure. Full database backups typically take the most time to perform because they copy all of the data in a database. Consequently, they require more storage space and impact overall performance significantly.

It is important to estimate the size of the full database backup for appropriate disk management. A backup operation cannot complete if sufficient disk space is not available for the resulting backup files. SQL Server 2000 optimizes the storage of a full backup by only storing the data in the database. This results in a backup file that is smaller than the actual database from which it was generated. For example, a database could be 100 MB but only have 70 MB of data in it. Knowing the volume of data in a database before performing the backup can be very important when working in an environment where storage space is limited. The sp_spaceused system-stored procedure is used to determine the size of the data in a database. When executed against a database from Query Analyzer, it returns information about the amount of space occupied by the data in a database, as shown in Figure 7-1.

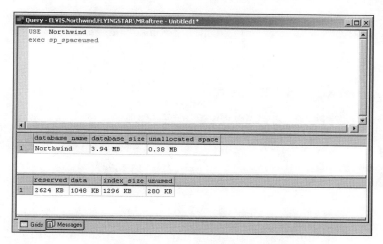

Figure 7-1   SQL Statement sp_spaceused executed in a Query window

Differential Database Backup Operation

The **differential database backup** is significantly different from the full database backup in that it only backs up the data pages that have changed since the last full database backup was performed. The resulting backup files are smaller, and this type of operation executes faster than a full backup.

There are a few considerations to take into account when determining the viability of using a differential backup. If the amount of data that has changed since the last full database backup is relatively small, then differential backups are more efficient for the system, because they save on space, time, and processor consumption. Consider a scenario where a small portion of data gets changed quite frequently (like a table containing project status information). In this situation, differential backups would be very effective since they execute faster than full backups, and therefore affect performance less.

The differential database backup operation is used in addition to a full database backup. Since differential backups capture all of the data changes since the last full backup, a new differential backup will include the information from any previous differential backups performed after the last full backup. As a result, subsequent differential database backups require more storage space because they include all of the changes from the last differential backup, as well as any new data modifications.

Differential database backups are typically scheduled more frequently than full database backups. For example, if you perform full backups once a week on Sunday nights, you might perform a differential backup every weeknight.

Database restoration with differential backups is only available when used in conjunction with the full database backup. In the event of system failure, you would first restore the most recent full backup, and then you would restore the last differential database backup. Transaction log backups are applied last if they are being used. This will be addressed in detail in the next section.

 When a full database backup is performed, any previous differential backups become irrelevant because all of the data is contained in the full backup.

Transaction Log Backup Operation

The **transaction log backup** operation allows transaction logs to be backed up. Recall from Chapter 4 that the transaction log keeps a record of the operations that have occurred against a database. When restoring a transaction log, SQL Server 2000 applies the transactions stored in the log to the current database. Transaction logs allow for point-in-time recovery because they can be used to recover all of the transactions within them to a particular hour and second.

Transaction log backups typically use fewer processor resources to complete than either full database backups or differential backups. Therefore, transaction log backups can occur on a more frequent basis without degrading the performance of the SQL Server. By using frequent transaction log backups, data loss is minimized because a more granular level of backup is maintained. For example, if transaction logs are backed up every hour, then the most data that could possibly be lost in the event of a system failure is one hour's worth of user activity.

It is important to note that transaction logs by themselves cannot restore a database. Transaction log backups need to be applied, in the order in which they were made, to the last full database backup or differential database backup. All preceding transaction log backups must also be applied before restoring the current transaction log.

 The purpose of the transaction log is to record any operations against a database that have occurred since a full database backup or a differential database backup was performed. As a result, a transaction log backup cannot take place during a full database backup or a differential database backup process. This ensures the integrity of events that must occur to restore the database.

SQL Server 2000 allows the application of transaction logs to the backup database to aid the recovery. In the event that you need the transaction log backups, and a transaction occurs over two separate transaction log backups, it is important to apply all of them. If a recovery is completed without the final transaction log that contains the later portion of a transaction that has occurred over two transaction log backups, the transaction will be rolled back. SQL Server 2000 will see this transaction as incomplete because the final transaction log has not been applied, and the remaining portion of the transaction resides on the final transaction log. If the recovery takes place without the final transaction log, we are at a point where the final transaction log backup cannot be applied to the recovered database. The rule still applies here: a transaction log backup alone cannot restore a database. The important thing to keep in mind is that the database should not be recovered until the last transaction log has been applied. If a transaction log other than the last transaction log has been applied, and the recovery is completed, the only option is to start the recovery process over again.

File Backup Operation

Remember that a database can reside on multiple physical files, and that these files can be logically grouped into an object called a filegroup. A file backup operation can be used to back up only the data residing on a single file or filegroup of a database. File backup operations are less taxing on performance than full backups and provide the advantage of decreased recovery time in the event of a disk failure.

File backups are useful when you are working with very large databases. A two terabyte database that powers a large retail Web site would take a significant amount of time to fully back up, especially if you are using a tape drive that only writes at a rate of 100 MB per minute. When databases grow to sizes so large that full backups simply aren't feasible, file backups can be used to back up each data file regularly. Large amounts of data also impact the time required to recover from a system failure.

Consider a situation where two RAID 5 hard drive arrays each hold a different data file for the same database. A file backup is used to back up each file. If one of the arrays fails, only a single file backup (that doesn't contain all of the data in the database) needs to be restored. This is faster than restoring from a full backup. To recover a file with a file backup, you would first restore the file backup and then apply any transaction log backups to it.

SQL SERVER 2000 RECOVERY MODELS

Each database on an instance of SQL Server 2000 is configured to use a **recovery model**. The recovery models are provided to simplify recovery planning and backup and restore operations. Each model addresses different needs, including:

- Minimizing data loss in the event of a failure
- The amount of disk space available to stored backups
- Impacting performance of the system

A recovery model is chosen based on the needs of an individual database. Each recovery model is used by a database to determine what type of backups will be used to restore it in the event of a failure. Table 7-1 outlines the three recovery models available in SQL Server 2000 and their benefits and limitations:

Table 7-1   SQL Server 2000 Recovery Models

Recovery Model	Benefits	Work Loss Exposure	Recover to Point in Time?
Simple	Permits high-performance bulk copy operations and requires minimal space usage	Changes since the most recent database or differential backup must be redone	Can recover to the end of any backup. Then changes must be redone.
Full	No work is lost due to a lost or damaged data file. Can recover to any point in time.	Normally none. Changes since the most recent backup would have to be redone.	Can recover to any point in time
Bulk-logged	This allows high-performance bulk copy operations and minimal log space usage	If the log fails, or any bulk operations occurred after the last log backup, only those changes after the last backup would need to be redone. Otherwise none.	Can recover to the end of any backup. After that, changes must be redone.

Simple Recovery

The simple recovery model requires the least administration. It recovers data up to the point of the most recent full or differential backup. Transaction log backups are not used in this model, and therefore transaction log space is kept at a minimum. The simple recovery model is the easiest to manage, since it requires a less complex set of operations (only full and differential backups). However, this model exposes a database to significantly more lost data, since backups are performed less frequently. Consider the backup scheme illustrated in Figure 7-2.

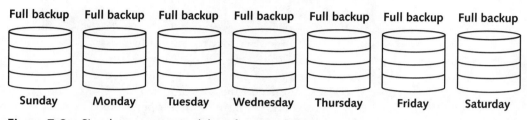

| Full backup | Full backup | Full backup | Full backup | Full backup | Full backup | Full backup |
| Sunday | Monday | Tuesday | Wednesday | Thursday | Friday | Saturday |

Figure 7-2   Simple recovery model performing full backups everyday

In this scenario, a full database backup is performed everyday (probably after regular business hours). This backup scheme is quite simple and easy to administer in that the full backup operation is performed daily. Since the backup operations are only run once a day, and after hours at that, there is no performance impact on the users of the database. However, in this scenario, a full day's data is lost in the event of a system failure. Although restoration is simple in this scenario (because only a single restore operation is performed when using a full backup file), all of the changes made since the last full backup would be lost.

Large databases take a long time to back up, and the resulting backup files can be quite large. Over time, storing several large full backup files could reduce large amounts of available disk space. Additionally, if the database is very large, a full backup operation could take hours to perform. Very few mission-critical databases are used only during regular business hours. Consequently, performing a long-running full backup operation while users are accessing the database can severely impact performance. A backup scheme that only performs full backups is a poor solution in mission-critical environments.

This scenario could be marginally improved by using differential backups in addition to full backups. Consider the scenario in Figure 7-3.

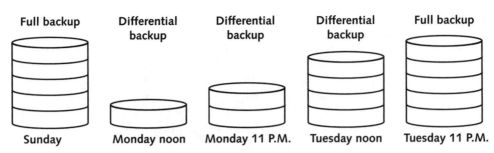

| Full backup | Differential backup | Differential backup | Differential backup | Full backup |

| Sunday | Monday noon | Monday 11 P.M. | Tuesday noon | Tuesday 11 P.M. |

Figure 7-3   Simple recovery model performing both full and differential backups

In this situation, a differential backup is performed twice a day, with a full backup every other day. This scheme will limit data loss to only a half day's worth of user activity. Differential backups execute faster than full backups because only the data pages that have changed since the last full backup are copied. However, over time, differential backups increase in size because users continue to modify data. Consequently, the first differential backup will execute faster than subsequent operations. The performance impact is minimal for the first operation, but increases with each additional differential backup.

Restoring a database after a system failure in this scenario is a little more complex than a scheme in which only full backups are performed. First, the most recent full backup must be restored, and then the most recent differential backup is applied to restore the database to the state it was in when the last differential backup was performed.

These scenarios are typical when using the simple recovery model; however, they are severely limited in that data exposure is quite high. Mission critical databases typically require more robust backup schemes to limit data loss.

Full Recovery and Bulk-Logged Recovery

The full recovery model is regarded as the model of choice to restore a database to an earlier point in time. The full recovery model uses full backups, differential backups, and transaction logs to restore a database to a point in time very close to when a system failure occurred. For example, in a scenario using either of these models, a database is recovered by first restoring a full and differential backup, and then applying transaction logs in the order in which they were backed up. This allows the database to be returned to the state it was in when the last transaction in the log was committed.

These recovery models provide the most robust scheme available for minimizing data loss in the event of a system failure. It is superior to the simple recovery model because it allows transaction logs to be used to recreate a database, which allows the database to be restored to a point in time (up to the last committed user transaction in the log). Additionally, when a transaction log is backed up, it can be truncated since the operations it contains will be stored in a backup file. This is important because transaction logs can grow to sizes larger than a database if not truncated regularly.

Location of the Transaction Log

It is strongly recommended that the transaction log for a mission-critical database be placed on a separate physical disk than the data. This way, if a hard drive housing a data file fails, the transaction log can be backed up after the failure and then applied to any existing full or differential backups to restore the database.

Transaction Logs in the Bulk-Logged Recovery Model

Bulk-logged Recovery is very similar to the full recovery model in that it provides optimal performance and limited exposure to data loss. The differentiating factor between the two models is how operations are logged. In the full recovery model, every single user action is recorded in the transaction log. In the bulk-logged model, large operations like CREATE INDEX statements and bulk data inserts (using the bcp utility discussed in detail in Chapter 9) are only minimally logged. For example, if a bulk import of 1000 customer records is performed, it is stored as a single entry in the transaction log instead of as 1000 individual inserts. While this results in smaller transaction logs, it also prevents restoring a database to a point in time. In a bulk-logged scenario, if a system failure occurs in the middle of a bulk operation, the actions that occurred as part of the bulk operation cannot be recovered (because the operations are handled as single units of activity).

Implementing a Backup Scheme with Transaction Logs

A backup scheme that incorporates transaction logs is typical in scenarios with a high volume of data changes, where data loss must be kept to a minimum and database performance must not be impacted by frequent, large backup operations. Consider the scenario illustrated in Figure 7-4.

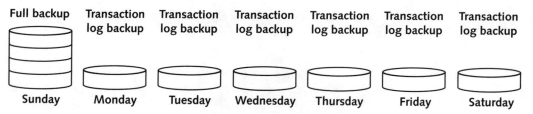

Figure 7-4   Full recovery model performing both full and transaction log backups

In this scenario, a full backup is performed on Sunday, and the transaction log is backed up daily. By backing up the transaction log regularly, its size is kept to a minimum, because once it has been backed up it can be truncated. Since the size of the log will remain relatively small (compared to the size of the database) it can be backed up quickly, impacting performance of the database less than a full or differential backup. Much like differential backups, transaction log backups require a full backup as a baseline.

When a system failure occurs in this scenario, the full database backup must be restored, then Monday's transaction log backup is applied, and then Tuesday's, etc. In a situation where there are several transaction log backups, the restoration process requires more care and time, resulting in more overall system downtime. Differential backups can be used to help alleviate this problem.

In systems with a very high volume of transaction processing, the transaction log can become quite large. When transaction log backups are performed, the size of the log is controlled with minimal impact on database performance. Consider the scenario illustrated in Figure 7-5.

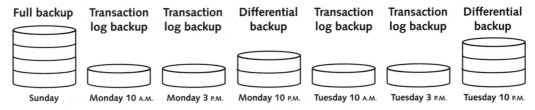

Figure 7-5   Full recovery model performing both full, differential, and transaction log backups

In this scenario, transaction log backups are performed every weekday at 10 A.M. and 3 P.M. A differential backup is performed at 10 P.M., each weekday. Notice that a full backup is done over the weekend on Sundays. The differential backup executed late at night simplifies the restoration process for the database and probably doesn't impact users, who are presumably off the system at that hour.

In the event of a failure, the full backup would be restored first, then the most recent differential backup, and then the transaction log backups performed since the differential backup are applied in the order in which they were created. In this backup scheme, a maximum of two transaction log back ups will be required to restore the database if needed. This minimizes the time required to bring the database back to a usable state and consequently has less impact on the users.

In a very large database, file backups would be used instead of differential backups to limit recovery time. File backups require the transaction log backups to be maintained in order to restore a file backup to a point in time. Consider the scenario in Figure 7-6.

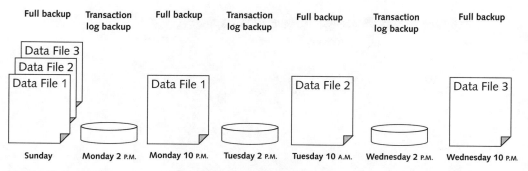

Figure 7-6   Full recovery model performing both full, file, and transaction log backups

In this situation, a different file is backed up each weeknight, and a transaction log backup is performed in the middle of each weekday. If File 1 suffered a hardware failure on Wednesday night at 8 P.M., the file backup for File 1 could be restored and then all of the transaction log backups performed since the File 1 backup could be applied to allow recovery to a specific point in time. The downside of this backup scheme is that you have to maintain several transaction log backups to be able to recover. This is different from the differential backup, which negates the need for transaction log backups performed before them.

Configuring the Recovery Model of Databases

As we discussed at the beginning of this section, the recovery model of a database specifies the types of operations you can use to restore it in the event of a failure. Depending on the complexity of the backup scheme used by a database, one of three recovery models can be selected.

To select a recovery model for an individual database, right-click on the database in Enterprise Manager and click Properties from the context-sensitive menu. When the Database Properties window appears, click the Options tab to access the screen shown in Figure 7-7.

Using the Recovery Model list, you can specify either full, bulk-logged, or simple recovery models.

The same task can be accomplished with the ALTER DATABASE T-SQL statement and the SET RECOVERY clause. The statement adheres to the following syntax:

```
ALTER DATABASE <Database Name>
SET RECOVERY <FULL | BULK_LOGGED | SIMPLE>
```

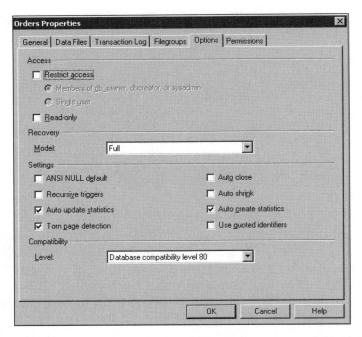

Figure 7-7   Configuring the database recovery model in Enterprise Manager

To configure the Northwind database to use the full recovery model, you could use the following statement:

```
ALTER DATABASE Northwind
SET RECOVERY FULL
```

With a recovery model chosen and a backup plan in place, the process of implementing the backup plan can begin. Before performing any backups, you must first create backup devices on which to store the backup information.

BACKUP DEVICES

SQL Server 2000 requires all database and log backups to be stored on objects called backup devices. **Backup devices** are files on hard drives or other disk storage media (like tapes) that are used to stored backups. Two common types of backup device types supported in SQL Server 2000 are disk devices and tape devices.

Disk Devices

Disk devices are Windows files that reside on hard drives or other storage media on a network. They can be accessed as if they were any other operating system file residing on a network. Disk backup devices can reside on the local machine or anywhere on the network, and they expand and shrink depending on the size and number of backups stored within them.

It is strongly recommended that disk devices reside on a different machine than the one running the instance of SQL Server 2000. Storing database backups on a remote machine prevents a disk failure from ruining both the database and its backups. A single disk device could be used to store backups from multiple instances of SQL Server 2000 running on remote computers. This would provide a central repository for database and log backups within a corporate network.

Tape Devices

Tape backup devices allow backups to be stored on tapes in a local tape drive. Since SQL Server 2000 does not support backing up to remote tape devices, the tape drive housing the tape device must be physically connected to the local computer. Though tapes are a less expensive storage medium, if a network contains multiple SQL Server 2000 instances, each computer running SQL Server 2000 will need its own tape drive(s).

A single database backup can be stored on multiple tapes. If a tape becomes full in the middle of a backup, SQL Server 2000 will prompt you to put a new tape in the drive and continue the backup when you are ready.

Microsoft Tape Format

Regardless of the device type used, database and log backups are stored in the same format. SQL Server 2000 writes backups in the **Microsoft Tape Format (MTF)**. MTF is a standard backup format developed by Microsoft to allow backups from multiple sources to be stored on the same media. Using MTF allows SQL Server 2000 backups to be stored on the same tapes as Windows NT and Windows 2000 backups. The MTF unit that stores various backups is called a **media**. Each backup stored on a single MTF media is contained within a unit called a **backup set**, as illustrated in Figure 7-8. In this example, a single MTF media is housing two SQL Server 2000 backups and two Windows 2000 backups.

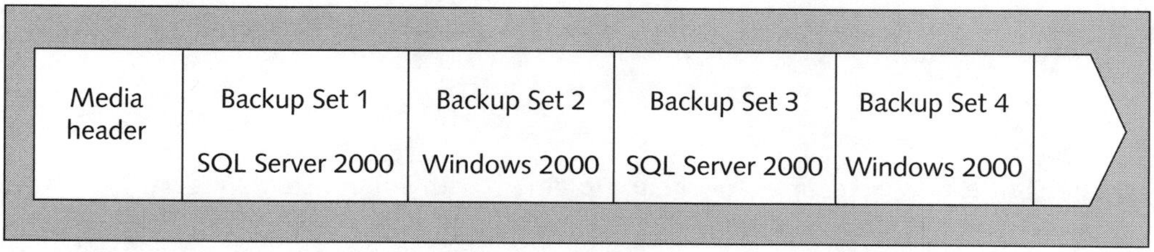

Media header	Backup Set 1	Backup Set 2	Backup Set 3	Backup Set 4
	SQL Server 2000	Windows 2000	SQL Server 2000	Windows 2000

Figure 7-8   Microsoft Tape Format (MTF) structure

A database administrator must have a thorough understanding of backup and restore architecture and recovery planning. This knowledge is indispensable when one is tasked with defining a backup scheme and selecting an appropriate recovery model. Once a feasible plan is in place, it can be implemented by performing its various tasks.

Managing Database Backups

As with most administrative tasks in SQL Server 2000, you can use the GUI provided by Enterprise Manager or equivalent T-SQL statements to perform the various backup and restore operations. This section covers device creation and the different backup and restore operations. By examining the individual tasks in detail, you will be prepared to tactically execute the backup and recovery scheme to prepare for and recover from database failures.

Performing Backups with Enterprise Manager

Enterprise Manager provides intuitive interfaces to simplify the process of managing and performing backups. Before a database backup can be performed, a backup device must exist for the data to be backed up to.

To create a new backup device in Enterprise Manager, click the Backup item in the Management folder. Right-click on Backup and click the New Backup Device option from the context-sensitive menu. This activates the Backup Device Properties window shown in Figure 7-9.

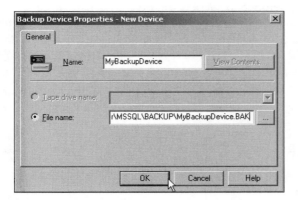

Figure 7-9   Creating a new backup device with Enterprise Manager

From this screen, you can specify the name and type of backup device that you wish to create. Tape drives connected to the local computer are automatically detected and are available through the "Tape drive name" option. In a file backup, the "File name" option is selected. By default, the name of the device will also be used as the device filename.

For example, the filename for a disk device named MyBackupDevice will be MyBackupDevice.BAK. The default location for disk backup devices is the SQL Server 2000 backup directory for the current instance, but they can be placed on any directory available to the Windows account that the SQL Server 2000 instance runs on. Once a device is available, any of the backup operations may be performed.

The SQL Enterprise Manager allows you to create a backup by right-clicking on a database, highlighting All Tasks and clicking the Backup Database option in the context-sensitive menu. This launches the SQL Server Backup window shown in Figure 7-10.

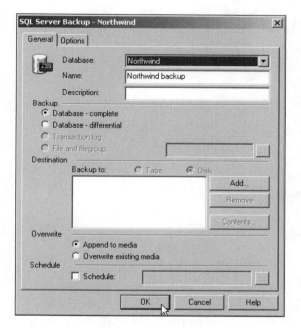

Figure 7-10   SQL Server Backup window

This screen allows you to choose the type of database backup you would like to perform such as complete (full), differential, transaction log, or file and filegroup.

The available backup operations are enabled based on the recovery model of the database. For example, the Northwind database is configured for the simple recovery model, so only the complete and differential options would be available, as shown in Figure 7-10.

The screen also allows you to specify whether the backup operation should overwrite any existing backups on a device. This is helpful if disk space is limited and historical backups are not required, because a single device can grow very large as more and more backups are written to it. From this screen, you can also schedule the backup operation to occur on specific days at specific times.

In order to back up the database, you must specify a location where the backup will reside. Click Add to access the Select Backup Destination window shown in Figure 7-11.

Figure 7-11   Select Backup Destination window

This window allows a directory to store a file backup or select an available backup device. Once a valid location is selected, the backup operation can be performed or scheduled for later execution.

Performing Backups with Transact-SQL

Though it is more common to use Enterprise Manager to configure and perform backups, it is important to know the T-SQL statement equivalents of the various backup operations.

Creating Backup Devices with Transact-SQL

The sp_adddumpdevice system-stored procedure is used to create a new backup device using T-SQL. This procedure must be run from the Master database, and it adheres to the following syntax:

```
USE master
EXEC sp_adddumpdevice '<Type of Device>', '<Device Name>',
  '<Device Location>'
```

In the following example, a new device called MyBackup is created in the 'C:\Backups\Databases\' local directory:

```
USE master
EXEC sp_adddumpdevice 'disk', 'MyBackup',
'C:\Backups\Databases\MyBackup.BAK'
```

Creating Backups with T-SQL

The BACKUP T-SQL statement is used with various options to perform full and differential database backups as well as transaction log backups.

To perform a full or differential database backup, the BACKUP DATABASE statement is used. This statement adheres to the following syntax:

```
BACKUP DATABASE <Database Name>
FILE = <Filename>     (optional)
FILEGROUP = <Filegroup Name> (optional)
TO <Device Name>
WITH <Option Setting>  (optional)
```

Some of the common options used in the WITH clause and their implications are listed in Table 7–2.

Table 7-2   Common BACKUP DATABASE Options

Option	Description
DIFFERENTIAL	Specifies that the operation should perform a differential database backup
INIT I NOINIT	Specifies whether or not to overwrite existing backups on a device. The INIT option causes SQL Server 2000 to overwrite any existing backups. The NOINIT clause is the default (you don't have to specify it) and it causes the backup to be appended to any existing backups on a device.
RESTART	This option is used when a system failure occurs in the middle of a backup operation. It will cause SQL Server 2000 to resume the operation from where it left off.

The following statement creates a full backup of the Northwind database and stores it on a device called NorthwindBaK:

```
BACKUP DATABASE Northwind
TO NorthwindbaK
```

A common backup practice involves overwriting old backups on a device to preserve storage space. The following statement performs a full backup of the Northwind database to the NorthwindbaK device, and it overwrites any existing backups residing on the device:

```
BACKUP DATABASE Northwind
  TO NorthwindbaK
  WITH INIT
```

A differential database backup is performed using the WITH DIFFERENTIAL option. The code below could be used to perform a differential backup of the Northwind database and store it on the NorthwindbaK backup device:

```
BACKUP DATABASE Northwind
  TO NorthwindbaK
  WITH DIFFERENTIAL
```

The BACKUP LOG statement is used to back up transaction logs with T-SQL. Its syntax is the same as that of BACKUP DATABASE:

```
BACKUP LOG <Database Name>
TO <Device Name>
WITH <Option>
```

For example, to back up the transaction log of the Northwind database to a device called NorthwindLogbaK you could use the following statement:

```
BACKUP LOG Northwind
   TO NorthwindLogbaK
```

RESTORING DATABASES

Databases can be restored from a backup or set of backups using both Enterprise Manager and T-SQL statements. In the event of a system failure, it is up to the database administrator to restore any full, differential, and transaction log backups in the right order and to a certain point in time if applicable.

Restoring Databases with Enterprise Manager

Databases are restored in Enterprise Manager using the Restore database window shown in Figure 7-12. To access this screen, right-click on a database in Enterprise Manager, highlight All Tasks, and click the Restore Database option in the context-sensitive menu.

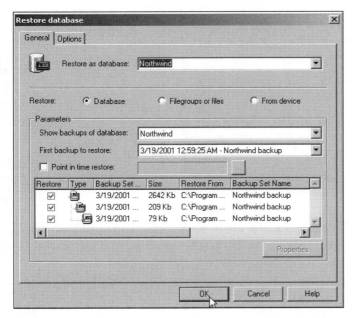

Figure 7-12   Restore database window

From this screen you can choose the database and the types of backups you want to restore. SQL Server 2000 maintains information about backups in the msdb system database. Consequently, Enterprise Manager is able to display a list of full backups in the "First backup to restore" list box. It can also automatically identify the chain of backups for a single database and the correct order in which to restore them. In Figure 7-12, SQL Server 2000 has detected and defaulted to a restoration plan based on the last full backup. The grid shows three separate backups, a full backup, a differential backup, and a transaction log backup that were performed in that order. Notice how the nodes are displayed in a tree structure to present the relationship between the different backups.

The Options tab of the Restore database window, shown in Figure 7-13, allows advanced restore operations to be performed.

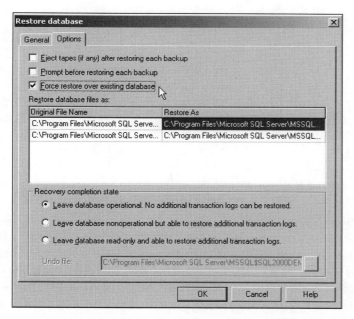

Figure 7-13   Options for performing customized restoration operations

In the example above, the "Force restore over existing database" option is checked. This option allows a backup from a database to be restored onto a different database. It is useful when you want to copy a database to an existing database on another computer. The "Recovery completion state" options allow you to control the state of the database after the restore operation completes. For example, if there is a very large full backup and 15 transaction log backups to restore a database, you could bring the database to a read-only state after the full backup is restored. This allows users to access the database for read operations while the 15 transaction logs are being applied to it.

Restoring Databases with Transact-SQL

The same recovery tasks can be accomplished with various T-SQL statements. The RESTORE T-SQL statement is used to recover different backups should the need arise. It adheres to the following syntax:

```
RESTORE DATABASE <Database Name>
FILE = '<Filename>' (optional for file backups)
FILEGROUP = '<Filegroup Name>'
(optional for file backups)
  FROM <Backup Device>
WITH <Option Name>
```

The following example restores a full backup of the Northwind database stored on a backup device called NorthwindbaK:

```
RESTORE DATABASE Northwind
  FROM NorthwindbaK
```

The next example restores a full database backup and then a differential database backup on the Northwind database. It allows this by specifying the WITH NORECOVERY clause when restoring the master database. The NORECOVERY option tells the database engine that more backups will be applied after the current restore operation executes. It also prevents uncommitted transactions from being rolled back because additional transaction log backups may be restored that commit them. As a result, the NORECOVERY option must be specified for each restore operation except the final one in the sequence. After the last restore operation completes, the database should be available for user interaction, so you don't need to specify the NORECOVERY option.

Notice how the NORECOVERY option is specified in the full backup restore because the differential database must be applied before the database can be made available to users. Another thing to note is the WITH FILE = 2 in the second RESTORE statement. In this example, the full backup and the differential backup are stored on a device called NorthwindbaK. Assuming that these two backups were the only ones ever stored on the device, the FILE = 2 specifies that the second backup on the device should be used.

```
RESTORE DATABASE Northwind
  FROM NorthwindbaK
  WITH NORECOVERY
RESTORE DATABASE Northwind
  FROM NorthwindbaK
  WITH FILE = 2
```

The next example restores a full backup and transaction log backup. In this example, the database is recovered to a particular point in time using the STOPAT clause. This is useful in cases of user error where you know the time that a user made an error, because you can restore a database right up to the minute before the error. The code specifies two devices to restore the backups from because this scenario assumes the transaction log backups are stored on a separate device from the database backup.

```
RESTORE DATABASE Northwind
   FROM NorthwindbaK
   WITH NORECOVERY
RESTORE LOG Northwind
   FROM NorthwindLogbaK
   WITH RECOVERY, STOPAT = 'December 28, 2001 10:58 AM'
```

The SQL Server 2000 recovery architecture is very flexible, and the previous examples have only touched on the most common scenarios supported by it. So far we have discussed backup and recovery planning and implementation, but another common administrative chore is regularly checking the consistency of databases.

DATABASE CONSISTENCY AND THE DBCC STATEMENT

System and software errors can cause low-level errors in the data and page allocations of a database. To combat this problem, the DBCC T-SQL statement is used. The DBCC CHECKDB statement performs consistency checks of the data and data pages within a database and identifies, and in some cases automatically fixes, problems it discovers.

DBCC CHECKDB validates the consistency of everything in a database. For each table in a database (including its indexes), DBCC CHECKDB checks that:

- Index and data pages are linked correctly on a hard drive
- Indexes are arranged in their proper sort order
- All pointers are valid
- Data is spread out evenly across pages

In addition to performing regular database backups, a sound maintenance plan should include period consistency checks using the DBCC CHECKDB statement. It adheres to the following syntax:

```
DBCC CHECKDB
   ( '<Database_name>' ,
      <NOINDEX >                     (optional)
          <REPAIR Options:
 | REPAIR_ALLOW_DATA_LOSS
      | REPAIR_FAST
      | REPAIR_REBUILD
   >
 )
WITH <Other Options>
```

Consider the following example:

```
DBCC CHECKDB ('Northwind', NOINDEX)
```

In the example above, a consistency check is performed without checking the nonclustered indexes on user-defined tables in the Northwind database. The NOINDEX option will result in shorter execution time of the statement, thus impacting performance less.

When specified with one of three REPAIR options, the DBCC CHECKDB statement will repair errors it encounters while performing its consistency checks.

 When DBCC CHECKDB is run without a REPAIR option, it will only report errors it has found and will not attempt to fix them.

The REPAIR_FAST option causes the statement to perform minor repairs that are not time-consuming, such as repairing extra keys in nonclustered indexes. These repairs can be done quickly and without the risk of losing data. The REPAIR_REBUILD option performs all of the repair activities of the REPAIR_FAST option as well as more time-consuming fixes like rebuilding indexes. REPAIR_REBUILD fixes more problems but runs slower than the REPAIR_FAST option. Like the REPAIR_FAST option, REPAIR_REBUILD performs its fixes without jeopardizing any data in a database.

The REPAIR_ALLOW_DATA_LOSS option performs all of the checks of the errors that the REPAIR_REBUILD option does. On top of that, REPAIR_ALLOW_DATA_LOSS fixes allocation and structural problems at the page and row level. The activities it performs can result in data loss since physical storage space is reorganized in the process. Being the most comprehensive of all the repair options, REPAIR_ALLOW_DATA_LOSS takes the longest time to run, impacting performance the most.

 The REPAIR_ALLOW_DATA_LOSS option requires that the DB run in single user mode. Consequently, the database is inaccessible to users when repairing errors with DBCC CHECKDB and the REPAIR_ALLOW_DATA_LOSS option.

In the following example, the Pubs database is checked for errors and repaired accordingly. The highest level of error checking is performed through the REPAIR_ALLOW_DATA_LOSS repair option.

```
DBCC CHECKDB ('Pubs', REPAIR_ALLOW_DATA_LOSS)
```

Consistency checks using DBCC CHECKDB should be performed regularly on all databases to detect errors early and correct them before they make the database unusable. A thorough backup strategy should include regularly scheduled consistency checks prior to backing up databases. This will ensure that the backed up database does not have allocation or consistency errors.

Managing regular backups and consistency checks can be a complex and time-consuming task. To streamline the process of deploying and regularly running these types of operations, SQL Server 2000 has a utility called the Database Maintenance Plan Wizard that allows a database administrator to schedule backups and consistency checks easily to meet the needs of any database.

DATABASE MAINTENANCE PLANS

One feature of SQL Server 2000 is the Database Maintenance Plan Wizard, which aids in the creation of a database strategy that is right for your personal or corporate needs.

To access the Database Maintenance Plan Wizard, navigate to the Management folder in Enterprise Manager, right-click Database Maintenance Plans and click the New Maintenance Plan in the context-sensitive menu. The wizard will launch, showing the screen in Figure 7-14.

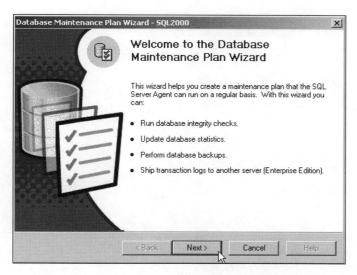

Figure 7-14   Database Maintenance Plan Wizard

The first step in creating a maintenance plan is to select the database you wish to regularly maintain. Click Next on the splash screen, and the Select Databases screen appears, as shown in Figure 7-15.

The Update Database Optimization Information screen shown in Figure 7-16 allows various optimization procedures to be configured and scheduled. From this screen, you can reorganize data and index pages, update distribution statistics used by the query analyzer, and even shrink databases to release unused disk space.

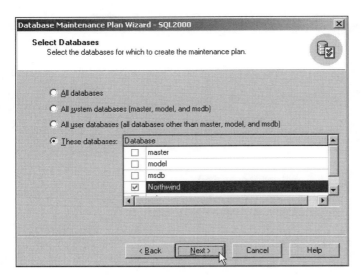

Figure 7-15   Selecting databases

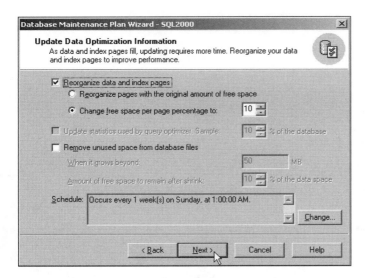

Figure 7-16   Updating data optimization information

Different activities in a maintenance plan can have their own execution schedule. A schedule option is available on almost every page of the Database Maintenance Plan Wizard. Clicking Change on any of these screens launches a simple interface for configuring a schedule, as shown in Figure 7-17.

The next screen in the Database Maintenance Plan Wizard, shown in Figure 7-18, is the Database Integrity Check screen.

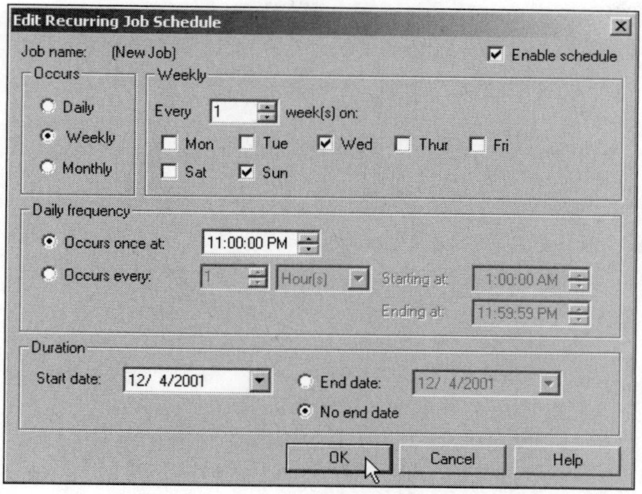

Figure 7-17   Edit Recurring Job Schedule window

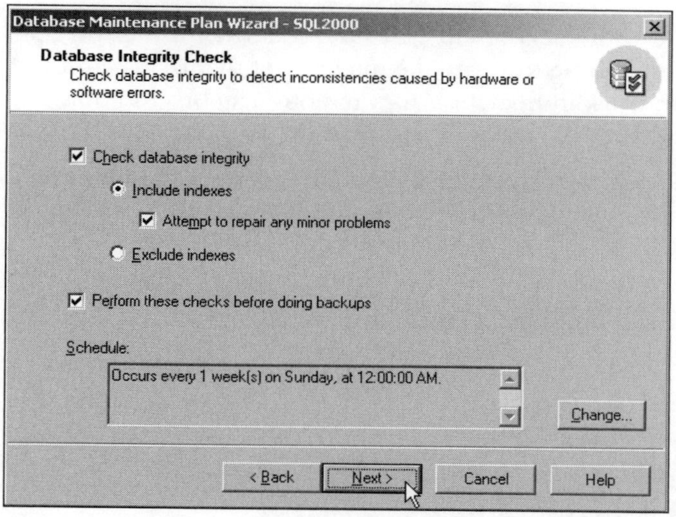

Figure 7-18   Checking database integrity

This screen allows the scheduling of the database integrity operations that check the database integrity to detect inconsistencies caused by hardware or software errors. You may choose to perform the checks prior to doing backups to ensure that the data being backed up is validated and repaired prior to the backup.

The next screen in the Database Maintenance Plan Wizard, shown in Figure 7-19, prompts you for a database backup plan.

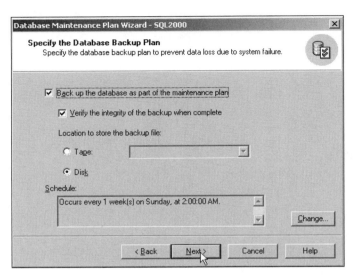

Figure 7-19   Specifying the database backup plan

You may choose to add your backup scheme to the database maintenance plan through this screen. You may also choose to verify the integrity of the database once it has completed (to ensure that a backup operation to a remote network location can complete successfully and that no file corruption was caused by traveling over the network).

The next step in the Database Maintenance Plan Wizard (if you choose to include database backups in the plan) allows you to specify the backup disk directory, as shown in Figure 7-20.

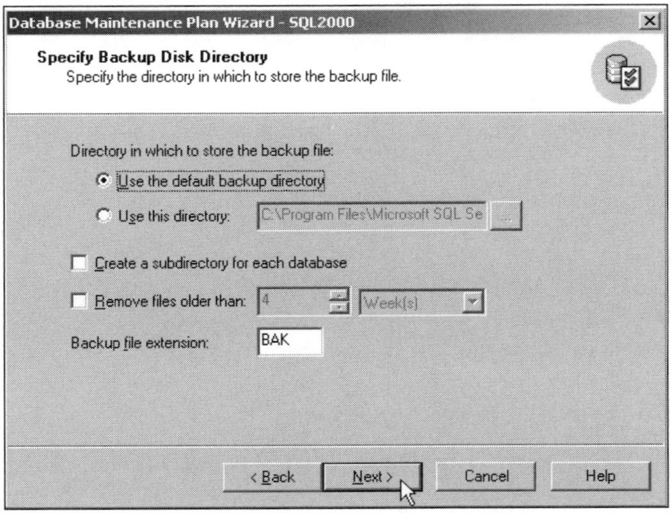

Figure 7-20   Specifying the backup disk directory

From this interface, you can specify the directory in which backups will be created. Additional configurations cause the maintenance plan to delete backups past a certain age or organize backups for different databases in different folders.

The same options are available for including transaction log backups as part of a maintenance plan. The next screen of the wizard, shown in Figure 7-21, prompts for transaction log backup requirements.

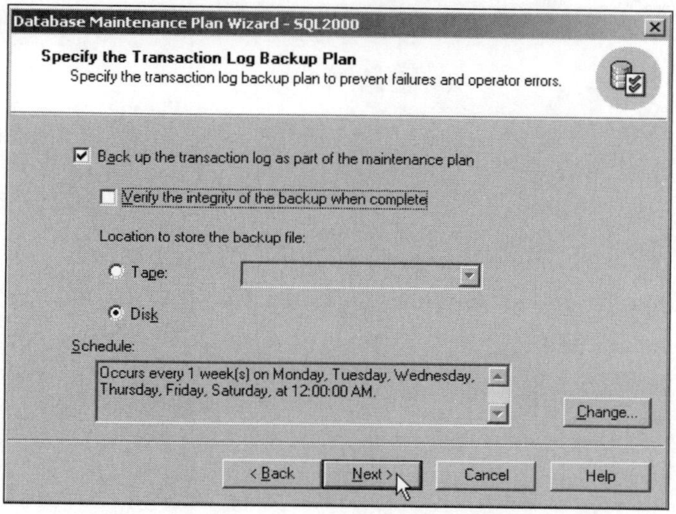

Figure 7-21   Specifying the transaction log backup plan

You can set the location of any transaction log backup from this screen. You also have the same types of options that were available with database backups in the previous steps.

The Reports to Generate screen, shown in Figure 7-22, allows you to specify a directory in which to store a text-based report generated each time the maintenance plan executes. This screen also allows you to manage disk usage of the reports by specifying the amount of time before reports are deleted. In addition to being stored on a hard drive, the reports can be sent directly to an administrator's e-mail box.

The last step in creating a maintenance plan through the wizard is specifying how and where to store the maintenance plan execution histories. As seen in Figure 7-23, histories can be written to the msdb.dbo.sysmaintplan_history table on the local server or a remote server.

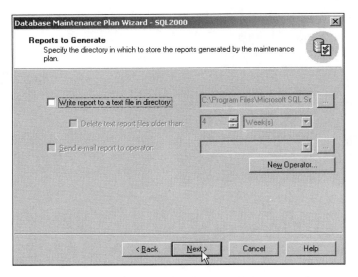

Figure 7-22   Configuring database maintenance plan reports

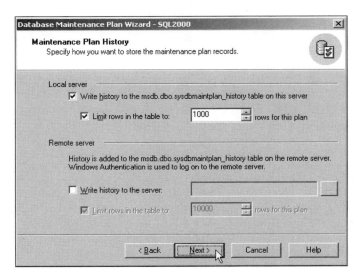

Figure 7-23   Maintenance Plan History screen

The Database Maintenance Plan Wizard is a powerful tool that can help you implement a backup scheme in minutes. Having the various operations of a backup plan scheduled to execute regularly also limits administrative overhead. The wizard can also be used to configure log shipping, a powerful feature of SQL Server 2000.

STANDBY SERVERS AND LOG SHIPPING

A warm standby server is a backup computer that is kept in sync with a computer supporting a production environment. They are used to recover the production database in the event of a hardware failure or to offload query processing by providing a read-only database for queries and reports. The simplest way to set up a backup server is to acquire a computer identical to the production server, install SQL Server 2000 Enterprise Edition on it, and copy the production databases to it regularly. A standby server can limit system downtime because backups from the production databases can be applied to it quickly, eliminating the need to repair failed hardware on the production server before bringing the database back online. The simplest warm standby servers are maintained by applying database backups to a remote server as they are performed (keeping the two machines somewhat in sync). The downside of this is the extra maintenance overhead for a database administrator. To simplify the process, SQL Server 2000 provides a feature known as log shipping.

Log Shipping

Log shipping is the process by which transaction logs are backed up from one database, copied to a remote SQL Server 2000 computer, and applied to an identical remote database. In the log shipping architecture, there are three entities that interact:

- A source server that houses a production database whose transaction log backups will be applied to one or more standby database servers

- One or more destination servers, which will receive transaction log backups from the source server and apply them to a local database

- A monitor server that is responsible for coordinating the log shipping process

Figure 7-24 outlines the basic log shipping architecture.

In this scenario, there are four servers that take part in the log shipping process. Server 1 is a source server and contains the database that the destination servers will maintain a copy of. Servers 3 and 4 are both destination servers and will regularly apply transaction logs they receive from the source server in order to remain in sync with it. Notice how the source server (Server 1) copies its transaction log backup files to the destination servers so that they can apply them.

Server 2 is the monitor server in this example. It continuously polls the source server for information about when it has shipped transaction log backups. It also polls the destination servers to gather information about when the transaction logs from the source server have been applied.

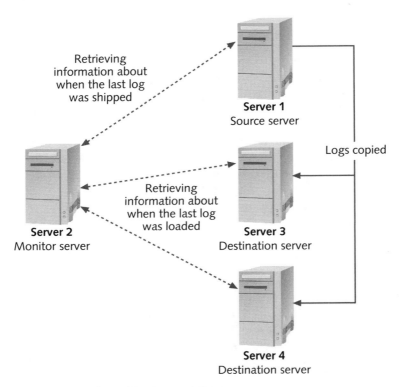

Figure 7-24   Log shipping architecture

Maintaining this information on the monitor server allows a time threshold to be set for applying transaction log backups to destination servers. The threshold refers to the time between when the source server reported the last transaction log backup and when a destination server last applied a copied log. If the threshold is exceeded, the monitor server generates "out of sync" alerts to inform an administrator of problems with the log shipping process.

The Database Maintenance Plan Wizard, discussed earlier, is used to configure log shipping to maintain standby servers automatically.

CHAPTER SUMMARY

- ☐ SQL Server 2000 provides a robust backup and recovery architecture that allows operations to be tailored to meet the individual needs of different systems. Transaction log backups can be used to recover a failed database all the way up to a specific time or even a specific transaction. This limits a database's exposure to data loss powerfully enough to meet the needs of even the most rigorous environments (like bank or financial institution databases).

❏ Backups are not the only tool for ensuring the integrity and consistency of data. Over time, small errors can occur within a database. The DBCC CHECKDB T-SQL statement is used to detect and repair these types of problems. This statement can repair poorly allocated index and data pages, improper index sort orders, etc.

❏ The SQL Server 2000 Database Maintenance Plan Wizard provides a time-saving interface for configuring recurring backup and consistency checking operations. Through a series of simple configuration screens, a database administrator can easily configure a backup plan and schedule its various operations. The wizard can also be used to configure log shipping.

❏ Log shipping is a powerful feature of SQL Server 2000 that maintains a warm standby server by automatically copying transaction log backups from a production database to a remote SQL Server 2000 instance and applying each log backup to a database that is kept in sync with the production system.

7

KEY TERMS

backup devices — Files on hard drives or other disk storage media (like tapes) that are used to store backups.

backup set — The unit in Microsoft tape format that houses a backup from a single source like SQL Server 2000 or Windows 2000/NT.

differential database backup — A type of backup that records only the changes made to the database since the last full database backup. The differential backup is smaller than the full database backup and consequently does not affect performance as much as a full database backup.

full database backup — A type of backup that creates a full copy of all of the data in a database.

log shipping — The process by which SQL Server 2000 can automatically apply transaction logs to a separate database, keeping a standby server in sync with the production server.

media — The largest unit in Microsoft Tape Format, it can house multiple backups from both Windows 2000/NT and SQL Server 2000.

Microsoft Tape Format (MTF) — A standard backup format developed by Microsoft to allow backups from multiple sources to be stored on the same media.

recovery model — The model by which you recover the backed up database. Recovery models include simple, full, or bulk-logged.

transaction log backup — A backup of the transaction log.

REVIEW QUESTIONS

1. Which T-SQL statement can be used to identify all of the errors in the Northwind database?

   a. `sp_dberrors 'Northwind'`

   b. `DBCC CHECKDB('Northwind')`

   c. `DBCC 'Northwind'`

   d. `DBCC DBERROR('Northwind')`

2. You need to back up an instance of SQL Server 2000 that resides on a network. One computer on the network has a tape drive that is available over the network and is used to backup the Windows 2000 network file server. A second computer on the network has ample disk space and is available to the SQL Server 2000 instance. The computer on which the instance is installed also has plenty of room on its hard drive. What is the best scenario to back up this database?

   a. Back up the data to the tape device across the network.

   b. Back up the data to a disk device on the remote server across the network.

   c. Create a new device on the disk that houses the database and back up the data there.

   d. none of the above

3. Log shipping can accomplish which of the following? Choose all that apply.

   a. off-load querying to another server

   b. provide a synchronized backup server

   c. create a new transaction log protocol

   d. none of the above

4. True or False: A tape device must have a physical tape that is large enough to store the entire contents of the backup. SQL server database backups cannot be segmented over two or more tapes.

5. Which database recovery model allows for the best performance and minimal use of log space?

   a. simple recovery

   b. bulk-logged recovery

   c. full recovery

   d. file or filegroup restore

6. Which database recovery model uses full and differential backups, but not transaction log backups?

   a. simple recovery

   b. bulk-logged recovery

   c. full recovery

7. True or False: Log shipping can be configured through the Database Maintenance Plan Wizard.

8. True or False: File backups don't require transaction logs to recovery a database.

9. _____ is a record of the transactions that have occurred against the database since the completion of the last transaction log backup.

   a. Index log

   b. Statistics log

   c. Replication log

   d. Transaction log

10. Which type of backup operation is typically used when working with very large databases?

    a. full database

    b. file backup

    c. differential database

    d. transaction log

11. True or False: A differential database backup records only those changes made to the database since the last transaction log backup.

12. Which of the following cannot be used as a database device?

    a. a file on the local computer

    b. a file on a network computer

    c. a tape in a tape drive connected to the local computer

    d. none of the above

13. What is the proper order of operations when restoring a database that uses full, differential, and transaction log backups in its backup scheme?

    a. transaction log(s), then the last differential backup, then the last full backup

    b. the last full backup, then transaction log(s), then the last differential backup

    c. the last full backup, then the last differential backup, then any of transaction log backups that have been performed since the last full backup

    d. the last full backup, then the last differential backup, then any of transaction log backups that have been performed since the last differential backup

14. True or False: SQL Server 2000 backups and Windows 2000 backups can be stored on the same physical tape.

15. Which backup scheme provides point-in-time recovery and the least recovery time?

    a. using both differential backups and transaction log backups with full backups

    b. using just transaction log backups with full backups

    c. performing a single full backup every night

    d. using user differential backups with full backups

16. Which of the following commands creates a new disk backup device named CustomerBackup in the 'C:\Backups' directory on the local computer?

    a. USE MASTER
       EXEC sp_adddumpdevice 'disk', 'CustomerBackup',
       'C:\Backups\CustomerBackup.dat'

    b. USE NORTHWIND
       EXEC sp_adddumpdevice 'disk', 'CustomerBackup',
       'C:\Backups\CustomerBackup.dat'

    c. USE MASTER
       EXEC sp_adddumpdevice 'CustomerBackup', 'disk',
       'C:\Backups\CustomerBackup.dat'

    d. USE MASTER
       EXEC sp_adddumpdevice 'disk',
       'C:\Backups\CustomerBackup.dat', 'CustomerBackup'

17. Which statement backs up up the Northwind database to a device called NorthwindBackup?

    a. BACKUP DATABASE Northwind USING NorthwindBackup

    b. BACKUP DATABASE Northwind (DEVICE='NorthwindBackup')

    c. BACKUP DATABASE Northwind TO NorthwindBackup

    d. BACKUP Northwind TO NorthwindBackup

18. Which of the following statements backs up the Northwind database to a device called NorthwindBackup and removes all existing backups on the device?

    a. BACKUP DATABASE Northwind TO NorthwindBackup
       WITH NOINIT

    b. BACKUP DATABASE Northwind TO NorthwindBackup
       WITH INIT

    c. BACKUP DATABASE Northwind USING NorthwindBackup
       WITH NOINIT

    d. USE MASTER
       BACKUP DATABASE Northwind TO NorthwindBackup
       WITH NOINIT

19. Which statement performs a differential backup on a database called Accounting and appends the backup to a device called AccountingBackup?

    a. `BACKUP DATABASE Accounting TO AccountingBackup`
       `WITH DIFFERENTIAL`

    b. `BACKUP DATABASE Accounting TO AccountingBackup`
       `WITH DIFFERENTIAL, INIT`

    c. `BACKUP DATABASE DIFFERENTIAL Accounting`
       `USING AccountingBackup`
       `WITH NOINIT`

    d. `USE MASTER`
       `BACKUP DATABASE Accounting TO AccountingBackup`
       `TYPE = 'DIFFERENTIAL'`

20. Which statement backs up the transaction of the Northwind database to a device called MyBackup?

    a. `BACKUP LOG Northwind ON MyBackup`

    b. `BACKUP DATABASE LOG Northwind TO MyBackup`

    c. `BACKUP LOG Northwind TO MyBackup`

    d. `BACKUP LOG Northwind TO DEVICE('MyBackup')`

21. Which statement performs a file backup of the Customer_Data_1 file in the Customer database to the CustomerBackup disk device?

    a. `BACKUP DATABASE Customer`
       `TO CustomerBackup`
       `WITH FILE = 'Customer_Data_1'`

    b. `BACKUP DATABASE Customer('Customer_Data_1')`
       `TO CustomerBackup`

    c. `BACKUP DATABASE Customer`
       `FILE = 'Customer_Data_1'`

    d. `BACKUP DATABASE Customer`
       `FILE = 'Customer_Data_1'`
       `TO CustomerBackup`

22. Which statement restores a full backup of the Northwind database from a device named NorthwindBackup?

    a. `RESTORE DATABASE Northwind`
       `FROM NorthwindBackup`

    b. `RESTORE FULL DATABASE Northwind`
       `FROM NorthwindBackup`

    c. `RESTORE DATABASE Northwind`
       `USING NorthwindBackup`

    d. `RESTORE DATABASE Northwind`
       `TO NorthwindBackup`

7

23. Which set of statements restores a full backup of the Northwind database from a device named NorthwindBackup and then applies a differential backup of the same database from a device named NorthwindDiff?

    a. ```
       RESTORE DATABASE Northwind
       FROM NorthwindBackup
       WITH RECOVERY
       GO
       RESTORE DATABASE Northwind
       FROM NorthwindDiff
       WITH RECOVERY
       ```

    b. ```
       RESTORE DATABASE Northwind
       FROM NorthwindBackup
       WITH NO RECOVERY
       GO
       RESTORE DATABASE Northwind
       FROM NorthwindDiff
       WITH RECOVERY
       ```

    c. ```
       RESTORE DATABASE Northwind
       FROM NorthwindDiff
       WITH NORECOVERY
       GO
       RESTORE DATABASE Northwind
       FROM NorthwindBackup
       WITH RECOVERY
       ```

    d. ```
       RESTORE DATABASE Northwind
       TO NorthwindBackup
       WITH DIFFERENTIAL ON 'NorthwindDiff'
       ```

24. A full backup of the Northwind database is performed on Sunday night. It is stored on a device called NorthwindBackup. A differential backup is performed on Tuesday morning and written to the same device (NorthwindBackup). If the system fails on Tuesday afternoon, which set of statements could be run to recover the database to the point in time when the differential backup was performed?

    a. ```
       RESTORE DATABASE Northwind
       FROM NorthwindBackup
       WITH NORECOVERY
       GO
       RESTORE DATABASE Northwind
       FROM NorthwindBackup
       WITH FILE = 1, RECOVERY
       ```

    b. ```
       RESTORE DATABASE Northwind
       FROM NorthwindBackup
       WITH NORECOVERY
       GO
       RESTORE DATABASE Northwind
       FROM NorthwindBackup (FILE = 2)
       WITH RECOVERY
       ```

c. RESTORE DATABASE Northwind
   FROM NorthwindBackup
   WITH NORECOVERY
   GO
   RESTORE DATABASE Northwind
   FROM NorthwindBackup
   WITH FILE = 2, RECOVERY

d. RESTORE DATABASE Northwind
   TO NorthwindBackup
   WITH DIFFERENTIAL ON 'NorthwindBackup (FILE = 2)'

25. Which system database stores information about database maintenance plans for historical purposes?

a. Master

b. Model

c. Tempdb

d. msdb

7

HANDS-ON PROJECTS

Project 7-1

In this exercise, we will use Enterprise Manager to perform a full backup of the Northwind database on the local instance of SQL Server 2000. As part of the operation, we will create a new backup disk device to house the full backup.

To create a new backup disk device and perform a full backup of the Northwind database:

1. Launch Enterprise Manager by clicking **Start**, highlighting **Programs**, highlighting **Microsoft SQL Server**, and clicking on **Enterprise Manager**.

2. Navigate to the **Management** folder of the local SQL Server 2000 instance.

3. Right-click the **Backup** option and click the **New Backup Device** option from the context-sensitive menu.

A backup device must exist before you can perform a database backup. For simplicity, in this exercise we will create the device on the local computer, though in a production environment, we recommend using a remote machine to store devices.

4. The Backup Device Properties window should appear with the default MSSQL\BACKUP directory in the "File name" text box. In this example, we are backing up the Northwind database. Enter **NorthwindBackup** into the Name text box. The filename should now read "…\MSSQL\BACKUP\NorthwindBackup.BAK".

5. Click **OK** to create the device. The device should now appear in the right-hand window of the Enterprise Manager.

6. Right-click the newly created device in Enterprise Manager and click **Backup a Database** in the context-sensitive menu.

7. The SQL Server Backup window appears. Choose the **Northwind database** from the Database list box.

8. Choose the **Database – complete** option in the Backup section of the window.

9. We will select our database device from the Destination section of the window. Click **Add**.

10. Choose the **Backup device** option.

11. Choose the **NorthwindBackup Device** from the list box and click **OK**. Verify that the screen looks like the one in Figure 7-25.

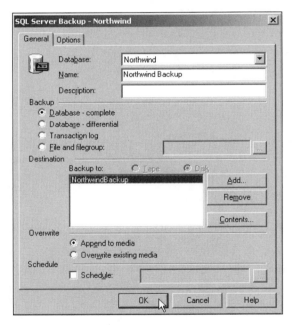

Figure 7-25   Performing a full backup of the Northwind database

12. Click **OK** in the SQL Server Backup window.

13. A window displaying the progress of the backup appears and then a message box should appear stating, "The backup operation has been completed successfully." We have just successfully backed up the Northwind database. Click **OK** to close the message box.

14. View the contents of the completed backup by double-clicking the **NorthwindBackup** device in Enterprise Manager.

15. Click the **View Contents** button to verify that the full backup was performed, as shown in Figure 7-26. Close the **View Contents** screen, the **Back-up Device** screen, and **Enterprise Manager** when done.

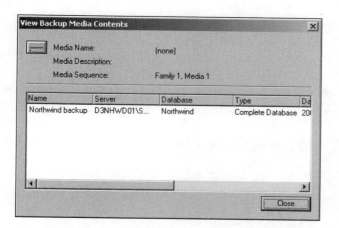

Figure 7-26 Viewing the contents of the NorthwindBackup device

Project 7-2

In this exercise, we will use Enterprise Manager to perform a differential backup and a transaction log backup of the Northwind database on the local instance of SQL Server 2000. As part of the operation, we will append the differential database backup and the transaction log backup to the NorthwindBackup backup device introduced in Project 7-1.

To perform a differential and a transaction log backup of the Northwind Database and append them to an existing device:

1. Launch Enterprise Manager by clicking **Start**, highlighting **Programs**, highlighting **Microsoft SQL Server**, and clicking **Enterprise Manager**.

2. Navigate to the **Management** folder of the local SQL Server 2000 instance and expand the Back-up node.

3. Right-click the **NorthwindBackup** backup device (created in Project 7-1) and click the **Backup a Database** option from the context-sensitive menu.

4. The SQL Server Backup window appears. Select the **Northwind** database from the Database list box.

5. Select the **Database – differential** option in the Backup section of the window.

6. Ensure that the **Append to media** option is selected in the Overwrite section of the window. This tells SQL Server 2000 to add the backup to the device without overwriting existing backups on the device.

7. Click **OK** in the SQL Server Backup window.

7

8. A window displaying the progress of the backup appears, and then a message box should appear stating, "The backup operation has been completed successfully." We have just successfully created a differential backup of the Northwind database. Click **OK** to close the message box.

9. View the contents of the completed differential backup by double-clicking the **NorthwindBackup** item device in Enterprise Manager and then clicking the **View Contents** button in the Backup Device Properties screen. There should now be two backups on the device, as shown in Figure 7-27.

10. Close the **View Contents** screen and then the **Back-up Device Properties** screen when done.

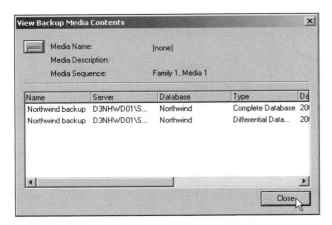

Figure 7-27   The NorthwindBackup device now has both the full and differential backup on it

 We will now append a backup of the transaction log to the NorthwindBackup device. In order to backup the transaction logs of a database, the recovery model of the database must be either full or bulk-logged. The Northwind database is configured for the simple recovery model by default, so it must be changed before the transaction log backup can be performed.

11. Change the recovery model by right-clicking the **Northwind** database item in Enterprise Manager and clicking **Properties** in the context-sensitive menu.

12. Click the **Options** tab of Database Properties window and choose **Full** from the Model list box in the Recovery section of the window. Click **OK**. The database is now configured properly for transaction log backups. Return to the devices listed in the Backup node under the Management folder in Enterprise Manager.

13. Right-click the **NorthwindBackup** device and click the **Backup a Database** option in the context-sensitive menu.

14. The SQL Server Backup window appears. Select the **Northwind** database from the Database list box.

15. Select the **Transaction log** option in the Backup section of the window.

16. Verify that your screen looks similar to the one in Figure 7-28, and click **OK** to perform the log backup.

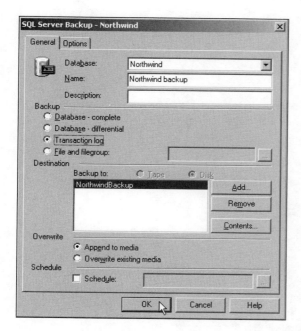

Figure 7-28 Performing a transaction log backup of the Northwind database

17. A window displaying the progress of the backup appears and then a message box should appear stating, "The backup operation has been completed successfully." Click **OK** to close the message box. We have just successfully created a transaction log backup of the Northwind database.

Project 7-3

In this exercise, we will restore the backups of the Northwind database performed in Project 7-1 and 7-2. We will use Enterprise Manager to restore the database from the NorthwindBackup disk device on which it is stored.

To restore the full backup of the Northwind database using Enterprise Manager:

1. Launch the SQL Server Enterprise Manager by clicking **Start**, highlighting **Programs**, highlighting **Microsoft SQL Server**, and clicking **Enterprise Manager**.

2. Right-click on the **Northwind** database, highlight **All Tasks**, and then click the **Restore Database** item in the context-sensitive menu.

3. Check to make sure the **Restore as database** list box has the **Northwind** database selected.

4. The window should show the most recent backups for the Northwind database by default, as shown in Figure 7-29.

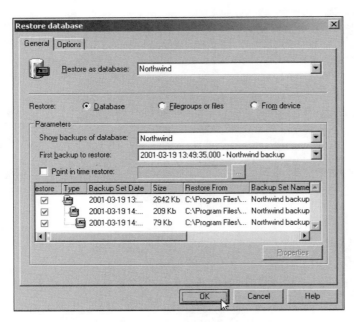

Figure 7-29   Restoring a database with backups

 The information about database backups is maintained in the msdb system database. This allows Enterprise Manager to display various backups for you, thus saving time and effort.

5. Select the **Options** tab of the Restore database window, and check the **Prompt before restoring each backup** option, as shown in Figure 7-30.

6. Click **OK** in the Restore database window to start the restore process.

7. Click **OK** as the various prompts appear when each backup is restored.

8. Click **OK** in the Restore Successful message box and close the Enterprise Manager when done.

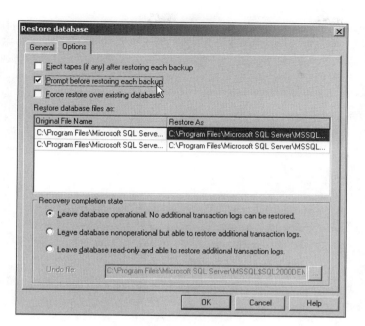

Figure 7-30   Setting restore options

Project 7-4

To create a database backup maintenance plan for the Northwind database using the Database Maintenance Plan Wizard:

1. Launch the SQL Server Enterprise Manager by clicking **Start**, highlighting **Programs**, highlighting **Microsoft SQL Server**, and clicking **Enterprise Manager**.

2. Navigate to the **Managment** directory, right-click the **Database Maintenance Plans** operation, and choose **New Maintenance Plan** from the context-sensitive menu.

3. The first screen explains the operations that can be set during the setup of the maintenance plan. Click **Next** when ready.

4. The next screen (Select databases) allows you to select the databases that will be included in the maintenance plan. Choose the **Northwind database** by clicking the check box next to it in the database list. Click **Next** to continue.

5. The next screen allows you to reorganize data and index pages, update statistics used by the query optimizer, and remove unused space from the database files. For the purposes of this example, we are focused on the scheduling of the database backups and will not choose any of these options. Click **Next** to continue.

6. This screen allows you to check the integrity of the database to detect inconsistencies. It is wise to check the integrity of the database before each backup, so we will do so here. Check the **Check database integrity** option and then check

Exclude indexes to speed up the integrity operation. Also check the **Perform these checks before doing backups** option to ensure that consistency errors are discovered and repaired prior to backing up the database. Your screen should look like Figure 7-31.

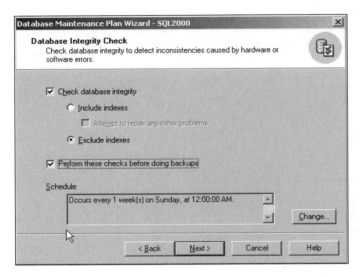

Figure 7-31   Database integrity checking options in the Database
Maintenance Plan Wizard

Leave the schedule alone for now, as our main purpose is to check the database integrity prior to backup. Click **Next** to continue.

7. The next screen allows you to schedule the backup as part of the maintenance plan and verify the integrity of the database after the backup has completed. Select both options. The location of our backup file will be on disk as opposed to tape.

8. Click **Change** to alter the schedule for the backup operation.

9. Using the Edit Recurring Job Schedule screen, modify the schedule so that the operations occur daily at 2:00 A.M., as shown in Figure 7-32. Click **Next** to continue.

10. We will use the default directory to store our backup file, and we will remove files older than five weeks. Make the appropriate changes on this screen, so that yours matches the one shown in Figure 7-33. The backup file extension should remain as the default (.BAK). Click **Next** to continue.

11. We are going to backup the transaction log every four hours, since we are making a complete database backup every morning. Check the **Back up the transaction log as part of the maintenance plan** check box. Make the appropriate schedule change to have the transaction log backed up every four hours. Check the **Verify the integrity of the backup when complete** option. Click **Next** when complete.

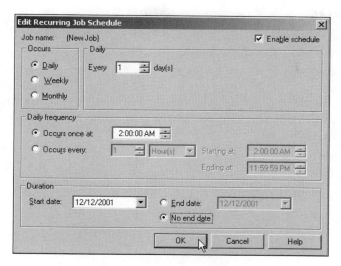

Figure 7-32   Scheduling the backup operations

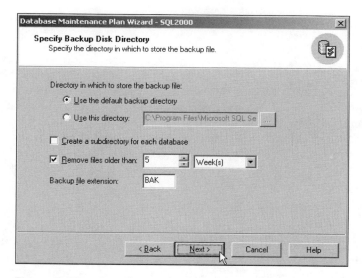

Figure 7-33   Specifying a backup disk directory in the Database Maintenance Plan Wizard

12. The next screen asks you to specify the location for the transaction log's storage. Use the default backup directory. Configure the screen to remove files older than one week to avoid having transaction log backups taking up too much available disk space over time. We will use the default backup file extension of TRN. Make these changes to this screen and click **Next**.

13. The next screen allows you to configure where reports of the maintenance plan are stored. Keep the default log directory and delete files older than four weeks (the length of time that our oldest database is still stored in this example). Click **Next** to proceed.

14. On the Maintenance Plan History screen, configure the plan to use the local server to store the maintenance plan records and limit the rows in the table to 1000 rows again to conserve space. Click **Next**.

15. The next screen displays the options you chose throughout the wizard. Specify the Plan Name as **Northwind Backup Maintenance Plan**. Verify that all your configurations are correct and click **Finish**. A plan has now been created that we can edit at any time by double-clicking the plan name in the right-hand window of Enterprise Manager.

16. Close **Enterprise Manager** when done.

 Make sure the SQL Server Agent is running prior to the execution of any of the operations specified in the plan.

CASE PROJECTS

Case One

Consider a situation where you are the SQL database administrator for a small company with limited free disk space available on its network. The company is growing at a very fast pace, but has little funds to allocate to new hardware; although a currently unused tape drive and spare tapes are a form of data storage available. A database is used to support the company's 24-hour customer support objectives. The database is backed up at a regular interval at 12:00 A.M. daily, and a differential database backup is scheduled to occur at 1:00 P.M. each day. The transaction log backup is scheduled to occur at 6:00 P.M., also on a daily basis. You are receiving messages regularly, stating that the transaction log is full. Based on your knowledge from this chapter and SQL Server Books Online what is the best strategy to resolve your company's issue?

Case Two

Consider the situation where a critical database in your company resides on a disk that has failed at 10:05 P.M. The transaction log backup and database backup were on another disk. The last database backup was at 8:00 P.M. that evening and the transaction log gets backed up every hour on the hour. How would you restore the database to the state it was in at 10:00 P.M?

Case Three

Assume that your company is implementing their disaster recovery strategy and that they would like you to determine and implement a plan that would limit system downtime to under one hour. Using your knowledge from this chapter and SQL Server Books Online, how will you deliver the desired results to your employer?

8

SECURITY IN SQL SERVER 2000

> **After reading this chapter and completing the exercises you will be able to:**
> ♦ Understand the security architecture of SQL Server 2000
> ♦ Manage logins, users, and roles
> ♦ Manage permissions
> ♦ Control access with database objects and ownership chains
> ♦ Audit SQL Server 2000

In most database systems, a flexible security infrastructure is required to control access to various types of data, which often require different security models. SQL Server 2000 offers a robust security architecture that can handle even the most complex security models.

Integration with Windows user accounts and groups offers increased ease of management when providing access to database users. SQL Server 2000 instances can be configured to allow access to Windows user accounts and groups. In addition to Windows accounts, SQL-based logins (managed by SQL Server 2000 rather than a Windows domain) can be created to allow non-Windows users to connect to database instances. Both of these types of users are considered logins by SQL Server 2000 and are granted access only at the instance level. These logins must be mapped to database users to provide access to individual databases residing on an instance. To simplify management, you can add Windows groups as logins, providing access to numerous individuals through a single security context. You can also define SQL Server roles, to group users who need similar permissions to a database. This is especially helpful when an applicable Windows group is not available. Roles are assigned permissions, and the users and Windows groups that are members of the roles inherit those permissions.

You can also specify permissions directly for database users (which are mapped to Windows users and groups, as well as SQL Server logins). Permissions control access to database objects and administrative functions. Once a security model is established and permissions are set, user activity can be audited for analysis. Auditing is the process of tracking actions performed by users. Security actions, like successful and failed login attempts, are recorded through auditing to preserve a historical record of activity.

Every network environment has different users and groups set up to control access to different resources like file servers, printers, and e-mail. In the SQL Server 2000 security scheme, the resources are database objects (like tables and views) and administrative T-SQL statements (like CREATE DATABASE). Each instance of SQL Server 2000 will have different security requirements, depending on the types of users needing access and the types of data stored in the databases. You should always identify and document the various users and groups that will need access to SQL Server 2000 prior to implementing security. Before implementing an effective security scheme, it is imperative to understand how SQL Server 2000 handles security.

SECURITY ARCHITECTURE IN SQL SERVER 2000

The security features of SQL Server 2000 provide authentication and authorization functionality. **Authentication** is the first stage of security, and it identifies a user based on the login information they provide. Authentication only verifies that a user can connect to a SQL Server 2000 instance. It does not provide access to databases and their objects. **Authorization** is the second stage of security, and it occurs when database permissions are checked to determine which actions a particular user can perform within a database.

This dual-phase approach to user validation is implemented in SQL Server 2000 through various user-access objects, including logins, database users, and roles. Logins provide access to the instance, and are, in turn, mapped to database users to provide access to various databases housed within the instance. The two-step process is illustrated in Figure 8-1.

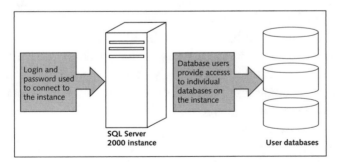

Figure 8-1 Authentication and authorization through logins and database users

Both Windows users and Windows groups can be added as logins. Using Windows groups (both global and local) simplifies administration by allowing access to be controlled at the group level, instead of managing access rights on each individual user in a group. When an applicable Windows group does not exist, a SQL Server role can be created that will group users together to provide permissions to a database. Roles are simply user-defined groups of users that can have permissions applied to them within SQL Server 2000 databases.

Consider the diagram shown in Figure 8-2. Notice how there are various users and groups defined in the network environment. In this scenario, there is a Windows local group called Accounting that contains some individual users as well as a Windows global group called Finance. There is also a Windows user without a group affiliation and a UNIX user who will need access to SQL Server 2000 as well. Notice how the Windows-based users and groups work transparently with SQL Server 2000. To provide access to a user without a Windows account (UNIXJoe in this example), a SQL Server 2000-based user account is created, allowing the user to explicitly provide credentials when accessing an instance and its databases. Also notice, how a SQL Server role is used to group the users within SQL Server. In this example, all of the users except DOMAIN\Jsmith are members of the Order Entry role. Permissions can be applied to the role and inherited by its members to control access to databases.

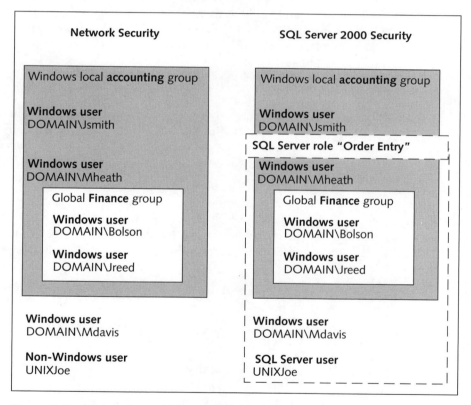

Figure 8-2   Network security mapped to SQL Server security

Logins

Authentication is implemented using logins in SQL Server 2000. **Logins** are SQL Server 2000 objects that allow users to connect to the instance. As we have already discussed, SQL Server 2000 is tightly integrated with the Windows operating system, and as such, Windows users and groups can be easily added as logins to SQL Server 2000. SQL Server 2000 can also manage its own logins to provide access to users without a Windows account.

Authentication Modes

A SQL Server 2000 instance can run in Windows Authentication Mode and Mixed Authentication Mode. Windows Authentication Mode allows users to connect to SQL Server 2000 instances using their Windows user account (a user account from a Windows NT or Windows 2000 domain). Mixed Authentication Mode allows both Windows accounts and SQL Server logins to be used to connect to instances.

Windows Authentication Mode

When Windows authentication is used, SQL Server calls out to the Windows domain to validate the account. When a user tries to connect to an instance of SQL Server 2000 without specifying a user name or password, Windows Authentication Mode is used. If the Windows credentials of the user are flagged as a valid login for a SQL Server 2000, then the user is allowed to connect to the instance.

When an instance is configured to use Windows Authentication Mode, any credentials (user name and password) explicitly provided by a user are ignored and the Windows credentials of the user are validated. Windows Authentication Mode provides several advantages over native SQL Server authentication. In addition to limiting administration of a user to a single location (within a Windows domain), Windows authentication provides the following benefits:

- Secure validation of credentials through Windows and encryption of passwords passed over the network

- Windows password requirements, like password expiration and minimum password length

- Automatic locking out of accounts that repeatedly fail to connect (for example, repeatedly providing a wrong password)

- Native auditing capabilities of Windows accounts

Mixed Authentication Mode

In Mixed Authentication Mode, either a Windows-based account or a SQL Server 2000-based login can be used to connect to an instance. Mixed Authentication Mode is provided for backward compatibility with older applications designed to utilize SQL

Server-based logins. It is also necessary for situations where users connecting to an instance of SQL Server 2000 do not have a Windows domain account (for example, a user who works on a UNIX computer). SQL Server authentication is used when an instance is configured for Mixed Authentication Mode and a user specifies user name and password information when attempting to connect to an instance. If no credentials are explicitly provided, then Windows Authentication Mode is used.

Changing the Authentication Mode of a SQL Server 2000 Instance

Once an authentication mode is specified for a SQL Server 2000 instance, it can be modified easily through Enterprise Manager. To modify the authentication mode, right-click on the instance in Enterprise Manager and choose Properties from the context-sensitive menu. Click the Security tab of the SQL Server Properties window to access the screen shown in Figure 8-3.

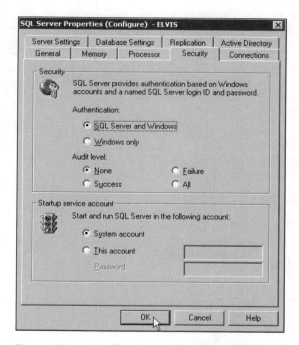

Figure 8-3   Configuring authentication mode for an instance

Choose the "Windows only" option to configure the instance to run in Windows Authentication Mode. Choose the SQL Server and Windows option to configure the instance for Mixed Authentication Mode.

Managing Logins in SQL Server 2000

Authentication is the first step in accessing databases in a SQL Server 2000 instance and verifies that the user can connect to the instance. Before accessing various databases on the instance, the user must first have a valid login and be able to connect to the instance. Depending on the authentication mode implemented in an instance, Windows users and groups can be added as logins (in Windows and Mixed authentication modes), and user-defined SQL Server logins (in Mixed Authentication Mode) can be created to provide access to users without a Windows account. To manage login information, expand a registered server in Enterprise Manager, expand the Security folder, and click the Logins item. Figure 8-4 shows the default view for logins in an instance of SQL Server 2000.

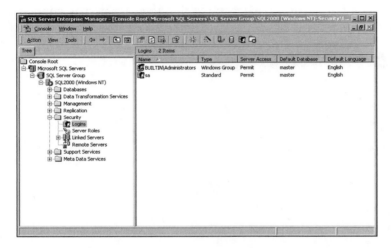

Figure 8-4   Default logins in Enterprise Manager

 By default, a SQL Server 2000 instance has logins set up for the sa SQL Server login and the local computer's BUILTIN\Administrators group. These logins provide system administrator privileges so that administrative users can connect to the instance after it has been installed, but before it has been configured with individual logins.

Creating Logins with Enterprise Manager

To create a login in a SQL Server 2000 instance, right-click on the Logins item in the security folder and click the New Login item. This brings up the SQL Server Login Properties screen shown in Figure 8-5.

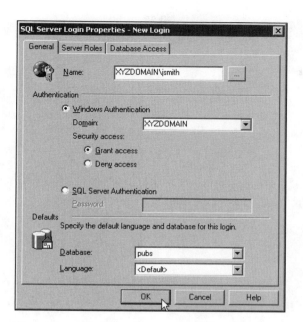

Figure 8-5   SQL Server Login Properties screen

If Windows authentication is selected, a Windows domain and either a user or a group are specified to provide access to the instance. In this example, the Jsmith user from the domain XYZDOMAIN is being added as a login on an instance of SQL Server 2000. The syntax for adding a Windows user or group is DOMAINNAME\userorgroupname. By default, a new login is granted access to an instance, but you could explicitly deny access to Windows users or groups as well. Notice that you can specify a default database and language for the login as well. When a default database is specified, the login will automatically use the database specified.

However, this process does not give database access permission to the login, it merely forces a particular database to be chosen when the user connects to the instance. This same interface can be used to create SQL Server 2000 logins used in Mixed Authentication Mode. If this is required, a password must be supplied, and the Domain name qualification in the login name is not needed. For example, if the user Jsmith did not have a Windows user account, you could add a SQL Server login and name it Jsmith.

To delete a login in Enterprise Manager, right-click on the login and choose **Delete** from the context-sensitive menu.

All of these functions can also be performed through T-SQL statements.

Managing Logins with T-SQL Statements

SQL Server 2000 provides several system-stored procedures for adding Windows users and groups as logins and creating SQL Server 2000-based logins for an instance. These procedures are available only to system administrators.

Windows-Based Logins The sp_grantlogin system-stored procedure is used to add Windows users and groups to a SQL Server 2000 instance. It has the simple syntax of:

```
EXEC sp_grantlogin 'DOMAINNAME\userorgroupname'
```

To grant access to the Windows user Jsmith in the XYZDOMAIN domain, you could use:

```
EXEC sp_grantlogin 'XYZDOMAIN\Jsmith'
```

The sp_denylogin system-stored procedure is used to deny access to a particular Windows user or group, without removing its SQL Server login entries. It has the simple syntax of:

```
EXEC sp_denylogin 'DOMAINNAME\userorgroupname'
```

To deny access to the Windows user Jsmith in the XYZDOMAIN domain, you could use:

```
EXEC sp_denylogin 'XYZDOMAIN\Jsmith'
```

The sp_revokelogin system-stored procedure is used to remove a login for a Windows user or group. It has the simple syntax of:

```
EXEC sp_revokelogin 'DOMAINNAME\userorgroupname'
```

To remove the login for the Windows user XYZDOMAIN\Jsmith from an instance of SQL Server 2000, you could use:

```
EXEC sp_revokelogin 'XYZDOMAIN\Jsmith'
```

SQL Server 2000-Based Logins The system-stored procedures used to add and remove logins for SQL Server authentication are: sp_addlogin and sp_droplogin. The sp_addlogin stored procedure has the following syntax:

```
EXEC sp_addlogin 'SQLServerloginname', 'password',
'defaultdb', 'DEFAULTLANGUAGE'
```

To create a login for SQL Server authentication, use the sp_addlogin stored procedure and specify both the login name and password parameters, which are not optional. For example, to add a login named Owilson with a password of '02031965', whose default database is Pubs, use the following call:

```
EXEC sp_addlogin 'Owilson', '02031965', 'Pubs'
```

This login could be removed easily by using the sp_droplogin system-stored procedure. It takes the login name as its only parameter:

```
EXEC sp_droplogin 'Owilson'
```

Remember that logins are only the first line of control in the SQL Server 2000 security architecture. Logins need to be mapped to database users to provide access to the data and functionality provided by each database.

Other Stored Procedures for Working with Logins As we saw in the Enterprise Manager interface for creating new logins, both a default database and default language can be set for each new or existing login. The sp_defaultdb and sp_defaultlanguage stored procedures are used to specify a default database and language for a login. They implement a similar syntax:

```
EXEC sp_defaultdb 'loginname', 'databasename'
```

And

```
EXEC sp_defaultlanguage 'loginname', 'language'
```

To change the default database and language for a login named Bridget, use the following code:

```
EXEC sp_defaultdb 'Bridget', 'Northwind'
GO
EXEC sp_defaultlanguage 'Bridget', 'english'
```

8

DATABASE USERS

Database users are individual accounts stored within each database that control access to database objects through permissions. A login has a database user in each database to which it requires access. Permissions are then applied to the database user to control access to objects in the database. User actions within a database are checked against permissions assigned to the user before they are permitted. If the user is not authorized to perform the action, then an "Insufficient Permissions" error is returned to the user.

Database users are mapped to Windows users, Windows groups, and SQL Server logins. All of the permissions within the database are controlled at the user level. The database user is first used to authenticate the user to the database when it initially connects. Once connected, each statement that the user attempts to run is checked against the permissions applied to the database user account.

Windows groups added as logins to SQL Server 2000 instances can help aid in organizing and controlling access for multiple users. Often, there is not an applicable Windows group for users who require the same access to data. SQL Server 2000 alleviates this problem with user-defined database roles.

Roles

Roles allow you to group database users (and even logins) who perform similar functions and to apply permissions for the group instead of the individual users. Roles also allow both Windows and SQL Server logins to be grouped together, which eases administration in diverse network environments. For example, you could create a database role called Accounting that contains the database users mapped to the Windows group Finance and various SQL Server logins (given to outside financial consultants who don't need Windows user accounts in the domain). You could apply permissions to the role to access tables containing sensitive financial information and just add members to the role. This simplifies security administration by eliminating the need to apply complex permissions to each user who requires them. SQL Server 2000 provides a predefined set of fixed roles at both the database level and the instance level, but user-defined roles can only be defined in databases.

Fixed Server Roles

Fixed server roles are associated with Windows and SQL Server logins defined for an instance. They are used to provide special permissions, like configuring instance-wide settings and creating databases that cannot be explicitly provided to individual logins. Table 8-1 outlines the set of predefined fixed server roles provided with SQL Server 2000.

Table 8-1   Fixed Server Roles

Fixed Server Role	Description
sysadmin	Allowed to perform any action in SQL Server
serveradmin	Allowed to configure instance-wide settings and shut down the instance
setupadmin	Allowed to manage linked servers and startup procedures
securityadmin	Allowed to manage logins and provide CREATE DATABASE permissions to them, read error logs, and change passwords
processadmin	Allowed to manage running processes in SQL Server 2000
dbcreator	Allowed to create, modify, and delete databases
diskadmin	Allowed to manage disk files
bulkadmin	Allowed to use the BULK INSERT statement to perform mass imports of data

To add logins to a fixed server role, click on Server Roles under the Security folder in Enterprise Manager. Right-click on a fixed server role and click the Properties item from the context-sensitive menu. This brings up the Server Role Properties window shown in Figure 8-6. Click Add to choose the logins to add to the roll.

Any login that belongs to a role can add other logins to it.

Fixed Database Roles   There are also several predefined roles in each database that provide sets of permissions for the database users who belong to them. Table 8-2 outlines the fixed database roles available in all user-defined databases.

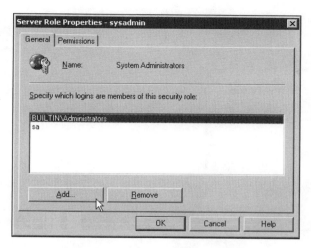

Figure 8-6 Adding logins to fixed server roles

Table 8-2 Fixed Database Roles

Fixed Database Role	Description
db_owner	Allowed to perform all of the operations permitted to the other roles, as well as activities to maintain and configure the database
db_accessadmin	Allowed to manage database users mapped from Windows users, Windows groups, and SQL Server logins
db_datareader	Allowed to see (read access) all data in all of the user-defined tables in a database
db_datawriter	Allowed to insert, update, and delete data from all user-defined tables
db_ddladmin	Allowed to create, modify, and remove all database objects, like tables and views
db_securityadmin	Allowed to manage roles and role membership, as well as to apply permissions to database users and roles
db_backupoperator	Allowed to back up the database
db_denydatareader	Not allowed to view data in the database
db_denydatawriter	Not allowed to modify data in the database
Public	The default role of which every database user is a member. If a user does not have permission to access an object like a table, then the permissions of the public role are checked as a last resort.

Unlike server roles, custom database roles can be created to accommodate special groups of users who require identical access to the database. For example, the Windows marketing and inside sales groups may require the same access permission to data stored in a database to work on promotions. You could create a database role called Promotions and assign the appropriate permissions to it. The Windows groups could then be added to it to inherit the access rights.

To create a custom role in a database with Enterprise Manager, expand a database, right-click on the Roles item, and choose New Database Role from the context-sensitive menu. This brings up the Database Role Properties window shown in Figure 8-7.

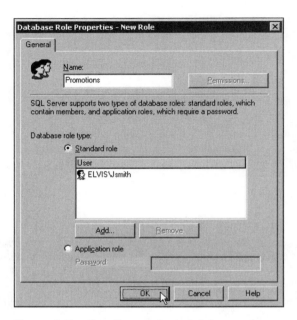

Figure 8-7   Creating custom database roles

In this screen, you can specify the new role name and associate users with the role. Once the role is created (by clicking OK), you can specify permissions within the database.

To create a new database role with T-SQL, use the sp_addrole system-stored procedure with the following syntax:

```
sp_addrole 'newrolename', 'owner'
```

Owner is an optional parameter that can be either a valid database user or role name. By default, the owner of roles is dbo. To create a new role called Promotions in the Northwind database, use the following code:

```
USE Northwind
GO
EXEC sp_addrole 'Promotions'
```

Application Roles

Application roles are special roles that don't contain users. They are used by applications to connect to SQL Server 2000 databases. These are used primarily when an application is managing user authentication itself but still requires access to the database. For example, a reporting application could manage users itself (outside of

SQL Server 2000) and only show certain reports to certain users, but the application itself must connect to a database to generate the reports. An application role with read-only permissions to certain tables in the database could be created for the reporting application.

Creating Database Users

You can create database users using either Enterprise Manager or T-SQL statements. The only prerequisite for creating a database user is that a login must already exist on the instance.

To create a database user with Enterprise Manager, expand a database, right-click on the Users item, and click the New Database User item from the context-sensitive menu. This brings up the Database User Properties window shown in Figure 8-8.

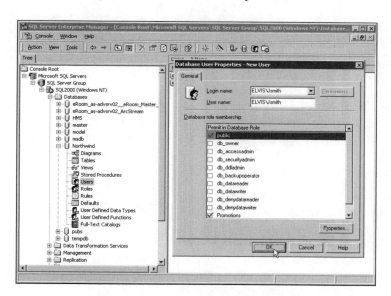

Figure 8-8   Creating database users with Enterprise Manager

From this screen, select a login (ELVIS\Jsmith in this example) to map the new database user to. The user name will default to the login name, but it can be altered if needed. Role membership can also be assigned when the user is created using this interface. Individual user permissions (discussed later in this chapter) are available after the database user has been created.

To create a database user using T-SQL, map a login to a database user with the sp_grantdbaccess system-stored procedure. Use the sp_addrolemember system-stored procedure to add database users to roles within the database. These stored procedures must be run in the database in which the new user is being added. They have the following syntax:

```
EXEC sp_grantdbaccess 'loginname', 'dbusername'
```

And

```
EXEC sp_addrolemember 'rolename', 'dbusername'
```

For example, to add the database user shown in Figure 8-8 (ELVIS\Jsmith) to the Northwind database as a member of the Promotions role, use the following T-SQL statement:

```
USE Northwind
GO
EXEC sp_grantdbaccess 'ELVIS\Jsmith', 'ELVIS\Jsmith'
GO
EXEC sp_addrolemember 'Promotions', 'ELVIS\Jsmith'
```

DBO and the Guest Database User

Every database in an instance of SQL Server 2000 can have two special users. The **database owner (dbo)** is a special user that has permissions to perform all database activities. This user exists in every database and can not be removed. Members of the sysadmin fixed server role use the dbo user. Additionally, the dbo user owns any objects created by a member of the sysadmin fixed server role. These objects are referenced as dbo.objectname in T-SQL statements.

The **guest user** is a special account that allows database access to a login without a mapped database user. Permissions can be applied to it as if it were any other user. It is useful if there are several people who only need access to the database for a short period of time. For example, a company who constantly has temporary workers performing data entry may assign appropriate permissions to the guest user and elect to have the various temps access the database through it. Unlike the dbo user, the guest user can be deleted from all databases except master and tempdb.

 The guest user is not created by default in new databases.

At this point, we have discussed the purposes and management of various objects required to access SQL Server 2000 instances and databases, including logins, roles, and database users. In the next section, we explore the permissioning system implemented in SQL Server 2000 databases and how object-level access is controlled within each database.

PERMISSIONS

SQL Server 2000 uses a complex permissioning system to control database access at a very granular level. Every action within a database, including accessing and altering data and modifying database objects, requires a specific permission. There are three types of permissions that can be used to control user access within a database. They are:

- *Object permissions:* allow access/modification to data as well as the execution of stored procedures and user-defined functions
- *Statement permissions:* allow access to certain object-creation T-SQL statements like CREATE DATABASE and CREATE TABLE
- *Implied permissions:* permissions only available through predefined roles

Object Permissions

As implied by their name, **object permissions** in databases allow users to work with objects and they can be granted to users or roles for database objects. These types of permissions allow users to insert, update, delete, and select data from tables and views. Object permissions can be granted on individual columns in tables and views, and they can also be applied to stored procedures and user-defined functions to allow users to execute them.

Insert and delete operations affect entire rows of data and can only be applied at the table level.

Statement Permissions

Statement permissions are used to allow users to create databases and database objects. This type of permission is applied to the statement itself. Access to the following statements are controlled through statement permissions:

- CREATE DATABASE
- BACKUP DATABASE
- BACKUP LOG
- CREATE TABLE
- CREATE VIEW
- CREATE RULE
- CREATE DEFAULT
- CREATE PROCEDURE
- CREATE FUNCTION

Implied Permissions

Implied permissions are special privileges that are provided through membership to a user-defined role. These are often permissions that cannot be explicitly provided to individual users. For example, the db_securityadmin predefined database gives its members permissions to manage the permissions of other users. Adding a user to a predefined role is the only way to provide certain types of permissions.

Implied permissions are also provided through database object ownership. For example, the owner of a table (the user who created the table) is given permission to perform insert, update, delete, and select operations against the table.

Applying Permission

Permissions within databases are hierarchical and, consequently, are inherited through group and role membership. Since a database role can contain users, groups, and other roles, permissions could be applied to a high-level role, and all of the users and groups associated with that role would receive the rights assigned to it. For example, consider a scenario where a database has a role called Sales. This role contains two other roles as members: Sales-East and Sales-West. These roles contain regional salespeople as members from two regions. If all sales personnel, regardless of region, need access to a table called Customer, permissions could be granted to the Sales role and inherited by the user Jsmith, who is a member of the Sales-East role. Hierarchical permissioning limits the amount of maintenance required to control access to databases, but is important to understand how permissions are applied and how conflicting permissions for a single user are handled to properly manage access to a database.

Managing Permissions in Databases

Both statement and object permissions can be assigned to users, groups, and roles within a database. Each permission can be granted, denied, or revoked.

When a permission is granted to a user (for example INSERT permission on the Customer table), the user is able to perform the operation in the database. Since permissions are assigned at all levels in the security hierarchy (users, groups, and roles) and inherited based on role memberships, there may be the need to limit access to an individual or role. In this case, permissions need to be denied to a user.

For example, the Promotions database role has permission to insert, update, and delete data in two tables: Customer and Campaign. User Dclune is a member of the Promotions role and needs full access to the Campaign table, but he is only doing data entry into the Customer table and should not be allowed to change or delete existing data. By default, Dclune inherits the permissions assigned to the Promotions role. To override the role permissions inherited by Dclune without affecting other members of the role, you could deny the Dclune user UPDATE and DELETE permissions on the Customer table. The denied permissions at the user level take precedence over conflicting permissions assigned at the role level.

Permissions already granted or denied are removed by revoking them. Revoking disallows access at a user or role level, but it doesn't prevent permissions from being inherited from role hierarchies like denying does.

Managing Statement Permissions Most statement permissions are easily managed through Enterprise Manager. To administer statement permissions within a database, right-click on the database in Enterprise Manager and choose the Properties item from the context-sensitive menu. When the database Properties window appears, click on the Permissions tab, as shown in Figure 8-9.

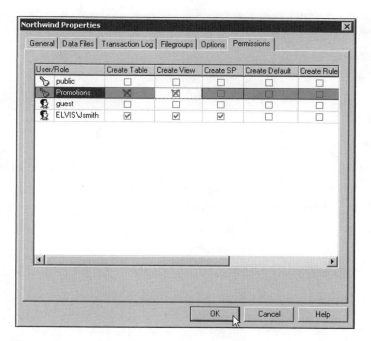

8

Figure 8-9 Granting statement permissions in Enterprise Manager

In this example, the ELVIS\Jsmith user is granted permission to create tables, views, and stored procedures. Granted permissions are signified by a green check in this interface. Notice also, that all database roles are available here for statement permissioning. In Figure 8-9, the Promotions role has been denied permission to create tables and views. Denied permissions are signified by red "X" marks in each check box. The unchecked boxes signify a permission that is neither granted nor denied. When a check box is toggled to blank from another setting, SQL Server 2000 revokes the permission.

Statement permissions can also be granted through T-SQL statements. The GRANT statement provides permissions to users and roles and adheres to the following syntax:

```
GRANT <STATEMENT (S)> TO <USERS, GROUPS or ROLES>
```

Multiple statements can be applied in a single GRANT operation by separating each statement with a comma. Similarly, you can grant multiple users and roles the statement permissions by separating their names with commas. In the following example, both the user ELVIS\Jsmith and the Promotions role are granted permission to use the CREATE TABLE and CREATE VIEW statements within the Northwind database.

```
USE Northwind
GO
GRANT CREATE TABLE, CREATE VIEW TO Promotions,
[Elvis\Jsmith]
```

The DENY statement explicitly denies permissions to users and roles and adheres to the following syntax:

```
DENY <STATEMENT (S)> TO <USERS, GROUPS or ROLES>
```

The following statement denies the use of the CREATE PROCEDURE statement to a role called Accounting in the Northwind database.

```
USE Northwind
GO
DENY CREATE PROCEDURE TO Accounting
```

The REVOKE T-SQL statement is used to revoke existing statement permissions for a user or role. It adheres to the following simple syntax:

```
REVOKE <STATEMENT (S)> TO <USERS, GROUPS or ROLES>
```

The following T-SQL statements are used to revoke CREATE TABLE statement permission from a user called Jsmith in the Northwind database:

```
USE Northwind
GO
REVOKE CREATE TABLE TO Jsmith
```

 The REVOKE T-SQL statement removes existing GRANT or DENY statement permissions. If neither of these permissions exist, the statement executes with no effect.

Managing Object Permissions   Object permissions are managed in a similar way to statement permissions. In fact, the interface in Enterprise Manager is strikingly similar for both object and statement permissions, and the same T-SQL statements are used to administer them.

To apply object permissions in Enterprise Manager, expand a database and then click the Users node. Right-click on a user and choose Properties from the context-sensitive menu. When the Database User Properties window appears, click the Permissions button to access the interface for assigning an object permissions, as shown in Figure 8-10. This interface displays a list of all objects in the database and various permission check boxes for each object. Only the applicable permissions (based on an object's type) are available. For example, a stored procedure only has a check box for EXECUTE permission, but not SELECT, INSERT, UPDATE, or DELETE.

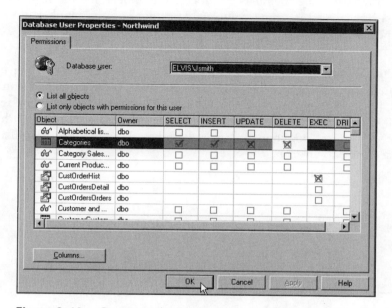

Figure 8-10 Granting object permissions in Enterprise Manager

The interface elements are the same as those for statement permissions. A green check signifies that a particular permission is granted to a user, and a red "X" signifies that the permission is denied. These settings are toggled back and forth by clicking the check box multiple times. In Figure 8-10, the Windows user Elvis\Jsmith is granted SELECT and INSERT permission on the categories table and denied UPDATE and DELETE permissions.

Object permissions are managed by the same set of T-SQL statements as statement permissions. The syntax used is slightly different, however, because database objects must be specified.

```
GRANT <PERMISSION(S)> ON <OBJECTNAME> TO <USER or ROLE
NAME>
```

To provide a user named Sean full access to a table named Products, use the following syntax:

```
GRANT SELECT, INSERT, UPDATE, DELETE ON Products TO Sean
```

The syntax is similar for both the REVOKE and DENY statements when administering object permissions.

Resolving Permission Conflicts

As discussed earlier in this chapter, permissions are handled in a hierarchical fashion, meaning that users and roles that are members of another role inherit the permissions applied to that role. As security becomes more complex, depending on the number of users and roles as well as possible overlapping permissions, conflicts can arise. SQL Server 2000 has a specific set of rules that it uses to handle permission conflicts.

SQL Server 2000 always applies deny permissions first when evaluating a particular action for authorization. Denied permissions always take precedence over conflicting granted permissions at the user or role level. Additionally, when permissions are revoked, SQL Server 2000 simply removes the previous granted or denied permission. Other permissions inherited from role memberships or applied directly to the user are still applied. Consider the scenario shown in Figure 8-11.

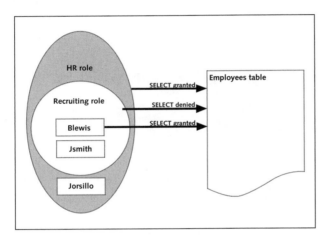

Figure 8-11   Conflicting permissions

In this situation, the user Blewis is a member of the Recruiting role, which is, in turn, a member of the HR role. Notice that conflicting SELECT permissions are applied. Both the Blewis user and the HR role have been granted SELECT permission on the Employees table. However, since the Recruiting role has been denied SELECT permission on the Employees table, both the Blewis and Jsmith users (members of the Recruiting role) may not perform SELECT operations against the table. Since the Jorsillo user is a member of the HR role (which has been granted SELECT permissions to the employees table), it can access the Employees table.

Object permissions are not the only way to control access to data in a SQL Server 2000 database. Database objects like views and stored procedures can be used to hide certain pieces of data or perform operations like inserting data into tables.

IMPLEMENTING SECURITY THROUGH DATABASE OBJECTS

Various programmable database objects can be designed to limit data access to users. Views provide filtered or composite views of tables with which users can interact. Stored procedures, user defined functions, and triggers can perform complex operations on multiple tables without requiring that the user know the underlying table structure. Another important security factor associated with database objects is the idea of ownership. The user who creates an object owns it, but in databases where multiple users are creating tables, views, and stored procedures, the chain of ownership will impact how permissions are checked and applied.

Securing Data with Views

As discussed in Chapter 4, views can be defined to provide either a filtered set of table columns or a limited set of data rows from underlying tables. A common use of a view is to create a special representation of a table that does not contain certain sensitive information. For example, a table named Employee includes name and contact information as well as personal information, like social security number and age. A view could be created that has the contact information but not the sensitive information. Users could then be granted permissions on the view to access the underlying data stored in the Employee table.

Securing Data with Stored Procedures and User-Defined Functions

Stored procedures and user-defined functions allow sets of T-SQL statements to be stored and executed as a single unit. They are typically used to enforce business rules or perform logic. Stored procedures are often used to encapsulate data modification operations like inserts and updates. For example, a single stored procedure called UpdateEmployee could perform updates to both the employee and salary tables in a transaction. In this case, a user could be granted EXECUTE permission on the procedure without being granted permissions to the tables that it affects.

Controlling Access with Triggers

Triggers are similar to stored procedures in that they contain saved groups of T-SQL statements. Triggers are not called directly however, so permissions cannot be granted directly to use them. Instead they are controlled by insert, update, and delete permissions on the table with which they are defined. Consider a situation where a user in the OrderManagement role inputs orders into a table called Order. Every time a new order is entered, the Inventory table must be updated to reflect the current stock level for certain products. However, the OrderManagement role should not have direct access to the Inventory table. In this scenario, a trigger that automatically updates the Inventory table when a new row is added could be created on the Order table. This way, only insert permissions on the Orders table need to be granted to the member of the OrderManagement role.

Understanding Ownership Chains

Database objects like stored procedures and views are based on other objects in the database. Stored procedures and views provide a way for users to access underlying objects but bypass the permissions set on those objects. The hierarchy of underlying objects and their owners is checked to determine access. Views can be based on other views and tables, and stored procedures can be based on other stored procedures, views, and tables. The hierarchy of underlying objects is known as an **ownership chain**. As is implied in the name, object ownership has a lot to do with ownership chains.

As we discussed earlier in this chapter, objects are owned by the users who create them. In most databases, a single user creates (and therefore owns) all of the objects. In this scenario, the ownership chain is simple. Consider the situation where a view called CustomerNames is based on a table called Customer. If the same user owns both objects, then only the permissions on the view (and not the table) are checked when a user accesses the view. Similarly, if a stored procedure called UpdateAddress updates data in a table called Address, and both objects are owned by the same user, then permissions are only checked on the stored procedure when a user executes it. In more diverse database environments where several users are creating objects, ownership chains become more complex.

When the same user who created a view or stored procedure does not own the underlying objects for the view or stored procedure, the ownership chain is considered broken. In these situations, permissions are checked on the objects whose predecessor in the ownership chain is owned by a different user. This allows the user who created the underlying object to maintain control over it.

When an ownership chain is not broken (all objects owned by the same user), permissions only need to be granted at the top level of the hierarchy. For example, the user Jsmith creates a view called CustomerView based on a table called Customer that it also owns. Jsmith could grant permissions to the user Dwang to use the view. When Dwang accesses the view, permissions on the underlying Customer table are not checked. In a broken ownership chain, the permissions of various objects are checked and can prevent access to users who have been granted permissions on an object in the chain. Consider the ownership chain illustrated in Figure 8-12.

Assume that Bill has granted a user named Henry EXECUTE permission on Procedure1. When Henry attempts to use the stored procedure, his permissions on Procedure1, Procedure2, Table1, and Table2 are checked to ensure that he has the appropriate permissions to access all of the underlying objects. Henry's permissions on View1 are not checked because the object above it in the ownership chain (Procedure1) is owned by the same user (Bill). Also note that even though Bill owns Table2, Henry's permissions on it are checked because the object above it in the ownership chain (Procedure2) is owned by a different user (John).

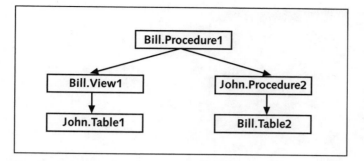

Figure 8-12   Ownership Chain

So far we have discussed the architecture of SQL Server 2000 security, including authentication through logins and authorization through statement and object permissions. In most environments, security is a top priority and, in addition to controlling access to databases, there is often a requirement to record events to preserve a history of actions against an instance of SQL Server 2000.

AUDITING SECURITY IN SQL SERVER 2000

Auditing security events in SQL Server 2000 allows a historical record of activity to be made for later review. This is helpful to identify attempts by users to violate security policies. You can configure a SQL Server 2000 instance to audit login attempts in order to track users connecting it. Each time a user attempts to log in to the instance, the attempt is written to the Windows application log and the SQL Server error log. This is helpful in identifying failed login attempts and, consequently, tracking down potential security risks. To configure login auditing for an instance, right-click on it in Enterprise Manager and choose Properties from the context-sensitive menu. Click on the Security tab of the SQL Server Properties (Configure) window as shown in Figure 8-13.

Four options are presented in the Audit level section of this screen:

- *None:* disables auditing for the instance
- *Success:* records successful login attempts
- *Failure:* records failed login attempts
- *All:* records both successful and failed login attempts

 You must restart the instance to begin login auditing if it is not already running.

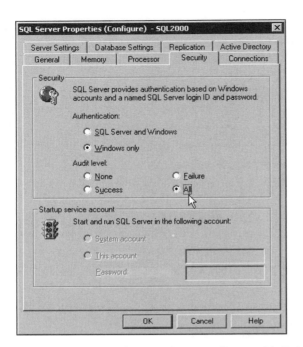

Figure 8-13   Configuring login auditing with Enterprise Manager

C2 Auditing

Class C2 is a rating granted by the National Computer Security Center (NCSC) for products that have been evaluated against the Department of Defense Trusted Computer System Evaluation Criteria (TCSEC). The Class C2 evaluation criteria is the minimum security rating required by many government agencies and offices (branches of the military, IRS, Federal Reserve, intelligence agencies, etc.) and by many corporations.

Systems evaluated for a C2 rating provide for discretionary access (need-to-know) protection and accountability of subjects and objects through audit capabilities. This means that based on the permissions on various objects (tables, columns, stored procedures, etc), the system will either authorize or deny access to other users.

A system rated at Class C2 provides a Trusted Computing Base (TCB) that implements the following mechanisms:

- User identification and authentication to control general system access
- Discretionary access control to protect objects and allow users to distribute access to those objects as appropriate
- Auditing to enforce general user accountability

In order for SQL Server 2000 instances to be C2 compliant, they must be run in the evaluated configuration to be assured that these mechanisms operate as intended.

When a SQL Server 2000 instance is operating in C2 mode, auditing will record events to a file in the \mssql\data subdirectory below the installation directory for default instances of SQL Server 2000, or the \mssql$instancename\data subdirectory for named instances of SQL Server 2000.

When C2 auditing is configured, SQL Profiler can be used to monitor object-level permissioning events as they occur. It can also be used to open and inspect the trace files created by C2 auditing. C2 auditing can be enabled using the sp_configure stored procedure to set the 'c2 audit mode' server setting to 1.

 Setting up SQL Server 2000 within a Windows network in a C2 certified mode is a very complex task. For more information on the C2 certified configurations supported with SQL Server 2000, visit the SQL Server homepage at *www.microsoft.com/sql*.

CHAPTER SUMMARY

8

❑ SQL Server 2000 has a flexible and scalable security architecture capable of supporting the full spectrum of requirements from 10 users to 10,000 users. Validating user activity is implemented as a two-part process consisting of authentication and authorization. Authentication is the process by which users are allowed to connect to an instance of SQL Server 2000 and is handled through the use of the login security object. Authorization is the process by which access to databases, objects, and statements is validated. Logins require a separate database user account in each database to gain access. Object and statement permissions are assigned at the database level to users. Roles are an organizational unit in databases that allows users to be grouped together and share a set of permissions. SQL Server 2000 is capable of meeting rigorous C2 certification standards for security and auditing.

KEY TERMS

application roles — Special roles that can be assigned permissions and used by applications to access databases.

authentication — The first stage of security, responsible for verifying that a user can connect to a SQL Server 2000 instance.

authorization — The second stage of SQL Server 2000 security, responsible for checking permissions to determine which actions a particular user can perform within a database.

Class C2 — A security rating granted by the National Computer Security Center (NCSC) for products that have been evaluated against the Department of Defense Trusted Computer System Evaluation Criteria (TCSEC).

database owner (dbo) — A special database user that exists in every database and has permissions to perform all activities on that database.

database user — An account within a database that is mapped to a login to provide access to the database.

fixed server roles — A set of predefined roles that are available in SQL Server 2000 instances to provide access to common instance-wide administrative functionality. They provide special permissions, like configuring instance-wide settings and creating databases, that cannot be explicitly provided to individual logins.

guest user — A special account that can be used by people who have a login on an instance but don't have a mapped database user for the database they wish to access.

implied permissions — Special privileges that are provided by membership to a user-defined role.

Login — A SQL Server object that provides connection access to an instance of SQL Server 2000 (authentication). Logins can be based on Windows users and groups defined natively in SQL Server 2000.

object permissions — Permissions that allow users or roles to access objects in a database. Object permissions are applied to a user to control INSERT, UPDATE, and DELETE actions against tables. They are also used to allow users to execute stored procedures and user-defined functions.

ownership chain — A hierarchy of dependent objects. For example, a view based on a view that is based on two tables. An ownership chain is considered "broken" if all of the objects are not owned by the same user.

roles — The equivalent of user groups in SQL Server 2000. Roles are used to administer permissions in a single location for multiple users (when an applicable Windows group is not available).

statement permissions — Permissions that allow users to execute certain T-SQL statements like CREATE TABLE and CREATE VIEW.

REVIEW QUESTIONS

1. What SQL Server 2000 object do you use to organize users who perform similar functions and require the same permissions?

    a. groups

    b. roles

    c. families

    d. none of the above

2. True or False: Statement permissions allow users to insert data into a table.

3. Which statement will allow a Windows user named Bill from the XYZ domain to connect to an instance of SQL Server 2000?

   a. EXEC sp_grantlogin 'Bill', 'XYZ'

   b. EXEC sp_addlogin 'XYZ\Bill'

   c. EXEC sp_grantlogin 'XYZ\Bill'

   d. EXEC sp_addlogin 'Bill', 'XYZ'

4. True or False: A SQL Server login is automatically locked if too many failed login attempts are made with it.

5. Which function(s) are members of the sysadmin fixed server role able to perform?

   a. configure instance-wide settings

   b. create databases

   c. manage disk files

   d. all of the above

6. Which statement will create a SQL Server login named JohnDoe?

   a. EXEC sp_addlogin 'JohnDoe', '12345'

   b. EXEC sp_addlogin '12345', 'JohnDoe'

   c. EXEC sp_grantlogin 'JohnDoe'

   d. EXEC sp_login 'JohnDoe', '12345'

7. Members of which pre-defined database role(s) are allowed to insert, update, and delete data from all user-defined tables?

   a. db_owner

   b. db_datareader

   c. db_datawriter

   d. a and b

   e. b and c

8. Which of the following cannot be granted as a statement permission?

   a. CREATE DATABASE

   b. DBCC CHECKDB

   c. BACKUP DATABASE

   d. CREATE TABLE

9. Which database role are all users a member of by default?

   a. guest

   b. public

   c. db_datareader

   d. db_datawriter

8

10. Which object cannot be used to control the way users access data?

    a. view

    b. trigger

    c. index

    d. stored procedure

11. True or False: The dbo user cannot be removed from any database.

12. Which account allows a login without a mapped database user to access database objects?

    a. public

    b. dbo

    c. sa

    d. guest

13. Which statement allows a user named Robin to add records to a table named Customer?

    a. GRANT INSERT TO Robin

    b. REVOKE DELETE ON customer TO Robin

    c. GRANT UPDATE ON customer TO Robin

    d. GRANT INSERT ON customer TO Robin

14. What is an application role?

    a. a role containing users who access databases through the same client application

    b. a predefined role that only allows Windows users and groups to be members

    c. a role without members, used exclusively by an application to connect to a SQL Server 2000 database.

    d. none of the above

15. Which of the following is a government certification standard for security and auditing?

    a. ANSI-92

    b. C2

    c. ISO9000

    d. C12

16. A user named Colleen is granted access to SELECT from the Products table. She is also a member of the Managers role, which has been denied select permissions on the Products table. Given the circumstances, will Colleen be able to perform SELECT operations against the Product table?

    a. yes

    b. no

17. Which statement adds the user Deirdre to a role named Corporate?

    a. sp_addrole, 'Corporate', 'Deirdre'

    b. sp_addrolemember 'Deirdre', 'Corporate'

    c. sp_grantdbaccess 'Deirdre', 'Corporate'

    d. sp_addrolemember 'Corporate', 'Deirdre'

18. Which system–stored procedure is used to remove a login from a SQL Server 2000 instance?

    a. sp_droplogin

    b. sp_revokelogin

    c. sp_grantlogin

    d. sp_denylogin

19. What is the name of the condition where dependent objects (e.g., a view based on a table) do not have the same object owner?

    a. severed linkage

    b. Mixed Authentication Mode

    c. broken ownership chain

20. Which statement will allow a database user named Kostas to use a stored procedure named UpdateInventory?

    a. GRANT SELECT ON UpdateInventory TO Kostas

    b. GRANT EXECUTE ON UpdateInventory TO Kostas

    c. GRANT EXCUTE TO Kostas ON UpdateInventory

    d. GRANT SELECT TO Kostas ON UpdateInventory

8

HANDS-ON PROJECTS

Project 8-1

To create a new Windows 2000 user and add a login to an instance of SQL Server 2000 (to keep things simple, we will create a Windows local user on the same machine as the database instance):

1. Click **Start**, highlight **Programs**, highlight **Administrative Tools**, and click the **Computer Management** item.

2. Expand the **Local Users and Groups** node in the Computer Management window, right-click on the **Users** folder and choose **New User** from the context-sensitive menu, as shown in Figure 8-14.

3. Create an account named **securitytest** in the New User window.

4. Provide a password that is easy to remember.

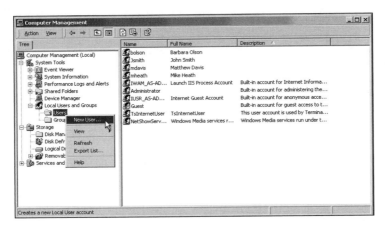

Figure 8-14 Create a new local user in Windows 2000

5. Uncheck the **User must change password at next logon** option. Ensure that your entries are similar to those in Figure 8–15.

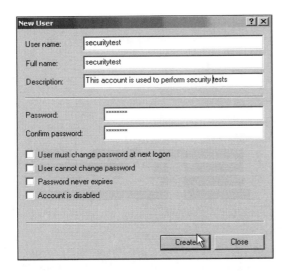

Figure 8-15 Windows 2000 New User screen

6. Click **Create** to create the account.

7. Click **Close** to exit the New User window. Notice that the securitytest user now appears in the list of local users. Close the Computer Management window when done.

8. Open Enterprise Manager and double-click on your local instance of SQL Server 2000.

9. Expand the Security folder, right-click on the **Logins** node, and choose **New Login** from the context-sensitive menu.

10. In the New Login window, click the **...** button next to the name text box to access a list of available Windows users and groups.

11. Ensure that your local computer is selected in the **List Names From** list box at the top of the screen.

12. Click on the **securitytest** user in the list of names (you may have to scroll down) and then click **Add**. Your screen should look like the one shown in Figure 8-16.

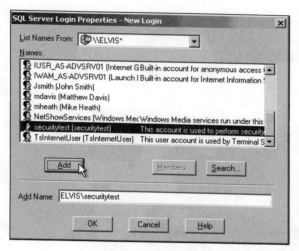

Figure 8-16   Selecting a Windows user when creating a new login for SQL Server 2000

13. Click **OK** when you are finished.

14. Click **OK** to create the login. Leave Enterprise Manager open for the next project.

Project 8-2

To add the securitytest user we created in Project 8-1 to roles and give it access to the Northwind database:

1. In Enterprise Manager, expand the **Security** folder of your local instance and then click the **Logins** node.

2. Right-click on the computername\securitytest login on the right side of the screen and choose **Properties** from the context-sensitive menu.

3. Change the default database for the login to **Northwind** by selecting it from the **Database** list box.

8

Setting the default database does not provide access to it. It is used to specify which default database to perform actions against, but it does not grant permission to the login to access the database in any way.

4. Click the **Database Access** tab to map the login to database users.

5. Click the **Permit** check box for the Northwind database, as shown in Figure 8-17.

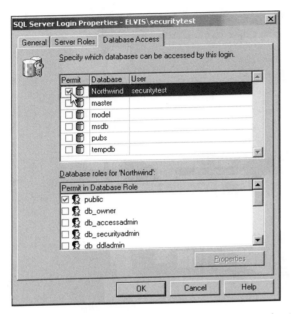

Figure 8-17   Providing database access to a login

6. Click **OK** to apply your changes.

7. Expand the Northwind database folder in Enterprise Manager and click the **Users** node.

8. Right-click the **securitytest** user in the list of users, highlight **All Tasks**, and then click **Manage Permissions**.

9. In the Database User Properties window, scroll down to the **Shippers** table in the list of objects.

10. Click the **SELECT** check box (make sure to set it to a green check) for the Products table as shown in Figure 8-18.

11. Click **OK** to finish the process.

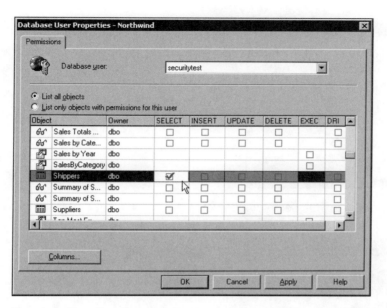

Figure 8-18   Granting database permissions in Enterprise Manager

Project 8-3

To access SQL Server 2000 as the securitytest user we created in Project 8-2, and test the permissions we set up previously:

1. Log out of Windows 2000 and log back in to the local machine as the securitytest Windows user.

2. Start Query Analyzer by clicking **Start**, highlighting **Programs**, highlighting **Microsoft SQL Server**, and then clicking **Query Analyzer**.

3. When the Connect to SQL Server window appears, click on or type the name of your local SQL Server 2000 instance (SQL2000 is the example used in Figure 8-19).

4. Select **Windows authentication**, as shown in Figure 8-19.

5. Click **OK** to connect to the instance.

6. Select the Northwind database and type the following query in the query window:

```
SELECT *
FROM Shippers
```

7. The query should execute properly and return the appropriate results, as shown in Figure 8-20.

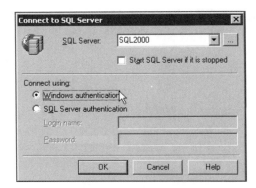

Figure 8-19   Connect to SQL Server window

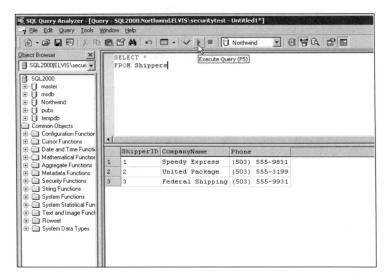

Figure 8-20   The securitytest user is able to perform SELECT operations in the
Shippers table

8. Now execute the following query in Query Analyzer:

```
DELETE Shippers
WHERE ShipperID = 1
```

9. This statement causes an error because the securitytest user does not have
DELETE permission on the Shippers table.

10. Now execute the following query in Query Analyzer:

```
INSERT INTO Shippers
VALUES ('New Shipping Company', '(555)-555-555')
```

11. This statement causes an error because the securitytest user does not have INSERT permission on the Shippers table.

12. Close Query Analyzer and log out of Windows. Don't save the queries.

Project 8-4

To create user-defined database roles to further demonstrate the hierarchical permissioning system of SQL Server 2000:

1. Log in to Windows with an administrative account capable of managing permissions.

2. Start Enterprise Manager by clicking **Start**, highlighting **Programs**, highlighting **Microsoft SQL Server**, and clicking **Enterprise Manager**.

3. In Enterprise Manager, double-click the local instance, expand the **Databases** folder, then expand the Northwind folder.

4. Right-click on the **Roles** node and choose **New Database Role** from the context-sensitive menu.

5. Type **Shipping** as the name for the new role.

6. Click **Add** to access a list of available users to add as members of the new role.

7. Choose the securitytest user from the list and click **OK**. Your screen should look like Figure 8-21.

8

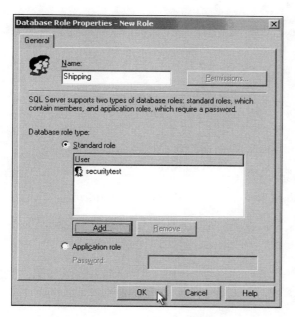

Figure 8-21   Creating a new database role in SQL Server 2000

8. Click **OK** to create the role.

9. Once the role is saved, permissions can be applied to it. Right-click the **Shipping** role from the list of roles in Enterprise Manager and choose **Properties** from the context-sensitive menu.

10. Click **Permissions** to access the interface for applying object permissions.

11. In the Database Role Properties window, scroll down to the **Shippers** table in the list of objects.

12. Click the check boxes to grant INSERT and DELETE permissions, as shown in Figure 8-22.

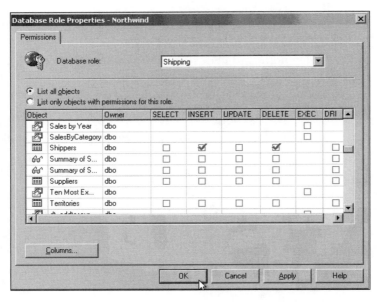

Figure 8-22   Granting object permissions to a database role

13. Click **OK** when done to close the permissions window.

14. Click **OK** again to close the Database Role Properties window.

 At this point the securitytest user has permissions applied directly to it and from the Shipping role that it is a member of.

Project 8-5

To test the permissions changes for the securitytest user (resulting from the role creation in Project 8-4) and to demonstrate how permissions are inherited:

1. Close all programs and log out of Windows.

2. Log back in to Windows as the securitytest local Windows user.

3. Start Query Analyzer by clicking **Start**, highlighting **Programs**, highlighting **Microsoft SQL Server**, and then clicking **Query Analyzer**.

4. When the Connect to SQL Server window appears, select or type the name of your local SQL Server 2000 instance.

5. Choose the **Windows authentication** option for connecting.

6. Click **OK** to connect to the instance.

7. Type the following query in the query window:

```
SELECT *
FROM Shippers
```

8. The query should execute properly and return the appropriate results because the securitytest user is granted SELECT permission on the table.

9. Now execute the following query in Query Analyzer:

```
INSERT INTO Shippers
VALUES ('ABCShipping Inc', '(503)-555-3456')
```

 A shipperid value is not required in the insert statement because ShipperID is an identity column in the table and automatically assigns the next available number.

10. This statement is now allowed because the securitytest user is a member of the Shipping database role that has INSERT permission on the Shippers table.

11. Now execute the following query in Query Analyzer:

```
DELETE Shippers
WHERE ShipperID = 4
```

12. This statement deletes the row you just inserted. It is allowed because the Shipping role has permissions to perform DELETE operations on the Shippers table and the securitytest user is a member of the role. Close Query Analyzer without saving the queries.

8

Project 8-6

To enable C2 auditing and use SQL Profiler to monitor the object-level permissioning events:

1. First, make sure you are logged into SQL Server 2000 as an administrative account (in case you are still connected with the securtytest login from the previous projects).

2. Start Query Analyzer by clicking **Start**, highlighting **Programs**, highlighting **Microsoft SQL Server**, and then clicking **Query Analyzer**.

3. When the Connect to SQL Server window appears, click on or type the name of your local SQL Server 2000 instance.

4. Select the **Windows authentication** option for connecting.

5. Click **OK** to connect to the instance.

6. Type the following query in the query window and execute it:

   ```
   EXEC sp_configure 'show advanced options', 1
   GO
   RECONFIGURE
   ```

 C2 auditing is an advanced option and is only visible if 'show advanced options' is set to 1.

7. Type the following query in the query window and execute it:

   ```
   EXEC sp_configure
   ```

   This returns a list of server options, including the "c2 audit mode" option, as shown in Figure 8-23. Notice the run_value of the option is set to 0.

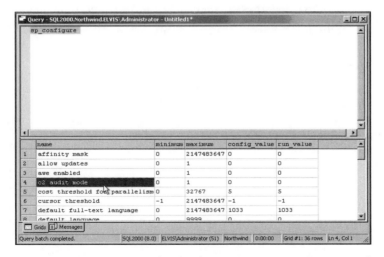

Figure 8-23   Viewing advanced server options in Query Analyzer

8. Type the following query in the query window and execute it:

```
EXEC sp_configure 'c2 audit mode', 1
GO
RECONFIGURE
```

9. The instance must be restarted to have this change take effect, so open **Enterprise Manager**, right-click on the instance, and choose **Stop** from the context-sensitive menu. Click **Yes** for the message dialog boxes.

10. Right-click on the instance again and choose **Start** from the context-sensitive menu.

11. Return to Query Analyzer and execute the following query:

```
EXEC sp_configure
```

The output from this procedure should now show that "c2 audit mode" is now set to 1 as its running value, as shown in Figure 8-24.

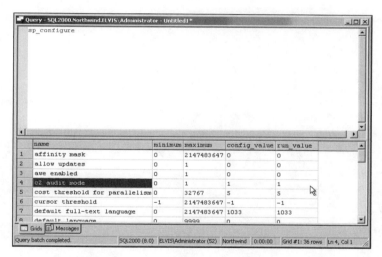

Figure 8-24   Confirm that the "c2 audit mode" option is set to 1

12. Open SQL Profiler by clicking **Start**, highlighting **Programs**, highlighting **Microsoft SQL Server**, and then clicking **Profiler**.

13. Click the **New Trace** button from the toolbar.

14. When the Connect to SQL Server window appears, click on or type the name of your local SQL Server 2000 instance.

15. Select the **Windows authentication** option for connecting.

16. Click **OK** to connect to the instance.

17. In the General tab of the Trace Properties window, name the trace by typing **Security Audit** in the Trace name text box.

18. Set the Template name to **Blank**.

19. Check the **Save to file** check box. When the file dialog comes up, click **Save** to save to a file called C:\Program Files\Microsoft SQL Server\MSSQL\Data\Security Audit.trc. Navigate to the Directory if it is not selected by default.

20. The General tab should look like Figure 8-25.

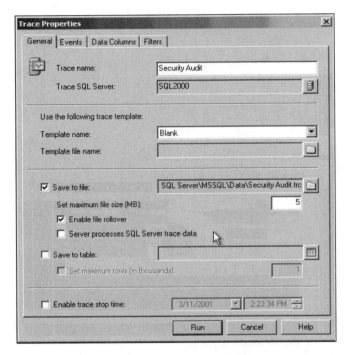

Figure 8-25   General tab for the Trace Properties window

21. Click the **Events** tab of the Trace Properties window and add the **Security Audit** group by double-clicking on it in the list. The screen should look like Figure 8-26.

22. Click the Data Columns tab and add the following columns to the trace:

- DatabaseName
- DBUserName
- Permissions
- ObjectName
- Success
- TextData

The window should like the one shown in Figure 8-27.

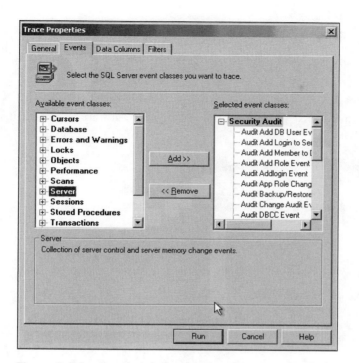

Figure 8-26   Events tab for the Trace Properties window

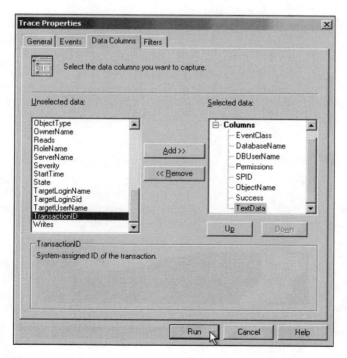

Figure 8-27   Data Columns tab for the Trace Properties window

23. Click **Run** to begin the trace.

24. Return to Query Analyzer, make sure the Northwind database is selected, and execute the following query:

```
SELECT *
FROM Shippers
```

25. Return to SQL Profiler to verify that the action was audited, as shown in Figure 8-28.

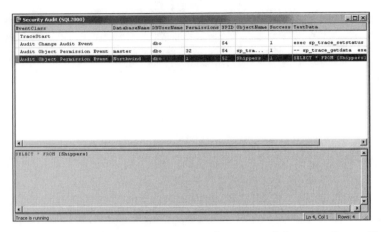

Figure 8-28   The query is captured as part of the security audit

26. Stop the trace and close Profiler. Close Query Analyzer without saving your queries. Close Enterprise Manager.

CASE PROJECTS

Case One

You have been hired as a consultant to help a company named Tweezer Inc. evaluate their potential network environment and to recommend how best to deploy SQL Server 2000. The company is planning to have 100 users on a Windows 2000 network and 10 users on a separate UNIX-based network. What security would you recommend and why? What are the advantages of the security mode you selected?

Case Two

Tweezer Inc. has just closed on their new office space and is getting ready to build out their planned network. They are now trying to understand how best to organize their various users to simplify security administration for their SQL Server 2000 databases. The IT manager asks you to come up with a document outlining the security architecture of SQL Server 2000, including the various objects used like users, groups, and roles, so that he can better understand the functionality available.

Case Three

Harpua Ltd. has a small user base on a Windows 2000 network. The users connect to a SQL Server 2000 database to manage data about company operations. Currently, there are two Windows global groups defined: HARPUA\Sales and HARPUA\inventory. These groups contain the Windows users who will need similar permissions in SQL Server 2000. In addition to that, there are two users who are not in these groups who need their own special set of permissions. These users are HARPUA\Trey and HARPUA\Mike.

The following are the data access requirements:

- HARPUA\sales and HARPUA\inventory groups need full access to the Customer, Orders, and Products tables.

- HAPRUA\sales needs full access to the SalesForecast table.

- HARPUA\inventory needs access to the ProductInventory table.

- HARPUA\Trey needs full access to the Customer, Orders, and Products tables.

- HARPUA\Mike just got promoted to DBA and needs full access.

How would you recommend implementing security in SQL Server 2000 to meet these requirements?

Case Four

Consider the broken ownership chain illustrated in Figure 8-29.

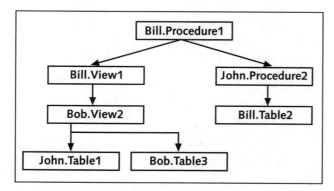

Figure 8-29   Broken ownership chain

In this scenario, Bill has created a powerful stored procedure (Procedure1) that generates a complex report. He grants execute permission on his procedure to a user named Althea, who requires access to the report. When Althea attempts to execute the procedure, she receives several errors signifying that she does not have the appropriate permissions to perform the operation. Which objects in the broken owner chain will Althea need permissions for before she can run Bill's Procedure1?

9

EXTRACTING AND TRANSFORMING DATA WITH SQL SERVER 2000

After reading this chapter and completing the exercises you will be able to:

♦ Understand the options in SQL Server 2000 for inserting from and extracting to external data sources

♦ Use the BULK INSERT statement and the BCP utility in SQL Server 2000 to move records into and out of tables and views

♦ Use the Data Transformation Services (DTS) interface to import and export data

♦ Create and save DTS packages to perform transformations and add workflow to packages

♦ Identify and implement an appropriate strategy for replicating data among instances of SQL Server 2000

♦ Understand and configure SQL Server 2000 XML support

SQL Server 2000 provides many ways in which to insert, extract, and transform the data in a given database. For high-performance insertion of large datasets, the bulk insert task and its accompanying Bulk Copy Program (BCP) utility are easy to use and highly effective. These utilities provide maximum speed and do not burden users by requiring them to set a large number of options. However, for greater control over the possible source and destination data sources and formats, the Data Transformation Services (DTS) provide an excellent means for transferring data. DTS is primarily used from Enterprise Manager and provides a simple and graphical yet flexible manner of moving data into, out of, or between SQL Server databases.

In addition, it is possible to perform almost any type of transformation during this process. Replication in SQL Server 2000 allows copies of data to be stored in multiple locations, with SQL Server 2000 performing the replication of changes throughout each. The sophisticated replication options available make it preferable to use SQL Server Replication to keep multiple data copies in synchronization instead of creating custom-defined synchronization strategies using BCP or DTS. In addition, new eXtensible Markup Language (XML) functionality in SQL Server 2000 makes it possible to move data into and out of the database in XML format. System administrators can choose to do this directly from the SQL Query Analyzer or through a Web browser connecting to Internet Information Services (IIS). This chapter will show you how to harness the power and flexibility of these methods of moving and manipulating data in your own database applications.

THE **BULK INSERT** STATEMENT

The **BULK INSERT statement** in SQL Server 2000 can be used to accomplish the high-performance insertion of large amounts of data into SQL Server tables or views from available data files. These files can contain data in the form of native SQL Server 2000 records (binary data) or in the form of text. However, the BULK INSERT statement cannot be used to accomplish the extraction of data from SQL Server 2000 tables or views. For extraction, the BCP utility, which is discussed in the next section, may be used instead.

Architecture

The OLE DB provider in SQL Server 2000 interprets the BULK INSERT statement natively. As a result, it is possible to use the bulk copy API from ODBC, OLE DB, SQL-DMO, and DB-Library-based applications. For example, you can perform the same bulk insert using a T-SQL statement written in the SQL Query Analyzer, a Visual Basic or Visual C++ application that uses the Distributed Management Objects (DMO), or an application that uses the Open Database Connectivity (ODBC) application-programming interface. The result is that the performance and functionality of a bulk insert is approximately the same, regardless of which type of application or interface initiates it.

BULK INSERT Statement Syntax

The BULK INSERT statement uses a simple syntax for inserting data from a file into a table. The statement is constructed as follows:

```
BULK INSERT [[ 'database_name'.] ['owner'].] {'table_name'
FROM 'data_file' }
  [ WITH
    (
      [BATCHSIZE [ = batch_size ]]
      [[,] CHECK_CONSTRAINTS ]
```

```
[[,]CODEPAGE[='ACP'|'OEM'|'RAW'|'code_page']]
[[,]DATAFILETYPE[=
  {'char'|'native'|'widechar'|'widenative'}]]
[[,]FIELDTERMINATOR[='field_terminator']]
[[,]FIRSTROW[=first_row]]
[[,]FIRE_TRIGGERS]
[[,]FORMATFILE='format_file_path']
[[,]KEEPIDENTITY]
[[,]KEEPNULLS]
[[,]KILOBYTES_PER_BATCH[=kilobytes_per_batch]]
[[,]LASTROW[=last_row]]
[[,]MAXERRORS[=max_errors]]
[[,]ORDER({column[ASC|DESC]}[ ,...n ])]
[[,]ROWS_PER_BATCH[=rows_per_batch]]
[[,]ROWTERMINATOR[='row_terminator']]
[[,]TABLOCK]
)
]
```

The destination table name, qualified by the database name, and the source data file are the only two parameters that must be specified for each BULK INSERT operation to succeed. The table name need only be qualified by the database name if the destination database is not the current database context in which the command is executed. Similarly, the owner name is only necessary when the current user is not the owner of the table or view into which the data are inserted. If the owner is required but not specified, SQL Server 2000 will return an error.

The destination database object may be a table or view. However, if the object is a view, all its columns must refer to the same base table to be used.

 The 'data_file' parameter is the full path of the data file on disk that contains data to copy into the specified table or view.

Each of the options that may be specified using the WITH clause are optional. However, if the data that are being inserted originate from an arbitrary data source, it is likely that several of the options will need to be specified as being different from the default options. Each of these options are described in Appendix B.

The BULK INSERT Statement in Action

To illustrate the use of the BULK INSERT statement, consider the following statement:

```
BULK INSERT Northwind.dbo.Customers
  FROM 'f:\marketing\customerlist.tbl'
  WITH
  (
     FIELDTERMINATOR = ';'
  )
```

9

This statement will insert records in the file f:\marketing\customerlist.tbl into the Customers table in the Northwind database. SQL Server 2000 will expect for the data to be in character format, with one line in the text file to correspond to one row in the database table. The values used for each column will be extracted from the data in the row, using the semicolon as a delimiter because this delimiter was specified in the FIELDTERMINATOR parameter.

If the number of columns in the Customers table is not the same as the number of values in any of the lines in the text file customerlist.tbl, SQL Server 2000 will generate an error. In addition, if the data fields are not present in the text file in the same order as the data columns in the database table, the data will be inserted into the wrong columns. Also, errors may result if the data type of the destination column is not compatible with data values in the source text file. To prevent these problems, a format file can be specified using the FORMATFILE parameter.

BULK INSERT Statement Usage Scenarios

The BULK INSERT statement is a high-performance way to insert data from a file into SQL Server 2000 using a standard T-SQL statement. It is best used when the data to be imported exist in a tabular, non-hierarchical format, such as a comma-delimited file. It can be used within a stored procedure as part of a data feed, and can be initiated by scheduling a job that executes the stored procedure. In addition, the BULK INSERT statement can be used if an event or program external to SQL Server 2000 initiates the data import. However, in that case, the use of the BCP utility should be considered. This utility will be discussed in more detail in the next section.

BULK INSERT Statement Performance

The BULK INSERT statement and the BCP are two high-performance ways to insert data into database tables in SQL Server 2000. However, there is an overhead associated with logging the insert of records using these methods. SQL Server 2000 incurs this overhead in order to ensure that the records inserted can be rolled back and, in the event of an error during insert, rolled forward. In order to optimize the performance of a bulk insert, it is possible to cause SQL Server 2000 not to log the inserts of the records. To do this, ensure that the following are true:

- The database option "select into/bulkcopy" is set to TRUE.
- The target table has no indexes, or if the table has indexes, it is empty when the bulk copy starts.
- The target table is not being replicated.
- The TABLOCK hint is specified.

 Only members of the sysadmin and bulkadmin fixed server roles can execute BULK INSERT statements.

BULK COPY PROGRAM

The **Bulk Copy Program (BCP)** included in SQL Server 2000 provides similar functionality to the BULK INSERT statement, which was discussed in the previous section. In addition to providing support for *inserting* records from data files, the BCP utility allows *extraction* of data from data tables and views to external files. To use the utility, one must execute the bcp.exe program found in the Microsoft SQL Server\80\Tools\Binn folder. Note that the syntax, presented later in this section, is similar to the syntax of the BULK INSERT statement. A key difference, however, is that it is necessary to specify a user name, password, database name, and server name when using the BCP utility. These are necessary because the BCP utility is executed from outside the context of a database login.

BCP Syntax

The BCP utility requires a slightly different syntax than the BULK INSERT statement, but uses similar parameters:

```
bcp {[[database_name.][owner].]{table_name | view_name} |
"query"}
  {in | out | queryout | format} data_file
  [-m max_errors] [-f format_file] [-e err_file]
  [-F first_row] [-L last_row] [-b batch_size]
  [-n] [-c] [-w] [-N] [-V (60 | 65 | 70)] [-6]
  [-q] [-C code_page] [-t field_term] [-r row_term]
  [-i input_file] [-o output_file] [-a packet_size]
  [-S server_name[\instance_name]] [-U login_id] [-P
password]
  [-T] [-v] [-R] [-k] [-E] [-h "hint [,...n]"]
```

As discussed earlier, it is possible both to insert and extract data using the BCP utility. This is why the parameters specified when using the BCP utility are slightly different than those specified when using a BULK INSERT statement. In addition to specifying a source or destination table or view name, when using the BCP utility, it is possible to specify a query that will act as the source of the data to be extracted. Note that it is not possible to insert data into the set of records produced by a query specified in the BCP statement. To obtain a similar result, it would be necessary to create a view that specifies the table and columns into which the records should be inserted. The BCP statement may then insert records into that view.

When using the BCP utility, it is necessary to use the IN or OUT keywords to specify whether the data are being inserted or extracted. If the IN keyword is used, the file specified will become the source file. If the OUT keyword is used, the file specified is the destination file for the data being extracted.

Because the BCP utility is invoked outside of SQL Server 2000, you must specify a server and user context in which the action should execute. You can accomplish this by specifying values for the following parameters:

```
[-S server_name[\instance_name]]
[-U login_id]
[-P password]
```

In this parameter listing, "server_name[\instance_name]" is the name of the server and the instance in which the BCP utility should execute.

 The "instance_name" portion of the parameter is only required if the instance of SQL Server 2000 is a named instance. This is required when installing SQL Server 2000 on a machine that has a previous version of SQL Server installed or one that already has a default (non-named) instance of SQL Server 2000 installed.

BCP in Action

To illustrate the use of the BCP utility, consider the following statement shown in Figure 9-1. It is executed at the MS-DOS prompt of a machine that has SQL Server 2000 installed.

This statement will copy the records in the Northwind database Orders table on the Test01\dev server into the c:\Recent Orders.txt file. Note that this statement can be executed from any machine that has a functioning installation of the SQL Server Client Tools. However, that machine must be on the same network as the Test01\dev machine or it will need to have an alias with the name Test01\dev in the client network utility. SQL Server 2000 will copy the data into character format, with the default column and row delimiters (the "Tab" character and the "Newline" character, respectively). Had the command been requesting all records in the Orders table, the keyword OUT would have been specified in place of QUERYOUT.

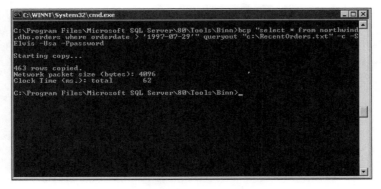

Figure 9-1   The BCP command to export order data

BCP Usage Scenarios

The same requirements that lead to the selection of the BULK INSERT statement for inserting large sets of data into SQL Server 2000 can be used to select the BCP utility. In addition, you should select the BCP utility when you need to export data from a SQL Server table into a data file and extensive transformations are not necessary. You may also choose the BCP utility instead of the BULK INSERT statement if an insert is required and the action can be more easily invoked from another machine or a program running outside of SQL Server 2000.

BCP Performance

Like the BULK INSERT statement, the BCP utility is a high-performance, batch-oriented mechanism for transferring large sets of records. Because both implement the Bulk Copy API, the performance of BCP will not differ much from the performance of the BULK INSERT statement. Each of the considerations that were discussed in reference to optimizing the performance of the BULK INSERT statement are relevant when using the BCP utility to insert data into SQL Server tables or views. Consider two main factors when attempting to optimize the performance of a data extraction: first, optimize the query that produces the output from the desired set of tables and views; and second, optimize the network speed and/or disk input/output.

9

DATA TRANSFORMATION SERVICES

The **Data Transformation Services (DTS)** are a set of features bundled together for use in Enterprise Manager. The functionality can be used to import data into or export data from tables or views. There are a variety of possible source and destination data types, including the most popular current relational database and flat-file data sources, as well as legacy data formats. In addition, it is possible to transform the data during the process of moving it from the source to the destination data locations.

Interface

SQL Server 2000 provides an intuitive, easy-to-use interface to the Data Transformation Services in the format of the Data Transformation Services Import/Export Wizard. This wizard exists in your SQL Server 2000 installation folder as \Microsoft SQL Server\80\Tools\Binn\dtswiz.exe. It can be invoked in one of the following ways:

- Right-click on the name of a server, database, or table in Enterprise Manager, and click on Import Data or Export Data in the All Tasks menu. See Figure 9-2.

- Click on the name of a server, database, or table in Enterprise Manager, click on the Action menu, and point to Import Data or Export Data in the All Tasks sub-menu.

- Click on Programs in the Start menu, click on Microsoft SQL Server in the sub-menu, and then click on Import and Export Data. See Figure 9-3.

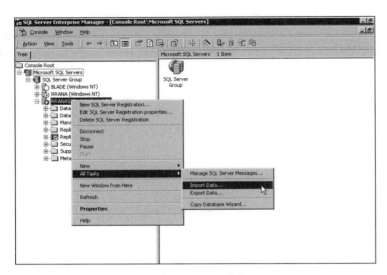

Figure 9-2   Invoking the DTS Wizard from Enterprise Manager

Figure 9-3   Invoking the DTS Wizard from the program group

Executing a Transformation Using DTS

The first two steps when executing a transformation using DTS are to correctly specify the source and target data repositories. Subsequently, it is necessary to specify several options about the data transfer and customer transformations. At a minimum, the user executing a transformation needs to select one or more tables or views to copy from the source to the target data repositories. By default, SQL Server 2000 performs a basic copy of the selected tables and views to the target. However, there are many options that one can set to change this behavior so that it meets almost any data transformation requirement.

Choosing a Data Source/Destination

After invoking the DTS Import/Export Wizard, it is necessary to identify both the source and target data repositories that will be involved in the data transfer/transformation. To identify each repository, specify the following:

- The type of data held in the data repository
- The physical location of the repository
- Any information required to gain access to the repository

The type of data may be specific to a database or other software vendor, or it may be based on a standard data format. The data formats supported by DTS include SQL Server 2000, Oracle, Access, Paradox, dBase, Excel, FoxPro, ISAM, ODBC, text data, and others. Figure 9-4 shows the window where you can choose the data source.

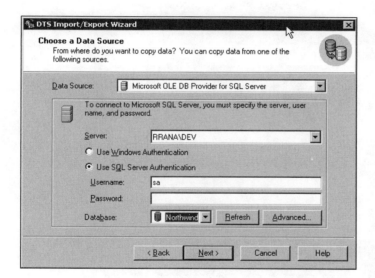

Figure 9-4   The Choose a Data Source dialog box in the DTS Wizard

The manner in which the physical location of the repository will vary depends on the data format of the repository. For instance, selecting a database server from the Server list box will specify the location of data in the SQL Server 2000 format. For this data format, it will also be necessary to specify the database on the server from which the data should originate or into which the data should be placed. The default database for the user executing the data transformation will be assumed if no other database is specified. To specify the data location of a text file, it will be necessary only to locate the file on the machine's file system, including network, hard disk, floppy drive, and CD-ROM locations.

If the data source or target repositories are secured by authentication, it may be necessary to specify a user name and password for SQL Server 2000 to gain access to the data repository.

For instance, it is necessary to specify the user name and password that will be used to access a SQL Server database. If the data repository has no security control, such as an Excel spreadsheet with no password protection, it will not be necessary to specify a user name and password before executing the data transformation.

Specifying Table Copy or Query

The Specify Table Copy or Query dialog box, shown in Figure 9-5, is the next step of the DTS Import/Export Wizard. One uses this dialog box after specifying the source and target data locations. In order to organize the vast number of transformation options, SQL Server 2000 has organized the types of data transfer/transformation into the following three options:

- Copy table(s) and view(s) from the source database
- Use a query to specify the data to transfer
- Copy objects and data between SQL Server databases

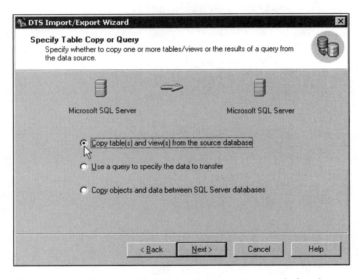

Figure 9-5   The Specify Table Copy or Query dialog box

To move the contents of one or more tables or views from the source to the target, click on the "Copy table(s) and view(s) radio button.

In the case of a non-relational database repository, the DTS utility considers a set of records to act as a table. Therefore, this option is available even when transferring data from a text file into SQL Server 2000. If this option is selected, SQL Server 2000 presents a list of the tables discovered in the source data repository. To select which ones should be moved into the target location, click the check box next to the name of the table, as shown in Figure 9-6.

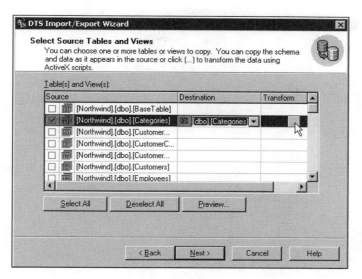

Figure 9-6   The Select Source Tables and Views dialog box

When one desires to transfer only specific columns and rows in the data source, the best option to choose is "Use a query to specify the data to transfer." This will allow entry of a valid T-SQL statement that references the tables and columns in the source repository. See Figure 9-7. Alternatively, it is possible to use the Query Builder to build the SQL statement. Double-click the tables and columns from the Source Tables list to select them. See Figure 9-8.

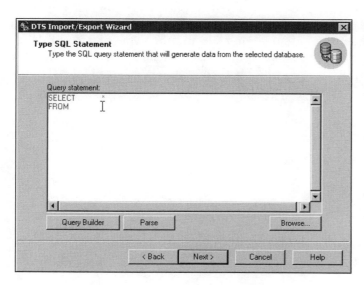

Figure 9-7   The Type SQL Statement dialog box

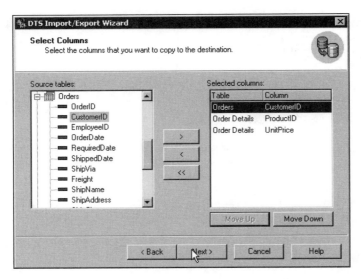

Figure 9-8   Using Query Builder to create SQL statements

After selecting the data objects in the source data repository that should be transferred to the target or creating a query that specifies the data to transfer, you will need to specify several options about the target data repository. It is necessary to specify the destination data table and columns into which the data will be inserted and to apply custom transformations to any or all of the data columns selected. By default, SQL Server 2000 will use an existing table as the target data table if one exists with the same name as the source table, and will automatically select the column mappings if the same columns exist in the target repository as in the source. See Figure 9-9. However, it is possible to change both the name of the destination table and the name of each of the destination columns. Changing the destination column names will be possible only if the table is new, or if the "Create destination table" radio button is selected and the "Drop and recreate destination table" check box is checked.

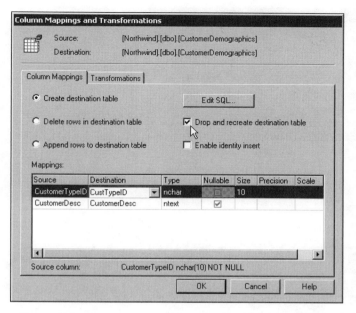

Figure 9-9   The Column Mappings tab in the Column Mappings and Transformations dialog box, which allows customization of destination column mappings

If the destination table is already suitable for the data transfer, the system administrator may click the "Delete rows in destination table" radio button or the "Append rows to destination table" radio button. If the table exists and the "Create destination table" radio button is selected, the administrator should click the "Drop and recreate destination table" check box to prevent SQL Server 2000 from raising an error that specifies that it cannot create a table that already exists.

To specify data transformations on the data columns that will be transferred, it is possible to write a custom VBScript or JScript. This custom script will replace the default script that SQL Server 2000 creates for each DTS package. To edit the default script, click the Transformations tab in the Column Mappings and Transformations dialog box, as shown in Figure 9-10. The expressions in this script that have the form DTSDestination("field") are the names of the columns in the target repository. It is possible to change these expressions to implement any custom logic in the transformation.

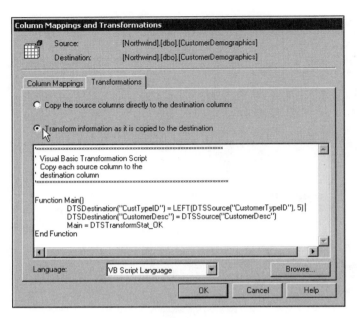

Figure 9-10   The Transformations tab in the Column Mappings and Transformations dialog box, which allows custom transformations to the source data

Copying Objects and Data Between SQL Server Databases

To move almost any type of object between one SQL Server database and another, click the "Copy objects and data between SQL Server databases" radio button in the Specify Table Copy or Query dialog box. This allows the transfer of any kind of database object from one instance of SQL Server 2000 to another. Note that because multiple SQL Server 2000 instances may be on a single machine, the source and destination SQL Server machines can be on the same physical computer.

Clicking the "Copy objects between SQL Server databases" radio button causes the Select Objects to Copy dialog box to appear, as shown in Figure 9-11. The first major option that one must select is how to handle the creation of the objects on the target SQL Server machine. If the objects do not already exist on the target machine, the "Create destination objects" check box should remain checked. If you are copying data to a machine that already has the database objects defined, you may uncheck the check box. However, it is still possible to create the destination objects if they already exist, but in this case the "Drop destination objects first" check box should be selected.

Use the "Copy data" option to specify whether the data in the objects (tables or views) should be moved over to the destination server. It is possible to deselect this option to create a blank copy of the objects on the target server. If you wish to copy the data, you can choose to either replace or append the data to any existing data on the target server.

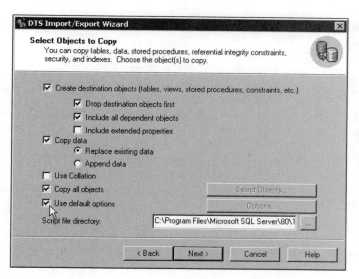

Figure 9-11   The Select Objects to Copy dialog box

Use the "Copy all objects" option to specify that all objects in the source database should be copied to the target database. Otherwise, it is possible to select which specific objects should be copied to the target database. By default one may select any tables, views, stored procedures, user defined functions, defaults, rules, and user defined data types. In addition, a system administrator can set several options that specify whether SQL Server 2000 should move users, roles, logins, permissions, and other objects with their parent objects. To specify these options, click the Use default options check box to deselect it.

Finally, it is possible to change the directory to which SQL Server 2000 will temporarily store the scripts used to accomplish the object transfer. If more than one concurrent DTS operation uses the same directory location, file locking may cause one or more of the operations to fail. Therefore, you should specify a unique file location in which to store these temporary scripts for each concurrent DTS object copy operation.

Saving DTS Packages

After selecting all the options necessary to specify the behavior of the data transformation desired, you have the option to run the transformation immediately, schedule the transformation to run at a later time or on a recurring schedule, or simply to save the package. These options are available in the "Save, schedule, and replicate package" dialog box shown in Figure 9-12. When you save a Data Transformation Services (DTS) package, you save all DTS connections, DTS tasks, DTS transformations, and workflow steps, and preserve the graphical layout of these objects on the DTS Designer design sheet. You may save the package in SQL Server, SQL Server Meta Data Services, as a Structured Storage File, or as a Visual Basic File.

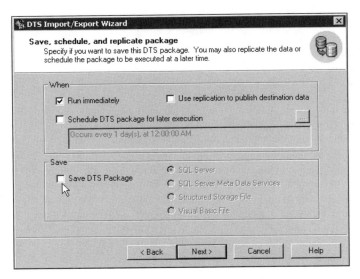

Figure 9-12   The Save, schedule, and replicate package dialog box

SQL Server

With this default save option, you can store a package as a table in the SQL Server msdb database. This allows you to store packages on any instances of SQL Server 2000 on your network; to keep a convenient inventory of saved packages in Enterprise Manager; and to create, delete, and branch multiple package versions during the package development process.

SQL Server Meta Data Services

With this save option, you can maintain historical information about the data manipulated by the package. However, Meta Data Services and the repository database must be installed and operational on your server. You can track the columns and tables that are used by the package as a source or destination. You can also use the data lineage feature to track which version of a package created a particular row. You can use these types of information for decision-support applications.

Structured Storage File

With this save option, you can copy, move, and send a package across the network without having to store the file in a SQL Server database. The structured storage format allows you to maintain multiple packages and multiple package versions in a single file.

Visual Basic File

With this save option, you can programmatically customize a package created in DTS Designer or the DTS Import/Export Wizard. The option scripts out the package as Visual Basic code, and you can later open the Visual Basic file and modify the package definition in your development environment.

Editing DTS Packages

To edit a DTS Package, open the package in the DTS Designer, which is available through Enterprise Manager. You can open the DTS Designer by right-clicking on a package and clicking Design Package in the menu. See Figure 9-13. The DTS Designer makes it possible to change all properties of the connections, data objects, and transformations specified using the DTS Import/Export Wizard. In addition, the DTS Designer allows more complex logic and functionality to be incorporated into the package through the use of FTP tasks, data-driven queries, and other advanced features not present in the DTS Import/Export Wizard. Combined with the workflow options available for specifying the necessary conditions for each task to execute, the DTS Designer allows the creation and saving of complex and complete data transformation packages. See Figure 9-14.

9

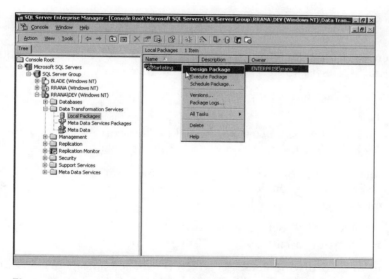

Figure 9-13   Invoking the DTS Designer from Enterprise Manager

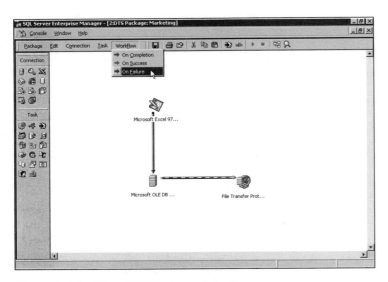

Figure 9-14 The DTS Designer interface

DTS in Action

To illustrate a common use of the DTS Import/Export Wizard, consider the following steps:

1. To open the Enterprise Manager, click Start, highlight Programs, highlight Microsoft SQL Server, then click Enterprise Manager.

2. Expand the group containing the SQL Server instance installed on the local machine.

3. Right-click on the local machine, then click Next on the Introduction screen, highlight All Tasks, and then click Export Data.

4. Ensure that the Data Source list box reads "Microsoft OLE DB Provider for SQL Server," and that the local machine name and instance name, if one exists, appears in the Server list box.

5. Use Windows or SQL Server authentication, depending on the configuration of security in your installation of SQL Server 2000.

6. Click on the Northwind database, which is installed automatically with SQL Server 2000, in the Database list box. Click Next at the bottom of the dialog box.

7. For the data destination, click on Microsoft Excel 97–2000.

8. For the file name, click on a folder location and type "DTS_Export.xls". Click Next.

If a message box appears warning that a script may not be valid, click Yes to have the wizard generate a default script.

9. Click the "Copy table(s) and view(s) from the source database" radio button. Click Next.

10. Click on the Customers table in the source column.

11. For the Customers table, click on the ellipses in the Transform column.

12. For the row CustomerID, click on <ignore> in the Destination column, so that the column will not be exported.

13. Click the Transformations tab, and then click the "Transform information as it is copied to the destination" radio button.

14. Make sure the values exported to the CompanyName and ContactName columns are uppercase, by changing the expression DTSSource("CompanyName") to Ucase(DTSSource("CompanyName")) and changing the expression DTSSource("ContactName") to Ucase(DTSSource("ContactName")).

15. Click OK, and then click Next in the Select Source Tables and Views dialog box.

16. Click Next to run immediately, and then click Finish after reviewing the summary information.

17. You should receive a message informing you that one table was successfully copied.

18. Click OK and Done, and then open the Excel spreadsheet.

19. Verify that all columns except the CustomerID were exported and that the CompanyName and ContactName columns appear in all capital letters.

REPLICATION

In the context of a relational database management system (RDBMS), **replication** is the act of keeping copies of the same data on multiple sites. This may involve only keeping copies on two sites, or keeping copies on hundreds of sites. SQL Server 2000 includes a complete set of features for managing how and when data should be replicated to multiple sites. In addition, the tools that SQL Server 2000 includes for replicating data allow a system administrator to have complete control over which data are replicated.

Uses of Replication

Each time that replication is used, a common goal is to make data available when and where it is needed. However, there are many specific uses of replication that will affect which type of replication is chosen and how it is implemented. The major uses for replication include:

- Allowing multiple locations to keep copies of the same data. This is useful when multiple sites need to read the same data or need separate servers for reporting applications.

- Separating transaction processing (read and write) applications from analytical processing (read-intensive) applications

- Allowing greater autonomy. Users can work with copies of data while disconnected, and then the changes can propagate to other databases when they are connected.

- Creating a scalable application that is based on strategically locating data that will be accessed

- Bringing data closer to individuals or groups. This can help to reduce conflicts based on multiple user data modifications and queries, because data can be distributed throughout the network, and you can partition data based on the needs of different business units or users.

- Using replication as part of a customized standby server strategy. Replication is one of a few choices for standby server strategy.

Replication Overview

Replication of data stored in relational databases is commonly described using a metaphor that is borrowed from the publishing industry. In this metaphor, data that are being replicated among multiple locations are compared to subscriptions that are published and distributed to multiple subscribers. Therefore, database servers participating in data replication can act as publishers, subscribers, and distributors. It is important to remember that a server may take on multiple roles in a replication configuration.

The **Publisher** is a server that makes data available for replication to other servers. In addition to being the server where you specify which data is to be replicated, the Publisher also detects which data has changed and maintains information about all publications at that site. Usually, any data element that is replicated has a single Publisher, even if it may be updated by several Subscribers or republished by a Subscriber.

Subscribers are servers that receive replicated data. Subscribers subscribe to publications, not to individual articles within a publication, and they subscribe only to the publications that they need, not necessarily all of the publications available on a Publisher.

The **Distributor** is a server that contains the distribution database and stores meta-data, history data, and/or transactions. The Distributor can be a separate server from the Publisher (remote Distributor), or it can be the same server as the Publisher (local Distributor). The role of the Distributor varies depending on which type of replication is implemented.

There are three basic types of replication. Each adopts a different strategy for ensuring that a single logical record that exists in multiple locations will remain synchronized in all locations. The method that should be chosen depends on several factors, including the frequency/stability of connectivity among locations, network speed between locations, the frequency of data changes at each location, the priority of having most recent data on all locations, and the extent to which data can be partitioned for updates among locations. These factors will be mentioned as each of the replication types are discussed. The three types of replication are:

- Snapshot replication
- Transactional replication
- Merge replication

The sections that follow discuss the strategy adopted by each type of strategy. Real-world scenarios that require replication are typically not completely optimized by any of these three replication strategies. Therefore, trade-offs must be considered, and it is often best to implement more than one type of replication concurrently.

Snapshot Replication

In **snapshot replication**, data and database objects are copied and distributed exactly as they appear at a moment in time. Snapshot replication does not require continuous monitoring of changes, because changes made to the published data are not propagated to the Subscriber incrementally. Subscribers are updated with a complete refresh of the data set at some future time. SQL Server snapshot agents create the snapshots, and SQL Server distribution agents apply the snapshots to the subscribers. This strategy may require more time to propagate data modifications to Subscribers, because all data are transferred at once. For this reason, snapshot publications are typically configured with schedules that replicate the data less frequently than other types of publications. See Figure 9-15.

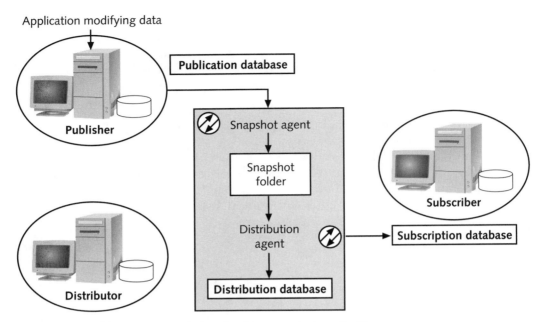

Figure 9-15   The components involved in snapshot replication

Usage Scenarios for Snapshot Replication

Because snapshot replication involves transferring an entire publication of data from the Publisher to each Subscriber, it is not appropriate for all replication scenarios. Snapshot replication is the best choice when the following are true:

- Most of the data are static and do not change often.

- It is acceptable to have copies of data that are out of date for some period of time.

- The total size of data publications to replicate is small.

- The sites are often disconnected, eliminating the possibility to send constant updates of data as in transactional replication.

Transactional Replication

In **transactional replication**, an initial snapshot of data is propagated from the Publisher to the Subscribers in a similar manner as in snapshot replication. However, when data modifications are made at the Publisher, the individual transactions are captured and propagated to Subscribers. In addition to the snapshot agent and distribution agent used in snapshot replication, a log reader agent that can run on the Publisher or the Distributor is involved in transactional replication (see Figure 9-16). The log reader agent takes changes to data in the publication database from the publication database's transaction log, and puts these into the distribution database on the Distributor. Because only individual transactions are propagated to Subscribers, the total amount of data transferred will be less than with snapshot replication, unless all data on the Publisher are modified.

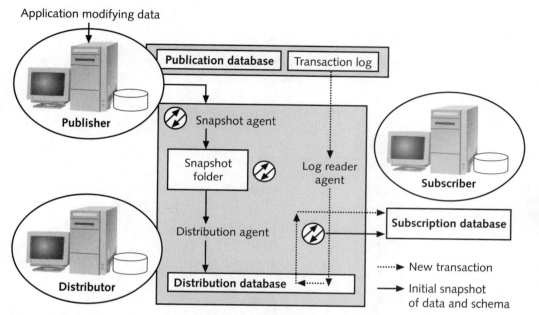

Figure 9-16   The components involved in transactional replication

Usage Scenarios For Transactional Replication

Because transactional replication involves more frequent transfer of data than snapshot replication, it may not be a good choice when the sites are only connected infrequently. In addition, it is not designed to resolve conflicts that could occur if the same data are modified at multiple sites independently of one another. However, transactional replication is an excellent choice when:

- Data modifications should be propagated to Subscribers within seconds of when they occur.

- Transactions should be atomic, meaning that either all or none of the related changes are applied at the Subscriber.

- Subscribers are connected to the Publisher most of the time.

- The application cannot tolerate out-of-date data on the Subscribers that receive the changes.

SQL Server 2000 Personal Edition and SQL Server 2000 Desktop Engine can be used only as a transactional replication Subscriber. These editions can be installed on any platform supported by SQL Server 2000. The Standard edition and Enterprise edition of SQL Server 2000, however, require Windows 2000 Server and Windows 2000 Advanced Server, respectively.

Merge Replication

In **merge replication**, data modifications can be made at each site. Data modifications made at the sites are later merged into a uniform result at a later time. Because the results are merged at a later time, the changes made to each site can be done online or offline. This type of replication is achieved after an initial snapshot from the Publisher is applied to the Subscribers, and SQL Server 2000 tracks the changes made at the Publisher and each Subscriber. These changes are tracked using a merge agent, which typically runs on the distribution server (as shown in Figure 9-17). Because multiple sites may update the same data before they next communicate, conflicts may arise. Therefore, a merge agent uses a conflict table on the publication database to store information about the conflicts, to consider the priorities of each of the servers participating in replication, and to resolve the conflicts.

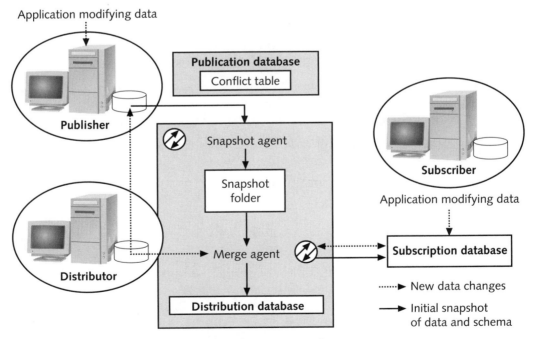

Figure 9-17   The components involved in merge replication

Usage Scenarios for Merge Replication

Because merge replication allows multiple sites to operate autonomously, it is a popular choice for organizations whose typical working data sets can be partitioned in a logical manner. For example, an organization whose sales data are geographically partitioned to sales offices in different locations may make use of merge replication. Merge replication is the best selection when:

- Multiple Subscribers need to update data at various times and propagate those changes to the Publisher and to other Subscribers.

- Subscribers need to receive data, make changes offline, and synchronize changes later with the Publisher and other Subscribers.

- The ability for each site to operate independently is critical.

Replication Tools

SQL Server 2000 provides several easy-to-use tools for establishing and configuring replication. Each of these tools is available through Enterprise Manager. Most take the form of wizards that allow the definition of Publishers, Distributors, Subscribers, subscriptions, and their properties. In addition, property dialog boxes, such as the Publication Properties dialog box, allow changes to be made to the replication configuration once it exists. In order to automate the configuration of replication to a different set of servers or archive the replication settings, it is possible to use Enterprise Manager to script out the configuration. The resulting T-SQL script then recreates the same replication environment.

Replication Wizards

Enterprise Manager provides access to several wizards and properties dialog boxes that simplify the establishment and maintenance of replication. In addition to viewing and modifying the replication properties, it is also possible to view the replication folder and Replication Monitor. These provide a useful way to monitor SQL Server replication and take action if necessary. Note that the Replication Monitor appears as a node under the server name in Enterprise Manager after replication is established.

The following replication wizards are the primary tools used to configure replication in SQL Server 2000:

- Configure Publishing and Distribution Wizard
- Create Publication Wizard
- Push Subscription Wizard
- Pull Subscription Wizard
- Disable Publishing and Distribution Wizard

Configure Publishing and Distribution Wizard   The Configure Publishing and Distribution Wizard is typically the first wizard that is invoked to establish replication. This wizard allows the specification of a server to use as a Distributor. In addition, it is possible to enable databases on the server as Publishers and identify servers to act as Subscribers. After running this wizard, changes to the established configuration can be made in the Publisher and Distributor Properties dialog box. To invoke this wizard, right-click the Replication folder under the server name node in Enterprise Manager and select Configure Publishing, Subscribers, and Distribution.

Create Publication Wizard   The Create Publication Wizard allows the creation of a publication. The wizard allows an administrator to specify what type of replication will be used to customize the replication options, including the data or database objects that should be replicated. If tables or views are being replicated, advanced options allow the horizontal and vertical filtering of the data to be replicated. This can help to optimize the performance of replication, as only the necessary data are transferred from the publisher to the subscriber. In addition, it is possible to specify which types of Subscribers are accessing the publication, which will enable SQL Server to determine the replication options that are available. After the publication is created using the Create Publication Wizard, changes to the publication can be made in the Publication Properties dialog box, which is accessible by right-clicking the publication in Enterprise Manager and clicking Properties in the menu.

Push Subscription Wizard   The Push Subscription Wizard allows the creation of a subscription to an existing publication. The subscription will be distributed to the Subscriber specified in this wizard. It is possible to later view the options selected for this push subscription in the Subscription Properties dialog box, which is opened by right-clicking the subscription in Enterprise Manager and clicking Properties in the menu.

Pull Subscription Wizard   The Pull Subscription Wizard allows the creation of a subscription to a publication requested by the Subscriber on the SQL Server specified in this wizard. After the subscription is created, the configuration options selected can be viewed in the Pull Subscription Properties dialog box, which is opened by right-clicking the subscription in Enterprise Manager and clicking Properties in the menu.

Disable Publishing and Distribution Wizard   The Disable Publishing and Distribution Wizard allows the removal of replication publications and the distribution service from the SQL Server machine. This removes the schedule for replication, the replication database, and any publications defined on the machine. Note that this also causes the Replication Monitor, visible as a node under the SQL Server machine in Enterprise Manager, to be removed.

Filtering Published Data

In order to make the best use of system and network resources and to optimize the performance of SQL Server 2000 replication, it is often necessary to filter the data published for replication. For example, a company table in a customer database may be replicated to several different sites. However, each site may need only a specific subset of the data present on the publisher. In this case, the data should be horizontally filtered so that each publication only includes the desired rows. If all of the data columns are not needed on the remote sites, it is possible to utilize a vertical filter as well. In addition to horizontal and vertical data filters, it is possible to create more complicated data filters based on dynamic conditions and joins relating records in multiple tables. By filtering published data, it is possible to:

- Minimize the amount of data sent over the network

- Reduce the amount of storage space required at the Subscriber

- Customize publications and applications based on individual Subscriber requirements

- Avoid or reduce conflicts that could result if the same data were sent to multiple Subscribers

 While row and column filters can be used with all three of the publication types, dynamic and join filters can be used only with merge replication.

Replication Performance Optimization

There are several application-specific and network-specific techniques for optimizing the performance of replication. The simplest way is to set a minimum amount of memory allocated to SQL Server 2000 by using the Min Server Memory option. This will prevent SQL Server 2000 from dynamically reducing the memory it uses at times of low activity and causing that memory not to be available when it is needed. In addition, using a separate disk drive for the transaction log on any server involved in replication will help to avoid the disk I/O bottleneck that can result from logging many operations.

Ensuring that the data that is replicated is then filtered as much as possible will also help to avoid unnecessary performance problems. Also, the snapshot folder should not exist on a drive that contains log files or database files. If the number of Subscribers is large, consider reducing the frequency of distributions. Avoid creation of unnecessary indexes and application logic triggers at the Subscriber. If agents are run very frequently, consider running them continuously instead. This will prevent the overhead associated with stopping and starting the agent.

HETEROGENEOUS QUERIES

A heterogeneous query retrieves, inserts, or updates data by joining together sets of data from multiple data source types. For example, it is possible to simultaneously retrieve customer records from an Oracle database and related order records from a SQL Server database. It is necessary to initiate a heterogeneous query from a SQL Server database that is linked to another data source. A linked server configuration allows remote server access and allows access of non–SQL Server data sources to be treated the same way as the access of SQL Server data sources.

Configuring a Linked Server

To configure a linked server definition, a SQL Server administrator specifies an OLE DB provider and an OLE DB data source. An OLE DB provider is a dynamic-link library (DLL) that manages and interacts with a specific data source. An OLE DB data source is any data file accessible through OLE DB. Although data sources queried through linked server definitions are usually databases, OLE DB providers exist for a wide variety of files and file formats, including text files, spreadsheet data, and the results of full-text content searches. Table 9-1 lists valid examples of an OLE DB provider and an OLE DB data source:

Table 9-1   OLE DB Providers and Data Sources

OLE DB Provider	OLE DB Source
Microsoft OLE DB Provider for SQL Server 2000	SQL Server database
Microsoft OLE DB Provider for Jet	Pathname of .mdb database file
Microsoft OLE DB Provider for ODBC	ODBC data source name (pointing to a particular database)
Microsoft OLE DB Provider for Oracle	SQL*Net alias that points to an Oracle database
Microsoft OLE DB Provider for Indexing Service	Content files on which property searches or full-text searches can be run

It is important for the SQL Server administrator to know that for a data source to return data through a linked server, the OLE DB provider (DLL) for that data source must be present on the same server as SQL Server machine. See Figure 9-18 for a depiction of how a linked server configuration functions.

Linked servers are typically used to handle distributed queries. When a client application executes a distributed query through a linked server, SQL Server 2000 breaks down the command and sends rowset requests to OLE DB. Rowsets are the central objects that enable all OLE DB data providers to expose data in tabular form. Conceptually, a rowset is a set of rows in which each row contains columns of data.

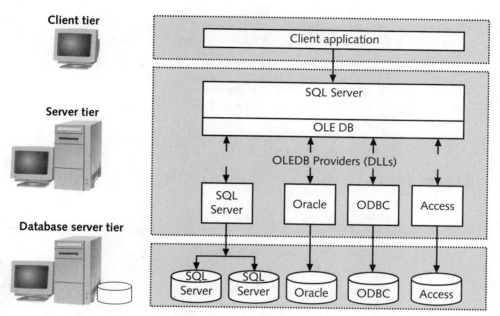

Figure 9-18   Linked server configuration

OLE DB then queries the provider for the rowset information. The provider, in turn, knows the specifics of calling the data source, opening the file, and returning the requested information. The rowset data is returned through the provider and OLE DB to SQL Server 2000, where it is reconstructed and returned to the client application as a result set and set of output parameters (if applicable).

Managing a Linked Server Definition

When setting up a linked server, register the connection information and data source information with SQL Server 2000. After registration is accomplished, it is possible to refer to the data source with a single logical name.

You can create or delete a linked server definition with stored procedures or through Enterprise Manager. In addition, it is possible to use stored procedures to manage linked server definition. To create a linked server definition using T-SQL, execute the sp_addlinkedserver system-stored procedure. To view information about the linked servers defined in a given SQL Server, use the sp_linkedservers system-stored procedure.

To delete a linked server definition, it is possible to use the sp_dropserver system-stored procedure. The syntax for using each of these system-stored procedures is presented here:

```
sp_addlinkedserver [@server =] 'server'
[,[@srvproduct =] 'product_name']
  [,[@provider =] 'provider_name']
[,[@datasrc =]'data_source']
  [, [@location =] 'location']
[,[@provstr =] 'provider_string']
  [, [@catalog =] 'catalog']
```

Arguments

[@server =] 'server'

is the name of the linked server to create. Server is sysname, with no default.

[@srvproduct =] 'product_name'

is the product name of the OLE DB data source to add as a linked server. Product_name is nvarchar(128), with a default of NULL. If SQL Server, provider_name, data_source, location, provider_string, and catalog do not need to be specified.

[@provider =] 'provider_name'

is the unique programmatic identifier (PROGID) of the OLE DB provider corresponding to this data source. Provider_name must be unique for the specified OLE DB provider installed on the current computer. Provider_name is nvarchar(128), with a default of NULL. The OLE DB provider is expected to be registered with the given PROGID in the registry.

[@datasrc =] 'data_source'

is the name of the data source as interpreted by the OLE DB provider. Data_source is nvarchar(4000), with a default of NULL. Data_source is passed as the DBPROP_INIT_DATASOURCE property to initialize the OLE DB provider.

[@location =] 'location'

is the location of the database as interpreted by the OLE DB provider. Location is nvarchar(4000), with a default of NULL. Location is passed as the DBPROP_INIT_LOCATION property to initialize the OLE DB provider.

[@provstr =] 'provider_string'

is the OLE DB provider-specific connection string that identifies a unique data source. Provider_string is nvarchar(4000), with a default of NULL. Provstr is passed as the DBPROP_INIT_PROVIDERSTRING property to initialize the OLE DB provider.

[@catalog =] 'catalog'

is the catalog to be used when making a connection to the OLE DB provider. Catalog is sysname, with a default of NULL. Catalog is passed as the DBPROP_INIT_CATALOG property to initialize the OLE DB provider.

The sp_ addlinkedserver system-stored procedure returns an integer value of 0 to indicate a successfully added linked server, and returns an integer value of 1 to indicate a failed attempt to create a linked server definition.

The sp_dropserver stystem-stored procedure has the syntax described by:

```
sp_dropserver [@server =] 'server'
[,[@droplogins =]{'droplogins' | NULL}]
```

Arguments

The following is the server to be removed. server is sysname, with no default. In this case, server must exist.

```
[@server =] 'server'
[@droplogins =] 'droplogins' | NULL
```

indicates that related remote and linked server logins for server must also be removed if droplogins is specified. @droplogins is char(10), with a default of NULL.

The sp_dropserver system-stored procedure returns an integer value of 0 to indicate that a linked server definition was successfully dropped, and returns a value of 1 to indicate that an attempt to drop a linked server definition failed.

The sp_linkedservers system-stored prodcedure is executed without any arguments, and returns an integer value of 0 to indicate success or a nonzero number to indicate failure. In addition, the list of currently configured linked servers is displayed in the query window. Table 9-2 describes the data returned by the sp_linkedservers system-stored procedure.

Table 9-2   Returned Data

Column Name	Data Type	Description
SRV_NAME	sysname	Name of the linked server
SRV_PROVIDERNAME	nvarchar(128)	Friendly name of the OLE DB provider managing access to the specified linked server
SRV_PRODUCT	nvarchar(128)	Product name of the linked server
SRV_DATASOURCE	nvarchar(4000)	OLE DB data source property corresponding to the specified linked server
SRV_PROVIDERSTRING	nvarchar(4000)	OLE DB provider string property corresponding to the linked server
SRV_LOCATION	nvarchar(4000)	OLE DB location property corresponding to the specified linked server
SRV_CAT	sysname	OLE DB catalog property corresponding to the specified linked server

9

Enterprise Manager provides an intuitive alternative for managing linked servers. The functionality available is the same as through the use of the stored procedures presented already.

To create a linked server definition using the Enterprise Manager console tree, expand the Security node, and then expand Linked Servers. Specify the name, provider properties, server options, and security options for the linked server. The valid options for these properties are the same as those used when executing the sp_addlinkedserver system-stored proecedure. To delete a linked server definition, right-click on the linked server and click Delete.

Executing a Distributed Query

To execute a distributed query against a linked server, include a fully qualified, four-part table name for each data source to query. This four-part name should be in the form

```
linked_server_name.catalog.schema.object_name.
```

For example, to execute a query that returns customer data from a SQL Server database and related order data from an Oracle database, the distributed query could look similar to the following:

```
SELECT    c.CustomerID,
          o.OrderID,
          o.OrderDate
FROM      SQLServer1.Northwind.dbo.Customers    AS    c,
          OracleSvr.Catalog1.SchemaX.Orders     AS    o
WHERE     o.CustomerID                    =    c.CustomerID
AND       o.OrderDate                     >    '05-MAR-2000'
```

XML SUPPORT IN SQL SERVER 2000

The standard data format eXtensible Markup Language (XML) is a format for marking up data with extensible tags that can be used by applications to determine the purpose of the data. Because XML data and their tags form a hierarchical data structure, XML is often used to represent complex data relationships. Therefore, it has become increasingly popular to transform relational database data into XML and vice versa. SQL Server 2000 has rich support for performing these types of transformations automatically.

In SQL Server 2000, it is possible to make a request for relational data in the form of XML and have the SQL OLE DB provider in SQL Server construct an XML document from the resulting data. In addition, it is possible to insert, update, or delete data in SQL Server using XML syntax to describe the data that should be inserted, updated, or deleted. Much of this functionality is available through stored procedures and general T-SQL statements that are executed against SQL Server 2000. However, there are also features that can be used directly from a browser and do not require writing T–SQL code. Some of these features include:

- Executing a T–SQL query in the URL window of a browser to retrieve the results as XML.

- Executing a query against a database object, such as a table or view, using the XPath query syntax.

- Defining an XML template with a T–SQL statement that can be executed to return a set of data in the form of XML.

- Defining an XML View that uses XML Data Reduced (XDR) syntax instead of T–SQL syntax.

In order for these features to function correctly, a machine running Internet Information Services (IIS) 5.0 on Windows 2000 must have access to the SQL Server database, which can be on another machine. In addition, configuration of the IIS is necessary to define from where the data will come and what security will be applied. These procedures will be described below.

Configuring Internet Information Services for XML Support

The XML support in Internet Information Services (IIS) is implemented as an Internet Services API (ISAPI) filter in the Internet Services Manager for Windows 2000. Internet Services Manager can be opened from the Administrative Tools, available on the Control Panel of a Windows 2000 machine. This can allow verification that the ISAPI filter is installed, or can be used to troubleshoot the ISAPI filter installations. However, Microsoft has created a Microsoft Managment Console (MMC) snap-in that will configure the XML support in IIS automatically. To invoke the MMC snap-in, click on Configure SQL XML Support in IIS from the Microsoft SQL Server program group off the start menu. A standard MMC snap-in should open, and the local machine should be displayed. It is from this interface that the XML support can be configured. See Figure 9-19.

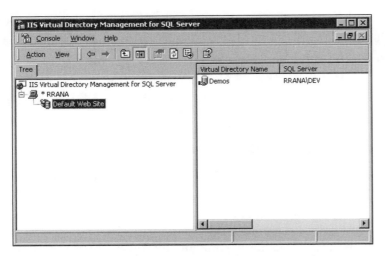

Figure 9-19 The MMC snap-in to configure SQL XML support in IIS

Virtual Directories

Internet Information Services 5.0 is included with Windows 2000. When SQL Server 2000 is installed to a machine running Windows 2000, the ISAPI filter **sqlisapi.dll** is copied to the machine and registered. The default location for this file is in \Program Files\Common Files\System\OLE DB\sqlisapi.dll, but the file may reside in another location. This filter can automatically intercept HTTP requests for XML data and pass these to SQL Server 2000 in the appropriate manner. If trouble is encountered when attempting to configure and use the XML support in SQL Server 2000, it is helpful to verify that this ISAPI filter is listed in the Internet Services Manager. To do this, click on the ISAPI Filters tab in the Properties dialog box for the Web site that is enabled for XML support. To access the Properties dialog box, right-click the Web site in the Internet Services Manager and then click on Properties.

To allow IIS to differentiate between request files that exist in conventional virtual directories and XML requests, it is necessary to create SQL virtual directories. There is no limit to the number of virtual directories that can exist in a Web site, and each may have its own templates and schema files, or may allow direct access to query objects in the database. Properties should be set on each virtual directory, such as the name and file location for files in the virtual directory, what type of security to use when users attempt to access the directory, the server and database from which the directory can pull data, what types of XML data access to allow, and the location of the sqlisapi.dll ISAPI filter mentioned previously.

The data access settings allow an administrator to configure:

- Whether typing a query in the URL window can cause the query to run in SQL Server. This should only be enabled if the virtual directory is configured for SQL or Windows authentication on the Security tab.

- Whether template queries can be executed by typing the URL that references the template

- Whether the XPath syntax can be used to reference a database object. If this option is enabled, it is possible to run ad hoc queries similar to those allowed when executing queries in the URL window. However, this type of query allows mainly data viewing operations, and is therefore not as large a security risk.

- Whether to allow posting of XML templates and queries using the HTTP Post method

Each of these settings is located on the Settings tab of the Demos Properties dialog box in MMC, as shown in Figure 9-20.

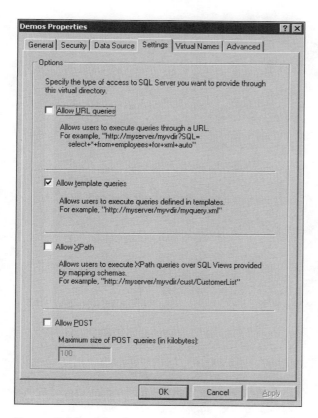

Figure 9-20   The Settings tab of the Demos Properties dialog box

Virtual Names

Correctly creating one or more virtual directories does not complete the configuration of XML support in SQL Server 2000. To allow SQL Server 2000 to differentiate among the different types of HTTP requests for XML data, it is necessary to create **virtual**

names. These virtual names each belong to a virtual directory and can fulfill one of three different types of data requests, as shown in Figure 9-21. These types are:

- Dbobject
- Schema
- Template

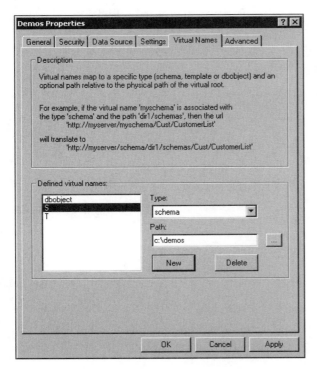

Figure 9-21   The Virtual Names tab of the Demos Properties dialog box

Dbobject

The dbobject virtual name type allows access to the objects in the underlying database if the Allow XPath option is selected for the virtual directory. This is possible using the syntax *http://server/vroot/dbobject/xpath*, where *server* is the name of the server, *vroot* is the name of the virtual directory, *dbobject* is the virtual name of type *dbobject*, and *xpath* is the XPath query that requests some data from a database object. An example is *http://localhost/demos/dbobject/Employees[@EmployeeID=1]/@LastName*. In this example, the XPath query Employees[@EmployeeID=1]/@LastName retrieves the value of the LastName column in the record of the Employees table where EmployeeID = 1.

Schema

The schema virtual name type allows access to data in the underlying database without the use of a T-SQL statement. In the folder defined by the path property for this type of virtual name, schema files that define the structure and relationships of database objects may be stored. These schema files are also called XML Views because it is possible to reference query them using the XPath syntax. The syntax for doing this is *http://server/vroot/vname/schema/xpath*.

Template

The template virtual name type allows access to an XML file that acts as a template if the "Allow template queries" option is selected for the virtual directory. The template must be located in the file folder specified in the Path property for the virtual name of type Template. This template stores a T-SQL statement that can optionally use parameters passed into the template in the URL. The syntax used to request that a template be executed is *http://server/vroot/vname/template*.

CHAPTER SUMMARY

There are a variety of data formats and methods for moving data into and out of SQL Server 2000. For one-time importing and exporting of data, the bulk insert task and BCP utility can be executed using T-SQL statements and Windows command-line statements. To apply user-defined transformations to data imports and exports, DTS packages can be managed in Enterprise Manager. In addition, Enterprise Manager can be used to configure replication to keep copies of the same data on multiple sites. If it is necessary to retrieve or to insert data in XML format, the FOR XML clause can be used in T-SQL statements. This functionality can be accessed using an HTTP request if IIS is properly configured using the sqlisapi.dll ISAPI filter and the "Configure SQL XML Support in ITS" MMC snap-in that comes with SQL Server 2000.

KEY TERMS

Bulk Copy Program (BCP) — This is an executable program used to move data into and out of SQL Server 2000.

BULK INSERT — A statement used in SQL Server 2000 to insert data into a table or view from a data file.

BULK INSERT Statement — A Transact-SQL (T-SQL) statement that executes a bulk insert.

Data Latency — A measure of how long it takes after data modifications are made on one server before they are reflected on a server to which the data are replicated.

Data Transformation Services (DTS) — A bundled set of features for importing, exporting, and transforming data using a variety of data formats and transfer methods.

DTS Designer — A tool available in Enterprise Manager that allows the creation and design of DTS packages.

DTS package — A set of DTS tasks that each move or transform data or perform related tasks.

Distributor — A server that participates in replication by moving data to Subscribers.

merge replication — A type of replication that allows changes made at different sites to be merged at a later time.

Publisher — A server that participates in replication by creating sets of articles, called publications, that will later be copied to Subscribers of the publications.

replication — The process of synchronizing copies of data stored in multiple sites.

snapshot replication — A type of replication that periodically copies entire publications as they exist at a moment in time.

SQL virtual directories — Namespaces that do not correspond to physical file folders, but are tracked by IIS so that requests can be forwarded to SQL Server 2000.

SQL Virtual Names — Sub-namespaces in IIS whose HTTP requests are forwarded to SQL Server 2000 as a specific type of request.

sqlisapi.dll — An implementation of the Internet Services API (ISAPI) filter that provides SQL-specific functionality to Internet Information Services (IIS).

Subscriber — A server that participates in replication by subscribing to publications of data.

transactional replication — A type of replication in which incremental changes made on the Publisher are sent to each Subscriber.

XPath — A syntax used to query an XML document based on naming the element whose data is desired.

REVIEW QUESTIONS

1. The BULK INSERT statement can be used to accomplish which of the following tasks? (Choose all that apply.)

   a. Insert data from an Excel spreadsheet into a SQL Server table.

   b. Insert binary data from a file into a SQL Server view.

   c. Insert comma-delimited character data from a file into a SQL Server table.

   d. Export data from a SQL Server table to a text file.

2. True or False: The BULK INSERT statement runs as a separate connection from other SQL statements executed in the same batch.

3. How should the performance of the BULK INSERT statement compare to the performance of the BCP utility?

   a. BCP should be faster.

   b. BULK INSERT should be faster.

   c. The two are approximately the same speed.

   d. It depends on whether the data is character data or binary data.

4. Which keyword is used in the BCP command to specify that data should be output from a query to a text file?

   a. OUT

   b. IN

   c. QUERYOUT

   d. No keyword is required because the query is a SELECT query that outputs data by default.

5. True or False: A single BULK INSERT or BCP command always executes as a single transaction.

6. Which of the following are required to ensure that a BCP operation is not logged? (Choose all that apply.)

   a. The recovery model is simple or bulk logged.

   b. The target table is not being replicated.

   c. The target table does not have any triggers.

   d. The target table is empty and has no indexes.

   e. The TABLOCK hint is specified.

7. What is the simplest way to modify a BCP operation so that data are not provided for each column in the destination table?

   a. Simply do not provide the data in the source file.

   b. If the missing columns do not occur at the end of the column list, create a format file using any text editor.

   c. Regardless of where the missing columns occur, create a format file using any text editor.

   d. If the missing columns do not occur at the end of the column list, create a format file by running the BCP utility.

   e. Regardless of where the missing columns occur, create a format file by running the BCP utility.

8. The Data Transformation Services support which type of data formats? (Choose all that apply.)

   a. SQL Server 2000

   b. ODBC Data Sources

   c. Excel

   d. Oracle

   e. binary data exported using BCP

9. True or False: A DTS package may be created directly from the DTS Designer without first using the DTS Import/Export Wizard.

10. True or False: If a DTS task fails, each subsequent task in the package will fail.

11. In which ways can a DTS Package be saved? (Choose all that apply.)

   a. to SQL Server

   b. to the Meta Data Services

   c. to a command-line script

   d. to a structured storage file

   e. to a Visual Basic file

12. Which is the default method for performing transformations in DTS?

   a. customizing the default SQL script used by DTS

   b. customizing the default JScript used by DTS

   c. customizing the default VBScript used by DTS

   d. customizing the VB code used by DTS

13. The Query Builder is available from which location in the DTS Import/Export Wizard?

   a. the Column Mappings tab in the Column Mappings and Transformations dialog box

   b. the Select Source Tables and Views dialog box

   c. the Type SQL Statement dialog box

   d. the Select Objects to Copy dialog box

14. Which of the following is responsible for resolving conflicts in replication?

   a. the merge agent

   b. the distribution agent

   c. the snapshot agent

   d. the log reader agent

   e. the publication agent

15. Which of the following types of replication is typically configured to execute with the least frequency?

   a. transactional replication

   b. merge replication

   c. snapshot replication

   d. hybrid replication

16. True or False: The Publisher may not be the same SQL Server machine as the Distributer.

17. True or False: To replicate data from a table to some servers running SQL Server and some running Oracle, it is necessary to create two publications.

18. The Replication Monitor contains which of the following? (Choose all that apply.)

   a. replication alerts

   b. Publishers

   c. Agents

   d. Subscriptions

19. Which of the following will verify that XML support is configured in IIS?

   a. opening Query Analyzer and attempting to execute a SELECT T-SQL statement with the FOR XML clause

   b. verifying that the Microsoft Management Console snap-in ITS Virtual Directory for SQL Server has been installed

   c. checking that the file sqlisapi.dll is present under the \Program Files\Common Files\System\OLE DB folder

   d. opening Internet Services Manager and verifying that the sqlisapi.dll filter has been applied to the desired Web site

20. Which of the following are required for a Windows user to execute a T-SQL statement on a SQL Server instance from a browser? (Choose all that apply.)

   a. The sqlisapi.dll filter must be in place on the target Web site.

   b. There must be a SQL virtual directory on the Web site with permissions to execute URL queries.

   c. The user must have permissions in the SQL Server instance or anonymous access must be enabled.

   d. There must be at least one virtual name on the Web site with permissions to execute URL queries.

   e. The query must be a SELECT statement that uses the FOR XML clause, an INSERT statement, an UPDATE statement, or a DELETE statement.

9

HANDS-ON PROJECTS

Project 9-1

To use the BCP command-line utility to import the Investors.txt file into a table in SQL Server 2000, you will want to save the format file that SQL Server 2000 generates for you so that you can later perform the import of the Prospects.txt file into the same table, even though it will present data in a slightly different format. Before you begin, create a table called Investors in the Northwind database by executing the Investors_Table.SQL student file in Query Analyzer:

1. Open the command prompt from Windows 2000 by clicking on **Programs**, then **Accessories**, and then **Command Prompt** in the Start Menu or by clicking on **Start**, then **Run**, and then entering **cmd.exe**.

2. Switch to the file location where your BCP.exe utility is stored. This is typically \Program Files\Microsoft SQL Server\80\Tools\Binn.

3. Execute the following command:

   ```
   BCP northwind.dbo.investors in path\investors.txt
   -SServer\Instance —Usa -Ppassword
   ```

   Path is the path where you have located the Investors.txt student file, *Server\Instance* is the name of your server and instance of SQL Server 2000, and *password* is the password of the user "sa."

4. You will be prompted to enter the file storage type, prefix length, field length, and field terminator of each field. For each file storage type, enter **char**. For the field prefix lengths, enter **0**, as there are not field prefix values in the file Investors.txt. For the field lengths, enter the suggested value. This should be 50 for first and last names, 50 for MoneyToInvest, and 10 for PhoneNumber. For the field terminators, enter **\t**, the Tab character, for the first three fields. For the last field, enter **\n**, denoting that a new-line character will delimit each row.

5. The final question asks whether to save the format file. Click **yes**, and name a path and filename where the file should be stored. Note this information, as you will need it in a future exercise.

   SQL Server 2000 should notify you that nine rows were copied. Open **Enterprise Manager**. Expand your server, and expand the databases folder. Expand the Northwind database. Right-click **Investors**, highlight **Open Table** and then **Return all rows**. Verify that the records have been copied into the table. Now you will use the BCP utility to insert the contents of the Prospects.txt student file into the table. This will require modifying the format file you created, because the last two columns in this file, MoneyToInvest and PhoneNumber, have changed order.

6. Open the format file you saved in the previous step in any text editor.

7. In the fourth column, the field sizes are given. Switch the **50** and the **10** in the last two rows so that they trade places.

8. In the sixth column, the order of the columns in the database table is given. Switch the **3** and the **4** in the last two rows so that they trade places.

9. Execute the same command as in Step 3, except that you will change the filename from Investors.txt to Prospects.txt. Also, type the switch **–f***path******formatfile*, where *path**formatfile* is the path and name of the format file, that you created in Step 5.

   You should see a message printed to the command window that four records were copied. Following the same instructions after Step 5, verify that the rows have been inserted.

Project 9-2

To use the Data Transformation Services to create a package that imports data from an Access database into SQL Server 2000, you will use custom transformations to change the value imported for the AccountID column and to ensure that the names are in uppercase:

1. Open the **Accounts.MDB** Access database if you have Access installed on your machine. Look at the Accounts table. It has an AccountNumber column, a FirstName column, and a LastName column. Close Access when done.

2. Open **Enterprise Manager** and expand your server name in the Microsoft SQL Servers group.

3. Right-click on your server and click on **Import Data** under the **All Tasks** submenu. The DTS Import/Export Wizard should open. Click **Next**.

4. The first two dialog boxes will ask you to select the source and destination for the data import. For the source, click on **Microsoft Access** in the Data Source list box. Use the ellipsis below to select the file by browsing to the Accounts.MDB student file in the location that you have saved it. No user name or password is required, so click **Next**.

5. For the destination, click on **Microsoft OLE DB Provider for SQL Server**, which is the default, in the Destination list box. Select the current server in the server list box, and click on the Northwind database in the **Database** list box. Click **Next**.

6. Leave the default **Copy table and view from the source database** option selected. Click **Next**.

7. In the Select Source Tables and Views dialog box, leave the automatically selected **Northwind.dbo.Accounts** table selected. Click on the **Transform** ellipses next to the name of the table.

8. Click the **Transformations** tab and then click the **Transform information as it is copied to the destination** radio button.

9

9. In the function Main(), change the expression that assigns the destination AccountNumber field so that it concatenates the constant string ACC to each of the accounts. To do this, change the line that reads:

```
DTSDestination("AccountNumber")=DTSSource("AccountNumber")
```

to read:

```
DTSDestination("AccountNumber") = "ACC" &
DTSSource("AccountNumber")
```

10. To ensure all first names appear in upper case, change the expression that assigns the destination FirstName field. To do this, change the line that reads:

```
DTSDestination("FirstName") = DTSSource("FirstName")
```

to read:

```
DTSDestination("FirstName") = Ucase(DTSSource("FirstName"))
```

11. Repeat the previous step for the LastName field. Click **OK**.

12. Click **Next** to complete the Select Source Tables and Views dialog box.

13. Check the **Save DTS Package** option and leave the default of **SQL Server** as the storage type. Click **Next**.

14. Name the Package **AccountImport**, and click **Next**.

15. Review the DTS import summary and click **Finish**. After viewing the successful completion message, click **OK** and then click **Done**.

16. Verify that the data are in the Accounts table and that the transformations were applied correctly. Close Enterprise Manager when done.

Project 9-3

To use the DTS Designer to modify the package you created in the previous lab and include a task that will create a backup of the imported file when the import is complete:

1. Open **Enterprise Manager** and expand your server name in the Microsoft SQL Servers group.

2. Expand the **Data Transformation Services** folder in the tree list, and click on **Local Packages**. You should see the AccountImport package that you created in the last project.

3. Open a text editor and create a batch file that you will put on the root of your hard drive. For the contents of the batch file, enter the following:

```
copy path\Accounts.mdb path\Accounts_old.mdb
```

Note that *path* is the file location to which you have saved the Accounts.mdb file. The file must be on a read–write disk. Save the file as **DTS_Complete.bat** on the root of your hard drive.

4. In Enterprise Manager, right-click on the AccountImport package, and select **Design Package**. This will open the DTS Designer.

5. From the toolbar on the left, drag an **Execute Process Task** to the white space in the DTS Designer.

6. For the description, enter **Backup file when complete**. For the Win32 process, browse to and click on the batch file you created in Step 3.

7. Click **OK**. This will close the Execute Process Task Properties dialog box.

8. Holding down the Ctrl key, click on both the connection to SQL Server and the **Execute Process** task. On the Workflow menu above, click on **On Success**. You should now see a green arrow going from the SQL Server connection to the Execute Process task.

9. Click on **Package**, and then click **Save** on the menu bar. Close the DTS Designer without closing Enterprise Manager.

10. In Enterprise Manager, expand the **Northwind** database, expand the Tables node, and click on the **Accounts** table. Press the **Delete** key, and confirm that you want to drop the table by clicking on **Drop All**.

11. Go back to the AccountImport package under **Local Packages** in **Data Transformation Services**.

12. Right-click on the package and click on **Execute Package**. You should verify that the data were again imported and that now a backup of the file imported named AccountImport_old.mdb exists in the same folder as the original file. Close Enterprise Manager when done.

Project 9-4

To demonstrate the configuration of replication in SQL Server 2000 (these instructions can be used as a guide for establishing transactional replication):

This example requires that you have two SQL Server machines or two instances of SQL Server 2000 on the same machine. At least one must be the Standard or Enterprise edition of SQL Server 2000. The other may be a Personal, Desktop, or Developer edition of SQL Server 2000 or a previous version of SQL Server.

1. Click **Start**, highlight **Programs**, highlight **Microsoft SQL Server**, and click **Enterprise Manager**. Expand the local SQL server instance.

2. Right-click on the **Replication** folder and click on **Configure Publishing, Subscribers, and Distribution** in the menu that appears. This will invoke the Publishing and Distribution Wizard. See Figure 9-22. Click **Next**.

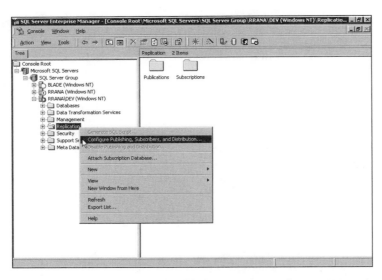

Figure 9-22   Invoking the Publishing and Distribution Wizard

3. In the Select Distributor dialog box shown in Figure 9-23, keep the default radio button selected, specifying that the local machine will be the distributor. Click **Next**. If you are prompted to change the account under which SQLServerAgent runs, use the MachineName\User syntax, and choose a user with administrative privileges on the machine. Stop and re-start SQL Server.

4. In the Configure SQL Server Agent dialog box, keep the default radio button selected, specifying that the SQL Server Agent service should start automatically. This will allow replication to occur unattended. Click **Next**.

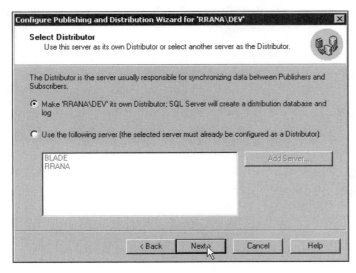

Figure 9-23   The Select Distributor dialog box

5. In the Specify Snapshot Folder dialog box, use the default location or specify any other location that you prefer. Note that if a remote Subscriber uses a pull subscription, the SQL Server Agent on that machine will need to run using an account that has access to this snapshot folder. Click **Next**.

 If a message box appears, click Yes to use the path specified.

6. In the Customize the Configuration dialog box, click the **No, use the default settings** radio button and click **Next**.

7. Click **Finish** to configure the server as a distributor. Click **OK** when the confirmation message box appears.

8. Enterprise Manager should present a notification that the Replication Monitor has been added to allow monitoring of all replication activity. Click **Close** when done.

9. Create a two-column table in the Northwind database and name it **ReplicationData**. Name one column **ID**. This will be an integer and will serve as the primary key. Name the second column **Text**. This will be a varchar(50) column. See Figure 9-24.

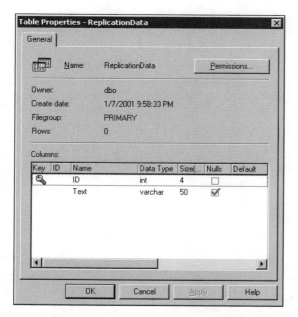

Figure 9-24 Sample table that will be replicated

10. Enter a few data records into the table.

11. Expand the Replication folder, right-click **Publications** and then click **New Publication**.

12. Click **Next** in the Welcome dialog box.

13. In the Choose Publication Database dialog box, click on **Northwind Database**, and then click **Next**.

14. In the Select Publication Type dialog box, click on **Transactional publication**, and then click **Next**.

15. Click on **Servers running SQL Server 2000** and deselect any other options. Click **Next** to proceed.

16. In the Specify Articles dialog box, click only the table that you created earlier, **ReplicationData**. Click **Next**.

17. Leave the default Publication Name and Publication Description in the Select Publication name and Description dialog box. Click **Next**.

18. In the Customize Properties dialog box, leave **No**, the default radio button, selected. Click **Next**.

19. Click **Finish** to create the publication.

20. SQL Server Enterprise Manager should confirm that the Publication was successfully created. Click **Close**.

21. Verify that the publication is present by opening the Publications node under the Replication folder in Enterprise Manager. See Figure 9-25.

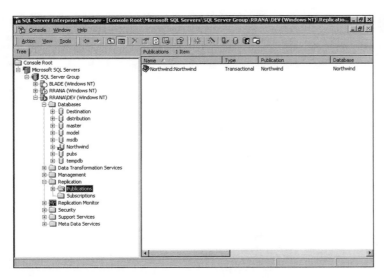

Figure 9-25   The publication listing under the Publications node

22. Right-click on the publication you created and click on **Push New Subscription** from the context-sensitive menu. This will invoke the Push Subscription Wizard. Click **Next**.

23. In the Choose Subscribers dialog box, select a second server or server instance to which the publication should be replicated. Click **Next**.

24. In the Choose Destination Database dialog box, click on the **Northwind** database as the database to which the data will be replicated. Click **Next**.

25. In the Set Distribution Agent Schedule dialog box, click on **Continuously**. This will cause updates to the data in the publication to be sent to the Subscriber immediately. Click **Next**.

26. In the Initialize Subscription dialog box, click the **Yes, initialize the schema and data** radio button and check the **Start the Snapshot Agent** check box. See Figure 9-26. This will initialize the snapshot so that updates on the Publisher can be replicated. Click **Next**.

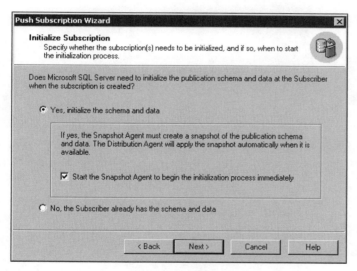

Figure 9-26   The Initialize Subscription dialog box

27. If the Start Required Services dialog box appears, verify that the SQLServerAgent is started. If it is not, start it, and click **Next**.

28. On the final dialog box, click **Finish** to verify that SQL Server should create the push subscription. Click **Close** when the confirmation message appears.

SQL Server should notify you that the push subscription was created. The subscription should appear on the right-hand side of Enterprise Manger when the publication name is selected in the tree view on the left. See Figure 9-27. Verify that the table now exists on the server acting as the Subscriber. Check to verify that when data are modified on the Publisher, the updates are replicated to the Subscriber.

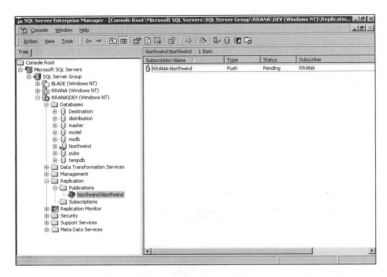

Figure 9-27   The push subscription in Enterprise Manager

Project 9-5

To configure the XML support to allow queries from the URL, you will test the configuration by entering a URL in your browser that should cause a query to execute:

1. Click **Programs** in the Start menu, then click on **Microsoft SQL Server**, and then click on **Configure SQL XML Support in IIS**.

2. You should see your computer name. Expand your computer and right-click on the **Default Web Site**.

3. Highlight **New**, then click on **Virtual Directory**. This will open the New Virtual Directory Properties dialog box. On the General tab, give the virtual directory the name **Demos**. Click on any folder you prefer, including the root of your hard drive, in the Local Path text box.

4. In the Security tab, leave the **Always log on as** option selected, and enter a SQL Server user name that has read access to the Customers table in the Northwind database. For example, you can enter **sa** in the username text box and enter the password in the **password** text box.

You may be prompted to confirm your password.

5. On the Data Source tab, click on the local SQL Server in the SQL Server text box.

6. Click on the **Northwind** database. If the database list is not available, recheck the server name, the user name, and the password on the previous tab.

7. On the Settings tab, click on the **Allow URL queries** option. Click **Apply** to apply the settings and **OK** to exit the Properties dialog box.

8. Open a browser and enter the following URL:

http://localhost/demos?sql=select+*+from+Customers+FOR+XML+auto&root=Root

You should see an XML document in your browser. If you see nothing, it is possible that your browser does not render the result because it is expecting HTML. In this case, select to view the source (procedure varies depending on browser). In Internet Explorer, the XML should appear in an expandable/collapsible tree view, as shown in Figure 9-28.

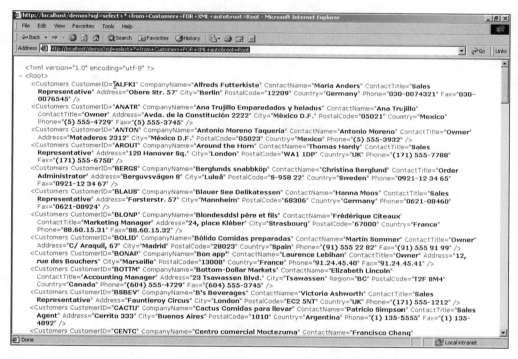

Figure 9-28   The XML output

Note that you can also use your machine name instead of "localhost." In addition, it is possible to choose any value for the variable "root." For example, it is possible to enter **root=Test**. This will only change the name of the root element in the resulting XML document.

CASE PROJECTS

Case One

Amy is responsible for the order fulfillment database in a warehouse. Because orders come from many different partners in the form of text files, Amy must create a data import that can be executed nightly. She knows that BCP is a high-performance way to import data from text files into SQL Server 2000 tables. However, the import will run at night, so speed is not crucial. In addition, there are several partners, and each provides the data in a slightly different format. Analyze the trade-offs between using BCP and DTS for the data import. State any assumptions you must make.

Case Two

A company has a sales team that is primarily responsible for educating its customers on the very complex product that it sells. Because much personal attention is necessary in this process, sales people travel to their customers' sites, and often are not connected to the corporate network. However, it is necessary for each salesperson to access primarily the data concerning customers in his or her region. The salesperson must be able to update customer data offline. The central office may update the data at the same time because inside sales representatives are sometimes in contact with decision makers over the phone. In addition, several product catalog changes are made once quarterly, and each sales representative should receive the updates. Suggest a replication strategy. Identify the roles that each participant will take. Is more than one replication type beneficial?

Case Three

Company A has decided that it is necessary to have a backup server to which applications and users can connect if the primary server experiences a failure. However, Company A has decided not to use SQL Server clustering. How else could the backup server be configured so that it stays up-to-date with the changes to data made on the primary server? How does the strategy vary if the tolerance for the data lost in the failure is data added in the last 10 minutes versus data added in the last day?

Case Four

Company B has a technical staff that is proficient in XML. However, the database administrator and his team of database developers have recently left the company, and no remaining staff members are familiar with structured query language. The company wishes to make simple product catalog content available on the Internet in the form of XML documents to which XSL style sheets will be applied. The company is running SQL Server 2000 and Windows 2000 Advanced Server. Create an implementation plan for providing the content using SQL Server 2000 and the XML functionality available in IIS. Decide whether database object, template, or schema virtual names should be used. Also suggest an authentication method for browsing the product catalog content.

10

AUTOMATING AND MONITORING SQL SERVER 2000

After reading this chapter and completing the exercises you will be able to:

♦ Configure SQL Server Agent to automate the administration of SQL Server 2000

♦ Create and configure jobs, alerts, and operators by using SQL Server Agent

♦ Monitor hardware resource usage and SQL Server activity by using the Windows System Monitor

These days, database administrators can expect to be involved in several different projects simultaneously. Since they are the owners of the most critical corporate asset (mission-critical data), database administrators are often responsible for several applications within an organization. Common applications include financials, human resources applications, and customer management systems. These additional responsibilities do not preclude the traditional database administrator tasks, however. On top of building new applications and supporting them, a database administrator is still expected to make sure the various databases within a network environment are running smoothly.

Routine backups and optimization tasks (like rebuilding indexes) have to be performed for every database in use. On top of that, most databases have administrative requirements that are specific to the database itself. Managing and performing these various tasks can be tedious and time-consuming. To help limit the actual time spent by a database administrator in performing these routine tasks, SQL Server 2000 tasks can be automated using native tools like SQL Server Agent and the Database Maintenance Plan Wizard (discussed in Chapter 7). In addition to scheduling administrative tasks, SQL Server Agent can also be used to monitor SQL Server 2000 instances and alert database administrators when predetermined performance thresholds are breached.

SQL SERVER 2000 AUTOMATION

SQL Server 2000 offers a robust infrastructure for automating administrative activity. **Automated administration** refers to a programmed response to a predictable administrative task (e.g., regular database backups) or event on the server. Leveraging this functionality in SQL Server 2000 frees database administrators to focus on tasks that cannot be predicted, like writing stored procedures to support a corporate Web site. Automatic maintenance reduces administrative costs as well. Performance problems can be detected and resolved before a system failure occurs, and, as we have already discussed, automating administrative tasks allows database administrators to use their working hours to contribute to more important initiatives.

SQL SERVER AGENT

The primary component responsible for automating administrative activity is the SQL Server Agent component. **SQL Server Agent** is a separate program that executes administrative tasks and generates alerts defined by database administrators. It is implemented as a service called SQLServerAgent in Windows 2000 and Windows NT. The SQL Server Agent can be used to perform the following operations:

- Execute administrative tasks
- Detect system conditions and automatically instigate measures to resolve problems
- Alert people in a variety of ways

These operations are configured through the use of objects called jobs, alerts, and operators. Figure 10-1 illustrates the basic relationship between these objects and SQL Server Agent.

The clock in Figure 10-1 represents the ability to schedule jobs to occur at specific times or repeatedly over a period of time.

Jobs

SQL Server Agent **jobs** are administrative tasks that are defined once and executed as many times as necessary. For example, a backup operation against the Northwind database could be a job. Jobs can be run manually, but they are more often scheduled. A job can be scheduled to run at a particular time, repeatedly on a regular schedule, or in response to an event or condition.

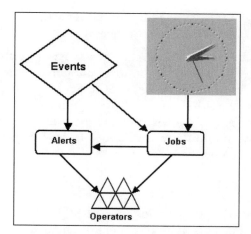

Figure 10-1   SQL Server Agent architecture

Jobs are not limited to a single operation. Instead, multiple dependent operations can be grouped into a single job. Each operation is called a **step**. A step in a job can be any one of the following:

- T-SQL statements

- Windows executable programs (.exe files)

- ActiveX scripts (shell scripts written in scripting languages like VBScript and JScript)

An important feature of jobs is that steps can be dependent. Depending on the success or failure of an individual step, additional steps can be executed or an entire job can be ended. SQL Server Agent automatically monitors jobs (and steps) for success or failure and can alert appropriate people if it is required. That brings us to another component in the SQL Server Agent architecture: Alerts.

Alerts

Alerts are actions on an instance of SQL Server 2000 in response to a particular event or performance condition. Alerts are commonly used to trigger notification of a problem to administrative users of a database known as operators (discussed in the next section). When configuring alerts to be triggered by events, we are referring to errors or messages that get written to the Windows application event log by SQL Server 2000. Performance conditions refer to various elements of server performance, like CPU utilization or hard drive statistics. The conditions are monitored through a special set of SQL Server 2000 counters and standard system counters, using the Windows System Monitor tool.

Alerts defined for particular events are triggered when a matching event is written to the Windows application event log. SQL Server Agent is notified when any Windows events occur, and new events are compared against the list of alerts defined for events.

10

If a match is found, then the alert executes any configured response actions, like sending an e-mail to the database administrator or executing a specific job.

Alerts defined for specific performance conditions are executed when a performance threshold is exceeded. SQL Server Agent constantly monitors configured performance metrics, like locks and the number of connections in use by SQL Server 2000. If a particular value exceeds a specified limit (e.g., the number of user connections exceeds 100), then the alert is triggered and any response operations are executed. Performance alerts are typically configured to notify administrative personnel. In SQL Server Agent terminology, administrators are known as operators.

Operators

Operators are users who are configured within an instance of SQL Server 2000 to receive notifications of particular jobs and alerts. Typically, operators are database administrators who have responsibility for one or more databases on an instance. An operator can receive notification in one of three ways:

- E-mail
- Pager
- The NET SEND command

E-mail Notification

E-mail notifications are provided through the SQL Mail service, discussed in Chapter 3. Contacting operators by e-mail is beneficial in that a history of the notifications is easily stored in the operator's mailbox. However, e-mail is not the fastest way to contact an operator. Depending on the volume of e-mails processed by a central e-mail server, or if the e-mail server is a large-scale public e-mail provider like Hotmail.com or Yahoo, e-mails are often backlogged and delivered minutes or even hours after they are actually sent. This can be a problem if the operator is being alerted to a serious, time-sensitive problem. Another limitation of e-mail notification is that an operator has to be in front of his or her e-mail client and constantly checking an inbox for new messages. In the dynamic work environments of today's corporations, people are usually not at their desks every minute of the workday, and important notifications can go unnoticed for a period of time.

 Wireless e-mail devices have begun to take hold in the business world these days. As a result, there are several mobile devices that provide the ability to send and receive e-mail from anywhere within a wireless carrier's network. Palm and Research In Motion (RIM) are two common manufacturers of these types of devices used today. Mobile technologies also make it possible to perform some administrative tasks from a remote location. For example, an application could be developed that allows an operator to execute a job or series of jobs against a server directly from a mobile device.

Pager Notification

Pager notification is actually an extension of the standard e-mail notification, in that only those pagers whose service providers handle e-mails for paging can be used. Pagers provide a better solution than e-mail in that they provide operators the ability to be away from their desks but still receive notifications right to their belt-mounted pagers. However, pagers still suffer the limitations of the e-mail systems that support them. In high-volume pager networks, messages may not be delivered in a timely fashion.

 In order for both pager and e-mail notification to work, SQL Server Agent must be configured with a MAPI mail profile to access a mail server. Creating mail profiles and configuring SQL Server Agent mail was discussed in detail in Chapter 3.

NET SEND Notification

Net send is a command line application in Windows 2000 and Windows NT, which automatically forces a message box to pop up on a computer screen when the user is connected to the network. This functionality is provided through the Windows 2000 and Windows NT service called Messenger. The **Messenger service** listens for messages sent across the network, receives messages addressed to the computer or user on the computer, and displays them in the form of a pop-up message box, as shown in Figure 10-2.

10

Figure 10-2   NET SEND message box

The NET SEND command allows users to create and send messages to the Messenger service running on another computer. SQL Server 2000 can use the NET SEND command to notify operators of job execution results and alerts. Net send messages are usually faster than e-mail–based notifications, and they provide the inherent benefit of popping up a message in the middle of a screen, regardless of the computer the user is using on the network. Net send messages are limited in that the user must be using a computer on the network to receive the message. Another limitation is that a historic record is not preserved, as when using e-mails. It is common to use Net send messages and e-mail notifications together to ensure that the message is received in a timely fashion and that all messages are stored for historical purposes (in the recipient's e-mail inbox).

Multiserver Automation

In an environment that has several instances of SQL Server 2000 supporting various corporate operations, centralized administration simplifies the process of maintaining multiple database servers. SQL Server 2000 provides these capabilities to allow database administrators to manage two or more servers and schedule multiple instance operations, like replication.

To configure multiple servers for centralized administration and automation, one master server and one or more target servers must be defined. Figure 10-3 illustrates the basic architecture of the multiserver automation.

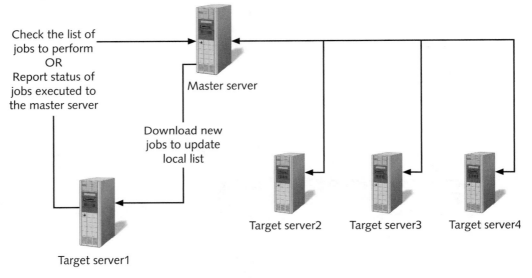

Figure 10-3   Multiserver automation architecture

The **master server** houses a complete list of the various operations (jobs) that must be performed on the various target servers. At regular intervals, each **target server** connects to the master server to determine if there are any changes to the list of jobs it maintains locally. If there are any differences, the new jobs are downloaded to the target server. The target server goes about its normal business and executes the jobs as their schedules require. When a job is executed on a target server, the target server connects to the master server and returns results of the job (success or failure).

For more information on setting up multiserver automation, refer to SQL Server Books Online.

CONFIGURING SQL SERVER AGENT

The SQL Server Agent service has several settings available at the service level. To configure the various properties of the SQL Server Agent component in Enterprise Manager, expand the Management folder under a registered instance, right-click on the SQL Server Agent node, and click Properties. This brings up the SQL Server Agent Properties window, as shown in Figure 10-4.

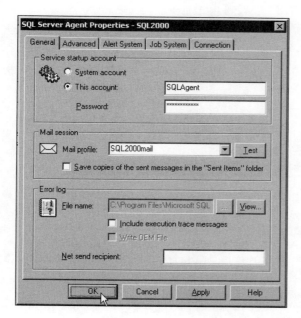

Figure 10-4   General tab of the Properties window SQL Server Agent

From this screen you can configure the account the SQL Server Agent service uses to log in. You can also configure the service to send e-mail by specifying a Windows mail profile. SQL Server Agent has its own error log that it uses to record problems encountered in its operations. Click the View button to access the error log. The error log also allows a Net send recipient to be defined. This recipient (specified in the form of a computer name on the network) will receive pop-up messages when new entries are logged to the SQL Server Agent error log.

Advanced Tab

The Advanced tab of the SQL Server Agent Properties window, shown in Figure 10-5, allows you to configure SQL Server Agent to monitor and restart the SQL Server and SQL Server Agent services if they unexpectedly stop.

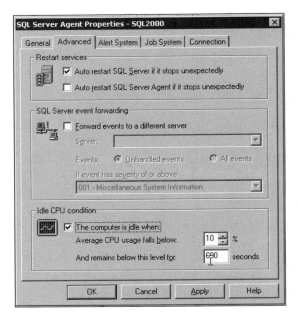

Figure 10-5   Advanced tab of the SQL Server Agent Properties window

 Automatically restarting services is recommended in a single server environment, because it limits system downtime in the event that a service terminates. However, if failover clustering is used, automatic restarting of the services must be disabled for clustering to work properly.

The event forwarding section provides various options for configuring a multiple server monitoring setup. Remember that alerts can be triggered from events that are written to the Windows application log. In a situation where there are several SQL Servers running on a single network, you could configure the server to forward all SQL Server 2000 related events to a single server. This way, alerts only need to be defined on a single central server to simplify administration.

The Advanced tab also allows a threshold to be specified to indicate when the instance is considered idle. This condition can be used to trigger maintenance jobs to fire automatically when the system is not fully utilized by users. Notice that you can specify a CPU usage percentage and a duration (in seconds). The default value is CPU utilization under 10% for 600 seconds (10 minutes).

Connection Tab

The Connection tab (shown in Figure 10-6) is where authentication credentials are specified for SQL Server Agent. Remember that SQL Server Agent is a separate service from the SQL Server service, and it must connect to the database just like any other user.

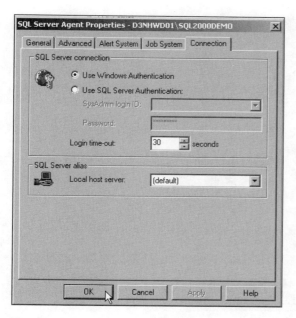

Figure 10-6   Connection tab of the SQL Server Agent Properties window

Typically, both the SQL Server Agent service and the SQL Server service will run under the same account, so Windows authentication would be used by SQL Server Agent to connect to the instance of SQL Server. All of the information regarding alerts, operators, and jobs is stored in the msdb database for a particular instance of SQL Server 2000, so it is imperative that SQL Server Agent be able to access this information in order to execute jobs and respond to alerts defined on the instance.

CREATING AND CONFIGURING JOBS, ALERTS, AND OPERATORS

In the following sections, procedures to create operators, jobs, and alerts are described in detail. Enterprise Manager has several simple graphical interfaces for creating and managing these objects. And, as with most functionality available through Enterprise Manager, equivalent T-SQL statements can be used to perform these same tasks.

Creating Operators

To create operators in Enterprise Manager, expand the Management folder, expand the SQL Server Agent node, right-click on the Operators node, and click the New Operator option from the context-sensitive menu. This brings up the New Operator Properties window. Figure 10-7 shows this window with sample information provided.

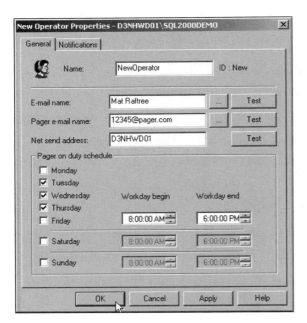

Figure 10-7   General tab of the New Operator Properties window

Use the General tab of the New Operator Properties window to specify a name for the new operator. This should be a logical name, since it is used for identification later when the operator is associated with jobs. As we have already discussed, operators can be contacted in one of three ways. Use this screen to specify e-mail, pager, and Net send addresses for an operator. You can also specify a schedule for when the operator will be on call to receive pages.

The Notifications tab, shown in Figure 10-8, allows you to specify which alerts and jobs should contact the operator. By default, events with a severity level of 19 or higher are logged in the Windows application log by SQL Server 2000, but the alert or job list will show any custom alerts that are defined on the server.

From this tab you can also activate or deactivate the operator by using the "Operator is available to receive notifications" check box. When this option is unchecked, the operators will not be notified, regardless of the schedule defined for them. This is useful when operators are away on business trips or out of the office for vacation. They can simply be reactivated when they return to reassume their operational responsibilities.

Creating Operators with T-SQL Statements

SQL Server 2000 provides several system-stored procedures for managing operators in the SQL Server Agent notification system. Since the msdb database stores all of the information about operators, alerts, and jobs, all of these procedures must be run from the msdb database.

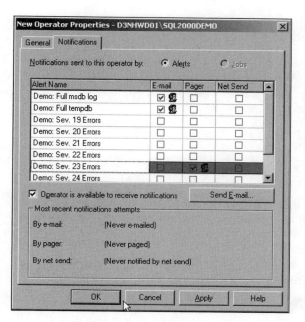

Figure 10-8   Notifications tab of the New Operator Properties window

10

The sp_add_operator system-stored procedure is used to add new operators. It adheres to the following syntax:

```
sp_add_operator [ @name = ] 'name'
  [ , [ @enabled = ] enabled ]
  [ , [ @e-mail_address = ] 'e-mail_address' ]
  [ , [ @pager_address = ] 'pager_address' ]
  [ , [ @weekday_pager_start_time = ] weekday_pager_start_
time ]
  [ , [ @weekday_pager_end_time = ] weekday_pager_end_time ]
  [ , [ @saturday_pager_start_time = ] saturday_pager_start_
time ]
  [ , [ @saturday_pager_end_time = ] saturday_pager_end_
time ]
  [ , [ @sunday_pager_start_time = ] sunday_pager_start_
time ]
  [ , [ @sunday_pager_end_time = ] sunday_pager_end_time ]
  [ , [ @pager_days = ] pager_days ]
  [ , [ @netsend_address = ] 'netsend_address' ]
  [ , [ @category_name = ] 'category' ]
```

The following example creates a new operator named John Smith. Notice that e-mail and pager addresses have been specified, but the Net send address has not. The procedure only requires that you include the parameters that you are specifying a value for.

```
USE msdb
EXEC sp_add_operator @name = 'John Smith',
  @enabled = 1,
  @e-mail_address ='jsmith@xyzcompany.com',
  @pager_address = '1234567@pagercompany.com',
  @weekday_pager_start_time = 060000,
  @weekday_pager_end_time = 183000,
  @pager_days = 62
```

The start and end times are specified in a six-digit format, where each pair of digits represents hours, minutes, and seconds respectively. In the example above, the weekday start time is specified as 060000, meaning 6:00 AM. The weekday end time is specified as 183000, meaning 6:30 PM.

The pager_days parameter specifies the days on which the operator can receive pager notifications. It takes a bitmask value, representing the days on which an operator is available. Table 10-1 shows the various day values.

Table 10-1   Day Values for the Pager_days Parameter

Value	Day	Value	Day
1	Sunday	16	Thursday
2	Monday	32	Friday
4	Tuesday	64	Saturday
8	Wednesday		

The value for the pager_days parameter is the sum of the values from the associated days. In the example, John Smith is available only on weekdays, and the value specified for the pager_days parameter value is 62 because the sum of 2 + 4 + 8 + 16 + 32 equals 62. A value of 0 means the operator is not available on any day, and a value of 127 signifies the operator is available every day of the week.

Updating Operators in T-SQL

The sp_update_operator system-stored procedure is used to modify the properties of existing operators. It accepts the same parameters as the sp_add_operator procedure, but it requires that the name parameter be a valid existing operator.

```
sp_update_operator [@name =] 'name'
  [, [@new_name =] 'new_name']
  [, [@enabled =] enabled]
  [, [@e-mail_address =] 'e-mail_address']
  [, [@pager_address =] 'pager_number']
  [, [@weekday_pager_start_time =] weekday_pager_start_time]
  [, [@weekday_pager_end_time =] weekday_pager_end_time]
  [, [@saturday_pager_start_time =] saturday_pager_start_
time]
```

```
[, [@saturday_pager_end_time =] saturday_pager_end_time]
[, [@sunday_pager_start_time =] sunday_pager_start_time]
[, [@sunday_pager_end_time =] sunday_pager_end_time]
[, [@pager_days =] pager_days]
[, [@netsend_address =] 'netsend_address']
[, [@category_name =] 'category']
```

The following example updates the previously created operator named John Smith. Notice that e-mail has been changed. Also, the hours available for John Smith are changed to 6:00 AM to 5:30 PM. The pager_days parameter value of 127 means that John Smith is available seven days a weeks for notifications.

```
USE msdb
EXEC sp_update_operator @name = 'John Smith',
  @e-mail_address ='jsmith@newcompany.com',
  @pager_address = '12345@pager.att.com',
  @weekday_pager_start_time = 080000,
  @weekday_pager_end_time = 173000,
  @pager_days = 127
```

Viewing and Deleting Existing Operators in T-SQL

The sp_help_operator system-stored procedure is used to return information about all or one of the operators defined in the msdb database for an instance of SQL Server 2000. It adheres to the following syntax:

```
sp_help_operator [ [ @operator_name = ] 'operator_name' ]
```

When called without any parameters, the procedure returns a result set containing the configurations for all operators in the system. If the operator_name parameter is specified, only the information of that particular operator is returned. Figure 10-9 shows the results returned when the following T-SQL code is executed from Query Analyzer:

```
USE msdb
EXEC sp_help_operator
```

To delete an existing operator, you would use the sp_delete_operator system-stored procedure. It adheres to the following syntax:

```
sp_delete_operator [ @name = ] 'name'
```

For example, the following code would delete the operator name John Smith from the msdb database.

```
EXEC sp_delete_operator 'John Smith'
```

Now that you have a thorough understanding of how operators are managed in SQL Server 2000, the next sections discuss how to create the jobs and alerts that a particular operator can be associated with for notification.

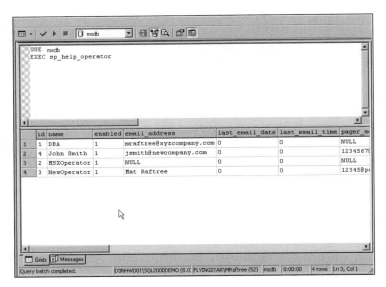

Figure 10-9   Results of the sp_help_operator system-stored procedure

Creating Jobs

New jobs are created in Enterprise Manager by expanding the Management folder, expanding the SQL Server Agent node, right-clicking on the Jobs node, and selecting the New Job option from the context-sensitive menu. This brings up the New Job Properties window shown in Figure 10-10.

Figure 10-10 contains sample job information.

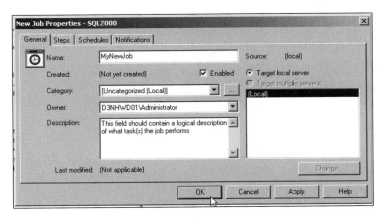

Figure 10-10   General tab of the New Job Properties window

The General tab allows you to specify high-level information about a new job. This is where a new job is named and given a description. Jobs can also be logically organized using the category field. There are several predefined categories that are used for administrative jobs that perform replication or database maintenance, but custom categories are easily created using this interface.

Jobs are disabled by clicking the Enabled check box to unselect it. This is useful if the job needs to be tested or if you need to prevent it from running temporarily. The job owner field specifies a login that is responsible for the job. The owner defaults to the current user, but it can be any valid login on an instance of SQL Server 2000. The "Target local server" option is used when a master server is used to centrally manage jobs across multiple target servers.

Only members of the sysadmin fixed server role can modify a job owned by another user.

Recall from our earlier discussion that each job is made up of one or more steps. Steps are the individual actions that are performed in a certain order to execute a job. The Steps tab of the New Job Properties screen, shown in Figure 10-11, will show a list of all the steps in a particular job.

10

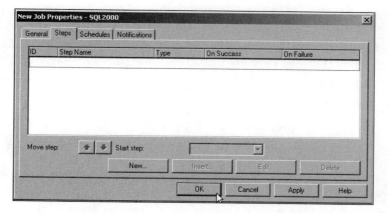

Figure 10-11   Steps tab of the New Job Properties window

Most jobs will be simple enough to perform with a single step. For example, a regular backup of a database or a once-a-week DBCC REINDEX call to rebuild the indexes of a database could be jobs with a single step. However, there may be requirements in complex environments that require multiple-step jobs to be executed. Consider a scenario where a reporting database needs to be updated regularly with data from three different production databases. In this situation, you might create a job with three steps, where each step copies the data from one of the databases to the reposting system.

Managing Job Steps

To create individual steps for a job, click the New button from the Steps tab of the New Job Properties window. This activates the New Job Step window, as shown in Figure 10-12. This window allows you to specify the type of job and the actual commands that should be executed as part of the step.

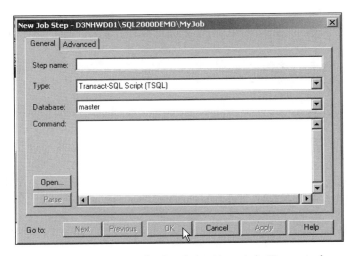

Figure 10-12   General tab of the New Job Step window

A logical name is specified to help identify the step, and then the type of the step is selected from the Type list. As we have discussed previously, there are three general types of steps:

- T–SQL statements
- Windows executable programs (.exe files)
- ActiveX scripts (shell scripts written in scripting languages like VBScript and JScript)

In addition to these, there are also some pre-defined step types associated with replication. For the sake of simplicity, we will only be dealing with the custom steps in this chapter.

When T-SQL script is chosen, a database is specified from the provided list and the actual T-SQL statement is typed into the Command field. In Figure 10-13, a new T-SQL step named Delete old orders is created with a T-SQL statement that deletes records in the Orders table of the Northwind database that have a shippeddate value that is before 01/01/1995.

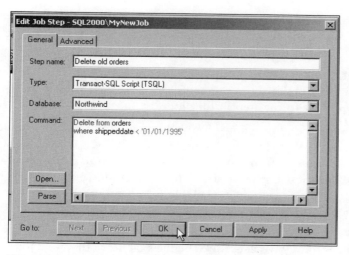

Figure 10-13   Sample information in the Edit Job Step window

To utilize a saved T-SQL script stored in a file, use the Open button to locate the file on the network. The Parse button allows you to check the syntax of the statement without actually executing it.

The Advanced tab of the New Job Step window, shown in Figure 10-14, provides additional options to further control each step in a job.

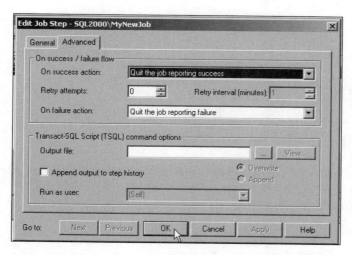

Figure 10-14   Advanced tab of the New Job Step window

10

From this tab you can specify what happens after the step executes. Notice how you can specify different actions for success and failure conditions. You can configure steps to retry executions from this tab as well.

In the case of a T-SQL step (as in the example we are discussing), there is a set of T-SQL specific options. With these options you can configure the T-SQL statement to write its output to a file or append it to the step history log.

One or more steps can be added to a single job and executed in an order that you specify. This simple architecture allows for a high degree of flexibility. For example, you could run four related T-SQL statements in a single job. You can also define steps of differing types to be run in the same job. For example, a single job could have a T-SQL statement step and a CMD Exec step that calls an executable program on the computer.

Scheduling Jobs

To manage the schedules for a job, select the Schedules tab from the New Job Properties window. The Schedules tab, shown in Figure 10-15, allows you to create new schedules and manage existing schedules.

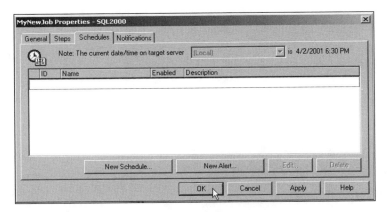

Figure 10-15   Schedules tab of the New Job Properties window

Each job can have one or more schedules associated with it, and each schedule can be easily enabled and disabled using this interface. To add a new schedule for the job, click the New Schedule button to access the New Job Schedule window, shown in Figure 10-16.

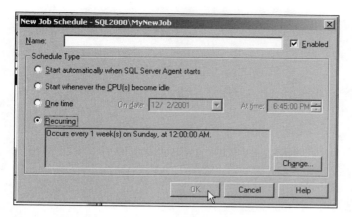

Figure 10-16   New Job Schedule window

Each schedule must have a name specified for it. In addition to that, there are four scheduling options for a job:

- Start the job whenever the SQL Server Agent service starts.
- Start the job when the CPU is in an idle condition.
- Start one time only by specifying a date and time.
- Start the job according to a recurring schedule.

Multiple schedules can be created and used together. For example, for a job that rebuilds indexes and updates statistics, you could have one schedule that runs the job on Sunday night, when system utilization is low, and you could have another schedule that executes the job if the CPU becomes idle. By using both schedules you can ensure that the job will run at least once a week (on Sunday night), regardless of activity on the server, but it will also take advantage of system lulls to execute the job more frequently.

Configuring Job Notifications

The automation system powered by the SQL Server Agent service keeps a log of all job and step history. This information can be helpful when debugging jobs and when verifying that jobs have executed successfully. In addition to this, various operators can be configured to receive notifications of jobs as they execute. To configure operators for jobs, click the Notifications tab of the New Job Properties window, as shown in Figure 10-17.

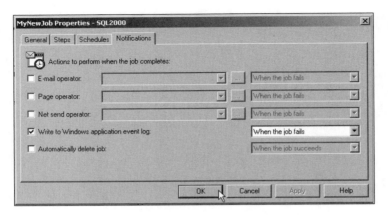

Figure 10-17   Notifications tab of the New Job Properties window

From this screen you would typically assign various operators to receive notifications via e-mail, pager, and NET SEND command. To send an e-mail notification to an operator, check the E-mail operator option, and then select an operator from the list box to the right. The notification can be configured in three ways:

- When the job fails
- When the job succeeds
- Every time the job executes regardless of success or failure

Typically, notifications for jobs are sent when the job fails to alert an operator to repair any problem with the job. By default, each job writes an event to the Windows application log when it fails. We will discuss how to configure an alert to listen for these events in the application log and notify an operator in a later section.

Creating Jobs with T-SQL Statements

There is a set of system-stored procedures that can be used to create and manage jobs. They each address the various options available through the Enterprise Manager user interface when creating jobs. Consider the sp_add_job system-stored procedure that is used to create a new job.

```
sp_add_job [ @job_name = ] 'job_name'
  [ , [ @enabled = ] enabled ]
  [ , [ @description = ] 'description' ]
  [ , [ @start_step_id = ] step_id ]
  [ , [ @category_name = ] 'category' ]
  [ , [ @category_id = ] category_id ]
  [ , [ @owner_login_name = ] 'login' ]
  [ , [ @notify_level_eventlog = ] eventlog_level ]
  [ , [ @notify_level_e-mail = ] e-mail_level ]
  [ , [ @notify_level_netsend = ] netsend_level ]
```

```
[ , [ @notify_level_page = ] page_level ]
[ , [ @notify_e-mail_operator_name = ] 'e-mail_name' ]
[ , [ @notify_netsend_operator_name = ] 'netsend_name' ]
[ , [ @notify_page_operator_name = ] 'page_name' ]
[ , [ @delete_level = ] delete_level ]
[ , [ @job_id = ] job_id OUTPUT ]
```

Notice how the procedure has a long list of parameters that map directly to the various options on the General and Notifications tabs of the New Job Properties window in Enterprise Manager. To create a job named BackupJob, on an instance of SQL Server 2000, that notifies an operator named John Smith via e-mail when the job fails, you would use the following syntax:

```
USE msdb
EXEC sp_add_job @job_name = 'BackupJob',
  @enabled = 1,
  @description = 'My Backup Job',
  @notify_level_e-mail = 2,
  @notify_e-mail_operator_name = 'John Smith'
```

The numeric values associated with the various notify_level parameters are outlined in Table 10-2.

Table 10-2 Notify Level Values for sp_add_job System-Stored Procedure

Value	Description
0	Never Notify
1	Notify when the job is successful
2	Notify when the job fails (this is the default value)
3	Notify whenever the job runs

In the previous code example, the notify_level_e-mail parameter is set to 2, meaning that the operator will only be notified if the job fails.

Adding Job Steps with T-SQL The sp_add_jobstep system-stored procedure is used to add steps to a job. It adheres to the following syntax:

```
sp_add_jobstep [ @job_id = ] job_id | [ @job_name = ] 'job_
name'
[ , [ @step_id = ] step_id ]
{ , [ @step_name = ] 'step_name' }
[ , [ @subsystem = ] 'subsystem' ]
[ , [ @command = ] 'command' ]
[ , [ @additional_parameters = ] 'parameters' ]
[ , [ @cmdexec_success_code = ] code ]
[ , [ @on_success_action = ] success_action ]
[ , [ @on_success_step_id = ] success_step_id ]
```

```
[ , [ @on_fail_action = ] fail_action ]
[ , [ @on_fail_step_id = ] fail_step_id ]
[ , [ @server = ] 'server' ]
[ , [ @database_name = ] 'database' ]
[ , [ @database_user_name = ] 'user' ]
[ , [ @retry_attempts = ] retry_attempts ]
[ , [ @retry_interval = ] retry_interval ]
[ , [ @os_run_priority = ] run_priority ]
[ , [ @output_file_name = ] 'file_name' ]
[ , [ @flags = ] flags ]
```

To add a step to the job named BackupJob from the last example, use the following syntax:

```
USE msdb
EXEC sp_add_jobstep @job_name = 'BackupJob',
 @step_name = 'Delete old orders',
 @subsystem = 'TSQL',
 @command = 'Delete from orders where shipped-
date < 01/01/1995',
 @database_name = 'Northwind',
 @retry_attempts = 5,
 @retry_interval = 5
```

This statement will create a T-SQL job step called "Delete old orders," which executes the T-SQL statement provided in the @command parameter. Notice also that the step will retry itself five times in the event of failure, with a timeout of five minutes between retry attempts.

Adding Job Schedules in T-SQL To add a job schedule to a job in T-SQL, use the sp_add_jobschedule system-stored procedure. It adheres to the following syntax:

```
sp_add_jobschedule
[ @job_id = ] job_id, | [ @job_name = ] 'job_name',
 [ @name = ] 'name'
[ , [ @enabled = ] enabled ]
[ , [ @freq_type = ] freq_type ]
[ , [ @freq_interval = ] freq_interval ]
[ , [ @freq_subday_type = ] freq_subday_type ]
[ , [ @freq_subday_interval = ] freq_subday_interval ]
[ , [ @freq_relative_interval = ] freq_relative_
interval ]
[ , [ @freq_recurrence_factor = ] freq_recurrence_
factor ]
[ , [ @active_start_date = ] active_start_date ]
[ , [ @active_end_date = ] active_end_date ]
[ , [ @active_start_time = ] active_start_time ]
[ , [ @active_end_time = ] active_end_time ]
```

To create a schedule called NewSchedule for the BackupJob job, you would use the following syntax:

```
USE msdb
EXEC sp_add_jobschedule @job_name = 'BackupJob',
 @name = 'NewSchedule',
 @freq_type = 4,
 @freq_interval = 1,
 @active_start_time = 230000
```

The freq_type parameter, with a value of 4, specifies that the schedule includes every day of the week, and the freq_interval parameter, with a value of 1, means that the jobs runs once a day. In this case the job will execute at 11:00 PM (active_start_time = 230000).

You should now be familiar with creating and managing jobs from both Enterprise Manager and through T-SQL system-stored procedures. Jobs can be set up to perform a wide array of tasks for administering SQL Server 2000 instances. For each job, multiple operators can be configured to receive notifications regarding the outcome of job executions. As we will see in the next section, operators can also be associated with alerts, so that certain events in a SQL Server 2000 instance can be captured and appropriate administrative personnel can be contacted to resolve any issues associated with the event.

Creating Alerts

Remember from our earlier discussion, that alerts are used to respond to events as well as performance conditions. You can define various alerts in the SQL Server Agent system to notify operators when particular events are written to the Windows application log. For example, an alert could be set up to notify an operator when any event of a certain severity occurs. Similarly, you can set alerts to respond to various performance counters provided through SQL Server 2000.

To create a new alert using Enterprise Manager, expand the Management folder, expand the SQL Server Agent, right-click the Alerts node, and click New Alert from the context-sensitive menu. This activates the New Alert Properties window, shown in Figure 10-18.

10

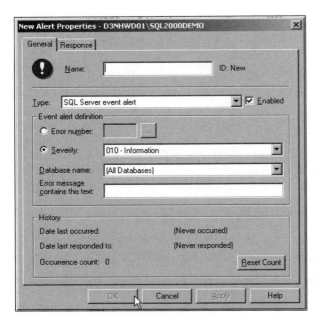

Figure 10-18   New Alert window

This screen can be used to configure both event-based alerts as well as performance con-
dition-based alerts. By default, the window is ready to accept a SQL Server event alert.

SQL Server Event Alerts

SQL Server 2000 traps and reports certain events to the Windows application log. Each
error that SQL Server 2000 reports is stored in the sysmessages table of the master database. By default there are over 3700 different messages stored in this table. Each of these
has a unique error number and a severity level, as well as descriptive information. The
higher the severity of the error, the greater the impact on the system. Table 10-3 outlines the various severity levels for SQL Server error messages.

Table 10-3   SQL Server Error Severity Levels

Severity Level	Description
1 – 10	Informational messages. For example, there are several level 10 messages that report information about various replication events.
11-16	Errors caused by users and correctable by them. For example, a level 11 message is used when a user misspells a table name in a T-SQL statement.
17	Insufficient Resources. For example, a query that fails because it requires more locks than are available.
18	Nonfatal Internal Error Detected. These errors indicate an internal software problem that did not result in a user losing his or her connection.
19	SQL Server Error in Resource. Similar to severity level 17, but deals only with limits that are not configurable by an administrator. These types of errors must be corrected by administrators.
20	SQL Server Fatal Error in Current Process. A fatal error encountered in a single process (user connection). Errors at this level only affect a single process, so the database itself should still be operational for other users.
21	SQL Server Fatal Error in Database (dbid) Processes. An error that affects all processes running on the database. The database itself is probably not damaged when one of these errors occurs.
22	SQL Server Fatal Error Table Integrity Suspect. An error noting that a hardware or software error has damaged a table.
23	SQL Server Fatal Error Database Integrity Suspect. An error noting that an entire database has been damaged by a hardware or software error.
24	SQL Server Fatal Error Hardware Error. An error noting that a media failure has likely occurred. This usually requires that the media be replaced and the database(s) be restored from backups.
25	SQL Server Fatal Error. An error that reports that the SQL Service has terminated abnormally.

10

You can also create user-defined error messages that have their own unique error number and one of the available severity levels. These errors can be raised using T-SQL system-stored procedures, triggers, or even jobs.

Any logged errors with a severity of 17 or higher should be configured to alert an administrator, since they deal with hardware or software errors and should be addressed. To configure all messages of severity 24 to notify an operator, you would first fill the New Alert Properties window with the information shown in Figure 10-19.

The name of the alert is set to Severe Error Alert (Level 24). Notice that the Type box is set to SQL Server event alert. Since we are trapping all errors of severity 24, simply specify the severity by selecting from the list. You can set alerts on a specific error number or based on the message containing some text as well. Alerts can be further limited to individual databases by using the Database name list arrow.

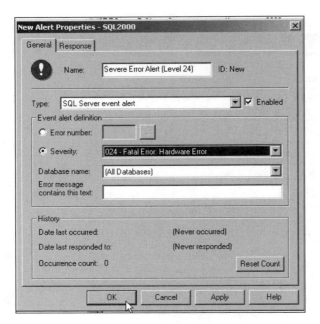

Figure 10-19 Creating a SQL Server event alert

Each alert can also be configured to notify operators of the event using the Response tab of the New Alert Properties window, shown in Figure 10-20. This tab shows all of the available operators who could be notified by the alert. Configure each operator by selecting the appropriate check boxes (E-mail, Pager, Net send). Also notice that a job could be run when the event occurs. This is useful if you can predict certain problems and resolve them by automatically running a job.

Performance Condition Alerts

Alerts can also be configured to fire when a threshold on some performance metric is breached. Performance conditions are set against certain performance counters. **Performance counters** are individual metrics that are measured by SQL Server 2000. Each performance counter is grouped into an object known as a **performance object**. An example of a performance object is SQL Server:General Statistics. This object has various counters, including User Connections. Later in this chapter, we will identify several of the most useful performance objects and their performance counters.

To set a performance condition alert, make the appropriate selection from the Type list box in the New Alert Properties screen, as shown in Figure 10-21.

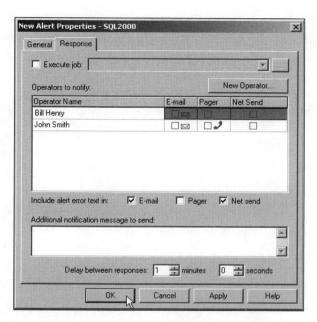

Figure 10-20   Notifications tab of the New Alert Properties window

10

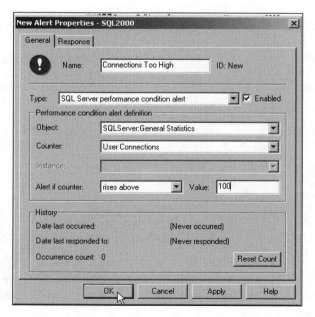

Figure 10-21   Creating a SQL Server performance condition alert

Since performance condition alerts are considerably different from event alerts, notice that the window itself changes when you make the selection in the Type list box. Selecting a performance object from the Object list box automatically causes the Counter list box to populate with associated performance counters for the performance object.

Depending on which counter you are monitoring, a threshold could be created to fire if a counter value rises above, falls below, or becomes equal to a specified value. In the example shown in Figure 10-21, the alert is set to fire if the number of user connections exceeds a value of 100.

Notifications for performance condition alerts are configured the same way that they are for SQL Server event alerts.

 Some performance counters have multiple instances. For example, a performance counter Percent Log Used, in the SQLServer:Databases performance object, would have a separate instance for each database so that you could monitor the transaction logs of individual databases.

Creating Alerts with T-SQL

Alerts can also be created using the sp_add_alert system-stored procedure. It adheres to the following syntax:

```
sp_add_alert [ @name = ] 'name'
 [ , [ @message_id = ] message_id ]
 [ , [ @severity = ] severity ]
 [ , [ @enabled = ] enabled ]
 [ , [ @delay_between_responses = ] delay_between_responses
 ]
 [ , [ @notification_message = ] 'notification_message' ]
 [ , [ @include_event_description_in = ] include_event_desc
ription_in ]
 [ , [ @database_name = ] 'database' ]
 [ , [ @event_description_keyword = ] 'event_description_ke
yword_pattern' ]
 [ , { [ @job_id = ] job_id | [ @job_name = ] 'job_name' }
 ]
 [ , [ @raise_snmp_trap = ] raise_snmp_trap ]
 [ , [ @performance_condition = ] 'performance_
condition' ]
 [ , [ @category_name = ] 'category' ]
```

The same procedure is used to create both SQL Server event alerts and performance condition alerts. As you would expect, only the parameters required for a single type of alert are required when using the procedure. For example, the following statement will create a performance-based alert on the User Connections counter of the SQLServer:General Statistics performance object.

```
EXEC sp_add_alert @name = 'Connections Too High',
@enabled = 1,
@performance_condition = 'SQLServer:General Statistics|User
  Connections||>|100'
```

This example creates an event alert that is triggered only by the error number 903:

```
EXEC sp_add_alert @name = 'Trapping Error 903',
@message_id = 903
```

Notifications are added to alerts using the sp_add_notification system-stored procedure. It adheres to the following syntax:

```
sp_add_notification [ @alert_name = ] 'alert' ,
  [ @operator_name = ] 'operator' ,
  [ @notification_method = ] notification_method
```

You simply specify the name of the alert that you wish to add the notification to and the operator name to notify. The notification_method parameter is used to specify how to contact the operator. The three methods: e-mail, pager, and Net send are assigned the values 1, 2 and 4 respectively. The notification_method parameter takes the sum of any of the notification options you choose. For example, if you wished to only notify via e-mail (1) and Net send (4), then you would specify 5 for the value of the notification_method parameter.

The following example adds a notification for an alert named Trapping Error 903. It names John Smith as the operator and specifies that he should only be notified via e-mail (notification_method = 1).

```
USE msdb

EXEC sp_add_notification
     @alert_name = 'Trapping Error 903',
     @operator_name = 'John Smith',
     @notification_method = 1
```

WINDOWS PERFORMANCE MONITOR AND SQL SERVER 2000

When SQL Server 2000 is installed on Windows 2000 or a Windows NT server computer, several performance objects and their associate performance counters are installed. These performance counters, as well as some of the native Windows 2000 performance objects and counters, are invaluable when determining where system bottlenecks occur. The Windows System Monitor program is used to create traces and monitor specific counters. You can start the Windows System Monitor by clicking Start, highlighting Settings, clicking Control Panel, double-clicking Administrative Tools, and double-clicking the Performance item. This brings up the default Windows System Monitor, as shown in Figure 10-22.

10

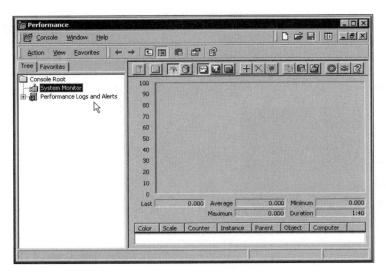

Figure 10-22   Windows System Monitor

You can add the performance counters you wish to monitor by clicking the Add button, which has the Plus sign on it. This opens the Add Counters window, shown in Figure 10-23.

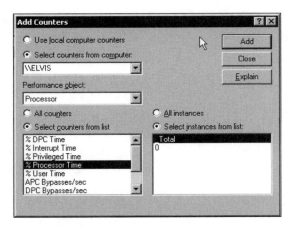

Figure 10-23   Add Counters window of Windows System Monitor

Click Add, then Close to add the counters to your monitoring session. When you have finished specifying counters, the Windows System Monitor window should show various lines being graphed, as shown in Figure 10-24.

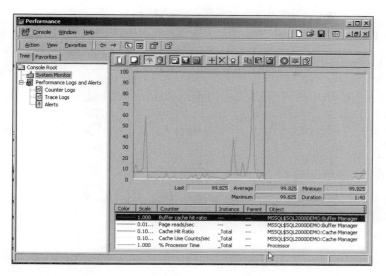

Figure 10-24   Windows System Monitor tracking multiple counters

Monitoring for Bottlenecks with Windows System Monitor

10

Windows System Monitor can be used to evaluate hardware conditions that effect the overall performance of the SQL Server 2000. There are three main categories of hardware resources that can commonly cause bottlenecks in server performance. They are CPUs, memory, and I/O subsytem.

CPU

In large multi-user environments, CPU processing power can become a limiting factor in overall performance. If a system doesn't have enough processing power to handle the volume of activity, then users will experience poor performance. Each individual process in SQL Server 2000 can only run on a single processor, but simultaneous processes can be run on different CPUs to increase overall throughput of the system. In order for performance to improve based on multiple processors, a system must be running many concurrent processes. Large transaction-processing databases will often benefit from adding processors because of the high volume of concurrent activity. Increasing the speed of existing processors will almost always improve performance, because the heavy lifting that the processor performs can be done quicker, allowing more transactions to be handled in a shorter period of time.

When determining if the CPU is causing a bottleneck on a server, use the % Processor Time performance counter from the Processor performance object in Windows System Monitor. If the counter is consistently at 75% or higher, then the CPU is probably part of the cause in a poorly performing system.

Adding additional processors to a system that is experiencing performance problems due to poorly performing queries will not solve the problem. Since a single process must run on a single CPU, a poorly performing query will still run slowly if you add an extra processor to the SQL Server 2000 system.

There are limits to the performance gains achieved through adding or upgrading processors. Other things can cause bottlenecks in servers, including the amount of available memory and how SQL Server 2000 instances are using it. Also, the I/O subsystem (hard drives supporting an instance) is a common performance bottleneck.

Memory and Cache Hits

The amount of memory available to SQL Server 2000 is a very important value when optimizing performance. In general, the more memory the better, especially when working in large multi-user environments. SQL Server 2000 caches data so that it can be read from memory instead of a disk drive. It is always faster to access the cache than it is to read information directly from hard drives.

SQL Server 2000 instances will dynamically allocate memory as needed, but in some cases, the total amount of memory is limiting the ability of the instance to optimize its operations. To determine if there is a sufficient amount of memory available and being used by a SQL Server 2000 instance, check the following counters:

- Total Server Memory (KB) of the SQL Server:Memory Manager performance object

- Buffer Cache Hit Ratio of the SQL Server:Buffer Management performance object

The Total Server Memory (KB) counter shows you how much memory an instance of SQL Server 2000 is using. If the value is close to the maximum amount of memory on the computer and performance is still slow, then additional memory will probably boost performance.

The Buffer Cache Hit Ratio counter shows the percentage of data retrievals that are performed against the cache (in memory) instead of the hard drives of the server. This number should be as high as possible to ensure that a SQL Server 2000 instance has enough memory to cache data and therefore increase the overall data retrieval performance by not accessing hard drives directly. A value of 90% is optimal, however, some systems may never achieve this rate due to their design (if they don't reuse data pages often). If the Buffer Cache Hit Ratio is less than 90%, and SQL Server 2000 is using as much physical memory as is available on the server, then increasing the amount of memory will probably improve performance.

I/O Subsystem

One of the most common performance bottlenecks in SQL Server 2000 systems, is the I/O subsystem. These types of bottlenecks are directly related to the capabilities of the hard drives on the server. The number of I/O operations that a hard drive can perform is limited. For example, a single hard drive may only be capable of performing 100 random I/O operations per second. A random I/O operation is typically performed when searching for a piece of data on a data file in a database. If there are more requested operations than the limit of 100 per second, then the requests are queued and performance degrades. This decrease is caused by the increased latency of operations. When an operation is delayed by the I/O subsystem, locks are held longer than they should be and processes sit idle, waiting their turn in the queue. This results in an overall decrease in SQL Server 2000 performance.

The important performance counters to watch when monitoring for a possible I/O subsystem bottleneck are found in the Logical Disk and Physical Disk performance objects. The following performance counters of the Physical Disk object monitor disk latency:

- Avg. Disk Sec/Transfer
- Avg. Disk Sec/Read
- Avg. Disk Sec/Write

These counters display the amount of time it takes for the drive to perform a read or write operation. In general, if any of these counters is showing a value greater than 20 milliseconds (.0200 seconds) then you probably do have an I/O subsystem bottleneck. These types of problems are easily resolved by adding hard drives to the system and configuring the database to use the additional hard drives through filegroups.

There are too many performance counters to even begin to list them in this book, but it is strongly recommended that you read SQL Server Books Online to find out more. A nice feature of Windows System Monitor is that you can get specific information on each counter by pressing the Explain button in the Add Counter window, as shown in Figure 10-25.

10

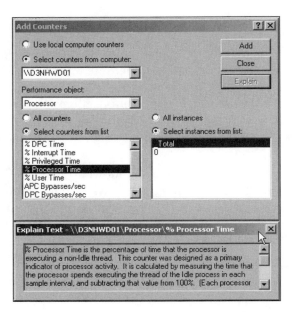

Figure 10-25   Getting counter information using the Explain button

Chapter Summary

❑ The SQL Server Agent service provides a robust and flexible facility for automating and monitoring SQL Server 2000 instances. Using jobs, recurring operations can be configured and scheduled to run automatically by the SQL Server Agent service. This frees up significant amounts of time for the average database administrator, allowing him or her to perform other duties, like optimizing queries and designing new databases.

❑ Alerts are a powerful component of the SQL Server Agent architecture that allow different events and performance conditions to trigger notifications to administrative personnel. This is very important when severe errors occur that require an immediate response from an administrator to correct the problem. Alerts can be based on events that SQL Server 2000 writes to the Windows application log, or they can be defined for certain SQL Server 2000 performance counters.

❑ Performance counters are added to the server when you install SQL Server 2000. These counters can be used in conjunction with the Windows System Monitor to identify performance bottlenecks involving the CPU, memory, and I/O subsystems.

KEY TERMS

automated administration — A programmed response to a predictable administrative task (e.g., regular database backups) or event on the server.

jobs — Administrative tasks that are defined once and executed as many times as necessary.

master server — An instance of SQL Server 2000 that houses a complete list of the various operations (jobs) that must be performed on various target servers when using multiserver automation.

Messenger service — A Windows service that listens for messages sent across the network, receives messages addressed to the computer or user on the computer, and displays them in the form of a pop-up message box. This service is utilized by the NET SEND command to enable messaging.

Net send — A command line application in Windows 2000 and Windows NT, which automatically forces a message box to pop up on a computer screen when the user is connected to the network.

operators — Users who are configured within an instance of SQL Server 2000 to receive notification regarding jobs and alerts.

performance counters — Individual metrics that are measured by SQL Server 2000 and grouped in performance objects.

performance objects — A grouping mechanism used to categorize related performance counters.

SQL Server Agent — A separate program that executes administrative tasks and generates alerts defined by database administrators.

step — A single operation in an administrative job. Steps can be in the form of T-SQL statements, executable files, or ActiveX scripts.

target server — An instance of SQL Server 2000 that connects to the master server and receives jobs scheduled to be run locally when using multiserver automation.

10

REVIEW QUESTIONS

1. Which system database is used by the SQL Server Agent service to store information about jobs, alerts and operators?

   a. master

   b. model

   c. msdb

   d. tempdb

2. Which of the following operations is not performed by the SQL Server Agent service?

   a. automatically allocate memory to SQL Server 2000

   b. execute administrative tasks

   c. detect system conditions and automatically instigate measures to resolve problems

   d. alert people in a variety of ways

3. Which system–stored procedure is used to create a new job?

   a. sp_add_new_job

   b. sp_insert_job

   c. sp_add_job

   d. sp_add_jobstep

4. By default, events with a severity level of _____ or higher are logged to the Windows application log by SQL Server 2000.

   a. 10

   b. 15

   c. 17

   d. 19

5. A single job is made up of one or more of what object?

   a. task

   b. step

   c. operation

   d. command

6. The NET SEND command is powered by which Windows service?

   a. SQL Server service

   b. SQL Agent service

   c. Messenger service

   d. MS-DTC service

7. Job steps can be implemented in which of the following ways?

   a. T-SQL statements

   b. Windows executable programs (.exe files)

   c. ActiveX scripts

   d. all of the above

8. True or False: A performance counter contains numerous individual performance metrics called performance objects.

9. Which of the following is required in order for operators to receive alerts to pagers?

   a. The SQL Server 2000 instance must have a modem available to make pager calls.

   b. The SQL Server Agent service must be configured to dial out of the network.

   c. The paging company must accept pages via e-mail.

   d. Each pager phone number must be registered in the msdb database.

10. Which T-SQL statement creates an operator named Bill, who is available via pager from 6:00 AM to 6:00 PM, seven days a week?

    a. ```
    USE msdb
    exec sp_add_operator @name = 'Bill',
     @pager_address = '1234567@pagercompany.com',
     @weekday_pager_start_time = 060000,
     @weekday_pager_end_time = 18000,
     @pager_days = 127
    ```

    b. ```
    USE master
    exec sp_add_operator @name = 'Bill',
     @pager_address = '1234567@pagercompany.com',
     @weekday_pager_start_time = 060000,
     @weekday_pager_end_time = 18000,
     @pager_days = 127
    ```

    c. ```
    USE msdb
    exec sp_add_operator @name = 'Bill',
     @pager_address = '1234567@pagercompany.com',
     @weekday_pager_start_time = 000600,
     @weekday_pager_end_time = 001800,
     @pager_days = 127
    ```

    d. ```
    USE msdb
    exec sp_add_operator @name = 'Bill',
     @pager_address = '1234567@pagercompany.com',
     @weekday_pager_start_time = 060000,
     @weekday_pager_end_time = 18000,
     @pager_days = 7
    ```

11. True or False: SQL Server Agent can be configured to automatically restart the SQL Server service if it fails.

12. Jobs can be scheduled to execute based on which of the following criteria?

    a. when the SQL Server Agent services starts

    b. when the computer is considered to be in an idle state

    c. a complex schedule defined with days of the week and time of day

    d. all of the above

10

13. When monitoring for a CPU bottleneck, which of the following performance counters should be used?

    a. Processor:% Processor Time

    b. Physical Disk:Avg. Disk Sec/Write

    c. Physical Disk:% Processor Time

    d. Processor:Avg. Disk Sec/Write

14. True or False: A slow-running query will benefit from additional CPUs being added to a SQL Server 2000 system.

15. I/O subsystem bottlenecks are caused by which of the following?

    a. CPUs that are too weak

    b. not enough hard drives to handle the volume of operations

    c. too much RAM available to SQL Server 2000

    d. all of the above

16. What does the Buffer Management:Buffer Cache Hit Ratio performance counter allow you to diagnose?

    a. whether an instance has too many users connected to it

    b. whether an instance has enough memory allocated to cache data effectively

    c. whether an instance needs additional CPUs

    d. whether an instance requires additional hard drives

17. Which T-SQL statement will create a step in a T-SQL job named NewJob on a database called Accounting that deletes orders that are older than 11/15/2001?

    a.
```
USE msdb
  EXEC sp_add_jobstep @job_name = 'NewJob',
    @step_name = 'Delete old orders',
    @subsystem = 'TSQL',
    @command = 'Delete from orders where date < 11/15/2001',
    @database_name = 'Northwind'
```

    b.
```
USE Accounting
  EXEC sp_add_jobstep @job_name = 'NewJob',
    @step_name = 'Delete old orders',
    @subsystem = 'TSQL',
    @command = 'Delete from orders where date < 11/15/2001',
    @database_name = 'Northwind'
```

    c.
```
USE msdb
  EXEC sp_add_jobstep @job_name = 'NewJob',
    @step_name = 'Delete old orders',
    @subsystem = 'TSQL',
    @command = 'Delete from orders where date < 11/15/2001',
    @database_name = 'Accounting'
```

```
d. USE Accounting
   EXEC sp_add_jobstep @job_name = 'NewJob',
    @step_name = 'Delete old orders',
    @subsystem = 'TSQL',
    @command = 'Delete from orders where date < 11/15/2001',
    @database_name = 'Accounting'
```

18. True or False: A target server receives and stores all of the jobs used by other instances of SQL Server 2000 when using multiserver automation.

19. True or False: A single operator can receive duplicate messages from the same job via both e-mail and the NET SEND command.

20. Which of the following operations can trigger a SQL Server event alert?

    a. an event of a certain severity is written to the Windows application log

    b. when the CPU utilization surpasses a configured threshold

    c. when a user misspells the name of an object in a query

    d. when a scheduled time occurs

21. When running Windows System Monitor, you find that the Physical Disk:Avg. Disk Sec/Read counter is returning values consistently over 30 milliseconds. What does this mean?

    a. The buffer cache is large enough to provide optimal performance.

    b. The I/O subsystem is overloaded and is causing a bottleneck.

    c. The CPUs are causing a system bottleneck.

    d. The I/O subsystem is sufficient for the volume of activity on the server.

22. Operators can be notified by a job under which of the following conditions?

    a. the job fails

    b. the job succeeds

    c. the job finishes regardless of success or failure

    d. all of the above

23. Which T-SQL statement will return a list of all operators in the msdb database?

    a. ```
       USE msdb
       EXEC sp_help_operator
       ```

    b. ```
       USE msdb
       EXEC sp_list_operators
       ```

    c. ```
       USE msdb
       EXEC sp_help_operator 'ALL'
       ```

    d. ```
       USE msdb
       EXEC sp_help 'operators'
       ```

10

HANDS-ON PROJECTS

Project 10-1

In this project, you will create two new operators using the Enterprise Manager interface for one of them and T-SQL statements for the other. To keep things simple, the operators we define will only be contacted via Net send messages.

To create a new operator in Enterprise Manager:

1. To start Enterprise Manager, click **Start**, highlight **Programs**, highlight **Microsoft SQL Server**, and then click **Enterprise Manager**.

2. Expand the local instance of SQL Server. Then expand the Management folder, expand the **SQL Server Agent** node, right-click on the **Operators** node and click **New Operator** from the context-sensitive menu.

3. When the New Operator Properties window appears, name the first operator **Operator 1**.

4. Configure the operator to receive Net send messages by typing the local computer name in the **Net send** address text box as shown in Figure 10-26.

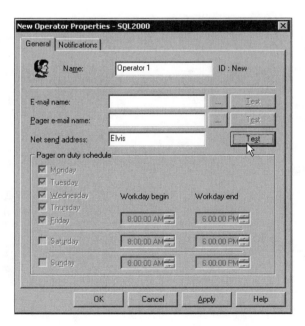

Figure 10-26   New Operator Properties window

In Figure 10-26, the local computer name is Elvis, so that value in the Net send address text box ensures that pop-up messages will appear on this local computer when the operator is notified via the NET SEND command. To discover your local computer name, you can look at the registered default instance in Enterprise Manager. Notice in Figure 10-27 how Elvis is the name of the registered instance. This is also the valid computer name to be used with Net send notifications.

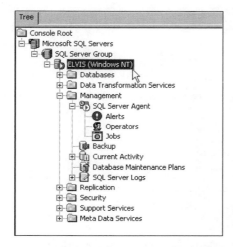

Figure 10-27   Reading the local computer name from Enterprise Manager

5. Click **Test** to perform a test of the NET SEND command to the name you specified in Step 4.

6. Click **OK** when the confirmation appears.

7. The Net send message should appear as a pop-up message box as shown in Figure 10-28. Click **OK** to close the pop up message.

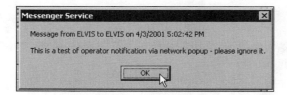

Figure 10-28   Test Net send message

8. Click **OK** on the New Operator Properties window to create the new operator named Operator 1.

To create an operator using T-SQL statements and Query Analyzer:

1. To start Query Analyzer, click **Start**, highlight **Programs**, highlight **Microsoft SQL Server**, and then click **Query Analyzer**.

2. When the Connect to SQL Server window appears, click on or type the name of your local SQL Server 2000 instance.

3. Click on the **Windows authentication** option for connecting.

4. Click **OK** to connect to the instance.

5. Type the following query in the query window:

```
USE msdb
EXEC sp_add_operator @name = 'Operator 2',
    @netsend_address = 'Your Local Computer Name'
```

6. Execute the query by clicking the **Execute Query** toolbar button or pressing **F5**.

7. Now type the following query in the query window to confirm the creation of Operator 2.

```
USE msdb
EXEC sp_help_operator
```

8. Execute the Query by clicking the **Execute Query** toolbar button or pressing **F5**.

9. The results of the query should contain both of the operators we created in this exercise.

10. Close Query Analyzer and Enterprise Manager when you are finished.

Project 10-2

In this project, you will create a simple job containing one step, and you will schedule it to run weeknights at midnight. One of the operators created in Project 10-1 will be configured to receive notifications when this job is run.

To create a new job in Enterprise Manager:

1. To start Enterprise Manager, click **Start**, highlight **Programs**, highlight **Microsoft SQL Server**, and then click **Enterprise Manager**.

2. Expand your local instance of SQL Server, then expand the Management folder, expand the **SQL Server Agent** node, right-click on the **Jobs** node, and click the **New Job** item from the context-sensitive menu.

3. In this example we will be scheduling a regular execution of the sp_who system-stored procedure, which returns information about which processes and users are connected to an instance of SQL Server 2000 at the time of execution. Configure the General tab of the New Job Properties window with the information shown in Figure 10-29. Type **Who is on the server** in the Name field and add a description for which operations will perform in the Description field. The Category and Owner fields should be left as the defaults.

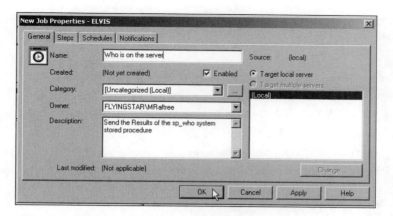

Figure 10-29   General tab of the New Job Properties window

4. Click the **Steps** tab to add a new step to the job.

5. Click **New** to access the New Job Step window.

   In the General tab, configure the fields to match the values shown in Figure 10-30. The step will be a T-SQL script, since we want to run the sp_who system-stored procedure. Give it a logical name and enter the T-SQL statement in the Command field.

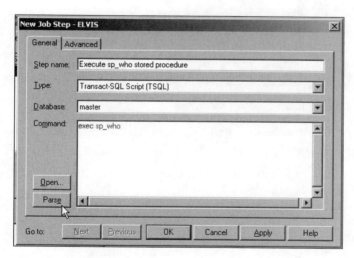

Figure 10-30   New Job Step window

6. Click **Parse** to verify the syntax.

7. When a message box appears saying that parse succeeded, close it by clicking **OK**.

8. Click the **Advanced** tab of the New Job Step window.

9. In the Output file field type **C:\JobOutput.txt** (or specify a more convenient path from the local machine).

10. Click **OK** to add the new step.

11. Click the **Schedules** tab and then click **New Schedule** to access the New Job Schedule window.

12. Name the schedule **Weekday Nights**.

13. Click **Change** to edit the schedule of the job.

14. Using the Edit Recurring Job Schedule window, configure the schedule to fire the job at 7:00 PM each weekday night, as shown in Figure 10-31.

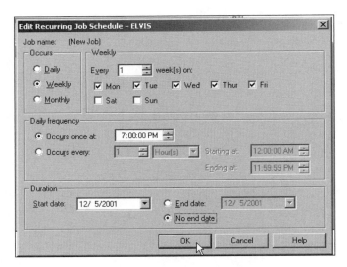

Figure 10-31   Edit Recurring Job Schedule window

15. Click **OK** to save the schedule and then **OK** again to commit your changes.

16. Click the **Notifications** tab of the New Job Properties window.

17. Add **Operator 1** as a new Net send operator, and configure the notification to execute whenever the job completes.

18. Click **OK** to add the job, and close the **New Job Properties** window.

 Leave Enterprise Manager open if you are going on to Project 10-3.

Project 10-3

To manually execute the job we created in Project 10-2 and inspect the job history and the output file we specified for the job:

1. In Enterprise Manager, expand the **Management** folder, expand the **SQL Server Agent** node, and click on the **Jobs** node.

2. Right-click on the **Who is on the server** job and click the **Start Job** item from the context-sensitive menu.

 If SQL Agent is not running, an error message will appear. To continue, start SQL Server Agent.

3. The Net send message box should appear alerting you that the job has finished and was successful. Figure 10-32 shows a sample pop-up message. Click **OK** to close the message box.

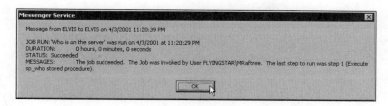

Figure 10-32 Net send notification pop-up message

4. Repeat Steps 2 and 3 twice to create a few more historical records of its execution.

5. Right-click on the **Who is on the server** job in Enterprise Manager and click the **View Job History** item from the context-sensitive menu.

6. Examine the history for the job in the Job History window. Figure 10-33 shows an example of what this window may look like.

10

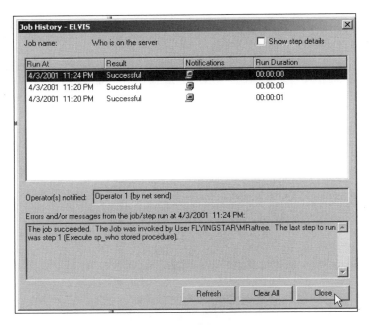

Figure 10-33   Job History Window

7. Click **Close** to exit the window.

8. To access the output file we created for the job step in Project 10-2, we will have to access the Windows file system. Remember that the output file is named C:\JobOutput.txt. Click **Start**, then click **Run**.

9. Type **C:\JobOutput.txt** into the Open text box and click **OK**.

You can use any local path to store the JobOutput.txt file.

10. The output text file should open, and you can examine the output of the various executions of the sp_who system-stored procedure.

11. Close the JobOutput.txt file.

Project 10-4

In this exercise we will add a custom error message and number, and then we will configure an alert for the new error we have defined.

To add a new SQL Server message in Enterprise Manager:

1. Click the **Tools** button in Enterprise Manager, and then click the **Manage SQL Server Messages** option.

2. Click the **Messages** tab of the Manage SQL Server Messages window.

3. Click the **New** button to add a new SQL Server message.

4. In the New SQL Server Message window, add your own message in the Message text box and be sure to check the option to **Always write to Windows event log**. Figure 10-34 provides an example of what the screen should look like when you make these changes.

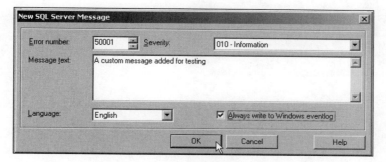

Figure 10-34 New SQL Server Message window

5. Click **OK** twice to create the new message (Message 50001).

To create a new SQL Server Event Alert for the message you just created:

1. In Enterprise Manager, expand the **Management** folder, expand the **SQL Server Agent** node, right-click on the **Alerts** node, and click the **New Alert** item from the context-sensitive menu.

2. In the New Alert Properties screen, name the alert **Custom Error Alert**.

3. In the Event alert definition section of the General tab, click on the **Error number** radio button and specify the error number of 50001 that you created previously. The message you specified for the error number should appear on the screen, as shown in Figure 10-35.

10

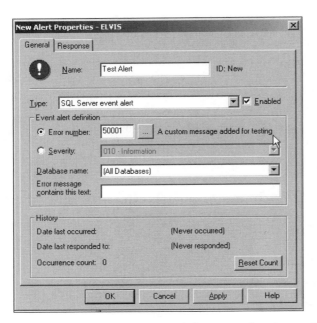

Figure 10-35   General tab of the New Alert Properties window

4. Click the **Response** tab to set up notifications for the alert.

5. Specify that Operator 1 should be notified via Net send by checking the appropriate check box.

6. Click **OK** to save the new alert. Click **Yes** on the message box asking if the error should always invoke the alert.

To test the alert by forcing the 50001 error using the RAISE ERROR T-SQL statement:

1. Start **Query Analyzer** and log in to the local instance of SQL Server 2000.

2. Type the following command in the query window and press **F5** to execute it.

```
RAISERROR (50001,10,1)
```

The RAISERROR T-SQL command allows you to force a particular error to be logged. It is often used when applications want to integrate directly with the Windows application log. It is also useful for testing alerts.

3. A pop-up message should appear on your screen, because the alert was triggered when the error was raised in the previous step. Close the pop-up window by clicking **OK**.

To access the Windows 2000 application log:

1. Click **Start**, highlight **Programs**, highlight **Administrative Tools**, and click the **Event Viewer** item.

2. Click the **Application Log** item in the tree on the left. Your screen should look like Figure 10-36.

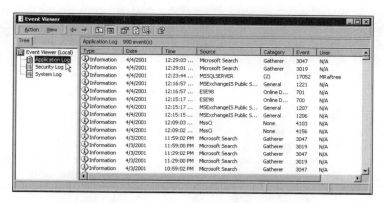

Figure 10-36   Windows 2000 Application Event Log

3. Double-click the most recent entry in the log, where the Source column says MSSQLSERVER. You can see that your custom error was logged in the Event Properties window, as shown in Figure 10-37.

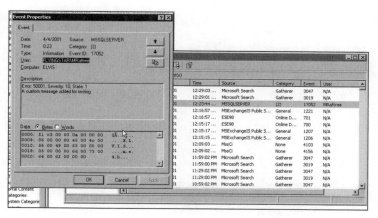

Figure 10-37   Event Properties window

4. Close **Event Viewer**, **Query Analyzer**, and **Enterprise Manager**.

CASE PROJECTS

Case One

As DBA of a large SQL Server 2000 database system, you have been tasked with developing and implementing a monitoring scheme for your company's customer database. You do not know for sure if the hardware supporting the database is sufficient. On top of that, your company only has 50 concurrent user licenses for the customer management application that accesses the SQL Server 2000 database. You must keep track so that you don't violate your licensing agreement. What types of things should you monitor?

Case Two

Your company currently has three SQL Server 2000 instances operating on its network to support various systems, including financial and inventory management applications. Your job as database administrator puts all of these systems in your hands. You want to establish an automation and monitoring scheme that allows you to manage all of the servers from a central location. Using the information in this chapter, and more information in SQL Server Books Online, come up with a plan for implementing this. Be sure to discuss the steps required to set up such an environment.

Appendix

EXAM OBJECTIVES FOR MCSE/MCDBA CERTIFICATION

Exam #70-228: Installing, Configuring, and Administering Microsoft SQL Server 2000 Enterprise Edition

Installing and Configuring SQL Server 2000

Objectives	Chapter: Section	Hands-on Project(s)
Install SQL Server 2000	Chapter 2: Installing SQL Server 2000	Discussed in Chapter 2
Upgrade to SQL Server 2000	Chapter 2: SQL Server 2000 Upgrades	Process described in Chapter 2
Perform a custom upgrade	Chapter 2: SQL Server 2000 Upgrades	Discussed in Chapter 2 (in Chapter scenario)
Upgrade to SQL Server 2000 from SQL Server 6.5	Chapter 2: Upgrading from SQL Server 6.5	Discussed in Chapter 2
Upgrade to SQL Server 2000 from SQL Server 7	Chapter 2: Upgrading a SQL Server 7 Installation	Process described in Chapter 2
Create a linked server	Chapter 3: Linked Servers	Process described in Chapter 3 with screen shots and applicable code examples Project 3-4
Configure SQLMail and SQLAgentMail	Chapter 3: Configuring E-mail for SQL Server 2000	Process described in Chapter 3 (Section includes screen shots and code examples) Project 3-3
Configure network libraries	Chapter 2: Networking Libraries	Described in text Chapter 2
Troubleshoot failed installations	Chapter 2: Troubleshooting Installations and Upgrades	Described in text in Chapter 2

Creating SQL Server 2000 Databases

Objective	Chapter: Section	Hands-on Project(s)
Attach and detach databases	Chapter 5: Attaching and Detaching Databases	Project 5-5 Covered extensively in text for Chapter 5
Create and alter databases	Chapter 5: Creating a Database	Project 5-1 and extensively in chapter text
Add filegroups	Chapter 5: Managing Files and Filegroups	Project 5-1 and extensively in chapter text
Configure filegroup usage	Chapter 5: Managing Files and Filegroups	Project 5-1 and extensively in chapter text
Expand and shrink a database	Chapter 5: Shrinking a Database	In Chapter 5: Case project 3 as well as text (examples and screen shots)
Set database options by using the ALTER DATABASE or CREATE DATABASE statements	Chapter 5: Configuration Settings	In chapter examples
Size and place the transaction log	Chapter 4: Transaction Logs Chapter 5: Expanding a Database	In Chapter 5: Case project 1 as well as text (examples and screen shots)
Create and manage objects. Objects include constraints, indexes, stored procedures, triggers, and views.	Chapter 4: Database Objects Chapter 5: Database Objects	Extensively in text of Chapter 5 Projects 5-2, 5-3, 5-4

Managing, Monitoring, and Troubleshooting SQL Server 2000 Databases

A

Objective	Chapter: Section	Hands-on Project(s)
Optimize database performance	Chapter 6: Optimizing Databases	All of Chapter 6 hands-on projects
Indexing	Chapter 6: Indexing Recommendations	Project 6-1
Locking	Chapter 4: Transactional Locking Chapter 6: Diagnosing Database Problems	Project 4-1 Project 6-3
Recompiling	Chapter 6: Execution Plan Caching	In chapter examples

Objective	Chapter: Section	Hands-on Project(s)
Optimize data storage • Optimize files and filegroups • Manage database fragmentation	Chapter 6: Page Splits and Fragmentation Chapter 6: Placing indexes and tables	Several in chapter examples
Modify the database schema	Chapter 4: Tables Chapter 5: Adding Columns to Database Tables Chapter 5: Creating and Modifying Database Objects with T-SQL	Several in chapter examples
Perform disaster recovery operations • Perform backups • Recover the system state and restore data • Configure, maintain, and troubleshoot log shipping	Chapter 7: Backup and Restore Operations Chapter 7: Log Shipping Chapter 7: SQL Server Recovery Models	Project 7-1, 7-2, 7-3, 7-4
Perform integrity checks • Database Maintenance Plan Wizard • Database Consistency Checker (DBCC)	Chapter 7: Database Maintenance Plans	Extensive in chapter example And Projects 7-3 and 7-4
Troubleshoot transactions and locking by using SQL Profiler, SQL Server Enterprise Manager, or SQL	Chapter 4: Transactional Locking Chapter 6: Diagnosing Database Problems	Project 6-3 Project 6-4

Extracting and Transforming Data with SQL Server 2000

Objectvies	Chapter: Section	Hands-on Project(s)
Set up Internet Information Services (IIS) virtual directories to support XML	Chapter 9: XML Support in Microsoft SQL Server 2000	Project 8-4
Import and export data • bulk insert task • bulk copy program • Data Transformation Services (DTS) • heterogeneous queries	Chapter 9: The BULK INSERT Statement Chapter 9: Bulk Copy Program (BCP) Chapter 9: Data Transformation Services (DTS)	Project 8-1
Develop and manage Data Transformation Services (DTS) packages • Convert data types	Chapter 9: Data Transformation Services (DTS)	Project 8-2 Project 8-3

Objectvies	Chapter: Section	Hands-on Project(s)
Manage linked servers • Manage OLE DB providers • Configure security mapping	Chapter 3: Linked Servers	Project 3-4
Configure, maintain, and troubleshoot replication services	Chapter 9: Replication	Extensive hands-on activities in the chapter

Managing and Monitoring SQL Server 2000 Security

A

Objective	Chapter: Section	Hands-on Project(s)
Configure mixed security modes or Windows Authentication (considerations include client connectivity, client operating system, and security infrastructure)	Chapter 8: Authentication Modes Chapter 3: Security Tab	In chapter examples
Create and manage logins	Chapter 8: Logins	Project 8-1 and numerous examples in text
Create and manage database users	Chapter 8: Database Users	Project 8-2 and numerous examples in text
Create and manage security roles. Roles include application, database, and server • Add and remove users from roles • Create roles in order to manage database security	Chapter 8: Roles	Project 8-4 Project 8-5
Enforce and manage security by using stored procedures, triggers, views and user-defined functions	Chapter 8: Implementing Security through Database Objects Chapter 4: Views	Project 4-2
Set permissions in a database. Considerations include object permissions, object ownership, and statement permissions.	Chapter 8: Permissions	Project 8-2 and extensively in chapter
Manage security auditing. Methods include SQL Profiler, SQL Trace, and C2 auditing.	Chapter 8: Auditing Security in SQL Server 2000 Chapter 6: SQL Server Profiler	Project 8-6

Managing, Monitoring, and Troubleshooting SQL Server 2000

Objective	Chapter: Section	Hands-on Project(s)
Create, manage, and trouble-shoot SQL Server Agent jobs	Chapter 10: Creating Jobs	in chapter example Project 10-2 Project 10-3
Configure alerts and operators by using SQL Server Agent	Chapter 10: Creating Operators, Creating Alerts	in chapter example Project 10-1
Optimize hardware resource usage. Resources include CPU, disk I/O, and memory • Monitor hardware resource usage by using the Windows System Monitor • Resolve system bottlenecks by using the Windows System Monitor	Chapter 10: Windows Performance Monitor and SQL Server 2000	in chapter example Project 10-4
Optimize and troubleshoot SQL Server system activity. Activities include cache hits, connections, locks, memory allocation, recompilation, and transactional throughput. • Monitor SQL Server system activity by using traces • Monitor SQL Server system activity by using the Windows System Monitor	Chapter 4: Transactional Locking Chapter 6: Diagnosing Database Problems	Project 6-3 Project 6-4 Chapter 10 in chapter example

Glossary

after trigger — A trigger configured to fire after data modification statements are run.

American National Standards Institute (ANSI) — An organization of American industry and business groups that develops trade and communication standards for the United States. Through membership in the International Organization for Standardization (ISO) and the International Electrotechnical Commission (IEC), ANSI coordinates American standards with corresponding international standards.

AppleTalk ADSP — Library allowing clients on an AppleTalk network to communicate with SQL Server. It is not supported with named instances of SQL Server 2000 and it will not be supported in future releases of SQL Server.

application roles — Special roles that can be assigned permissions and used by applications to access databases.

Application Service Provider (ASP) — A company that hosts and supports software for its customers or provides an application that can be "leased" by its customers.

attribute — A piece of information that describes a data entity. For example, for a customer entity, the associated attributes could consist of name, address, and phone number.

authentication — The first stage of security, responsible for verifying that a user can connect to a SQL Server 2000 instance.

authorization — The second stage of SQL Server 2000 security, responsible for checking permissions to determine which actions a particular user can perform within a database.

automated administration — A programmed response to a predictable administrative task (e.g., regular database backups) or event on the server.

availability — The ability of a system to be constantly accessible by it's users. Using redundant technologies like failover clustering increases availability.

backup devices — Files on hard drives or other disk storage media (like tapes) that are used to store backups.

backup set — The unit in Microsoft tape format that houses a backup from a single source like SQL Server 2000 or Windows 2000/NT.

Banyan VINES — This library supports Banyan Vines clients. It is not supported with named instances of SQL Server 2000 and it will not be supported in future releases of SQL Server.

branch node — A mid-level node in an index. Branch nodes are traversed to quickly locate specific rows of data.

Bulk Copy Program (BCP) — This is an executable program used to move data into and out of SQL Server 2000.

BULK INSERT — A statement used in SQL Server 2000 to insert data into a table or view from a data file.

BULK INSERT Statement — A Transact-SQL (T-SQL) statement that executes a bulk insert.

cascading delete — Records in a foreign key table are automatically deleted when the primary key rows are removed.

cascading update — Changes to a primary key field are automatically made to related foreign key fields.

checkpoint — An event that causes data modifications stored in the transaction log to be committed to disk. When a checkpoint occurs, all changes to data that have occurred since last checkpoint (and have not yet been committed to disk) are written to disk. Checkpoints can be triggered automatically by SQL Server 2000 if the instance is configured for this (recovery internal set to zero). They can also be triggered by an explicit recovery interval (specified by an administrator), or when requested by a user or a system shutdown.

Class C2 — A security rating granted by the National Computer Security Center (NCSC) for products that have been evaluated against the Department of Defense Trusted Computer System Evaluation Criteria (TCSEC).

cluster group — Term used to refer to shared sets of resources (usually hard drives) used by a SQL Server failover cluster.

clustered index — An index that physically sorts and stores the rows in a table. The leaf nodes of a clustered index store actual data rows.

code page — Defines the bit patterns that represent specific letters, numbers, and symbols. Some are single byte, consisting of 256 unique values. Others are double byte and offer over 65,000 unique values.

collation — Specifies the binary patterns that represent each character available and the rules by which characters are sorted and compared.

constraints — User-defined rules that help enforce the integrity of column data.

covered query — A query whose requested table columns (in its SELECT list) are all stored in a single index. Covered queries can bypass reading data from tables because all of the information it needs resides in the leaf nodes of an index.

Data Latency — A measure of how long it takes after data modifications are made on one server before they are reflected on a server to which the data are replicated.

Data Transformation Services (DTS) — A bundled set of features for importing, exporting, and transforming data using a variety of data formats and transfer methods.

database — A logical collection of data and objects that are used to support maintenance and use of that data.

database owner (dbo) — A special database user that exists in every database and has permissions to perform all activities on that database.

database user — An account within a database that is mapped to a login to provide access to the database.

deadlock — A situation arising when two users, each having a lock on one piece of data, attempt to acquire a lock on the other's piece. This circumstance causes the users to block each other indefinitely. To resolve this condition, SQL Server 2000 detects deadlocks and terminates one user's process.

default — A type of constraint that defines a default value for a column in a table.

default filegroup — The filegroup where space is allocated when a table or index does not explicitly define a filegroup.

delimited identifiers — Names that do not follow the rules for regular identifiers must be delimited with double quotes or square brackets.

differential database backup — A type of backup that records only the changes made to the database since the last full database backup. The differential backup is smaller than the full database backup and consequently does not affect performance as much as a full database backup.

disk striping — Also referred to as RAID 0, disk striping involves combining two or more hard drives into a single logical drive and writing chunks of data (stripes) across all of the disks in a round-robin fashion.

distributed partition view — A single queriable entity that is horizontally partitioned and housed on multiple physical computers.

distributed transactions — Transactions that group queries that affect data on multiple servers.

Distributor — A server that participates in replication by moving data to Subscribers.

domain — The valid range of values for a set of data.

DTS Designer — A tool available in Enterprise Manager that allows the creation and design of DTS packages.

DTS package — A set of DTS tasks that each move or transform data or perform related tasks.

entity — An object comprised of various pieces of data and stored in a database.

execution plan — The step-by-step instructions for executing a query in the most efficient way. Execution plans are generated by the query optimizer.

extended property — User-defined named value associated with an object in the database.

extended stored procedure — A function that is part of an external software object (DLL), which is coded using the SQL Server 2000 Extended Stored Procedure API. The function can then be called using Transact-SQL from SQL Server 2000, using similar statements to those used to execute Transact-SQL stored procedures. Extended stored procedures are often developed to provide functionality that is not supported by T-SQL.

extended stored procedure — A special type of stored procedure that is implemented in a dynamic-link library (DLL) and usually written in a language like Visual Basic or C++.

Extensible Markup Language (XML) — A language for creating documents containing structured information.

extent — Eight contiguous pages (64 KB). All physical space allocated to tables is done using extents.

federation — A group of servers that cooperate to process a single workload.

file — A physical operating system file that stores a database or transaction log.

filegroups — A named grouping of one or more physical data files.

fill factor — An attribute of an index that defines the amount of free space left on each page of the index when it is created or rebuilt.

fill factor — The amount of space left in an index page to account for future growth.

fixed server roles — A set of predefined roles that are available in SQL Server 2000 instances to provide access to common instance-wide administrative functionality. They provide special permissions, like configuring instance-wide settings and creating databases, that cannot be explicitly provided to individual logins.

foreign key — A column or set of columns that refer to another table for a valid set of values. Foreign keys are a way of enforcing a relationship between tables.

fragmentation — The inefficient use of physical storage that results from page splitting.

full database backup — A type of backup that creates a full copy of all of the data in a database.

guest user — A special account that can be used by people who have a login on an instance but don't have a mapped database user for the database they wish to access.

GUID — A globally unique identifier.

heartbeat — Simple network messages passed between nodes on failover clusters that are used to determine which nodes are operational.

hints — T-SQL directives used to manually control how an execution plan is generated by the query optimizer.

horizontally partitioned — A restriction of rows from a result set.

Hypertext Transfer Protocol (HTTP) — The most common protocol used to transfer information from Web servers to Web browsers. Because of this protocol, most URLs begin with HTTP://.

implied permissions — Special privileges that are provided by membership to a user-defined role.

index — A structure that increases the data retrieval performance of SQL Server 2000 by reducing the amount of I/O operations required to locate specific rows.

index row — Individual entries of an index that are stored in a page and contain a key value and a memory pointer to other pages used by the index.

instead of trigger — A trigger that runs in place of the data modifications that caused it to fire.

jobs — Administrative tasks that are defined once and executed as many times as necessary.

Kerberos — A system developed by MIT that lets two parties on a network communicate securely. Unlike in SSL, which uses two static keys (public key and private key), Kerberos generates a unique key for each communication session.

leaf node — The lowest level nodes in an index. Depending on the type of index (clustered or nonclustered), a leaf node will contain actual data rows or memory pointers to data rows.

locale — The Windows operating system attribute that defines certain behaviors related to language. The locale defines the code page, used to store and sort character data, as well as language-specific items such as the format used for dates and time and the character used to separate decimals in numbers.

locking — Process by which SQL Server 2000 ensures transactional integrity and database consistency by preventing users from accessing data being changed by other users, and by preventing multiple database users from modifying the same piece of data at the same time.

log shipping — Process by which transaction logs of a database are backed up and applied to a secondary database server. The goal of log shipping is typically to have a standby server (relatively in sync with the main server) that can be activated in the event of a primary server failure.

Login — A SQL Server object that provides connection access to an instance of SQL Server 2000 (authentication). Logins can be based on Windows users and groups defined natively in SQL Server 2000.

master database — A system database that stores login, configuration, and installed database information. The master database stores all system-stored procedures and information about extended stored procedures.

master server — An instance of SQL Server 2000 that houses a complete list of the various operations (jobs) that must be performed on various target servers when using multiserver automation.

media — The largest unit in Microsoft Tape Format, it can house multiple backups from both Windows 2000/NT and SQL Server 2000.

merge replication — A type of replication that allows changes made at different sites to be merged at a later time.

Messenger service — A Windows service that listens for messages sent across the network, receives messages addressed to the computer or user on the computer, and displays them in the form of a pop-up message box. This service is utilized by the NET SEND command to enable messaging.

Microsoft Data Access Components (MDAC) — The key technologies for enabling data access across a network. MDAC is installed as a suite of connectivity tools for accessing data in a variety of formats.

Microsoft Distributed Transaction Coordinator (MS DTC service) — A component of SQL Server 2000 that provides transaction management services that facilitate including several different sources of data in one transaction.

Microsoft Tape Format (MTF) — A standard backup format developed by Microsoft to allow backups from multiple sources to be stored on the same media.

Mixed Authentication Mode — One of two mechanisms used to validate user connections to SQL Server instances. Users are identified by their Windows domain logon or SQL Server logon information.

mixed extent — An extent that houses information from multiple tables or indexes on its pages.

model database — A system database that is used as a template for all user-defined databases.

MS Search service — A full text indexing engine that is bundled with SQL Server 2000. It generates and maintains full text indexes as well as handles queries that access them.

msdb database — A system database that stores scheduling and alert information.

Multi-Protocol — A single network library that offers support for TCP/IP, Named Pipes, and NWLink IPX/SPX. Multi-Protocol is not supported for named instances of SQL Server 2000.

Named Pipes — A network library that is required when installing SQL Server in Windows 2000 or Windows NT. Named Pipes permits access to shared network resources.

narrow index — An index that has very few (but at least one) key columns.

Net send — A command line application in Windows 2000 and Windows NT, which automatically forces a message box to pop up on a computer screen when the user is connected to the network.

node — A single computer running in a cluster configuration.

nonclustered index — An index that does not physically order the data in a table. Instead of data rows, pointers to data rows are stored in the leaf nodes of the index.

Northwind database — A sample user-defined database installed with SQL Server 2000.

NWLink IPX/SPX — The NWLink network library provides support for Novell NetWare clients connecting to SQL Server.

object permissions — Permissions that allow users or roles to access objects in a database. Object permissions are applied to a user to control INSERT, UPDATE, and DELETE actions against tables.

They are also used to allow users to execute stored procedures and user-defined functions.

OLE DB — The application programming interface (API) for accessing data stored in any format (databases, spreadsheets, text files, e-mail stores).

OLE DB Provider — A software component that provides access to data from a particular type of data source through the standard OLE DB API (e.g., SQL Server databases, Access databases, or Excel spreadsheets).

operators — Users who are configured within an instance of SQL Server 2000 to receive notification regarding jobs and alerts.

ownership chain — A hierarchy of dependent objects. For example, a view based on a view that is based on two tables. An ownership chain is considered "broken" if all of the objects are not owned by the same user.

page — The smallest unit of storage employed by SQL Server 2000, measuring only 8 KB.

page split — The process of handling a new insertion to a full index or data page. SQL Server 2000 creates a new page and then moves half of the data from the original page to the newly created one.

parallel scans — The process by which multiple CPUs are used to read data residing in multiple filegroups simultaneously.

parity — An integer's property of being odd or even. Parity checking is used to detect errors in binary-coded data. Parity information is used to rebuild lost data in a RAID 5 configuration.

performance counters — Individual metrics that are measured by SQL Server 2000 and grouped in performance objects.

performance objects — A grouping mechanism used to categorize related performance counters.

precision — The total number of decimal digits that can be stored in a numeric field in a table (both to the left and right of the decimal point).

primary file — Database file that holds the system tables and data.

primary filegroup — A filegroup that holds the primary data file and any other files not in an explicit filegroup.

primary key constraint — A type of constraint applied to a column or set of columns in a table to ensure that each row is unique. No two rows in a table can have the same values in the primary key column or set of columns.

procedure cache — The pool of memory allocated by SQL Server 2000 to store and reuse compiled execution plans.

Publisher — A server that participates in replication by creating sets of articles, called publications, that will later be copied to Subscribers of the publications.

pubs database — A sample user-defined database installed with SQL Server 2000.

query governor threshold — Signifies the maximum query cost a query can have while still being able to run. Query cost refers to the estimated time (in seconds) required for a query to be executed based on the hardware configuration of the computer.

query optimizer — The database engine component that generates efficient execution plans for SQL statements.

recovery model — The model by which you recover the backed up database. Recovery models include simple, full, or bulk-logged.

Redundant Array of Independent Disks (RAID) — A hard drive configuration where multiple physical disk drives are grouped to create a single logical drive. RAID allows for improved performance and fault tolerance through techniques like striping and mirroring.

regular identifiers — A set of naming rules for objects.

replication — A process that copies and distributes data to another and then synchronizes information between databases for consistency.

roles — The equivalent of user groups in SQL Server 2000. Roles are used to administer permissions in a single location for multiple users (when an applicable Windows group is not available).

root node — The top-level node of an index. This is the first node that is accessed when an index is being used to locate data.

rules — User-defined rules to enforce data integrity. Rules are provided for backward compatibility.

scalability — The ability to easily grow in size to support a growing user base. For example, XYZ Company sets up a database driven application and wants to have a system that not only works with the initially estimated user population size, but can be easily expanded to support the growing user population in one year, five years, or ten years.

scale — The maximum number for decimal digits stored to the right of the decimal point (applies to a numeric field in a table).

secondary files — Additional data files for a database.

Secure Sockets Layer (SSL) — A protocol that uses public key cryptography to enable encrypted, authenticated communications across the Internet.

service — An application that starts when a computer is booted up and continues to run while the computer is on. Services do not require graphic user interfaces and run invisibly to the user.

snapshot replication — A type of replication that periodically copies entire publications as they exist at a moment in time.

sort order — The set of rules used by a collation to define how characters are sorted and evaluated by comparison operations.

sp_lock — The system-stored procedure that displays current lock information, including which users hold locks and on which database objects the locks are held.

sp_recompile — The system-stored procedure that is used to force stored procedures and triggers to regenerate a more current execution plan.

sp_who — The system-stored procedure that returns information about current user and process activity.

SQL Server Agent — A separate program that executes administrative tasks and generates alerts defined by database administrators.

SQL Server Agent service (SQLServerAgent service) — The component of SQL Server 2000 that supports features allowing the scheduling of periodic activities (like database backups), or the notification to system administrators of problems that have occurred with the server.

SQL Server database engine (MSSQLServer service) — The SQL Server 2000 service manages all of the files that comprise the databases owned by an instance of SQL Server 2000. It is the component that processes all Transact-SQL statements sent from SQL Server 2000 client applications.

SQL virtual directories — Namespaces that do not correspond to physical file folders, but are tracked by IIS so that requests can be forwarded to SQL Server 2000.

SQL Virtual Names — Sub-namespaces in IIS whose HTTP requests are forwarded to SQL Server 2000 as a specific type of request.

sqlisapi.dll — An implementation of the Internet Services API (ISAPI) filter that provides SQL-specific functionality to Internet Information Services (IIS).

statement permissions — Permissions that allow users to execute certain T-SQL statements like CREATE TABLE and CREATE VIEW.

step — A single operation in an administrative job. Steps can be in the form of T-SQL statements, executable files, or ActiveX scripts.

stored procedures — A group of T-SQL statements that is compiled with a single execution plan.

stripe — An individual block of data used with disk striping.

Structured Query Language (SQL) — A language used to insert, retrieve, modify, and delete data in a relational database. SQL also contains statements for defining and administering the objects in a database. SQL is the language supported by most relational databases, and is the

subject of standards published by the International Organization for Standardization (ISO) and the American National Standards Institute (ANSI).

subscriber — A server that participates in replication by subscribing to publications of data.

system databases — A special collection of databases that store vital system information. The database engine uses system databases to operate.

System Process Identification Number (spid) — A unique number that is used to identify individual processes connected to SQL Server 2000.

table — A structure that stores information in a row and column format. A table is the most common database object and is used to store all data in a database.

table scan — A data retrieval operation requiring the database engine to read all of the pages in a table to find the rows that qualify for a query. The database engine performs table scans when a suitable index is not defined.

target server — An instance of SQL Server 2000 that connects to the master server and receives jobs scheduled to be run locally when using multiserver automation.

TCP/IP Sockets — The TCP\IP network library allows communication through standard Windows sockets. The default port for default instances of SQL Server 2000 is 1433. For named instances, a port will be dynamically assigned each time the service starts, unless a static port number is assigned. The proxy address allows SQL Server to listen for requests through a proxy server.

tempdb database — A system database that is used by the database engine for temporary processing and objects.

thread — An operating system component that allows multiple simultaneous requests to a multiuser application to execute as separate tasks. The SQL Server 2000 relational database engine leverages multiple threads to make use of multiple processors and optimize performance when multiple, concurrent user connections are performing operations. Threads ensure that some user connection is executing even when other connections are blocked (e.g., when waiting for disk reads and writes to complete).

trace — A specific session of monitoring performed with SQL Profiler.

trace template — A set of configurations for a trace. A trace template specifies which types of events to monitor as well as what information is captured with the events.

Transact-SQL (T-SQL) — The version of the SQL language implemented by Microsoft SQL Server 2000.

transaction log — A file that records all changes to a database before they are written to the database itself. Transaction logs allow for internal consistency and recoverability.

transaction log backup — A backup of the transaction log.

transactional replication — A type of replication in which incremental changes made on the Publisher are sent to each Subscriber.

trigger — A special type of stored procedure that automatically runs when data is inserted, updated, or deleted from a table. Triggers can be configured to run after data is modified or instead of the data modification statement.

Unicode — Unicode defines a set of letters, numbers, and symbols by using two bytes per character. Two-byte characters allow Unicode to offer more that 65,000 possible values compared to single-byte character sets, which only allow 256. Unicode includes characters for most modern languages.

uniform extent — An extent that stores information from only one object.

user-defined data types — A custom data type, based on a standard SQL Server 2000 data type, that can have rules and defaults embedded within it to enforce data validation logic.

user-defined database — *See* database.

user-defined filegroup — A named grouping of files other than the primary filegroup.

user-defined functions — A set of T-SQL statements that can be reused in other T-SQL scripts. User-defined functions can return a single value or a table structure.

vertically partitioned — Restriction of columns from a result set.

views — Logical tables that are based on Transact-SQL statements.

wide index — An index that has many key columns. For example, a large composite index that is based on seven columns in the table.

Windows Authentication Mode — One of two mechanisms used to validate user connections to SQL Server instances. Users are identified by their Windows user or group when they connect.

write-ahead transaction log — A log where data modifications are written prior to being committed to the database. When a transaction has been committed in the transaction log, then the data is persisted to the database.

XPath — A syntax used to query an XML document based on naming the element whose data is desired.

Index